HELP SEEK ~~~~~~~~~~~~~~~~~~~~ **S**

GOALS

HELP SEEKING IN ACADEMIC SETTINGS
GOALS, GROUPS, AND CONTEXTS

Edited by

Stuart A. Karabenick
University of Michigan & Eastern Michigan University

Richard S. Newman
University of California, Riverside

LAWRENCE ERLBAUM ASSOCIATES, PUBLISHERS
2006   Mahwah, New Jersey   London

Lawrence Erlbaum Associates, Inc., Publishers
10 Industrial Avenue
Mahwah, New Jersey 07430
www.erlbaum.com

Cover design by Tomai Maridou

Library of Congress Cataloging-in-Publication Data

Help seeking in academic setttings : goals, groups, and contexts /
    edited by Stuart A. Karabenick and Richard S. Newman.
        p. cm.
    Includes bibliographical references and index.
ISBN 0-8058-5219-0 (cloth : alk. paper)
ISBN 0-8058-5220-4 (pbk. : alk. paper)
1. Mastery learning.   2. Help-seeking behavior.   3. Questioning.
    4. Teacher-student relationships.   I. Karabenick, Stuart Alan
    II. Newman, Richard S. (Richard Stuart)
LB1031.4.H45 2006
371.3'9—dc22   2005054161
                                                            CIP

Books published by Lawrence Erlbaum Associates are printed on
acid-free paper, and their bindings are chosen for strength and
durability.

Printed in the United States of America
10   9   8   7   6   5   4   3   2   1

Contents

Foreword

I have been teaching introductory psychology since 1946 and have always been interested in ways of helping students learn more effectively. When behaviorism was followed by advances in cognitive psychology in the 1960s and 1970s, I realized that the theories and research in cognition could be of great help to students and began offering a course for freshman called "Learning to Learn." The course covered attention, memory, problem solving, anxiety, and self-management. To help assess its usefulness we compared the performance in later classes of students who had taken or not taken our course. Although effects were not large it was clear that our students had generally done better (McKeachie, Pintrich, & Lin, 1985). Students told others that the course had been helpful, and soon it was attracting upperclassmen as well as freshmen. A few years later our research group developed the Motivated Strategies for Learning Questionnaire (Pintrich, Smith, Garcia, & McKeachie, 1991) to help us determine what cognitive strategies and motivational characteristics were important for student achievement in different courses, such as biology, English, and psychology.

I traveled to other colleges giving talks and workshops stressing the importance of teaching students not only the subject matter but also the skills and strategies for learning the subject more effectively. In all that time I never thought about one of the most useful learning strategies—help seeking. And I was not unique. Even today some books on how to study do not mention help seeking. It was not until Karabenick and Sharma (1994) were carrying out their research that I saw that I had neglected one of the most useful strategies for learning. I realized that I, myself, frequently use this strategy (e.g., whenever I don't know how to do something on my computer, I call my daughter, rather than trying to read the manual).

Herb Simon once said that knowledge is like an area enclosed in a circle—with knowledge the area inside the circle and what is not known on the outside. The more knowledge we gain, the larger the circumference of the circle, and thus the more questions for further research. This book shows how much the circle of research on help seeking has expanded in the past few years. As Ruth Butler points out in chapter 2, help seeking was formerly regarded as a symptom of dependency and weakness. One may be afraid that peers or supervisors will think one incompetent if one asks for help. I recall that one of our Michigan PhDs who had not participated in our program for training psychology teachers called me from the West Coast frequently during his first year as a faculty member to ask how to handle one or another problem. He called me because he didn't dare ask any of his colleagues.

Now we see that help seeking can be a useful strategic tool of effective learners. We see that the kind of assistance the help seeker asks for as well as the kind of help that is given can have a good deal of impact on the seeker's ability to not only solve an immediate problem but also transfer that knowledge to future problem situations. Students in mastery-oriented classrooms are more likely to seek help that will facilitate their understanding; students in performance-oriented classrooms may be more likely to avoid asking for help or, when asking, to seek answers rather than understanding.

As Webb et al. discuss in chapter 3, "Help Seeking in Cooperative Learning Groups," giving an explanation can be as helpful (or more helpful) for learning and memory as receiving an explanation., and the level of help given can make a difference in later performance for the help seeker. We learn about the cultural, situational, and personality variables that constrain or facilitate effective help seeking and help giving. Kemper and Linnenbrink in chapter 4, Volet and Karabenick in chapter 5, and Sandoval and Lee in chapter 6 all point to the effect of the group, cultural, and organizational contexts that affect help seeking and help-giving behaviors. And chapters 7, 8, 9, and 10 describe the unique aspects of help seeking and help giving in academic advising, academic support services, the classroom, and computer-based tutoring. The final chapter, by Newman, discusses the major themes and points to interesting possibilities and needs for further research.

The audience for this book includes both students and teachers. We teachers need to help students understand that help seeking is not a sign of weakness but is rather an important learning strategy. We need to help them develop help-seeking strategies for gaining understanding rather than asking simply for the answer to a problem. I also hope this book will be used not only by teachers and students but also by the public in general. As indicated in the book, particularly in the chapter by Sandoval and Lee, help seeking is not confined to educational settings; it is a useful strategy in everyday life in all sorts of situations. Thinking about help seeking and help giving—becoming more aware of our own use or nonuse of these universal skills—can better our lives.

Finally, in reading most edited books I am conscious of differences in level and style as I go from chapter to chapter. This book seems to me to have a sequence of chapters that flow fairly smoothly from one to another, each demonstrating how the study of help seeking represents an important tributary that contributes to mainstream research on self-regulation.

—Wilbert McKeachie
Ann Arbor, Michigan

REFERENCES

Karabenick, S. A., & Sharma, R. (1994). Perceived teacher support of student questioning in college classrooms: Its relation to student characteristics and role in the classroom questioning process. *Journal of Educational Psychology, 86,* 90–103.

McKeachie, W. J., Pintrich, P. R., & Lin, Y.-G. (1985). Teaching learning strategies. *Educational Psychologist, 20,* 153–160.

Pintrich, P. R., Smith, D. A. F., Garcia, T., & McKeachie, W. J. (1991). *A manual for the use of the Motivated Strategies for Learning Questionnaire (MSLQ).* Ann Arbor: National Center for Research to Improve Postsecondary Teaching and Learning, University of Michigan.

Preface

Following Sharon Nelson-Le Gall's pioneering work in the 1980s, researchers have engaged in a sustained effort to integrate help seeking within the general framework of *self-regulated learning*. Help seeking is now considered an important learning strategy that is linked to students' achievement goals and academic performance. The publication of *Strategic Help Seeking: Implications for Learning and Teaching* (Karabenick, 1998), the first edited volume devoted to academic help seeking, combined early work (Dillon, Nadler, Nelson-Le Gall, van der Meij) with later contributions (Arbreton, Karabenick, Newman, Ryan). The volume also included chapters on help seeking in cultural and technological/information contexts. By all indications the book was well received. Research on help seeking and achievement goal theory continues unabated, some of it presented in Carol Midgley's recent publication (*Goals, Goal Structures, and Patterns of Adaptive Learning*, 2002). Increasingly, learning communities (teachers and support personnel) recognize the value of facilitating adaptive help seeking. Therefore, the time was right for a new edited volume that brings together contemporary work that is both theoretically and practically important.

Our goals in the present volume are to maintain high standards of scholarship and intellectual rigor, highlight current trends in research, and expand the amount of material devoted to application. Consistent with the initial volume, we hope this book will be of interest to educational researchers and teachers. In addition, we trust that its applied emphasis (i.e., technology, support services, organizations) appeals to other educational personnel. Contributors represent an internationally recognized group of scholars and researchers who provide both depth of analysis and breadth of coverage. Chapters examine: (a) help seeking as a self-regulated learning strategy and its relationship to achievement goal theory; (b) help seeking in collaborative groups; (c) culture and help seeking in K–12 and college contexts; (d) help seeking and academic support services (e.g., academic advising centers); (e) help seeking in computer-based interactive learning environments; (f) help seeking in response to peer harassment at school; and (g) help seeking in nonacademic settings such as the workplace. Readers will, we trust, come away not only with answers to who, why, and when learners seek help, but with questions of their own as well.

ACKNOWLEDGMENTS

Although not among the authors in the volume, we would like to acknowledge those whose work has contributed considerably to our understanding of help seeking in academic settings. These include James Dillon, Arie Nadler, Sharon Nelson-Le Gall, Allison Ryan, and Hans Van der Meij. Numerous colleagues, including Yi Guang Lin, Bill McKeachie, and Akane Zusho, participated with us in research endeavors on self-regulated learning strategies as assessed by the Motivated Strategies for Learning Questionnaire (MSLQ). We have benefited over the years from discussions with John Knapp, Martin Maehr, Michelle Potter, and Brian Murray. Lawrence Erlbaum Associates reviewers Judith Meece and Maryellen Weimer provided insightful comments and helpful suggestions. And, as have so many others worldwide, we gratefully acknowledge our friend and colleague Paul Pintrich, who was an inspiration in so many ways. With Paul, help seeking was a natural, reciprocal process of inquiry, collaborative learning, and development. We miss his intelligence, enthusiasm, and companionship, and consider ourselves fortunate to have shared, along with Liz, so many wonderful experiences.

REFERENCES

Karabenick, S. A. (Ed.). (1998). *Strategic help seeking: Implications for learning and teaching.* Mahwah, NJ: Lawrence Erlbaum Associates.
Midgley, C. (Ed.). (2002). *Goals, goal structures, and patterns of adaptive learning.* Mahwah, NJ: Lawrence Erlbaum Associates.

Contributors

Vincent Aleven
Carnegie Mellon University

Louise R. Alexitch
University of Saskatchewan

Ruth Butler
Hebrew University, Jerusalem

William Collins
University of Michigan

Marsha Ing
University of California, Los Angeles

Stuart A. Karabenick
University of Michigan & Eastern Michigan University

Toni Kempler
University of Michigan

Nicole Kersting
University of California, Los Angeles

Kenneth R. Koedinger
Carnegie Mellon University

Fiona Lee
University of Michigan

Elizabeth Linnenbrink
Duke University

Bruce M. McLaren,
Carnegie Mellon University

Kariane M. Nemer
University of California, Los Angeles

Richard S. Newman
University of California, Riverside

Brian Sandoval
University of Michigan

Brian C. Sims
University of Michigan

Simone Volet
Murdoch University

Noreen M. Webb
University of California, Los Angeles

Introduction

Stuart A. Karabenick
University of Michigan & Eastern Michigan University

When learners have trouble understanding text material, solving problems or completing assignments, they often rely on such strategies as rereading a text more slowly, organizing class notes, reviewing previous work, or searching for information available online. If these efforts are ineffective they may also turn to teachers, classmates, friends, or parents for assistance. Examples can range from very young children who ask adults for help placing letters into simple alphabet cutout puzzles to high school students' appeals to classmates for the correct solutions to quadratic equations. Until recently, such reliance on others was considered of little value and even stigmatized, with the admonition that truly independent learners are not supposed to need others to succeed. This pejorative view has changed, however. Recent theoretical developments and research indicate instead that help seeking can be an important self-regulated learning strategy, an essential implement in mature learners' "tool kits," and an activity engaged in by more motivated and better performing students (e.g., Butler, 1998; Karabenick, 1998, 2004; Karabenick & Knapp, 1991; Nelson-Le Gall & Resnick, 1998; Newman, 2000; Zimmerman & Martinez-Pons, 1990).

Evidence of this change in perspective—that seeking help can be an adaptive strategy—is suggested by its inclusion in elementary school report cards (e.g., "seeks help when needed"), in literature that advises parents about ways to foster their children's motivation and involvement in learning (e.g., Edwards, 2003), and in college students' study skills curricula (e.g., Collins-Eaglin & Karabenick, 1991, 1992; Vanderstoep & Pintrich,

2003). Help seeking has also been listed among the most important activities that contribute to university student success (University of Texas at Austin: www.utexas.edu/student/utlc/). In the chapters to follow, most discussions of this contemporary view acknowledge the identification by Nelson-Le Gall and her colleagues (Nelson-Le Gall, 1981, 1987, 1992; Nelson-Le Gall, Gumerman, & Scott-Jones, 1983) of instrumental help seeking (also called autonomous, adaptive, or strategic help seeking) as an important developmental skill. Unlike executive (also called expedient or excessive) help seeking, which is effort-avoidant, unnecessary, and perpetuates dependency, the goal of instrumental help seeking involves improving one's capabilities or increasing one's understanding, which can lead to greater autonomy. Although it is important to encourage learners to seek help, therefore, this functional distinction suggests that not all forms of help seeking are equally desirable.

In many respects, help seeking is similar to other self-regulated learning strategies that can improve knowledge and skill acquisition (e.g., rehearsal, organization, and elaboration). Learners must know how to use them (i.e., strategic knowledge) and when they are most appropriate; they also require the expenditure of resources (e.g., time and effort). There are also important differences, however, that fall into three general categories. One distinctive feature is that, unlike other strategies (e.g., rehearsal), help seeking can imply inadequacy and threaten self-worth (Covington, 1992; Nadler, 1983, 1998). Second, seeking help implies a social-interactive process (Newman, 2000) that can expose learners to public scrutiny. Being judged less capable by teachers, other students, or anyone in an evaluative position could be embarrassing (Shapiro, 1983). Third, seeking help can incur indebtedness to those providing it, creating the obligation to return the favor or provide some other form of compensation, except in cases where the help provided is role related (e.g., from an academic advisor or teacher) and such return favors are not expected. Individually or in combination, these costs can completely discourage students and other learners from seeking needed help (Fisher, Nadler, & Whitcher-Alagna, 1982), and consequently perceived costs have been the subject of numerous investigations. As for early influences, developmental research indicates that younger learners become increasingly aware of the price they could pay for seeking help, especially during whole-class activities. However, not until middle school with its greater emphasis on performance do perceived costs begin to affect their help-seeking decisions (Newman, 1990). Establishing adaptive learning environments involves understanding and reducing classroom and school practices that engender negative outcomes that inhibit help seeking as well as other self-regulated learning practices.

Consistent with other areas of self-regulated learning, achievement goal theory has framed much of this research (e.g., Karabenick, 2003, 2004;

Midgley, 2002; Ryan, 1998). Achievement goals are the purposes or reasons for engaging in achievement behavior (Kaplan, Middleton, Urdan, & Midgley, 2002). Goals are relevant because of their implications for the meaning of help seeking and can influence the value of its benefits and costs. As discussed in several contributions to the present volume, achievement goal orientations include mastery approach (a focus on learning and improvement, also called learning or task goals) and performance goals (also called ego or ability goals). Performance goals have been differentiated into performance approach (doing better than others) and performance avoid (not doing worse than others) orientations (Church, Elliot, & Gable, 2001; Harackiewicz, Barron, Pintrich, Elliot, & Thrash, 2002; Midgley, 2002; Pintrich, 2000a, 2000b; Skaalvik, 1997). Results of several studies indicate that for mastery-oriented learners, seeking help is viewed more positively as a way to improve and gain greater understanding—help from others represents another learning resource. By contrast, because of concerns about their abilities, having to seek help is more threatening for performance-oriented learners. Goal orientations also have different implications depending on the type of help: Mastery-oriented students are more likely to seek instrumental/autonomous help when needed, whereas those higher in performance approach and avoid goal orientations are more likely to avoid seeking help or to seek expedient help when they do (Arbreton, 1993, 1998; Butler & Neuman, 1995; Karabenick, 2003, 2004; Newman, 1991, 1994; Ryan, Hicks, & Midgley, 1997; Ryan & Pintrich, 1997).

In addition to personal orientations, achievement goal theory has also framed studies of learning contexts (e.g., classroom goal structure; Midgley, 2002). In accordance with a social-cognitive approach, context is typically assessed by student self-reports of teachers' intentional or inadvertent communications (e.g., Ryan, 1998; Ryan, Gheen, & Midgley, 1998; Turner et al., 2002). Considerable evidence indicates that associations between perceived goal structures and help seeking parallel those with students' personal goal orientations. At the individual level of analysis (i.e., ignoring differences between classes), students who perceive a greater emphasis on mastery goals are more likely to engage in instrumental/adaptive help seeking, whereas students who perceive classes as more performance focused tend to be more help-seeking avoidant. With regard to between-class differences, evidence also indicates that students in elementary school classes that they collectively perceive to be more mastery, or less performance, focused are less likely to avoid seeking needed help (Linnenbrink, 2005; Ryan, 1998; Ryan et al., 1998; Turner et al., 2002). And there is evidence that performance avoid goals are especially important for older learners. Specifically, college students in classes with greater perceived emphasis on performance-avoid goals felt themselves more threatened by help seeking and indicated they were less likely to seek it when needed (Karabenick, 2004). In summary, students' intentions to seek needed help depend both on how students perceive the classroom achievement goal structure and on their personal achievement goal orientations. Thus, increasing the likelihood of seeking needed help depends on reducing the perceived costs engendered when learners are concerned about not being as capable or performing worse than others.

Important for interpreting the effects of achievement goals and other influences is understanding the relation between help seeking and need. Although the effects of need would appear straightforward, the association is more complex and depends on how help seeking is assessed. To begin, need is a critical juncture in models of the help-seeking process (e.g., Gross & McMullen, 1983). According to these models, the help-seeking process is set in motion by a precipitating event, such as receiving a low exam grade; next, learners decide whether they need help. Doing so depends on several factors, which include causal attributions for the event that are help-relevant (e.g., that blame poor performance on lack of effort rather than lack of ability, bad luck, or prejudicial grading practices; Ames, 1983) and the proper calibration of need (Nelson-Le Gall, Kratzer, Jones, & DeCooke, 1990; Newman & Schwager, 1993). Once learners decide help is needed, the remainder of the process follows (e.g., deciding whether to seek help, selecting the source of help). The models recognize that the sequence may not be unidirectional (e.g., deciding on a source could precede the decision to seek help). They also acknowledge that learners may skip steps, or at least be unaware of them. For example, to account for executive (expedient) help seeking, the model would have to provide a path for help seeking in the absence of need (Nelson-Le Gall, 1987; Newman, this volume, chap. 9).

In addition to whether the presence or absence of need determines the kind of help seeking that occurs (i.e., instrumental/autonomous or executive/expedient), the level of need must be known (or assumed) when interpreting the presence or absence of help seeking itself. Consider the frequent experience of teachers asking, "Are there any questions?" Although the presence of questions can represent help seeking, their absence is ambiguous without knowing, or making assumptions about, whether students have understood the material. Disparaging student passivity (Good, Slavings, Harel, & Emerson, 1987) requires the assumption that students lacked comprehension but failed to seek needed help. An (ideal?) alternative is that students did not need to ask—that the material was so well organized and presented that everyone understood it. In the case of help seeking, in other words, such techniques as classroom observations alone may not be unambiguously informative (as would observing other behavior such as time on task). This is more than an incidental methodological matter but rather important for an adequate understanding of help-seeking research.

Most help-seeking research in instructional contexts (including that described in subsequent chapters) relies on self-reported help seeking as a proxy for direct observations. Self-reported help seeking has the advantage, especially for older learners whose experiences extend beyond the classroom, of sampling a wide range of learning contexts, but, as with direct observations, the level of need must still be taken into consideration when interpreting the results (see Karabenick & Knapp, 1991). In one study that examined the relationship between need and help seeking, college students reported both the incidence of their academic help seeking from a variety of sources (e.g., teachers, advisors) and the level of help they needed during the term (Karabenick & Knapp, 1988a). Interestingly, reported help seeking was not a direct function of the need for help. Highest rates of help seeking were instead reported at moderate levels of need and lowest at either very high or very low need levels. Low rates of help seeking by very needy students supported the generalization that those most in need are less likely to seek it, presumably because of their low levels of motivation or self-threat induced avoidance. The infrequency of self-reported help seeking by high-performing students with low need is explicable (i.e., they didn't need help) but, as with direct observation, leaves unresolved what those students *would have done* if they needed help.

Controlling the level of need is one way to approach the problem. In experimental studies, appropriate conditions are established by such techniques as presenting difficult tasks or norms that indicate relatively poor performance. There are two strategies used with self-reported help seeking. One involves assessing and statistically controlling for need when determining relations between help seeking and other variables (e.g., help seeking and students' use of other learning strategies; Karabenick & Knapp, 1991). Another approach relies on responses to statements that are need conditional—asking learners what they would do *if* they needed help. In essence, this conditional approach measures behavioral intentions under specified conditions, which have been closely linked to actual behavior when assessing attitudes in myriad areas (Ajzen & Fishbein, 1980). With the exception of studies that rely heavily on extensive process observations and qualitative analyses (see Webb et al. in chap. 3 and Kempler & Linnenbrink in chap. 4), the preponderance of contemporary learning-related help-seeking research has adopted this approach. Taking need into consideration, and the distinction between behavior and intentions, aids in understanding the seeming contradiction that more motivated and better performing students may be less likely to seek help (because they need it less) but more likely to seek more adaptive help when needed.

CURRENT CONTRIBUTIONS

Although not formally divided into sections, the following chapters sequentially focus on goals, groups, and contexts. The achievement goals framework is extensively discussed in the next chapter. Two chapters that follow are devoted to help seeking and group processes (collaborative and cooperative learning). Attention then shifts to several contexts that include help seeking: as affected by culture among international students and in noneducational organizations; in academic advising and support services; in computer-based interactive learning environments; and adaptive responses to threat (i.e., bullying).

We begin in chapter 2 with Ruth Butler's explication of the transition from help seeking as necessarily dependent to a potentially strategic and adaptive form of behavior. Achievement goal theory is then reviewed articulated with her proposed set of help-seeking orientations (autonomous, ability-focused, and expedient) and their implications for help-seeking behavior. Achievement goals and help-seeking orientations are used to help understand the potentially detrimental consequences of ability tracking and competition in and between schools. Based on evidence from a quasi-experimental study of students in Israeli schools, she describes how ability tracking can affect a school's achievement goal structure and thus help seeking in ways that are complexly moderated by students' ability levels. Butler complements her work on student help seeking with a motivational analysis of teachers' responses to student requests for help, summarizing approaches that include Batson's empathic concern, teachers' levels of social responsibility, Weiner's (1980) approach to attributions of responsibility, and teachers' achievement goal orientations and approaches to instruction. Butler concludes with a description of how contemporary public policy that increases interschool competition and accountability affects teacher help giving and student help seeking.

An extensive literature documents how students can learn from each other through such experiences as sharing their knowledge and skills, observing how others solve problems, and by giving and receiving help. In chapter 3, Noreen Webb, Marsha Ing, Nicole Kersting, and Kariane Nemer examine students' help-seeking and help-giving behavior within small groups. Webb's previous research on verbal interactions and learning in peer-directed groups includes the benefits for student achievement of receiving and applying explanations. Recent studies of collaborative learning in mathematics and science classrooms are reviewed and reanalyzed to focus on relationships between giving and receiving help, subsequent activity that processes the help received, and learning outcomes. The authors examine the types of help-seeking behavior that occur when students work collaboratively to solve problems, the effects of different types of help-seeking behavior on the help they receive, and how their subsequent use of help affects achievement outcomes. Attention then shifts to how teacher behavior influences student help seeking, the group dynamics that promote or inhibit different kinds of help seeking, and recommendations for effectively structuring classrooms and small-group work.

Building on work by Webb and other contributors to the collaborative learning literature, in chapter 4, Toni Kempler and Elizabeth Linnenbrink describe interaction patterns in groups, focusing on how the quality of group processes affects help seeking. Specifically, their detailed qualitative analyses discern the types of group interaction patterns that facilitate (e.g., active listening) or undermine help seeking (e.g., disrespectful behavior) and how help seeking depends on whether group members organize themselves to work cooperatively and synchronously or collaboratively in parallel on separate task components. The authors stress the need to recognize implicit help seeking in collaborative learning groups, which occurs when participants who lack comprehension acquire relevant information by virtue of their participation in the collaborative process. And they advocate that students would benefit from training to improve the quality of their group interactions and thus the likelihood of benefiting from their collaboration, including successful outcomes of their help-seeking behavior.

Cultural factors may determine the experiences that students have in collaborative groups, such as the type of groups students spontaneously form, their experiences in assigned groups, and whether they approach other students for help. General cultural dispositions, such as individualism and collectivism, as well as specific classroom norms, can affect whether and in what form students seek help. In chapter 5, Simone Volet and I review the impact of increasingly multicultural learning environments comprised of students with diverse prior educational experiences. One consequence of diversity is that cultural barriers may restrict the flow of useful information among students, including the potentially beneficial information communicated during helping interactions. Not only can help-seeking patterns depend on the presence of social barriers between students from different countries but also on those between students in varying indigenous groups within the same country. In addition to integrating help seeking and research on international student experiences, evidence from a transnational study is presented that examines the likelihood and types of help seeking by students in multicultural college and university classrooms in Australia and the United States.

Research on learning and performance in schools has for the most part progressed in relative isolation from the extensive nonacademic literature. In chapter 6, Brian Sandoval and Fiona Lee describe ways these separate literatures can profitably inform each other. For the present volume, the authors focus on organizational culture. Drawing on evidence that includes cross-cultural studies, they describe how individualistic norms inhibit, and collectivistic norms promote, help seeking both in laboratory studies and in a variety of organizations, from office furniture manufacturing teams to hospital surgical departments. In contrast to effects of individualistic norms, they discuss the desirable consequences of collectivist organizational norms that engender greater "psychological safety" and reduce concerns over appearing dependent, incompetent, or inferior. Correspondingly, they emphasize that collectivistic school norms contribute to more cooperative learning and the adaptive use of help seeking in schools, which parallel efforts to foster mastery achievement goals (Maehr & Midgley, 1996).

Academic organizations increasingly provide students with support services, including expanded academic advising and transition programs for college students. In chapter 7, Louise Alexitch describes the types of students more or less likely to seek help from academic advisors. Characteristics include students' motivational orientation, past experiences with seeking help, and gender in determining attitudes toward seeking help and in preferences regarding academic advising. She then focuses on formal (i.e., institutionally provided) helping resources in higher education contexts for guidance, direction, and strategies to help students succeed. These sources include faculty, academic advisors, career counselors, and program advisors. At issue is what academic advisors and faculty can do to meet the needs of students by providing effective help. Alexitch suggests strategies for reaching students with a variety of advising goals, as well as those who avoid advising entirely.

In chapter 8, William Collins and Brian Sims also focus on help seeking and academic support services in college and university contexts, in particular those designed to support students academically and ensure they have access to the help they need. In addition to the role of academic advising that Alexitch presents, many colleges and universities have extensive orientation and other transition programs that make available to students valuable resources and on-campus support. The underlying purpose is to give students the skills and motivation to ask for help rather than fail in isolation. The authors discuss implications of the help-seeking literature for these programs. According to Collins and Sims, an important route to students' willingness to ask for help is their understanding of the reasons for and means of doing so. As noted earlier, it would also be important that support service personnel be able to identify the various forms of help seeking and have an awareness of the kinds of obstacles that may make it less likely students will ask for help. In this context, Collins and Sims describe a specific high school to college transition program that, evidence suggests, accomplishes many of these objectives, which includes building self-regulated learning skills.

Although a good deal of research has examined children's reluctance to seek a teacher's assistance when they encounter academic difficulties, there has been little investigation of help seeking in the context of these social and emotional challenges present in academic contexts. In chapter 9, Richard Newman extends perspectives on help seeking within academic contexts to include social as well as academic challenges at school, specifically alienation, disaffection, and peer conflict, which includes physical threat and bullying. Clearly, under certain circumstances—most notably, situations of peer harassment—getting help from a teacher can be considered a highly motivated and self-regulated strategy of survival. Yet, for understandable reasons (e.g., being labeled a "tattletale"), that option is avoided. Importantly, Newman's contribution includes an extensive analysis of when seeking or not seeking help can be considered adaptive. Calibration of help seeking with the need for help (as discussed earlier) is a critical determinant of whether it is adaptive.

Any discussion of help seeking in schools would be incomplete without consideration of the virtually universal context of computer-related instruction. An early study demonstrated the facilitative effects on help seeking that computers potentially provided during task performance (Karabenick & Knapp, 1988b) and in the context of computer-mediated communication (Keefer & Karabenick, 1998). In chapter 10, Vincent Aleven, Bruce McLaren, and Ken Koedinger describe help seeking in computer-based interactive learning environments (ILEs). Such contexts, as well as most computer applications, provide help that ranges from on-line resources, which are often very general, to help that can be very specific and context dependent. When these are available, students may use the system's help functions effectively, but often students do not. In an important advance, Aleven and colleagues propose a comprehensive model of help-seeking skill that can more precisely evaluate how effectively students are seeking help and can improve their help-seeking skills. Indeed, the model could be applied to contexts other than computer-based interactive learning environments.

In the final chapter, Newman summarizes several trends suggested by the contributors to this volume. These include theoretical developments, assessment issues, and implications of help seeking for academic contexts. He concludes by offering an agenda for future work in the field. This includes ways the collective contributions to the present volume contribute to discussions of more adaptive uses of help to promote learning in classrooms and the acquisition of knowledge and skills in other contexts within academic settings. Newman also suggests how adaptive help seeking can contribute to success in organizational and work settings as well as a generalized approach to maximize the use of available resources in the most effective manner.

In sum, research over the past two decades has made considerable progress toward understanding the person and situation determinants of help seeking and the developmental trajectory of students' beliefs about its benefits and costs, the characteristics of students most likely to seek and avoid help, the effects of how students perceive relevant features of their classes and teachers, and students' help-seeking goals. Furthermore, rather than an isolated phenomenon, help seeking is now embedded within existing frameworks of self-regulation and achievement goal theory. Developments in those frameworks contribute to our understanding of help seeking, and, in complementary fashion, help-seeking research has expanded the strategies encompassed by those theoretical approaches to learning and motivation. Contributors to this volume considerably extend the boundaries of relevance for this area of inquiry and our understanding of the role of help seeking in facilitative learning and teaching environments.

REFERENCES

Ajzen, I., & Fishbein, M. (1980). *Understanding attitudes and predicting social behavior.* Englewood Cliffs, NJ: Prentice Hall.

Ames, R. (1983). Help-seeking and achievement orientation: Perspectives from attribution theory. In B. M. DePaulo, A. Nadler, & J. D. Fisher (Eds.), *New directions in helping: Vol. 2. Help seeking* (pp. 165–186). New York: Academic Press.

Arbreton, A. (1993). *When getting help is helpful: Developmental, cognitive, and motivational influences on students' academic help seeking.* Unpublished doctoral dissertation, University of Michigan, Ann Arbor.

Arbreton, A. (1998). Student goal orientation and help-seeking strategy use. In S. A. Karabenick (Ed.), *Strategic help seeking: Implications for learning and teaching* (pp. 95–116). Mahwah, NJ: Lawrence Erlbaum Associates.

Butler, R. (1998). Determinants of help seeking: Relations between perceived reasons for classroom help-avoidance and help-seeking behaviors in an experimental context. *Journal of Educational Psychology, 90,* 630–643.

Butler, R., & Neuman, O. (1995) Effects of task and ego achievement goals on help-seeking behaviors and attitudes. *Journal of Educational Psychology, 87,* 261–271.

Church, M. A., Elliot, A. J., & Gable, S. L. (2001). Perceptions of classroom environment, achievement goals, and achievement outcomes. *Journal of Education Psychology, 93,* 43–54.

Collins-Eaglin, J., & Karabenick, S. A. (1991, March). *Black males' survival in college: Countering overindividualistic socialization to increase the likelihood of employing the critical strategy of seeking academic assistance.* National Black Student Retention Conference, Las Vegas, NV.

Collins-Eaglin, J., & Karabenick, S. A. (1992, April). *Teaching students of color the strategy of seeking academic assistance as a critical component of the freshman year experience.* Conference on the Freshman Year Experience, Lexington, KY.

Covington, M. V. (1992). *Making the grade: A self-worth perspective on motivation and school reform.* New York: Cambridge University Press.

Edwards, M. (2003). *Increasing your child's motivation to learn.* Little Rock, AR: Center for Effective Parenting (www.parenting-ed.org).

Fisher, J. D., Nadler, A., & Whitcher-Alagna, S. (1982). Recipient reactions to aid. *Psychological Bulletin, 91,* 27–54.

Good, T. L., Slavings, R. L., Harel, K. H., & Emerson, H. (1987). Student passivity: A study of question-asking in K-12 classrooms. *Sociology of Education, 60,* 181–199.

Gross, A. A., & McMullen, P. A. (1983). Models of the help seeking process. In B. M. DePaulo, A. Nadler, & J. D. Fisher (Eds.), *New directions in helping: Vol. 2. Help seeking* (pp. 45–70). San Diego, CA: Academic Press.

Harackiewicz, J. M., Barron, K. E., Pintrich, P. R., Elliot, A. J., & Thrash, T. M. (2002). Revision of achievement goal theory: Necessary and illuminating. *Journal of Educational Psychology, 94,* 638–645.

Karabenick, S. A. (Ed.). (1998). *Strategic help seeking: Implications for learning and teaching.* Mahwah, NJ: Lawrence Erlbaum Associates.

Karabenick, S. A. (2003). Help seeking in large college classes: A person-centered approach. *Contemporary Educational Psychology, 28,* 37–58.

Karabenick, S. A. (2004). Perceived achievement goal structure and college student help seeking. *Journal of Educational Psychology, 96*(3), 569–581.

Karabenick, S. A., & Knapp, J. R. (1988a). Help-seeking and the need for academic assistance. *Journal of Educational Psychology, 80,* 406–408.

Karabenick, S. A., & Knapp, J. R. (1988b). Effects of computer privacy on help-seeking. *Journal of Applied Social Psychology, 18,* 461–472.

Karabenick, S. A., & Knapp, J. R. (1991). Relationship of academic help seeking to the use of learning strategies and other instrumental achievement behavior in college students. *Journal of Educational Psychology, 83,* 221–230.

Kaplan, A., Middleton, M. J., Urdan, T., & Midgley, C. (2002). Achievement goals and goal structures. In C. Midgley (Ed.), *Goals, goal structures, and patterns of adaptive learning* (pp. 21–53), Mahwah, NJ: Lawrence Erlbaum Associates.

Keefer, J. A., & Karabenick, S. A. (1998). Help seeking in the information age. In S. A. Karabenick (Ed.), *Strategic help seeking: Implications for learning and teaching* (pp. 219–250), Mahwah, NJ: Lawrence Erlbaum Associates.

Linnenbrink, E. A. (2005). The dilemma of performance goals: The use of multiple goal contexts to promote students' motivation and learning. *Journal of Educational Psychology, 97*(2), 197–213.

Maehr, M. L., & Midgley, C. (1996). *Transforming school cultures.* Boulder, CO: Westview Press.

Midgley, C. (Ed.). (2002). *Goals, goal structures and patterns of adaptive learning.* Mahwah, NJ: Lawrence Erlbaum Associates.

Nadler, A. (1983). Personal characteristics and help-seeking. In A. Nadler, J. D. Fisher & B. M. DePaulo (Eds.), *New directions in helping (Vol. 2): Help seeking* (pp. 303–340). New York: Academic Press.

Nadler, A. (1998). Relationship, esteem, and achievement perspectives on autonomous and dependent help seeking. In S. A. Karabenick (Ed.), *Strategic help seeking: Implications for learning and teaching* (pp. 61–93). Mahwah, NJ: Lawrence Erlbaum Associates.

Nelson-Le Gall, S. (1981). Help-seeking: An understudied problem-solving skill in children. *Developmental Review, 1,* 224–246.

Nelson-Le Gall, S. (1987). Necessary and unnecessary help-seeking in children. *Journal of Genetic Psychology, 148,* 53–62.

Nelson-Le Gall, S. (1992). Children's instrumental help-seeking: Its role in the social construction of knowledge. In R. Hertz-Lazarowitz & N. Miller (Eds.), *Interaction in cooperative groups: The theoretical anatomy of group learning* (pp. 49–68). New York: Cambridge University Press.

Nelson-Le Gall, S., Gumerman, R. A., & Scott-Jones, D. (1983). Instrumental help-seeking and everyday problem-solving: A developmental perspective. In A. Nadler, J. D. Fisher, & B. M. DePaulo (Eds.), *New directions in helping (Vol. 2): Help seeking* (pp. 265–283). New York: Academic Press.

Nelson-Le Gall, S., Kratzer, L., Jones, E., & DeCooke, P. (1990). Children's self-assessment of performance and task-related help seeking. *Journal of Experimental Child Psychology, 49,* 245–263.

Nelson-Le Gall, S., & Resnick, L. (1998). Help seeking, achievement motivation, and the social practice of intelligence in school. In S. A. Karabenick (Ed.), *Strategic help seeking: Implications for learning and teaching* (pp. 39–60), Mahwah, NJ: Lawrence Erlbaum Associates.

Newman, R. S. (1990). Children's help-seeking in the classroom: The role of motivational factors and attitudes. *Journal of Educational Psychology, 82,* 71–80.

Newman, R. S. (1991). Goals and self-regulated learning: What motivates children to seek academic help? In M. L. Maehr & P. R. Pintrich (Eds.), *Advances in motivation and achievement* (Vol. 7, pp. 151–183). Greenwich, CT: JAI Press.

Newman, R. S. (1994). Adaptive help seeking: A strategy of self-regulated learning. In D. H. Schunk & B. J. Zimmerman (Eds.), *Self-regulation of learning and performance: Issues and educational applications* (pp. 283–301). Mahwah, NJ: Lawrence Erlbaum Associates.

Newman, R. S. (2000). Social influences on the development of children's adaptive help seeking: The role of parents, teachers, and peers. *Developmental Review, 20,* 350–404.

Newman, R. S., & Schwager, M. T. (1993). Students' perceptions of the teacher and classmates in relation to reported help seeking in math class. *Elementary School Journal, 94,* 3–17.

Pintrich, P. R. (2000a). The role of goal orientation in self-regulated learning. In M. Boekaerts, P. Pintrich, & M. Zeidner (Eds.), *Handbook of Self-Regulation* (pp. 451–502). San Diego: Academic Press.

Pintrich, P. R. (2000b). Multiple goals, multiple pathways: The role of goal orientation in learning and achievement. *Journal of Educational Psychology, 92,* 54–555.

Ryan, A. M. (1998). *The development of achievement beliefs and behaviors during early adolescence: The role of the peer group and classroom contexts.* Unpublished doctoral dissertation. University of Michigan, Ann Arbor.

Ryan, A. M., Gheen, M., & Midgley, C. (1998). Why do some students avoid asking for help? An examination of the interplay among students' academic efficacy, teachers' social-emotional role and classroom goal structure. *Journal of Educational Psychology, 90,* 528–535.

Ryan, A. M., Hicks, L., & Midgley, C. (1997). Social goals, academic goals, and avoiding help in the classroom. *Journal of Early Adolescence, 17,* 152–171.

Ryan, A. M., & Pintrich, P. R. (1997). "Should I ask for help?" The role of motivation and attitudes in adolescents' help seeking in math class. *Journal of Educational Psychology, 89,* 329–341.

Shapiro, E. G. (1983). Embarrassment and help-seeking. In B. M. DePaulo, A. Nadler, & J. D. Fisher (Eds.), *New directions in helping: Vol. 2. Help-seeking* (pp. 143–163). New York: Academic Press.

Skaalvik, E. M. (1997). Self-enhancing and self-defeating ego orientation: Relations with task and avoidance orientation, achievement, self-perceptions, and anxiety. *Journal of Educational Psychology, 89,* 71–81.

Turner, J. C., Midgley, C., Meyer, D. K., Gheen, M., Anderman, E. M., Kang, Y., & Patrick, H. (2002). The classroom environment and students' reports of avoidance strategies in mathematics: A multimethod study. *Journal of Educational Psychology, 94,* 88–106.

VanderStoep, S. W., & Pintrich, P. R. (2003). *Learning to learn: The skill and will of college success.* Upper Saddle River, NJ: Prentice Hall.

Weiner, B. (1980). May I borrow your class notes? An attributional analysis of judgments of help giving in an achievement-related context. *Journal of Educational Psychology,72,* 676–681.

Zimmerman, B. J., & Martinez-Pons, M. (1990). Student differences in self-regulated learning: Relating grade, sex, and giftedness to self-efficacy and strategy use. *Journal of Educational Psychology, 82,* 51–59.

Chapter 2

An Achievement Goal Perspective on Student Help Seeking and Teacher Help Giving in the Classroom: Theory, Research, and Educational Implications

Ruth Butler
Hebrew University of Jerusalem

This chapter focuses on why students do, or often do not, ask teachers for help with their schoolwork. Seeking help when one cannot solve a problem alone seems preferable to giving up or continuing to persist unsuccessfully alone (Newman, 1991). In this case, evidence that students often refrain from asking questions or requesting help when they have difficulty with their schoolwork is both intriguing and disturbing (Dillon, 1982; Good, Slavings, Harel, & Emerson, 1987; Karabenick & Knapp, 1988; Newman & Goldin, 1990; van der Meij, 1988). Studies of help seeking in other contexts have also shown that people often do not seek help, even when doing so may alleviate real distress (see papers in DePaulo, Nadler, & Fisher, 1983). Such findings led Nadler (1991) to propose that the need for help creates a "help-seeking dilemma" that evokes conflicting needs, some of which can be met by seeking help whereas others can be satisfied by not seeking help. In this case, it is not surprising that much research has focused on identifying students' motives, or reasons for seeking and avoiding help, and on examining how these are influenced by characteristics of students and the classroom environment, and how they influence students' academic help seeking.

Over the last decade, attempts to address these questions have been dominated by achievement goal theory and the assumption that students' willingness or reluctance to ask for help depends on what they are striving to achieve, or, in other words, on their construction of the purposes, or goals of learning. In the first section of this chapter, I set the stage for analyzing the major contribution of goal theory by reviewing earlier approaches to help seeking and the seminal contribution of Nelson-Le Gall (1981, 1985). The second section reviews the contribution of achievement goal theory to understanding help seeking. It also addresses some limitations of this framework and the studies it has generated, and considers promising directions for addressing some of these limitations. The third section focuses on an important but hitherto largely neglected partner in the academic help-seeking process—the teacher. Specifically, I propose that achievement goal theory might also provide a framework for examining why some teachers might be more likely to undermine and others to support academic help seeking and suggest how teachers' support for student help seeking might be influenced by their own constructions of the purposes, or goals of teaching. In the final section, I summarize the rather clear educational recommendations that emerge from this review and come to the reluctant conclusion that current trends in educational policy are more likely to undermine than to support their implementation.

EARLY THEORY AND RESEARCH ON HELP-SEEKING: FROM DEPENDENCE TO ACTIVE COPING

Until the early 1980s there was remarkably little systematic, theory-driven research on help seeking, among either children or adults, in either academic or other settings. As others have noted, this probably had much to do with prevailing cultural values and attitudes, and the ways in which they permeated influential theories of developmental and social psychology (Nelson-Le Gall, 1981, 1985; Karabenick, this volume). Early views of help seeking were influenced by emphases, especially in North America, on the virtue and value of autonomy, persistence, and individual achievement. Such themes were reflected in the image of America as the land of opportunity in which anyone could succeed, given the necessary drive. Indeed, generations of children grew up on the ethos of the Little Engine That Could and the message that they can overcome even apparently insurmountable obstacles if they only try hard enough. Within psychology, they were notably reflected in McClelland's theory of need achievement, which he defined as the striving to succeed in competition with some standard of excellence, and expected to develop as a form of learned drive in families and cultures that valued and demanded self-reliance and independence (McClelland, 1953). From this perspective, it made sense to view help seeking as a form of dependency and thus as a rather maladaptive behavior that should be associated with low levels of need achievement and actual attainment (Beller, 1957; Winterbottom, 1958).

Not long afterward, and in large part in the wake of the Kitty Genovese affair in the early 1960s, social psychologists became interested in helping as a particular case of altruistic or prosocial behavior. Although it became clear early on that willingness to offer help depended on characteristics not only of the helper, but also of the context and the recipient (e.g., Latané & Darley, 1970; Wispé, 1978; Weiner, 1980), these recognitions did not initially inspire research on the other side of the coin—why people ask for help, who is more or less likely to do so in which circumstances, and how people's willingness or reluctance to solicit help are related to other aspects of their personality, adjustment, and behavior. In this case, it is not surprising that educational psychologists also did not study students' help seeking, even though the classroom is clearly a context in which participants regularly encounter difficulty, at least some of the time, in the presence of a presumably more competent other—the teacher—whose job it is to help students overcome difficulties and acquire skills and understandings.

In keeping with the notion that responding to another's difficulty by giving help is virtuous, but responding to one's own difficulty by seeking help is problematic, when social psychologists began to study help seeking, they initially focused on the costs of soliciting help. Possibly because the benefits of asking for help initially seemed rather obvious, researchers were more intrigued by the other side of the help-seeking dilemma—why people were often reluctant to ask for help, even when they were in real need, and even from professionals such as social workers, doctors, or therapists, whose job it is to provide help (e.g., Merton, Merton, & Barber, 1983). In brief, the guiding assumption was that the reluctance to seek help reflects the social stigma and internalized psychological costs associated both with being needy in the first place and with responding to need by seeking help rather than by following the example of the Little Engine and trying to overcome difficulty on one's own. Moreover, if people tend to construe help seeking as an admission of dependency and incompetence, help avoidance can be understood as a strategy for protecting and maintaining self-worth by concealing inadequacy.

This approach characterized many of the contributions to the first major edited book on help seeking (DePaulo et al., 1983). Particularly relevant in the present context, evidence began to accumulate that reluctance to ask for help does indeed increase as a function of perceived threat to self-worth. In brief, people were less likely to ask for help when others did not experience similar difficulty (Tessler & Schwartz, 1972), when requests for help were public rather than anonymous and private (Shapiro, 1983), and when they experienced difficulty in an area more, rather than less, central to their self-esteem (Nadler, 1987). In this case, findings that students were often reluctant to ask teachers or even peers for help with their schoolwork are not surprising, because requesting help in the classroom necessarily involves public admission of difficulty in a highly valued domain.

Against this background, two reviews by Nelson-Le Gall (1981, 1985) introduced a very different emphasis. Her main innovation lay in challenging earlier views of help seeking in children as a form of passive dependency and earlier emphases on helpers, rather than recipients, to make the hitherto neglected point that the capacity to mobilize resources and elicit help could be viewed, instead, as an "active and complex social activity that is essential to learning and achievement" (1981, p. 224). Specifically, Nelson-Le Gall distinguished between dependent, "executive" help seeking that is in evidence when children seek help merely to complete a task or to avert criticism and "instrumental" help seeking that is motivated by strivings to learn and to acquire skills and understandings. Executive help seeking is expressed in bids for direct help in the form of solutions or clear directions that facilitate task completion by mobilizing someone else to solve the problem. In contrast, instrumental help seeking is expressed in requests for indirect help, in the form of hints or explanations that advance understanding and support future independent mastery by clarifying methods and strategies or identifying difficulties.

Theoretically, this distinction led to the formulation of several hypotheses that were quite novel at the time and continue to serve as salient foci for research on academic help seeking. First, in contrast with earlier approaches, Nelson-Le Gall proposed that instrumental help seeking should be associated with superior, rather than inferior, achievement and adjustment and thus set the stage for conceptualizations of adaptive help seeking as an important self-regulatory strategy (Karabenick & Knapp, 1991; Newman, 1991). Second, she proposed that instrumental help seeking should increase, rather than decrease, with age, as children become more capable of identifying that they are having difficulty, of determining whether they really need help or can cope on their own, and of distinguishing between more or less adaptive help requests and more or less effective helpers. Finally, her focus on adaptive help seeking as an important but neglected phenomenon implied that it was interesting to ask not only why students do not ask for help but also why they do. In her second review, Nelson-Le Gall (1985) addressed this question by proposing that children's motives for help seeking are related to their motivation for learning. Extrapolating from the distinction between intrinsic and extrinsic motivation that dominated research on academic motivation at the time (Deci & Ryan, 1985; Harter, 1981), she proposed that children who experience learning as intrinsically interesting and worthwhile should be motivated to engage in instrumental seeking when they encounter difficulty. In contrast, students who perceive their engagement in school work as guided by strivings to gain approval and avoid sanctions and as regulated by external standards and controls should be more likely to engage in executive help seeking that can facilitate rapid and effortless task completion.

Interestingly, empirical examinations of relations between various aspects of intrinsic motivation for schoolwork and help seeking yielded somewhat equivocal findings. For example, Nelson-Le Gall and Jones (1990) found that although elementary school children who scored high on strivings for independent mastery for schoolwork demonstrated the greatest preference for indirect help in an experimental setting, only 25% of these children asked for help when they were not sure of the correct answer. Moreover, children who scored low on this scale (and thus high on dependence on the teacher) were not more likely to prefer direct than indirect help. In another study, Newman (1990) examined students' self-reported willingness to ask for help when they experienced difficulty in class. Surprisingly, independent mastery was negatively related to help seeking among children in the age range studied by Nelson-Le Gall and Jones and the predicted positive relation was confirmed only for students in Grade 7. Moreover, the relation between intentions to ask for help and students' scores on preference for challenging assignments, another aspect of intrinsic motivation for learning, was low at all ages. One implication of these somewhat equivocal findings is that the distinction between intrinsic and extrinsic motivational orientations for schoolwork may not suffice for understanding the motivational basis of help seeking, because these orientations are more relevant to understanding why students seek help than to understanding the other side of the help-seeking dilemma—what motivates them to actively avoid seeking help. Thus, concerns to protect and maintain self-esteem by avoiding admissions of incompetence are not a central component of either intrinsic or extrinsic motivation. Against this background, achievement goal theory offered a promising perspective for conceptualizing and examining students' motives not only for help seeking but also for help avoidance.

ACHIEVEMENT GOALS, REASONS FOR SEEKING AND AVOIDING HELP, AND ACADEMIC HELP SEEKING

This section is divided into several subsections. The first reviews the contribution of achievement goal theory to understanding students' help-related motives and behavior. The second applies goal theory to informing long-standing debates as to the relation between self-esteem and help seeking. The third and fourth sections address some continuing theoretical and empirical challenges by exploring (a) implications of a recent, expanded model of relations between goals for schoolwork, perceived costs and benefits of help seeking, and help-seeking strategies and (b) influences of school practices, and of ability grouping in particular, on students' motives for learning and help seeking.

A Goal-Oriented Perspective on Motives for Learning and Help Seeking: Theory and Research

Starting from the simple proposition that students' achievement-related cognitions and behaviors depend on what they want to achieve, or, in other words, on their constructions of the purposes or goals of activity, Nicholls (1984) distinguished between two kinds of motivational states or goal orientations. In one, which he termed task-involvement and which has affinities with intrinsic motivation, students strive to acquire worthwhile skills and understandings and derive satisfaction from learning and acquiring competence. In the other, which he termed ego-involvement, students strive to maintain self-worth by demonstrating superior, or masking inferior, ability and derive satisfaction from performing better than others. This distinction formed the basis for contemporary achievement goal theory and for similar distinctions between performance and learning goals (Dweck, 1986), or ability and mastery goals (Butler, 2000), the terminology adopted in this review.

Students differ in their personal motivational orientations for schoolwork, but goal theorists assume that the degree to which students pursue one or the other goal in any situation is also influenced by the degree to which the context conveys that the purpose of activity is to learn and acquire competence or to demonstrate superior ability (Ames, 1992). Thus, some researchers have manipulated goals experimentally and compared the effects of mastery goal conditions in which a task or activity was presented as an opportunity to learn with ability goal conditions in which it was presented as a valid measure of some valued ability (for reviews see Butler, 2000; Dweck, 1986; Jagacinski, 1992). Others examined students' perceptions of the degree to which their teacher values and encourages learning, progress, and engagement with meaningful and challenging material and thus creates a mastery classroom goal structure, or values relative ability and attainment, correct answers, and high test grades and creates an ability classroom goal structure (e.g., Midgley, 2002). By and large, studies that examined individual differences in goal orientations, perceptions of classroom goal structure, and experimentally induced goal conditions have yielded similar results. In brief, mastery goals tend to be associated with more positive processes and outcomes (for reviews see Ames, 1992; Dweck, 1986; Midgley, 2002). Most significant in the present context, mastery goals were associated with superior self-regulation and with more resilient and adaptive responses to failure, apparently because difficulty is perceived as challenging and diagnostic of the need to learn under mastery goals and as diagnostic of inadequate capacity under ability goals (Butler, 2000).

Against this background, it seemed that achievement goal theory could provide a parsimonious framework for conceptualizing motives both to seek and to avoid help and for predicting when students will be more likely to resolve the help-seeking dilemma by seeking or by avoiding necessary help (Ames, 1983a; Butler, 1992; Nadler, 1991; Newman, 1991). For example, Butler and Neuman (1995) reasoned that strivings to learn and acquire competence should orient students to perceive help seeking as an adaptive strategy for attaining their goals, as long as the help available is indeed relevant to learning. In contrast, salient ability goals should orient students to construe the need for help as threatening, to construe help seeking as evidence of inadequate ability, and to perceive help avoidance as an "adaptive" way of meeting their goals. In other words, mastery goals should be associated with one side of the dilemma—perceptions of the perceived benefits of help seeking for learning—and ability goals with the other—perceptions of perceived costs for self-esteem. They examined this reasoning in a study in which children in Grades 2 and 6 worked on difficult spatial puzzles in either a mastery goal condition in which they were told that the activity would give them an opportunity to learn how to solve difficult puzzles or an ability goal condition in which they were told that children who are good at solving such puzzles are very smart. Children were also told that they could ask for help as they worked. If they asked for the solution, the experimenter would solve the puzzle. If they asked for a hint, she would explain how to do a tricky part of the puzzle (e.g., "you can make a square by thinking of it as two triangles"); hints thus enabled children to acquire strategies relevant to solving later puzzles on their own.

Overall, children asked for more hints than solutions, but they requested hints far more often in the mastery than in the ability goal condition. Moreover, this was not because children in the more supportive mastery condition were less motivated to try to solve problems on their own, because average latency before asking for help was quite high and did not differ in the two conditions. The assumption that children in the mastery condition sought help because they were motivated to learn and acquire competence was further supported by the finding that children who asked for more hints for early problems subsequently solved more puzzles on their own than did children who did not ask for needed help. Interestingly, this was not the case in the ability condition. Thus, even if children who were encouraged to construe the activity as a measure of their ability did ask for hints, they apparently did not use them to learn new strategies. Further evidence that help seeking is perceived as a threat to self-worth under salient ability goals was provided when we asked children why others who had worked on the same puzzles did not always ask for help when they could not solve a puzzle alone. As expected, 65% of the children in the ability goal condition, as compared with only 24% in the mastery condition, spontaneously cited concerns with maintaining self-worth, and said, for example, that "he didn't want to look stupid" or "if you ask for help, that shows you're not smart."

This study provided preliminary evidence that students were more likely to resolve the help-seeking dilemma by engaging in adaptive help seeking when they pursued mastery goals, and by avoiding help when they pursued ability goals. Subsequent studies have confirmed that this seems to be the case also in natural, classroom settings. For example, in one comprehensive study, Ryan and Pintrich (1997) found that students' mastery orientation for math predicted their reported help seeking in math class both directly and by enhancing perceptions that asking for help promotes learning. In contrast, ability orientation predicted reported help avoidance by enhancing perceptions that teachers and peers might think one is dumb if one asks questions or requests help (see also Karabenick, 2003, 2004; Middleton & Midgley, 1997; Ryan, Hicks, & Midgley, 1997). Surprisingly, however, ability orientation was not always related also to help seeking (Ryan & Pintrich, 1997).

If help-related perceptions, intentions, and behaviors are influenced both by individual differences in students' orientations to schoolwork and by experimental manipulations of mastery versus ability goals, one would expect them also to be influenced by the degree to which the classroom environment emphasizes personal learning and progress, on the one hand, or relative achievement and ability on the other (Newman, 2000). Few studies have examined relations between actual teacher and classroom practices and students' goals. Studies have, however, examined perceived classroom goal structure, as reflected in the degree to which students perceive their teachers as emphasizing learning and understanding on the one hand, or relative attainment and ability, on the other. Perceived goal structure did indeed predict both students' personal mastery versus ability orientations for schoolwork and their self-reported classroom help seeking (Ryan, Gheen, & Midgley, 1998; Turner et al., 2002). A recent study on college students was unusual in that it examined both personal achievement goals and perceptions of the classroom goal structure (Karabenick, 2004). Results confirmed that even after controlling for personal goals, perceptions of the classroom context as encouraging learning and mastery were associated positively with willingness to ask for needed help and negatively with help-avoidance and perceptions of the classroom context as emphasizing relative ability predicted help avoidance.

At this point, it is relevant to note that some researchers have proposed that strivings to demonstrate superior ability and strivings to avoid the demonstration of inferior ability represent two distinct orientations, which they label performance-approach and performance-avoidance, respectively (e.g., Harackiewicz, Barron, Pintrich, Elliot, & Thrash, 2002). These authors also reviewed evidence to support their proposal that many of the negative effects of ability strivings can be attributed to salient strivings to avoid the demonstration of inferior ability, and that performance (or ability) approach orientation is actually associated with some positive processes and outcomes. In the present context, some researchers have ventured that ability-avoidance may undermine willingness to seek help more than does ability-approach orientation (e.g., Ryan & Pintrich, 1997). In contrast, Butler (2000) argued that both orientations reflect rather similar concerns with the level of one's ability and similar perceptions of difficulty as threatening to one's self-esteem (see also Midgley, Kaplan, & Middleton, 2001). Because the need for help necessarily arises when students experience difficulty, this analysis suggests the alternative proposal that strivings to excel and strivings to avoid failing relative to others will be similarly associated with perceptions of help seeking as a threatening admission of inadequate ability and with reluctance to seek needed help.

Results from the few studies that examined both orientations have not as yet resolved this debate. Thus, approach and avoidance orientations were highly correlated with one another and were highly and similarly associated with both perceived threat and help-avoidance, but ability-avoidance emerged as a stronger predictor of both outcomes (Karabenick, 2002, 2004; Middleton & Midgley, 1997). Another possibility is suggested by findings that ability-approach was positively and ability-avoidance negatively correlated with actual or perceived competence (e.g., Elliot & Church, 1997; Skaalvik, 1997). Thus, Butler (2000) ventured that chronic histories of academic success or failure may influence the degree to which students motivated by concerns about their ability strive mainly to demonstrate superior or avoid the demonstration of inferior ability and may contribute to explaining why ability-avoidance orientation is so maladaptive. In this case, they may also contribute to the strong relation between ability-avoidance and help-avoidance, as long as one can demonstrate that less able students are less likely to request needed help. As we shall show, however, research on the relation between competence and help seeking has yielded rather equivocal results. Moreover, there are grounds for venturing that achievement goal theory can contribute to resolving debates as to whether more or less able students are more likely to seek needed help.

Can Goal Theory Contribute to Clarifying the Relation Between Competence and Help Seeking?

There is some agreement that any association between students' actual or perceived academic competence and their willingness to seek needed help is mediated by perceived threat to self-esteem, but it is less clear whether such perceived threat is higher among more or less able students. As initially framed by Tessler and Schwartz (1972), the question is whether less able students seek less help because the admission of need threatens their already vulnerable self-concept or whether reluctance is greater among the more able, for whom the admission of need is inconsistent with their positive self-concept. Although one might think that this question can be resolved rather easily by simply examining the relation between competence and help seeking, studies have yielded conflicting results. Experimental studies tend to show lower levels of help seeking at higher levels of self-esteem (Nadler, 1987; Tessler & Schwartz, 1972), but Nelson-Le Gall and Jones (1990) found that school achievement did not moderate help seeking in a controlled setting. In contrast, in classroom studies low achievers were least likely to ask questions or to report that they ask for needed help (Good et al., 1987; Karabenick & Knapp, 1991; Newman, 1990; Ryan & Pintrich, 1997).

One possibility is that the relation between competence and perceived threat is influenced by the context, and specifically by the degree to which difficulty is likely to be construed as evidence of chronic low ability. The need for help may be particularly threatening for able individuals who encounter difficulty in experimental settings in the presence of strangers unfamiliar with their general capacities and achievement history. Thus, in such settings they may be more concerned than less able individuals to conceal difficulty as a way of preventing erroneous conclusions that they are generally incapable. In the classroom, however, both students and teachers should be unlikely to infer low ability when students who generally perform well ask for help, but should be quite likely to interpret bids for help by low achievers as evidence of incompetence. Indeed, in several classroom studies low achievers were more likely than high achievers to agree that they did not ask for help because of fears of appearing dumb (Karabenick & Knapp, 1991; Newman, 1990; Newman & Goldin, 1900; Ryan et al., 1997; Ryan & Pintrich, 1997). In a similar vein, Good and his colleagues (1987) interpreted their finding that low achievers asked most questions in kindergarten, but asked fewest questions in later grades, in terms of increasing awareness of the costs of help seeking for self-esteem. Thus, the most disturbing implication of classroom research is that students who are most in need of help seem to be least likely to request it (Newman, 1991).

The main contribution of goal theory is in implying that this does not always have to be the case. By definition, concerns to demonstrate superior ability and strivings to mask inferior ability are salient when students pursue ability goals, but not when they pursue mastery goals. In this case, low achievers should be reluctant to ask for help under salient ability, but not mastery goals. Moreover, if low achievers are more likely than high achievers to strive to avoid the demonstration of low ability and if ability-avoidance orientation is a particularly strong predictor of help-avoidance, low achievers may be more reluctant than high achievers to seek help under salient ability goals. Thus, to summarize, there are grounds for proposing first that ability goals will enhance perceived threat and undermine classroom help seeking relative to mastery goals at all levels of ability. Second, perceived competence should moderate help seeking under ability, more than mastery goals. There is indeed prior evidence that competence moderated persistence, interest, and information-seeking for challenging tasks in ability, but not mastery goal conditions (Butler, 1992, 1999; Dweck & Leggett, 1988).

This proposal is not inconsistent with the results of classroom surveys, because classrooms often emphasize ability rather than mastery goals (Ames, 1992; Nicholls, 1989). More direct support was provided by a study in which mastery orientation predicted help seeking at all levels of achievement and ability goal orientation predicted help avoidance among low, but not high, achievers (Ryan et al., 1997). In another study, however, ability orientation predicted help avoidance at all achievement levels (Ryan & Pintrich, 1997). To complicate the picture still further, a study by Butler and Neuman (1995) confirmed that initial skill level did not moderate adaptive help seeking in a mastery goal condition, but requests for needed help in an ability goal condition were less frequent at both low and high than at intermediate skill levels. Interestingly, in one of the few observational studies of classroom help seeking, Nelson-Le Gall and Glor-Scheib (1985) also found that average achievers asked the teacher for help more often than did either low or high achievers; Karabenick and Knapp (1988) also reported a curvilinear relation between achievement and the frequency with which college students asked for help with their studies. Thus, taken together, studies have confirmed that even low achievers engage in adaptive help seeking when they pursue mastery goals, but it is still not clear whether ability goals increase perceived threat and undermine help seeking mainly among low or also among high achievers. We return to this question later on.

To summarize, achievement goal theory provided a coherent framework for conceptualizing the help-seeking dilemma that has proven very useful in predicting students' perceptions of help seeking, their intentions to seek help in the classroom, their actual help-seeking behavior in controlled settings, and the conditions under which students of diverse abilities might be equally willing to ask the teacher for needed help. One should, however, note some limitations and unresolved questions. First, relations between mastery orientation and help seeking, although consistently positive, have ranged from quite low to quite high (Butler & Neuman, 1995; Middleton & Midgley, 1997; Ryan et al., 1997; Ryan & Pintrich, 1997). Thus, mastery goals do not always ensure that students will ask for needed help. In a similar vein, although ability orientation predicted perceptions of help seeking as threatening to self-worth in all studies and predicted help avoidance in most, contextual or personal ability goals were not always related to help seeking (Karabenick, 2002; Newman & Schwager, 1995; Ryan & Pintrich, 1997). Second, just as earlier emphases on the role of intrinsic versus extrinsic orientations to learning could be faulted for failing to address the self-esteem costs that are so influential in motivating students not to ask for help, studies guided by achievement goal theory could be faulted for focusing too narrowly on conflicting perceptions of help seeking as beneficial for learning versus threatening to self-worth and failing to consider other reasons why students might both seek and avoid help, including the extrinsic reasons examined in earlier studies.

Third, just as early approaches could be faulted for focusing on dependent or executive help seeking, some of the studies guided by achievement goal theory can be faulted for focusing exclusively on adaptive help seeking and failing to examine how students cope with difficulty when they do not ask for help of this kind. Thus, for example, studies have shown that ability-oriented students do not do seek help when they are having difficulty, but by and large have not shown what they do instead. Fourth, the findings just reviewed here imply that students' goals and help-seeking strategies are influenced by the classroom environment, but most classroom studies focused on students' perceptions of the classroom goal structure, rather than on actual educational practices. Finally, just as early theory and research could be faulted for focusing almost exclusively on helpers, research on academic help seeking can be faulted for focusing almost exclusively on help seekers, and paying less attention to the role of potential helpers, and in particular teachers. I address some of these issues in the following sections.

Motives for Seeking and Avoiding Help: Single or Multiple Help-Seeking Dilemmas?

In an attempt to address some of these limitations, Butler (1998) noted that students' reasons for seeking or avoiding help in both experimental and classroom settings did not fall neatly into only two categories of benefits for learning versus threats to self-esteem, respectively. Rather, students also attributed help seeking to desires to succeed, to avoid the embarrassment of erring, or to expedite task completion, and attributed reluctance to seek help not only to fears of appearing stupid, but also to desires to work things out for themselves or to perceptions that asking for help is too much bother, or that teachers do not like students to ask questions or might respond in ways that might embarrass students or require them to exert more rather than less effort (Butler & Neuman, 1995; Newman, 1990; Newman & Goldin, 1990; van der Meij, 1988). Indeed, van der Meij's finding that elementary school students were more likely to attribute help avoidance to strivings for independent mastery than to strivings to conceal poor ability suggests that early views of help seeking as a dependent behavior that is incompatible with mastery strivings might not be so mistaken after all.

On the basis of such findings, Butler (1998) proposed, first, that motives or reasons for avoiding help are multidimensional and, second, that different reasons for avoiding help in the classroom will be differentially associated with the use of different strategies for coping with difficulty. Specifically, she proposed three distinct orientations to help-avoidance; an ability-focused orientation whereby help-avoidance is indeed motivated by perceptions that requests for help serve as an admission of inadequate ability; an autonomous orientation, whereby students avoid help because of strivings for independent mastery; and an expedient orientation whereby help avoidance is motivated by perceptions that asking for help will not expedite task completion. She then reasoned that rather than representing similar kinds of costs, which, if salient, all result in the same outcome——reluctance to seek help—different motives for help-avoidance will be associated with qualitatively different patterns of coping with difficulty. Specifically, students who perceive help-avoidance as motivated by strivings for independent mastery should exhibit an autonomous pattern of help seeking and should be quite willing to ask for needed help as long as the context enables them to try to first overcome difficulty on their own and the help available is relevant to learning and is thus supportive, in the long run, of their autonomy. Moreover, such students should indeed use the help received to improve task mastery.

In contrast, students who believe that the main reason for classroom help-avoidance is that bids for help do not expedite task completion should be quite willing to ask for help that serves to solve the problem for them if this is at all possible. Thus, they should prefer direct rather than indirect help and should request help rather rapidly, without first attempting to overcome difficulty on their own. Such a pattern corresponds to definitions of executive help seeking (Nelson-Le Gall, 1981) or dependent overutilization of help (Nadler, 1998), but has been largely ignored in classroom surveys guided by goal theory. Finally, help-avoidance may seem more "adaptive" than either autonomous or executive help seeking to students who are concerned to mask inadequate ability. Continuing to fail is also problematic for such students, however, because failing is a clear sign of poor ability. Butler thus ventured that they may be tempted to resolve the dilemma between exposing inadequacy by failing and exposing inadequacy by asking for help by adopting an "avoidant-covert" pattern of behavior, whereby they do not ask for overt help but may be particularly likely to engage in more covert strategies, such as copying answers from peers or the back of textbook instead.

This expanded framework was first examined in two studies (Butler, 1998). In the first, more than 1,000 students in Grades 5 and 6 rated their agreement with various reasons why students in their math class did not ask the teacher for help when they were having difficulty solving a problem in math. As expected, items reflecting autonomous strivings for independent mastery, ability-focused concerns to mask low ability, or expedient perceptions that asking for help would incur disapproval or would not expedite task completion loaded on three distinct factors. Students were then identified as displaying clear autonomous, ability-focused, or expedient orientations, respectively, if high agreement with one scale was accompanied by low agreement with both of the other scales. Several months later, these students participated in a second, controlled study in which they worked on difficult numerical series problems, each of which consisted of two alternating series. To solve them, children needed to understand that there were two series and to identify which series led to the incomplete number before working out what operation they needed to perform to complete the series. This task was chosen because even students who did well in math class did not initially understand that there were two series. Overcoming difficulty thus depended on acquiring a new understanding that could also be applied to solving subsequent problems. Children were told that they could decide whether to ask for help, when to do so, and what kind of help they wanted; they could ask for a hint that would illustrate the rule of the series, or for directions how to compute the correct answer (e.g., multiply the last number by two). Thus, hints, but not directions, were relevant to learning. Children were also told that they could check their answers against the correct answer that was concealed under a flap, but should do so only after they had written an answer, and should not copy it if their answer was wrong. Violations of these rules were scored as cheating.

Children's bids for help, the time they spent trying to solve the problem alone before requesting help, and the frequency of cheating served to define three distinct styles of help seeking. An autonomous style was defined when students scored above the mean on requests for hints, below the mean on requests for directions, and above the mean on time spent trying to solve a problem on their own before asking for help, an executive style when they scored above the mean on requests for directions and below the mean on requests for hints and request latency, and an avoidant-covert style when children scored below the mean on requests for both kinds of help and above the mean on cheating. Most significantly, the results summarized in Table 2.1 confirmed that these styles were predicted by children's orientations to classroom help-avoidance. Children who attributed reluctance to ask for help in math class to autonomous strivings for independent mastery were

TABLE 2.1

Motives for Help-Avoidance and Style of Help Seeking

Help-Seeking Style	Orientation to Classroom Help-Avoidance		
	Autonomous	Expedient	Ability-Focused
Autonomous	79	35	34
Executive	13	50	17
Avoidant-covert	9	15	49
Correlation between requests for hints and later independent mastery	.53	.10	08
N	64	60	59

Note. Adapted from Butler (1998).

most likely to engage in autonomous help seeking. They also used the hints to learn; thus, the more often they asked for hints for early problems, the more likely they were to solve later problems on their own. In contrast, pupils with an expedient orientation to classroom help-avoidance displayed an expedient style of help seeking and their problem solving did not improve even if they asked for hints. Rather, they seemed to use hints much as they did directions, to expedite task completion rather than to learn. Finally, students who displayed an ability-focused orientation to classroom help-avoidance were least likely to request help of any kind and were most likely to copy the answer instead. Thus, an important contribution of this study was in demonstrating what students with different help-related perceptions do when they do not engage in adaptive help seeking.

One implication of this multidimensional conceptualization of motives for help avoidance is that students' reasons or motives for help seeking may differ along the same dimensions. Specifically, if students who construed help-avoidance in terms of strivings for independent mastery displayed an autonomous style of help seeking, they might also be particularly likely to construe help seeking as beneficial for learning. In a similar vein, if students with an expedient orientation to help-avoidance exhibited an executive help seeking style in a context in which this was legitimate and possible, one can venture that they will construe help seeking mainly in terms of strivings to expedite task completion. Finally, students with an ability-focused orientation might be most likely to attribute help seeking to strivings to maintain self-esteem by avoiding the embarrassment of failing. Preliminary support for this expanded framework was provided by Goldschmidt (1999), who asked elementary school students to respond to two separate questionnaires that assessed their agreement with reasons for seeking and avoiding help in math class, respectively. As expected, each questionnaire yielded three distinct autonomous, ability-focused, and expedient factors. Perhaps more significantly, reasons for seeking and avoiding help were strongly correlated. Thus, students who attributed help-avoidance to strivings for independent mastery attributed help seeking to strivings to learn and acquire competence, but not to strivings to expedite task completion or to avoid the stigma of failure. In a similar vein, students who agreed that students did not ask for help because of fears of appearing stupid also agreed that students ask for help because of fears of failing and students who endorsed expedient reasons for help-avoidance also endorsed expedient reasons for help seeking.

One intriguing implication is that the help-seeking dilemma is not always experienced as a conflict between perceptions that help seeking is beneficial for learning but threatening to self-esteem. Rather, it might be fruitful to consider the possibility of distinct autonomous, ability-focused, and expedient dilemmas, each of which incorporates distinct motives for both seeking and avoiding help, that create distinct help-seeking dilemmas. This framework has several interesting implications that might be explored in future research. Regarding relations between achievement goals and help seeking, one implication is that mastery versus ability goal orientations evoke autonomous versus ability-focused orientations to help seeking, and distinct conflicts between competing perceptions that both seeking and avoiding help can serve to satisfy strivings to attain independent mastery and to salvage self-worth, respectively.

Theoretically, this conceptualization contributes to reconciling the discrepancy between early views of help seeking as a dependent behavior that is incompatible with mastery strivings and later proposals that it is an adaptive learning strategy that should be favored by students who strive for mastery by suggesting that mastery orientation invites both kinds of perceptions. In a similar vein, identification of three distinct orientations to help seeking and three distinct help-seeking styles can serve to integrate research generated by achievement goal theory, which has focused on the distinction between mastery and ability orientations, with Nelson-Le Gall's work on the role of intrinsic versus extrinsic orientations to schoolwork. Achievement goal theorists also acknowledge that students may experience schoolwork mainly as a means to the end of attaining rewards or avoiding sanctions, and Nicholls (1989) identified a similar, work-avoidant orientation whereby students strive to get through the school day with as little effort as possible. In present terms, one can venture that extrinsic, work-avoidant orientations will be associated with an expedient orientation to help seeking that incorporates its own dilemma as to whether help seeking will facilitate effortless task completion, on the one hand, or invite disapproval or demands that students invest more rather than less effort, on the other.

Another implication is that learning contexts influence student help seeking by influencing both the relative salience of the perceived benefits versus costs associated with one or another goal orientation or classroom goal structure and the likelihood that students will actually exhibit their preferred style of coping with difficulty. For example, the variations across studies noted earlier in the strength of the association between mastery orientation and adaptive classroom help seeking may have been influenced by variations both in the degree to which teachers encouraged students to persist alone or to request needed help and in the ways in which they responded to bids for help. Experimental contexts in which students work on tasks in which it is necessary and possible to learn, can try alone for as long as they want, and can request and receive help relevant to learning provide ideal conditions for autonomous help seeking. Such conditions are, however, rare in the classroom, where even teachers who value student learning and progress must attend to many students, may not always be able to provide students with instrumental help, or may value effort to an extent that also conveys that students should not ask for help. Indeed, rates of adaptive help seeking tended to be higher in experimental than in classroom settings, even when the latter seemed to provide a mastery goal structure (Butler, 1998; Ryan, Gheen, & Midgley, 1998).

Similarly, an ability goal structure should invite an ability-focused orientation to classroom help seeking and conflicting perceptions that help seeking both threatens and may also serve to salvage self-esteem. One way to resolve this dilemma is to adopt avoidant-covert strategies such as cheating, copying, or casually asking peers what answer they got (Frey & Ruble, 1985; Nelson-Le Gall & Glor-Scheib, 1985). Students in such classes may, however, also ask for help if the costs of failing (and thus the perceived benefits of help seeking) are high and if, for example, they do not understand the material for an important test or fear that low grades will lead to demotion to a low ability track. This possibility might contribute to explaining why researchers such as Ryan and Pintrich (1997) found that ability orientation was not related to help seeking. Finally, given that many teachers ignore bids for direct help, or respond by demanding that students try again (Nelson-Le Gall & Glor-Scheib, 1985), work-avoidant students in some classrooms may also prefer to ask peers for the answer, or to use other covert strategies for completing assignments (Dowson & McInerney, 2001; Murdoch, Hale, & Weber, 2001). Such students might, however, be highly likely to ask for executive help when teachers respond to student difficulty by providing directives and solutions, as some tend to do (Brophy & Good, 1970).

Some other researchers have also begun to address some of the limitations noted earlier by incorporating a wider range of student goals, of motives for both seeking and avoiding help, and, most crucially, of the strategies students use when they encounter difficulty in the classroom. For example, Ryan, Gheen, and Midgley (1998) examined relations between students' social goals and classroom help seeking, and a recent study by Karabenick (2004) included measures not only of adaptive but also of expedient help seeking. Future classroom research could, however, benefit from modifying current reliance on self-report measures. Thus, incorporating classroom observations of student strategies, including ones like copying that students may not admit to using when asked directly, and of teacher communications about, and explicit responses to, student difficulty and bids for help (e.g., Turner et al., 2002) would provide a more comprehensive context for clarifying students' ongoing constructions of the purposes of learning and of the costs and benefits of different strategies for attaining their goals in the classroom.

SCHOOL PRACTICE, GOAL ORIENTATIONS AND HELP SEEKING: THE CASE OF ABILITY GROUPING

The foregoing discussion underlines the importance of considering contextual influences on students' help seeking. As noted earlier, students who perceived their teacher as valuing relative ability and achievement were more likely to pursue ability goals, to perceive help seeking as threatening to their self-esteem, and to report that they would refrain from requesting needed help. Although there is some agreement regarding the contextual features that create such an ability goal structure, few studies have directly examined relevant school or classroom practices. One such practice is ability grouping. Advocates of ability groups emphasize their potential for enabling students of diverse abilities to learn, progress, and develop positive motivation for schoolwork. In motivational terms, however, ability grouping should orient students to pursue ability goals for schoolwork by conveying that schools and teachers ascribe great importance to individual differences in ability (se also Anderman, Maehr, & Midgley, 1999). In this case, perceived threat and help avoidance should also be greater in schools that group students by ability.

Two features of the elementary school system in Jerusalem enabled examination of these predictions in a quasi-experimental design (Butler, in preparation). First, catchment areas are determined by the municipality to ensure that schools serve similar, socially diverse populations. Second, within- and between-class ability grouping is not common, and the latter, if used at all, is used mainly in math. As a result, it was possible to identify schools that served similar student bodies but differed as to whether they tracked students in math or taught math in mixed-ability classes in which students were not assigned to within-class ability groups. In this case, any school effects on students' goal orientations and help-related perceptions and behaviors in math class could be attributed with some confidence to grouping practices.

Because different kinds of grouping also provide students with different frames of reference for social comparison and self-appraisal (Reuman, 1989), considering the range of ability in the classroom might also clarify the relation between competence and help seeking. Evidence that tracking tends to undermine the academic self-concept of high achievers and enhance that of low achievers (Kulik & Kulik, 1992) is consistent with the Big-Fish-Little-Pond Effect identified by Marsh and his colleagues, whereby high achievers in selective schools had lower self-concepts than their counterparts in schools in which the average level of achievement was lower (e.g., Marsh & Hau, 2003). In this case, one can venture that the help requests of high achievers will be interpreted as a sign of incompetence when they study with similar high-ability others, but not when they attend mixed-ability classes in which they usually do better than most of their classmates. Conversely, as discussed earlier, help seeking by less able students should be perceived as a salient low-ability cue in mixed-ability classes, but may be less threatening when they study with similar low-ability others. Thus, to summarize, perceived threat and reluctance to ask for help might be more characteristic of low achievers in mixed-ability classes and of high achievers in homogeneous classes.

Results confirmed, first, that at all levels of competence students in tracked schools expressed higher levels of ability orientation for math, higher perceived threat, as reflected in agreement with ability-focused perceptions of help-avoidance, and less frequent classroom help seeking than did students in nontracked schools. Second, students in the top track did indeed report higher levels of perceived threat and lower levels of help seeking relative both to students in the bottom track and to their high achieving counterparts in nontracked schools. Interestingly, the prediction that perceived threat would be greater and willingness to seek needed help lower among low than high achievers in mixed-ability classes was only partially supported. Thus, although there was some tendency for high achievers to report more help seeking than low achievers in these classes, the latter reported asking the teacher for help as often as did students in the bottom track of tracked schools.

One possibility is that prior studies, which showed that low achievers sought less help, were conducted in schools that used within-class ability grouping. This practice is particularly detrimental to the self-esteem of low achievers (Reuman, 1989) and in present terms should increase their sense of perceived threat and undermine their willingness to ask for help. More generally, one can speculate that just as tracking reflects school emphases on the importance of relative ability and is often associated with school adherence to an elitist educational philosophy and with allocation of poorer resources to students in the lowest track (Ireson & Hallam, 2001; Oakes, 1985), the decision to *not* track students may reflect a schoolwide commitment to the progress and welfare of students regardless of their ability that might also support adaptive help seeking in all students. In all events, it seems clear that analyses of the influence of educational practices on help seeking should also consider how schools and teachers address student diversity, and particularly whether they choose to do so in segregated or more inclusive frameworks.

TEACHERS' MOTIVES FOR HELPING STUDENTS

So far, this review has followed research that emphasizes how individual differences in students' perceptions of the purposes of learning and of the benefits and costs of help seeking influence help seeking and the degree to which this is moderated by competence. In a similar vein, consideration of contextual influences has focused on how the classroom goal structure and school practices for addressing student diversity influence help seeking by influencing students' goals and attitudes toward help seeking. The likelihood that students will ask for help might, however, depend first and foremost on the ways in which the teacher responds to student difficulty and bids for help (Karabenick & Sharma, 1994).

Interestingly, we know very little about the factors that influence teachers' helping because research on help seeking in academic contexts has focused almost exclusively on help seekers—students—and has paid little attention to the teachers to whom they can turn for help. In addition, although there is a long history of research on helping behavior among adults, much has focused on contexts very different from the classroom. As noted earlier, systematic research on helping was sparked by the tragic case of Kitty Genovese, who was beaten to death in front of over 30 witnesses, none of whom intervened to try and save her. As a result, many studies followed Latané and Darley (1970) in examining why people do, or often do not, spontaneously offer help to strangers in a state of specific distress. In contrast, classroom helping and help seeking occur, or not, in the context of an ongoing relationship in which partners have knowledge, perceptions, attitudes, and expectations about one another, and students' need for help tends to be the rule rather than the exception.

Despite these differences, previous research is relevant to the themes of the present review because much has focused on trying to identify people's motives for helping and how these are related to their actual helping behavior. Thus, just as there are different motives for seeking help, people have different motives for offering help. In brief, people help others because this is in their own self-interest (Krebs, 1987), because they feel empathic concern for others and are motivated to relieve their distress and promote their welfare (Batson, 1998), or because they ascribe to norms, values, or principles of social responsibility that one should help others (Berkovitz, 1972). There is also evidence that motives matter. For example, the likelihood that people will offer help and do so consistently across different situations is influenced by the degree to which helping is motivated mainly by self-interest or by empathic concern (Batson, 1998). However, the degree to which more altruistic motives such as empathy and social responsibility maintain helping behavior over time seems to be related also to satisfaction of certain personal needs, such as strivings to promote understanding or professional proficiency (Omoto & Snyder, 1995).

It seems likely that similar motives and individual differences are at work also in the classroom. Some teachers may focus mainly on their students and thus be inclined both to empathize with their distress and difficulties and to assume responsibility for promoting their learning and development. Such teachers should also be motivated to offer students help relevant to promoting their learning, understanding and welfare. Although the down side of helping is that offers of help serve as a potent low-ability cue (Weiner, 1980), this might not be the case when teachers help in ways that convey that skills can be learned and ability can be acquired. For example, in one study, elementary school students read scenarios in which the teacher is going over homework and a student gives an incorrect answer (Butler, 1994). Students who read that the teacher then said "never mind; let's see if someone else can help out" inferred that the hypothetical student had far lower ability than did students who read that the teacher said, "never mind; let me help you see where you went wrong so we can work out the answer together." Moreover students in the latter but not the former condition predicted both that the teacher would call on the student again (and thus not "give up" on him or her) and that the student would be willing to try to answer questions in the next class (and thus would not "give up"). In other words, offers of adaptive help were interpreted as a "mastery" cue that students are capable of learning rather than as evidence of low ability.

More direct support for this analysis was provided by an interesting study in which student measures of perceived classroom goal structure and help-avoidance were complemented by observations of teacher discourse (Turner et al., 2002). Teachers in classes in which help avoidance was low and perceived mastery structure high were far more likely than those in high-avoidance, low-mastery classrooms to respond to student difficulty by offering encouragement, by giving them time and opportunity to think and answer questions, by providing appropriate scaffolds, and, in brief, by conveying that they were competent and capable of learning. Similarly, Brophy (1985) cited evidence that teachers who defined the teacher role in terms of promoting students' welfare and adjustment were particularly likely to experience empathic concern for troubled students and to spend time and effort trying to help them with cope with their problems.

Butler did, however, report one less encouraging result. When she asked teachers how they respond when their students err, only 15% said that they respond by offering adaptive help. Thus, although helping others to learn and develop would seem to be a defining feature of the teacher's role, some teachers may focus more on their own needs and concerns. For example, Ames (1983b) reviewed evidence that teachers differ in the degree to which they attribute student failure mainly to student characteristics, such as low ability, laziness, or home background, or also to their own teaching. He also reported that teachers differ in the degree to which their causal attributions for their own teaching reflect self-serving biases to attribute lessons that succeeded to their own skills and effort and lessons that failed to student misbehavior, low ability, or poor motivation.

Ames concluded that teachers differ in their sense of responsibility for student learning, and thus also in the degree to which they feel obligated to help students. In the present context, one can further characterize teachers with a low sense of responsibility as self-focused teachers who should be inclined to interpret and respond to student difficulty mainly in terms of the implications for themselves. Such teachers may experience student difficulty as threatening because it reflects poorly on their own competence, or as annoying because it interferes with their lesson plan or makes what they perceive as unreasonable demands on their time and attention. In this case, the ways in which they respond to needy students might also be guided by self-interest. In my work as a school psychologist I encountered quite a few teachers who preferred to refer struggling students to other professionals or schools rather than try to help them within the classroom. These teachers, were, however, very willing to "help" students during standardized achievement tests, which are used also as a measure of teacher and school effectiveness (Butler, 1996).

In a similar vein, to the extent that such self-focused teachers respond to student difficulty in the classroom, they may be particularly likely to tell students what to do, or call on other students to "help out" so that they themselves can continue teaching without interference. Brophy and Good (1970) did indeed find that some teachers preferred to provide students with direct instructions and solutions rather than engaging with them around their difficulty. Such responses should serve as a potent low-ability cue that might deter students from asking for help and encourage them to resort to covert copying and cheating or to executive help seeking instead. In present terms, they can also be interpreted as a rather self-centered response, which may then reinforce work avoidance and expedient perceptions in their students. Indeed, students' beliefs in the desirability and efficacy of effort were undermined when teachers responded to failure in such an expedient manner, but were enhanced when they responded with attempts to scaffold student understanding by providing adaptive help (Butler, 1994).

To summarize, this analysis, although speculative, implies interesting parallels between the different styles of student help seeking described earlier and possible differences in teachers' styles of helping. Specifically, it seems likely that teachers who respond to student difficulty by offering constructive help will encourage their students to engage in adaptive help seeking, those who find it easier just to give students the answer will encourage executive help seeking and over dependence on the teacher, and those who respond in ways designed to protect their own self-worth will encourage students to adopt what Butler (1998) termed avoidant-covert strategies.

Accordingly, one can speculate that just as help-seeking styles are grounded in students' reasons or motives for both help seeking and learning, teachers' help-related perceptions and styles may be closely bound up with their own constructions of their goals for teaching. Thus, the classroom is an achievement context not only for students, whose job is to learn, but also for teachers, whose job is to teach. In this case, teachers might differ in the degree to which they strive to develop understanding and proficiency not only in their students but also in themselves (mastery orientation), strive to demonstrate superior teaching ability or avoid the demonstration of difficulty and inferior ability (ability orientation), or are motivated mainly by extrinsic reasons such as long vacations or work-avoidant strivings to get through the day with little trouble and effort. In this case, one can venture further that teachers' goals for teaching will influence not only their own motives for and styles of helping students, but also the degree to which they create mastery, ability, or work-avoidant classroom goal structures. Thus, examining teachers' goals for teaching might shed new light on why different teachers promote different goal orientations and different strategies for coping with difficulty among their students.

No studies have conceptualized teachers' motivation in this way; more generally, research on teachers has not systematically considered how this might be informed by contemporary theories of motivation. The basic idea that teachers' motivation for teaching might influence students' motivation for learning is consistent, however, with the results of one recent study that demonstrated that individual differences in teachers' intrinsic versus extrinsic motivation for teaching were associated with the degree to which they endorsed teaching strategies supportive of students' intrinsic motivation for learning (Pelletier, Seguin-Levesque, & Legault, 2002). Further research might also examine the intriguing possibility that teachers' motivational orientations will also influence their own willingness to seek help. Thus, teachers who themselves strive to learn and acquire competence should be quite likely to engage in adaptive help seeking that can help them become more effective teachers. In contrast, teachers who pursue ability strivings should be inclined to protect their self-esteem by concealing difficulties or attributing them to causes over which they have no control and for which they need take no responsibility. In both cases, they should be reluctant to seek help. Finally, work-avoidant teachers, like work-avoidant students, might be most likely to try to get others to solve problems for them, and, for example, to refer troubled students to others, or to suggest that parents pay for extra tutoring.

To summarize, research has confirmed the important role of students' achievement orientations, but the potential of achievement goal theory for understanding teaching has not been tapped. The first challenge is to examine whether orientations toward the purposes or goals of teaching do indeed correspond, at least to some extent, with orientations towards the purposes or goals of learning. If this is the case, the present preliminary analysis of how individual differences in teachers' own achievement goals might influence teachers' helping and students' help-seeking strategies might provide a new framework also for studying other aspects of student and teacher behavior and the relations between them.

EDUCATIONAL POLICY AND SCHOOL REFORM

There is no doubt, first, that students are more likely to engage in adaptive help seeking when they pursue mastery goals than when they pursue ability, extrinsic, or work-avoidant goals, and second, that adaptive help seeking is indeed preferable to various alternative strategies for responding to difficulty. This conclusion converges with prior recommendations that schools should create mastery goal contexts because these are most consistently associated with positive educational processes and outcomes (Ames, 1992; Butler, 2000; Maehr & Midgley, 1996). Mastery contexts are also most likely to promote "equality of motivational opportunity" (Nicholls, 1989) and to enable students of diverse abilities and backgrounds to develop adaptive self-regulatory strategies, including help seeking, and positive engagement with their schoolwork. Another implication of this review is that it is important for schools to create mastery contexts also for teachers. Thus, I have ventured that just as students who pursue mastery goals are more effective and satisfied learners, teachers who pursue mastery goals may be more effective and satisfied teachers.

There is some consensus as to how teachers, classrooms, and schools can convey that it is more important and valuable to learn and acquire worthwhile knowledge, understandings, and skills than it is to strive mainly to achieve higher grades than others (for extended discussions see Ames, 1992; Maehr & Midgley, 1996; Newman, 2000; Nicholls, 1989; Ryan & La

Guardia, 1999). In brief, they need to develop meaningful curricula, provide engaging and challenging assignments, create activity structures that favor the collaborative construction of knowledge, and include students as genuine partners in the learning process. Teachers also need to provide opportunities for students to experience for themselves that difficulty can be a springboard for learning and development by providing them with appropriate scaffolds and responding to requests for assistance with constructive help. Teachers can provide such help also when it is not solicited, by giving students informative feedback that focuses their attention both on what they have achieved and on where and how they can improve (Butler, 1987, 2000). It is also clear that educational environments promote ability goals when they segregate students into groups or tracks on the basis of their presumed ability, administer frequent tests, evaluate students relative to others, construct assignments and tests that require and assess rote learning and lower order thinking and strategies, rather than the construction of knowledge, higher order problem solving, and deep processing strategies, use competitive and extrinsic incentives to motivate students, and discourage students from soliciting help.

Research on achievement goals thus converges with that generated by related approaches such as self-determination theory (Deci & Ryan, 1985) to provide policymakers with a clear and coherent set of principles for informing and guiding school reform. It is true that these principles are not easy to implement and require the patient investment of considerable resources, primarily in the professional training and development of educators, but this does not seem to be the main obstacle to their implementation. Rather, the climate among policymakers has shifted rather radically in the last decade, in the United States and in countries such as England and Israel, and has done so in ways that are diametrically opposed to the recommendations of motivation researchers.

Specifically, both the No Child Left Behind education law passed in the United States in 2002 and numerous recent blueprints for educational reform (e.g., Department for Education and Employment, 1999; National Task Force for the Advancement of Education in Israel, 2005) are organized around the assumption that raising educational standards can be best accomplished by (a) increasing competition between schools over students and resources by, for example, enabling parental choice of schools alongside school choice of students and encouraging principals to raise funds from nongovernmental sources and (b) increasing accountability by mandated standardized testing of all students. Some such initiatives also incorporate provisions for rewarding or imposing sanctions on schools and teachers in accordance with test results; these will also influence students by, for example, determining whether they are held back a year and whether they can enter higher education, or the school of their choice.

In motivational terms, the common denominator is that current trends should undermine mastery strivings and enhance ability strivings among students and teachers alike. Indeed, there is some evidence that when schools and teachers receive poor grades in such a competitive system, they behave much as do students who get low grades in competitive classrooms, and become less, rather than more, motivated and effective (Butler, 1996; Maehr & Midgley, 1996; Pelletier et al., 2002; Ryan & La Guardia, 1999). In the present context, such trends can also be expected to create environments in which teachers will be too pressured to provide students with constructive help and students will be too pressured to engage in adaptive help seeking. They should also create environments in which teachers themselves should be reluctant to seek help from colleagues, principals, or other professionals who could enable them to become more effective teachers. Thus, one must be concerned that although the educational recommendations that emerge from research on student motivation and academic help seeking are remarkably consistent, the likelihood that they will be adopted by policy makers at the present time seems rather slim.

REFERENCES

Ames, C. (1992). Goals, structures, and student motivation. *Journal of Educational Psychology, 84,* 261–271.

Ames, R. (1983a). Help-seeking and achievement orientation: Perspectives from attribution theory. In B. M. DePaulo, A. Nadler, & J. D. Fisher (Eds.), *New directions in helping: Vol. 2. Help-seeking* (pp. 165–186). New York: Academic Press.

Ames, R. (1983b). Teachers' attributions for their own teaching. In J. Levine & M. Wang (Eds.). *Teacher and student perceptions: Implications for learning* (pp. 105–124). Hillsdale, NJ: Lawrence Erlbaum Associates.

Anderman, E. M., Maehr, M. L., & Midgley, C. (1999). Declining motivation after the transition to middle school: Schools can make a difference. *Journal of Research and Development in Education, 32,* 131–147.

Batson, C. D. (1998). Altruism and prosocial behavior. In D. T. Gilbert, S. T. Fiske, & G. Lindzey (Eds.), *The handbook of social psychology* (4th ed., Vol. 2, pp. 282–316). New York: McGraw-Hill.

Beller, E. (1957). Dependency and autonomous achievement striving related to orality and anality in early childhood. *Child Development, 28,* 287–315.

Berkovitz, L. (1972). Social norms, feelings and other factors affecting helping and altruism. In L. Berkovitz (Ed.), *Advances in experimental social psychology* (Vol. 6, pp. 63–108). New York: Academic Press.

Brophy, J. (1985). Teachers' expectations, motives and goals for working with problem students. In C. Ames & R. Ames (Eds.), *Research on motivation in education, Vol. 2: The classroom milieu* (pp. 175–214). New York, Academic Press.

Brophy, J. E., & Good, T. L. (1970). Teachers' communications of differential expectations for children's classroom performance: Some behavioral data. *Journal of Educational Psychology, 61,* 365–374.

Butler, R. (1987). Task-involving and ego-involving properties of evaluation: Effects of different feedback conditions on motivational perceptions, interest and performance. *Journal of Educational Psychology, 79,* 474–482.

Butler, R. (1992). What young people want to know when: The effects of mastery and ability goals on social information-seeking. *Journal of Personality and Social Psychology, 62,* 934–943.

Butler, R. (1994). Teacher communications and student interpretations: Effects of teacher responses to failing students on attributional inferences in two age groups. *British Journal of Educational Psychology, 64,* 277–294.

Butler, R. (1996). Motivation in the classroom. In U. Last & S. Zilberman (Eds.), *Psychology in the school* (pp. 35–58). Jerusalem: Magnes Press. (In Hebrew)

Butler, R. (1998). Determinants of help seeking: Relations between perceived reasons for classroom help-avoidance and help-seeking behaviors in an experimental context. *Journal of Educational Psychology, 90,* 630–644.

Butler, R. (1999). Information-seeking and achievement motivation in middle childhood and adolescence: The role of conceptions of ability. *Developmental Psychology, 35,* 146–163.

Butler, R. (2000). What learners want to know: The role of achievement goals in shaping information seeking, learning and interest. In C. Sansone & J. M. Harackiewicz (Eds.), *Intrinsic and extrinsic motivation: The search for optimal motivation and performance* (pp. 161–194). San Diego, CA: Academic Press.

Butler, R. (in preparation). Effects of ability grouping on student motivation and help seeking.

Butler, R., & Neuman, O. (1995). Effects of task and ego achievement goals on help-seeking behaviors and attitudes. *Journal of Educational Psychology, 87,* 261–271.

Deci, E. L., & Ryan, R. M. (1985). *Intrinsic motivation and self determination in human behavior.* New York: Plenum.

DePaulo, B. M., Nadler, A., & Fisher, J. D. (Eds.). (1983). *New directions in helping: Vol 2. Help-seeking.* New York: Academic Press.

Department for Education and Employment. (1999). *The national curriculum.* London: DfEE/QCA.

Dillon, J. T., (1982). The multidisciplinary study of questioning. *Journal of Educational Psychology, 74,* 147–165.

Dowson, M., & McInerney, D. M. (2001). Psychological parameters of students' social and work avoidance goals: A qualitative investigation. *Journal of Educational Psychology, 93,* 35–42.

Dweck, C. S. (1986). Motivational processes affecting learning. *American Psychologist, 41,* 1040–1048.

Dweck, C. S., & Leggett, E. (1988). A social cognitive approach to motivation and personality. *Psychological Review, 95,* 256–273.

Frey, K. S., & Ruble, D. N. (1985). What children say when the teachers's not around: Conflicting goals in social comparison and performance assessment in the classroom. *Journal of Personality and Social Psychology, 48,* 18–30.

Goldschmidt, N. (1999). *Orientations to learning and help seeking in math.* Unpublished master's thesis, Hebrew University, Jerusalem.

Good, T. L., Slavings, R. L., Harel, K. H., & Emerson, H. (1987). Student passivity: A study of question-asking in K–12 classrooms. *Sociology of Education, 60,* 181–199.

Harackiewicz, J. M., Barron, K. E., Pintrich, P. K., Elliot, A. J., & Thrash, T. M. (2002). Revision of achievement goal theory: Necessary and illuminating. *Journal of Educational Psychology, 94,* 638–645.

Harter, S. (1981). A new self-report scale of intrinsic versus extrinsic orientation in the classroom: Motivational and informational components. *Development Psychology, 17*, 300–312.

Ireson, J., & Hallam, S. (2001). Ability grouping in education. London: Paul Chapman Publishing.

Jagacinski, C. M. (1992). The effects of task-involvement and ego-involvement on achievement-related cognitions and behaviors. In J. L. Meece & D. H. Schunk (Eds.), *Student perceptions in the classroom* (pp. 307–326). Hillsdale, NJ: Lawrence Erlbaum Associates.

Karabenick, S. A. (2002). Seeking help in large college classes: A person-centered approach. *Contemporary Educational Psychology, 28*, 37–58.

Karabenick, S. A. (2003). Seeking help in large college classes: A person-centered approach. *Contemporary Educational Psychology, 28*, 37–58.

Karabenick, S. A. (2004). Perceived achievement goal structure and college help seeking *Journal of Educational Psychology, 96*, 569–581.

Karabenick, S. A., & Knapp, J. R. (1988). Help-seeking and the need for academic assistance. *Journal of Educational Psychology, 80*, 406–408.

Karabenick, S. A., & Knapp, J. R. (1991). Relationship of academic help seeking to the use of learning strategies and other achievement behavior in college students. *Journal of Educational Psychology, 83*, 221–230.

Karabenick, S. A., & Sharma, R. (1994). Teacher support of student questioning in the college classroom: Its relation to student characteristics and role in the classroom questioning process. *Journal of Educational Psychology, 86*, 90–103.

Krebs, D. (1987). The challenge of altruism in biology and psychology. In C. Crawford, M. Smith, & D. Krebs (Eds.), *Sociobiology and psychology: Ideas, issues and applications* (pp. 81–118). Hillsdale, NJ: Lawrence Erlbaum Associates.

Kulik, C. L., & Kulik, J. A. (1992). Meta-analytic findings on grouping programs. *Gifted Child Quarterly, 36*, 73–77.

Latané, B., & Darley, J. (1970). *The unresponsive bystander: Why doesn't he help?* New York: Appleton-Century-Crofts.

Maehr, M.. L., & Midgley, C. (1996). *Transforming school culture*. Boulder, CO: Westview Press.

Marsh, H. W., & Hau, K. T. (2003). Big-Fish-Little-Pond effect on academic self-concept: A cross-cultural (26-country) test of the negative effects of academically selective schools. *American Psychologist, 58*, 364–376.

McClelland, D. C. (1953). *The achievement motive*. New York: Appleton-Century-Crofts.

Merton, V. Merton, R. K., & Barber, E. (1983). Client ambivalence in professional relationships: The problem of seeking help from strangers. In B. M. DePaulo, A. Nadler, & J. Fisher (Eds.), *New directions in helping: Vol. 2. Help-seeking* (pp. 14–44). New York: Academic Press.

Middleton, M., & Midgley, C. (1997). Avoiding the demonstration of the lack of ability: An under-explored aspect of goal theory. *Journal of Educational Psychology, 89*, 710–718.

Midgley, C. (Ed.). (2002). *Goals, structures and patterns of adaptive learning*. Mahwah, NJ: Lawrence Erlbaum Associates.

Murdock, T. B., Hale, N. M., & Weber, M. (2001). Predictors of cheating among early adolescents: Academic and social motivations. *Contemporary Educational Psychology, 26*, 96–115

Nadler, A. (1987). Determinants of help-seeking behavior: the effects of helper's similarity, task centrality and recipients' self-esteem. *European Journal of Social Psychology, 17*, 57–67.

Nadler, A. (1991). Help-seeking behavior: Psychological costs and instrumental benefits. In M. S. Clark (Ed.), *Review of personality and social psychology* (Vol. 12, pp. 290–312). New York: Sage.

Nadler, A. (1991). Help-seeking behavior: Psychological costs and instrumental benefits. In M. S. Clark (Ed.), *Prosocial behavior* (pp. 290–311). Thousand Oaks, CA: Sage.

Nadler, A. (1998). Relationship, esteem, and achievement perspectives on autonomous and independent help seeking. In S. A. Karabenick (Ed.), *Strategic help seeking: Implications for learning and teaching*. Mahwah, NJ: Lawrence Erlbaum Associates.

National Task Force for the Advancement of Education in Israel. (2005). National Education Program, Jerusalem Ministry of Education.

Nelson-Le Gall, S. (1981). Help-seeking: An understudied problem-solving skill in children. *Developmental Review, 1*, 224–246.

Nelson-Le Gall, S. (1985). Help-seeking in learning. In E. W. Gordon (Ed.), *Review of research in education* (Vol. 12, pp. 55–90). Washington, DC: American Educational Research Association.

Nelson-Le Gall, S., & Glor-Scheib, S. (1985). Help-seeking in elementary classrooms: An observational study. *Contemporary Educational Psychology, 10*, 58–71.

Nelson-Le Gall, S., & Jones, E. (1990). Cognitive-motivational influences on the help-seeking behavior of black children. *Child Development, 61*, 581–589.

Newman, R. S. (1990). Children's help seeking in the classroom: The role of motivational factors and attitudes. *Journal of Educational Psychology, 82*, 71–80.

Newman, R. S. (1991). Goals and self-regulated learning: What motivates children to seek academic help? In M. L. Maehr & P. R. Pintrich (Eds.), *Advances in motivation and achievement* (Vol 7, pp 151–183). Greenwich, CT: JAI Press.

Newman, R. S. (2000). Social influences on the development of children's adaptive help seeking: The role of parents, teachers and peers. *Developmental Review, 20*, 350–404.

Newman, R. S., & Goldin, L. (1990). Children's reluctance to seek help with homework. *Journal of Educational Psychology, 82*, 92–100.

Newman, R. S., & Schwager, M. T. (1995). Students' help seeking during problem solving: Effects of grade, goal, and prior achievement. *American Educational Research Journal, 32*, 352–376.

Nicholls, J. G. (1984). Achievement motivation: Conceptions of ability, subjective experience, task choice, and performance. *Psychological Review, 91*, 328–346.

Nicholls, J. G. (1989). *The competitive ethos and democratic education*. Cambridge, MA: Harvard University Press.

Oakes, J. (1985). *Keeping track: How schools structure inequality*. New Haven, CT: Yale University Press.

Omoto, A. M., & Snyder, M. (1995). Sustained helping without obligation: Motivation, longevity of service and perceived attitude change among AIDS volunteers. *Journal of Personality and Social Psychology, 68*, 671–686.

Pelletier, L. G., Seguin-Levesque, C., & Legault, L. (2002). Pressure from above and pressure from below as determinants of teachers' motivation and teaching behaviors. *Journal of Educational Psychology, 94*, 186–196.

Reuman, D. A. (1989). How social comparison mediates the relation between ability-grouping practices and students' achievement expectancies in mathematics. *Journal of Educational Psychology, 81,* 178–189.

Ryan, A. M., Gheen, M. H., & Midgley, C. (1998). Why do some students avoid asking for help? An examination of the interplay between students' academic efficacy, teachers' social-emotional role and the classroom goal structure. *Journal of Educational Psychology, 90,* 1–8.

Ryan, A. M., Hicks, L., & Midgley, C. (1997). Social goals, academic goals, and avoiding seeking help in the classroom. *Journal of Early Adolescence, 17,* 152–171.

Ryan, A. M., & Pintrich, P. R. (1997). "Should I ask for help?" The role of motivation and attitudes in adolescents' help-seeking in math class. *Journal of Educational Psychology, 89,* 329–341

Ryan, R. M., & La Guardia, J. G. (1999). Achievement motivation within a pressured society: Intrinsic and extrinsic motivations to learn and the politics of school reform. In T. Urdan (Ed.), *Advances in motivation and achievement* (Vol. 11, pp. 45–85). Greenwich, CT: JAI Press.

Shapiro, E. G. (1983). Embarrassment and help-seeking. In B. M. DePaulo, A. Nadler, & J. D. Fisher, (Eds.), *New directions in helping: Vol. 2. Help-seeking* (pp. 143–163). New York: Academic Press.

Tessler, R. C., & Schwartz, S. H. (1972). Help-seeking, self-esteem, and achievement motivation: An attributional analysis. *Journal of Personality and Social Psychology, 21,* 318–326.

Turner, J. C., Midgley, C., Meyer, D. K., Gheen, M., Anderman, E. M., Kang, Y., & Patrick, H. (2002). The classroom environment and students' reports of avoidance strategies in mathematics: A multi-method study. *Journal of Educational Psychology, 94,* 88–106.

van der Meij, H. (1988). Constraints on question-asking in classrooms. *Journal of Educational Psychology, 80,* 401–405.

Weiner, B. (1980). A cognitive (attribution)-emotion-action model of motivated behavior: An analysis of help-giving. *Journal of Personality and Social Psychology, 39,* 186–200.

Winterbottom, M. (1958). The relationship of need for achievement to learning experiences in independence and mastery. In J. A. Atkinson (Ed.), *Motives in fantasy, action and society* (pp. 453–478). Princeton, NJ: Van Nostrand.

Wispé, L. G. (Ed.). (1978). *Altruism, sympathy, and helping: Psychological and sociological perspectives.* New York: Academic Press.

Chapter 3

Help Seeking in Cooperative Learning Groups

Noreen M. Webb
Marsha Ing
Nicole Kersting
Kariane Mari Nemer
University of California, Los Angeles

Research on cooperative learning shows that working collaboratively with others has the potential to increase achievement (Slavin, 1990). However, simply putting students in small groups does not guarantee that they will interact with each other in ways that benefit learning (Bossert, 1988–1989; Webb & Palincsar, 1996). Much attention has been paid to help giving and receiving and the significant role these behaviors play in predicting how well students learn how to solve problems in cooperative groups. Previous research identifies several important categories of help-related behavior: the level of help exchanged (explanations rather than just answers) and whether recipients of help apply it themselves to the problem or task at hand (Webb & Palincsar, 1996).

From a theoretical perspective, *giving* explanations may promote learning by encouraging the explainer to reorganize and clarify material, to recognize misconceptions, to fill in gaps in his or her own understanding, to internalize and acquire new strategies and knowledge, and to develop new perspectives and understanding (Bargh & Schul, 1980; King, 1992; Peterson, Janicki, & Swing, 1981; Rogoff, 1991; Saxe, Gearhart,

Note, & Paduano, 1993; Valsiner, 1987; Webb, 1991). When explaining their problem-solving processes, students think about the salient features of the problem, which develops their problem-solving strategies as well as a metacognitive awareness of what they do and do not understand (Cooper, 1999). Giving nonelaborated help such as answers or calculations, on the other hand, is expected to result in fewer benefits because it involves less cognitive restructuring or clarifying on the part of the help giver. *Receiving* explanations may help students to correct misconceptions, to strengthen connections between new information and previous learning (Mayer, 1984; Sweller, 1989; Wittrock, 1990), and to bridge from the known to the unknown (Rogoff, 1990). Explanations from peers may be especially effective because students are likely to understand, and be familiar with, each other's misunderstandings, and can explain concepts in familiar terms (Brown & Palincsar, 1989; Noddings, 1985; Vedder, 1985; Vygotsky, 1981) and at a level that other students understand (Tharp & Gallimore, 1988). Receiving nonelaborated help, on the other hand, may not enable help receivers to correct their misconceptions or lack of understanding.

Vedder (1985) posed several conditions in order to maximize the efficacy of help received. He emphasized that help receivers must both have and take advantage of the opportunity to apply the explanation to the problem at hand. Through engaging with the material themselves after receiving explanations, the help receivers may generate self-explanations that assist them in understanding principles, constructing specific inference rules for problem solving, and repairing problematic mental models (Chi, 2000; Chi & Bassock, 1989; Chi, Bassock, Lewis, Reimann, & Glaser, 1989). In addition, these attempts to solve problems may lead to students engaging in self-monitoring of their own understanding and help them become aware of gaps in their knowledge (Chi & Bassock, 1989). If they do not attempt to apply explanations by solving problems on their own, students may maintain a false sense of competence. Furthermore, if a student makes a mistake while attempting to solve a problem on her own, this may help her groupmates to recognize her misconceptions and to provide additional information. Without firsthand knowledge that a student still cannot solve a problem alone, other group members may rely on a student's own assessment of whether she understands it (e.g., "I get it"), which may not be accurate (Shavelson, Webb, Stasz, & McArthur, 1988).

Previous research on the relationship between student help-related behavior and student learning in peer-directed small groups generally confirms these predictions. First, previous findings empirically confirm the power of giving elaborated explanations compared to giving nonelaborated help (Brown & Palincsar, 1989; Fuchs et al., 1997; King, 1992; Nattiv, 1994; Peterson et al., 1981; Slavin, 1987; Yackel, Cobb,

Wood, Wheatley, & Merkel, 1990). Second, researchers provide mixed evidence about the effectiveness of *receiving* explanations, finding weak and inconsistent relationships between receiving explanations and learning outcomes (Hooper, 1992; Nattiv, 1994; Ross & Cousins, 1995a,1995b; Webb, 1989, 1991; Webb & Palincsar, 1996). In analyses examining both the level of help received and the usage of help received, Webb, Troper, and Fall (1995; see also Webb & Farivar, 1999; Webb & Mastergeorge, 2003) found that the level of follow-up activity after receiving help strongly predicted achievement, confirming Vedder's (1985) expectations, and that carrying out high-level follow-up behavior required receiving explanations.

Researchers have paid much less attention to help *seeking* in cooperative settings. Cooperative learning studies that have addressed help seeking have usually examined the effectiveness of different types of requests for help. The type of request for help figures prominently in Nelson-Le Gall's (1981, 1985, 1992; Nelson-Le Gall, Gumerman & Scott-Jones, 1983) comprehensive, five-step model of children's help seeking in which the student experiencing difficulty must use effective strategies to elicit help, and in Newman's (1991, 1998) expanded model of adaptive help-seeking behavior in the classroom. In examining the ways in which students phrase requests for help, Wilkinson and colleagues showed that explicit, precise, and direct questions are more likely than vague and indirect questions to elicit explanations (Peterson, Wilkinson, Spinelli, & Swing, 1984; Wilkinson, 1985; Wilkinson & Calculator, 1982a, 1982b; Wilkinson & Spinelli, 1983; see also Webb & Mastergeorge, 2003).

Still, little research addresses how these different help-seeking requests shape students' experiences in cooperative groups. In the context of a semester-long program of cooperative learning in middle school classrooms, this chapter explores how students' help seeking influenced the help that they received, their use of the help received, and their eventual learning outcomes. We focus specifically on the group-work experiences and learning of students who sought help in two different ways: asking general questions that expressed confusion or lack of understanding versus asking specific questions about how to solve the problems. We analyze the discussions that took place during group work to shed light on the reasons for certain help-seeking and help-giving behaviors. In doing so, we examine the group dynamics that influenced students' help seeking and show that help seeking influenced, and was influenced by, group dynamics in a reciprocal fashion. We next describe the cooperative learning program implemented in seventh-grade mathematics classrooms and the design of the study. Then we present results of analyses describing help seekers and their learning outcomes, and analyses of group work experiences of students who sought help in different ways.

COOPERATIVE LEARNING PROGRAM AND STUDY DESIGN

Cooperative Learning Program

The cooperative learning program had four sequential sets of activities designed to develop students' ability to work effectively in small groups: inclusion activities (also called class building); activities to develop basic communication skills; activities to develop students' helping skills in work groups; and activities to develop students' ability to give explanations (Farivar & Webb, 1991). Due to the large number of activities, we spread them out over the course of a semester.

Developing Communications Skills.   Prior to the first curriculum unit (decimal operations: Phase 1), students carried out activities in class building and basic communications skills. For class building, students played games to learn classmates' names, interests, and aspirations. To develop basic communication skills, teachers introduced norms for group behavior, and the class discussed and made charts for posting in the classroom that summarized them (e.g., attentive listening, no put-downs, 12-inch voices—no yelling, equal participation by everyone, zero noise level signal; Gibbs, 1987). Classes also discussed and made charts of social skills to use in small groups: checking for understanding, sharing ideas and information, encouraging, and checking for agreement (Johnson, Johnson, & Holubec, 1988). Although these activities did not focus on help seeking, they set the stage for explanation giving by emphasizing understanding and sharing ideas, rather than focusing on the correct answers.

Developing Helping Skills.   Prior to the second curriculum unit (fractions: Phase 2), students carried out activities to develop their ability to help each other while working on problems in small groups. To introduce specific helping skills, the teacher displayed and discussed charts of behaviors for students to engage in when they did not understand how to solve a problem (help seekers) and when they gave help to another student (help givers). We based the help-seeking chart (shown in Table 3.1) on Nelson-Le Gall's (1981, 1985; Nelson-Le Gall et al., 1983) model of effective help seeking. For "employment of strategies to elicit help" (Nelson-Le Gall et al., 1983), we included the instruction to ask clear and precise questions to discourage students from asking general questions or making general statements of confusion. The chart for help givers (shown in Table 3.2) emphasized giving explanations rather than only the answer. It also gave examples of ways that the help giver could encourage the active participation of help seekers, such as inviting other students to ask for help, watching how students solved problems, and checking for help seekers' understand-

TABLE 3.1

Chart of Behaviors for Students Who Do Not Understand
How to Solve the Problem (Help Seekers)

Problem: Groups design their own restaurant menus with prices for entrees, desserts, and drinks. They each select a meal, and estimate the total cost for their entire group, including 8.5% sales tax and 15% tip.

Behavior	*Example*
1. Recognize that you need help.	"I don't understand how to calculate the sales tax."
2. Decide to get help from another student.	"I'm going to ask someone for help."
3. Choose someone to help you.	"I think Maria could help me."
4. Ask for help.	"Could you help me with the sales tax?"
5. Ask clear and precise questions.	"Our group's bill is $24.00. Why don't we just add $0.85 for the sales tax?"
6. Keep asking until you understand.	"So if the bill was $50.00, are you saying that the sales tax would be 8.5% of $50.00?"

Note. From "Helping and Getting Help: Essential Skills for Effective Group Problem Solving" by Sydney Farivar and Noreen M. Webb (1994), *Arithmetic Teacher, 41*(9), p. 522. Copyright 1994 by the National Council of Teachers of Mathematics. Reprinted by permission.

ing after receiving help. We included these steps to ensure that help givers gave the students who needed help an opportunity to try to solve the problems for themselves, as anecdotal observations in previous studies suggested that groups try to "help" by solving the problems for other students (Shavelson et al., 1988; Vedder, 1985).

Developing Explaining Skills. Prior to the third curriculum unit (percentages: Phase 3), students carried out activities designed to develop their ability to give explanations and to encourage the active participation of help seekers. In an activity adapted from a study by Swing and Peterson (1982), students performed skits in front of the class to demonstrate "good" helping and "unhelpful" helping behavior. In the skit for good helping, the help giver explained to the help seeker how to carry out the steps in solving a problem, gave her an opportunity to try to solve the problem, corrected her errors with explanations of what she should do and why, asked follow-up questions to make sure that she understood, and gave praise for work well done. In the skit for unhelpful helping, students gave each other only answers and did not describe how to solve the problem, told help seekers to hurry up, and placed their emphasis on getting the answer rather than on understanding how to solve the problem. The skits focused on the contrast between different kinds of help giving (a willingness to provide

TABLE 3.2

Chart for Students Who Do Understand How to Solve the Problem
(Help Givers)

Behavior	Example
1. Notice when other students need help.	See if anyone in your group needs help.
2. Tell other students to ask you if they need help.	"If you need help, ask me."
3. When someone asks for help, help him or her.	"I'll help you. What don't you understand?"
4. Be a good listener.	Let your teammate explain what he or she doesn't understand.
5. Give explanations instead of the answer.	"8.5% is not the same as $0.85. The sales tax is not the same amount of money for every bill. The bigger the bill is, the bigger the tax will be. So here we have to figure out 8.5% of $24.00. 10% of $24.00 is $2.40, so the sales tax will be a little less than that."
6. Watch how your teammate solves it.	
7. Give specific feedback on how your teammate solved the problem.	"You multiplied the numbers OK, but you have to be careful of the decimal point. If the bill is $24.00, the sales tax can't be $204.00."
8. Check for understanding.	"Tell me again why you think the sales tax is $2.04 instead of $204.00."
9. Praise your teammate.	"Good job!" "Nice work!" "You've got it!"

Note. Table from "Helping and Getting Help: Essential Skills for Effective Group Problem Solving" by Sydney Farivar and Noreen M. Webb (1994), *Arithmetic Teacher, 41*(9), p. 523. Copyright 1994 by the National Council of Teachers of Mathematics. Reprinted by permission.

elaborated help vs. an emphasis on speed and answers) and did not highlight differences in help-seeking behavior (e.g., asking specific vs. general questions). In both skits, help seekers asked what we now code as general questions ("Will you help me?" and "How did you get that?").

Design and Procedures of the Study

Sample. We implemented the cooperative learning program in six seventh-grade general mathematics classes (184 students) at an urban middle school in the Los Angeles metropolitan area. Students had little or no previous experience working collaboratively with other students. Two teachers each taught three classes. All classes had comparable entering student achievement levels and had similar mixes of student gender and ethnic background. All students except those in pre-algebra classes and in remedial or special needs classes, took these general math classes, so the classes represented a fairly wide range of achievement levels. The ethnic breakdown of students was 55% Latino, 26% White, 14% African-American, 3% Asian-American, and 2% Middle Eastern or Other. Nearly all students were proficient in English, although many were bilingual. Four of the six classes (two for each teacher) participated in all three phases of the program and served as the basis for the analyses we present here. The other two classrooms did not receive the full cooperative learning program and served as a comparison group; we do not analyze those classes here (see Webb & Farivar, 1994, for results concerning the contrast between the two comparison classes and the four classes that received the full program). We focus here on the 21 groups that had good-quality audiotape data for all three phases and few students absent on the days of recording.

Procedures. At the beginning of the semester, before any other activity, all classes completed a pretest on general mathematics achievement. Based on pretest scores, ethnic background, and gender, we assigned students to heterogeneous small groups that reflected the mix of backgrounds in the class as closely as possible. We defined three achievement strata in each class based on the pretest scores: high (top 25% of the sample), medium (middle 50%), and low (bottom 25%). We formed groups so that each had one high-achieving student, one low-achieving student, and two medium-achieving students.

At the beginning of each class period, the teacher introduced the whole class to the material for that day and solved a few example problems with the class. Students then worked within their small groups either on problems assigned in the textbook (general mathematics for Grade 7: Eicholz, O'Daffer, & Fleenor, 1989) or on teacher-prepared activities (e.g., calculating sales tax for meals selected from restaurant menus). The teacher reminded the class about the expectations for behavior, especially to consult each other first before asking her for help. The teacher circulated among groups, watching groups work and answering questions when necessary. At the end of each class period, groups turned in their classwork and spent 5 minutes completing and discussing their checklist of expected group-work behaviors. Periodically, the teacher discussed the groups' experiences in the whole-class setting. The teacher used a group reward structure to evaluate classwork: She randomly selected one student's paper from the group for grading.

On at least one day during each curriculum unit, we audiotaped classes working in small groups for the entire class period. During Phase 1 (multiplication with decimals), we taped students trying to determine the costs of long-distance telephone calls (e.g., "What would be the cost of making a 4-minute call to a number with a 755 prefix?"; Eicholz et al., 1989, p. 96) using a table with three columns: (a) the prefix of the telephone number, (b) the rate for the first minute of the telephone call for that prefix, and (c) the rate for each additional minute of the telephone call for that prefix. During Phase 2 (fractions), we taped students adding fractions with like or unlike denominators (e.g., 3/4 + 2/3). During Phase 3 (percentages), we taped students converting decimals to percents and percents to decimals (e.g., "Convert 0.36 to a percent" and "In order to find the sale price of a $12 shirt that is on sale for 25% off, convert 25% to a decimal").

Students completed a pretest at the beginning of each unit and a posttest at the end of each unit. For the statistical analyses correlating student behavior with student achievement, we focused on the posttest problems that corresponded to the material covered on the days of audio taping. This made it possible to link students' behavior and posttest performance on exactly the same content. Moreover, the posttest scores (and behavior codes, discussed later) we used in the analyses focused on the critical components of those problems, that is, the components that were central to solving the problem and those that caused students the most difficulty. In Phase 1, the posttest problem corresponding to the exercises the students completed on the day of taping was: "Find the cost of a 10-minute telephone call in which the first minute costs $0.30 and each additional minute costs $0.08." Determining the number of additional minutes in the telephone call (here, 9) constituted the critical component on this problem. In Phase 2, seven posttest problems paralleled those assigned to groups during the day of audio recording (addition of fractions with like and unlike denominators). We used adding the numerators and leaving the denominators unchanged (like denominators: Topic A) and determining the common denominator and converting the fractions to equivalent fractions with the common denominator (unlike denominators: Topic B) as the two critical components during our statistical analyses. In Phase 3, seven posttest problems paralleled group-work problems (converting between decimals and percents). The mean of the scores across these items served as the achievement score used in the analyses.

Coding of Verbal Interaction. Using transcripts of the group-work audiotapes, we identified and categorized student behavior. We coded students' indications of a need for help, the help received, and the activity students carried out after receiving help. Indications of a need for help included general requests for help about how to solve the problem or general statements of confusion ("How do you do that one?", "I don't get it."), requests for specific explanations or questions about specific components of the problem ("How did you get 29?", "Why is it over 12?"), and errors ("It's 13 times 30" instead of "13 times 29", "I got 6.4" instead of ".064"). In the statistical analyses, we used variables that consisted of a student's frequency of each category of a need for help summed over all problems attempted during group work.

We coded the help students received using a five-level rubric (consistent with the coding used by Webb, Nemer, Kersting, & Ing, 2004). The levels differ in the degree of elaboration and the extent of verbal labeling of the numbers and numerical rules given (see Table 3.3). We classified one level of help (Level 4) as high because it included at least some explanation of how to obtain the numbers and/or the meaning of the numbers and included at least some verbal labeling of quantities. Although we refer to Level 4 as high-level help throughout this chapter because it constituted the highest level we observed in this study, we acknowledge that it is not high in an absolute sense. Moreover, Level 4 help was heavily procedurally based, and rarely included any reference to, or explanation of, the underlying structure of the problem or the conceptual reasons for carrying out an arithmetic operation or procedure.

Finally, consistent with the coding used by Webb et al. (2004), we examined the nature of student verbalizations after receiving help. This included acknowledging help ("OK," Level 1) or signaling understanding ("OK, I get it," Level 1), carrying out work set up by others ("4 times 12 is 48," Level 2), and solving a problem without assistance or explaining to another student how to solve the problem (Level 3).

DESCRIPTION OF HELP SEEKERS AND THEIR LEARNING OUTCOMES

In this section we first compare the behavior and achievement outcomes of students who did or did not indicate a need for help. Then we explore further the students who sought help by examining the behavior and achievement of students who asked different types of questions.

Comparison of Students Who Did or Did Not Indicate a Need for Help

To set the stage for the primary focus in this study—students who needed help—we first give information about students who indicated a need for help relative to the other students in the sample. Table 3.4 gives the percentage of students who did or did not indicate a need for help. Phases 1 and 3 showed a similar pattern. In those phases, the majority of students indicated a need for help (as shown by asking general or specific questions, or making errors), and a substantial minority of students did not indicate a need for help but showed enough correct work to suggest that they understood how to solve part or all of the problem. In Phase 2, in contrast, fewer students indicated a need for help, and a majority of students showed at least some correct work.

TABLE 3.3

Levels of Help

			Examples	
Level	Description	Phase 1	Phase 2	Phase 3
			High	
4	Explanation that includes verbal labeling of at least one quantity	19 cents is for the first minute. And then each additional minute is 12 cents. For 5 minutes, the first minute is 19 cents, then the next 4 minutes will be 12.	You see how it has different denominators, so what you have to do is do the common multiples. Go, like, 4 then put 8 then 12 then 16. Then the same for 3, 6, 9, 12. When you do that, the lowest one that you have in common is 12.	You always move the decimal 2 spaces to the right when you're making it into a percent.
			Low	
3	Numerical procedure or series of calculations without verbal labeling of any quantity	It's 4 times 12.	3 plus 5 is 8.	And then you count 4 places which gives you 3.
2	Answer to all or part of the problem	29.	11/12	6.4%
1	Noncontent response	Do it like she said.	I don't know.	I got something else.
0	No response			

TABLE 3.4

Percentage of Students Who Did or Did Not Indicate a Need for Help

| | Phase 1: Decimals (n = 77) | Phase 2: Fractions (n = 74) | | Phase 3: Percent (n = 75) |
		Like Denominators (Topic A)	Unlike Denominators (Topic B)	
Indicated a need for help	61%	23%	28%	62%
Did not indicate a need for help				
Showed correct work	30%	68%	51%	24%
Showed no work	9%	9%	20%	14%

In all phases, the percentage of students who neither indicated a need for help nor provided any evidence about whether they understood how to solve the problem was fairly small. Because the students in this last group said very little during group work, we could ascertain little about their experiences. Furthermore, analyses of their pretest and posttest scores and their demographic characteristics (gender, ethnic background) showed no consistent pattern of differences with the other students. Consequently, we did not investigate these students further.

Comparisons of students who did versus did not indicate a need for help showed that students who indicated a need for help obtained lower pretest and posttest scores than students who did not indicate a need for help. These differences were statistically significant in Phases 1 and 2 (ranging from $p < .0001$ to $p = .028$) but not in Phase 3. In Phases 1 and 2, then, students who indicated a need for help during group work entered collaborative work with less knowledge than other students, and performed less well at the end. Students who indicated a need for help did not differ from other students in terms of gender or ethnic background. The remainder of this analysis, then, focuses on students who indicated a need for help.

Relationships Among Help-Seeking and Help-Receiving Behavior and Achievement

First we give descriptive information about help-seeking and help-giving behavior. We then present the partial correlations between help seeking, receiving help, and follow-up activity after receiving help and the level of achievement (posttest scores) among all students who indicated a need for help (by asking questions, making statements that signaled confusion or lack of understanding, or making errors). As can be seen in Table 3.5, students asked more general questions and made more errors, on the average, than they asked specific questions. Despite the instructions to phrase questions in specific ways, students asked few specific questions. Although it occurred infrequently, asking specific questions positively related to achievement, whereas asking general questions and making errors did not. In two of three phases, students who asked a greater number of specific questions obtained significantly higher posttest scores than students who asked fewer specific questions. The frequency of asking general questions was not statistically related to posttest scores, although the trend was negative in every phase. The frequency of errors was not related to achievement and did not show a consistent pattern across the phases.

The maximum level of help received was positively related to achievement in two of three phases. Students who received high-level help were more likely than other students to do well on the posttest. The maximum level of follow-up behavior after receiving help related positively to posttest scores in all phases. Students who solved at least one problem correctly without assistance or who explained how to solve the problem to another student obtained higher posttest scores than students who only carried out less active work after receiving help (carrying out work set up by others, acknowledging help, or not responding to help received).

To clarify the contrast between students who engaged in beneficial behavior (asking specific questions, receiving high-level help, carrying out high-level follow-up activity) and those who did not, Table 3.6 presents achievement data for those contrasting groups of students. In all cases, students who engaged in the beneficial behaviors showed higher posttest performance scores than students who did not. In Phase 1, differences between these two groups tested with analyses of covariance (using the Phase 1 pretest as the covariate) were statistically significant (ranging from $p < .001$ to $p = .03$). In Phase 2, the difference between students who engaged in beneficial behaviors and those who did not was in the expected direction for all contrasts but was statistically significant only for carrying out high-level follow-up activity ($p = .006$ for like denominators, $p = .007$ for unlike denominators, using the Phase 2 pretest as the covariate). In Phase 3 the differences between the two groups were statistically significant for help seeking and help receiving ($p = .04$) but only marginally significant for follow-up activity ($p = .08$).

DISTINGUISHING BETWEEN HELP-SEEKER SUBGROUPS

Students indicated a need for help in three ways: asking specific questions about how to solve the problem, asking general questions (or making general statements of confusion), and making errors. We subdivided students

Table 3.5

Partial Correlations[a] Between Behavior and Posttest Scores Among Students Who Exhibited Difficulty During Group Work

| | Phase 1: Decimals (n = 44)[b] | | | Phase 2: Fractions | | | | | | Phase 3: Percent (n = 46) | | |
| | | | | Like Denominators (Topic A) (n = 17) | | | Unlike Denominators (Topic B) (n = 21) | | | | | |
	M	SD	r	M	SD	r	M	SD	r	M	SD	r
Help-seeking behavior[c]												
Specific questions	.95	1.36	.47[h]	.58	.25	−.03	.38	.86	−.09	.26	.61	.35[g]
General questions	3.00	3.77	−.27	1.06	1.06	−.10	1.29	1.21	−.36	1.41	1.92	−.19
Errors	1.36	1.43	.23	1.00	1.31	.16	.86	1.15	.21	1.48	1.57	−.13
Maximum level of help received[d]	3.20	1.43	.31[g]	2.19	1.76	.43	2.19	1.50	−.04	2.46	1.49	.39[h]
Maximum level of follow-up behavior[e]	2.18	1.60	.62[i]	1.56	1.79	.61[g]	1.19	1.25	.58[h]	2.11	1.73	.29[g]

[a]Controlling for pretest scores.
[b]Sample sizes include students with non-missing data on all variables.
[c]Frequency of occurrence.
[d]Level of help received ranges from 0 to 4 (see text).
[e]Level of follow-up behavior ranges from 0 to 3 (see text).
[f]Significant at $p = .06$.
[g]Significant at $p < .05$.
[h]Significant at $p < .01$.
[i]Significant at $p < .001$.

TABLE 3.6

Posttest Performance for Different Patterns of Behavior Among Students Who Exhibited Difficulty During Group Work

| | Phase 1: Decimals (n = 44) | | | Phase 2: Fractions | | | | | | Phase 3: Percent (n = 46) | | |
| | | | | Like Denominators (Topic A) (n = 17) | | | Unlike Denominators (Topic B) (n = 21) | | | | | |
	n	M	SD	n	M	SD	n	M	SD	n	M	SD
Asked specific questions												
No	23	.13	.34	13	.51	.35	17	.29	.34	38	.61	.24
Yes	21	.48	.51	3	.55	.39	4	.44	.51	8	.82	.13
Received highest level of help												
No	16	.06	.25	10	.47	.28	17	.32	.39	27	.56	.25
Yes	28	.43	.50	6	.61	.44	4	.34	.31	19	.77	.15
Carried out highest level of follow-up behavior												
No	27	.04	.19	11	.36	.28	19	.25	.31	27	.58	.25
Yes	17	.71	.46	5	.87	.18	2	1.00	.00	19	.75	.19

who indicated a need for help into three subgroups based on these help-seeking behaviors: students who at some point asked specific questions (they may also have asked general questions and/or made errors), students who asked general questions but not specific ones (they may also have made errors), and students who made errors but did not ask any questions. Analyses of student behavior and performance showed a marked and consistent contrast between two of the three subgroups: the two subgroups of students who sought help (specific vs. general only). The third subgroup of students—those who made errors but did not seek help by asking questions (either specific or general)—did not show a consistent pattern of behavior or achievement across the phases and, consequently, we do not further consider these students in this chapter.

In the remainder of the chapter, then, we focus on the two subgroups of students who sought help. Our goal is to understand the differences in experiences and achievement outcomes for these two groups. We next present data on the success of the two subgroups of students in receiving high-level help and carrying out high-level follow-up behavior, as well as their achievement outcomes. Then we analyze the group work experiences of students in the two subgroups to uncover possible explanations for their differences in behavior and achievement outcomes.

Quantitative Comparisons Between Students Who Sought Specific Versus General Help

Next we present the percentage of students in each subgroup who received high-level help (Fig. 3.1) or who carried out high-level follow-up behavior (Fig. 3.2). In most phases, students who asked specific questions about how to solve the problem were more likely to receive high-level help and to carry out high-level follow-up behavior than were students who asked only general questions. In Fig. 3.3 we present the achievement results for students in each subgroup. Given these findings, it is not surprising that students who asked specific questions showed greater achievement than did students who asked only general questions (Fig. 3.3). What *is* surprising is that the benefits of receiving help and/or carrying out follow-up activity differed depending on the nature of students' help-seeking behavior. To see this in Figs. 3.4 and 3.5 we show the achievement results for students who were successful in obtaining high-level help (Fig. 3.4) or who carried out high-level follow-up behavior (Fig. 3.5). As the results show, even among students who received high-level help or engaged in high-level follow-up behavior, students who asked specific questions scored higher on the posttest than students who asked only general questions. Students who asked specific questions, then, were more likely to benefit from engaging in these high-level behaviors than were students who asked only general questions.

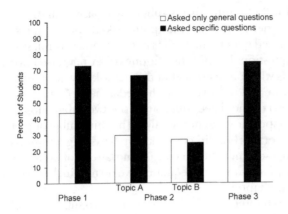

FIG. 3.1. Percent of students in each question category who received high-level help.

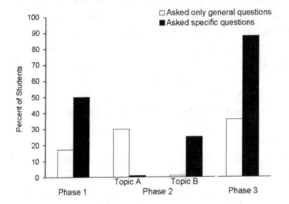

FIG. 3.2. Percent of students in each question category who carried out high-level behavior after receiving help.

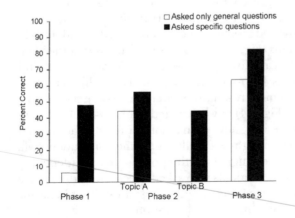

FIG. 3.3. Mean posttest performance of students in each question category.

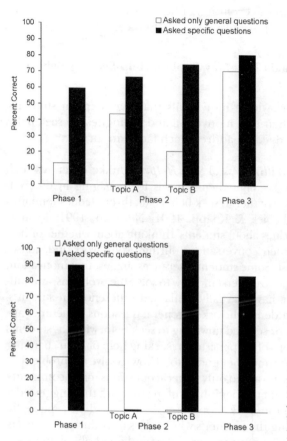

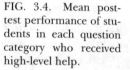

FIG. 3.4. Mean post-test performance of students in each question category who received high-level help.

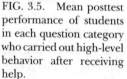

FIG. 3.5. Mean posttest performance of students in each question category who carried out high-level behavior after receiving help.

GROUP WORK EXPERIENCES OF STUDENTS WHO SOUGHT SPECIFIC VERSUS GENERAL HELP

The findings just presented show that students who asked only general questions exhibited different behavior and achievement outcomes from students who asked specific questions about how to solve the problem. In this section, we probe students' group-work experiences to understand why some students asked specific questions whereas others did not, why students who asked only general questions were less likely to receive high-level help and carry out high-level follow-up activity than students who asked specific questions, and why students who asked specific questions benefited more from engaging in high-level activity than did students who asked only general questions. In particular, we explore (a) factors within individuals that may explain differences in help seeking, (b) the role of groups' responses to help seeking in the evolution of help seekers' experiences during group work, and (c) help seekers' use of help received.

Factors Within Individuals That May Explain Help-Seeking Behavior

We examined two factors within individuals that may explain students' help-seeking behavior: their task motivation and willingness to seek help, and their level of knowledge. We address each factor in turn.

Task Motivation and Willingness to Seek Help.   Unlike other research that directly asked students about their reasons for engaging in different help-seeking strategies, or whether to seek help at all, through questionnaires or interviews (e.g., Karabenick & Knapp, 1991; Newman, 1991; Ryan & Pintrich, 1997), our only clues about students' thinking about whether or how to seek help come from their conversations during group work and, consequently, are indirect at best. Some student utterances suggest that motivation, both to work on the task and to understand how to solve the problems, and willingness to seek help may have partially explained differences in students' help-seeking behavior. Students who asked general questions sometimes appeared to lack motivation or seemed unwilling to seek help, whereas students who asked specific questions often persisted in seeking help or even changing the nature of their questions until they understood how to solve the problem.

First, several students who asked only general questions made comments early in the class period or at the beginning of group work that suggested a lack of motivation to do the work. For example, one student repeatedly muttered to himself during the teacher's whole-class introduction, "This is stupid. Stupid." Another student repeatedly complained about the heat ("Oh my God. Can we open this window?," "It's going to be hot until Sunday. I need an aspirin") and declared, "I can't work." Still another student complained that he couldn't work because his head hurt ("My head hurts ... I can't [work], I can't, I can't look at the first thing"). Only one student who asked specific questions ever voiced similar complaints at the outset of groupwork. This student had been in a fight before school and complained about pain ("My hand. My stomach hurts too bad") and said that he couldn't write ("I can't, because then it's going to hurt"). Despite his complaints, however, he did work on the task, including asking a specific question about adding fractions with like denominators.

Second, some students who asked only general questions—but none of the students who asked specific questions—admitted or showed during group work that they were (or had been) unwilling to seek help. For example, Student 1 admitted in the following that he did not understand how to solve the problem (lines 3, 5) and had copied others' work all along (line 7):

1	Student 1	Page 97. I don't want to do it.
2	Student 2	Why not?
3	Student 1	I don't know how.
4	Student 2	You don't? All you are going to do is 1 through 8 ... You know what we are doing right here?
5	Student 1	I don't.
6	Student 2	[It's] the same thing [that we were doing before].
7	Student 1	I don't even know what we are doing right here. I was copying you guys.

Not only did this student copy others' work, he misled the group by indicating on earlier problems that he "got it."

Another student (Student 4 in the excerpt that follows) voiced an incorrect answer, and one of his teammates, who suspected that he did not understand the problem and had copied from another student, pressed him to explain how he obtained his answer. Student 4, however, kept dodging her questions (lines 4, 6, 8, 10), seemingly reluctant to admit that he did not know how to solve the problem:

1	Student 3	How'd you get it? No, [another student's name], don't tell (pause) ... How'd you get it?
2	Student 4	Because you move this over and you put it right there. See?
3	Student 3	No, you move what over?
4	Student 4	I got it so don't worry.
5	Student 3	No, I want [to know] how did you get it, [student's name]?
6	Student 4	I got it.
7	Student 3	You got it because he told you?
8	Student 4	No.
9	Student 3	How did you get it then?
10	Student 4	'Cause I got it.
11	Student 3	How did you get it?

Shortly after this, he admitted that he did not understand and that he was "learning nothing" and proceeded to copy the other students' answers.

Students who asked specific questions, on the other hand, frequently showed persistence in seeking help and/or changes in help-seeking strategies that suggested they had motivation to work and learn. Students who asked specific questions showed greater persistence in seeking help than students who asked only general questions, as shown by repeated questions about the same issue (55% vs. 44% in Phase 1; 67% vs. 0% in Phase 2 for like denominators; 0% vs. 9% in Phase 2 for unlike denominators; 25% vs. 5% in

Phase 3). Moreover, a substantial number of students who asked specific questions changed the nature of their questions, for example, by asking questions that became increasingly specific (27% in Phase 1, 67% in Phase 2 for like denominators, 25% in Phase 3), whereas *none* of the students who asked only general questions changed the nature of their questions.

In the following example from Phase 1, a student who did not understand why another student used the number 29 in calculating the cost of a 30-minute long-distance telephone call persisted in asking questions until he understood. Over the course of five successive help-seeking attempts (listed below without teammate responses), his questions changed from general (2 questions) to specific (3 questions) and became increasingly focused on what he did not understand.

Student 5	(unclear) I don't get this.
Student 5	( ) I don't know. Could you ( ) repeat that again?
Student 5	I don't know how to do it. (pause) Prefix. So you, look, [it is prefix] 771 right here, and there is 30 minutes [in the call]. So why do you …
Student 5	Well, it's 30. 30. 30 minutes. But you are saying, do what?
Student 5	29? Why 29? This is 30.

In another example, Student 6 (below) pushed one of her teammates, Student 7, to explain how he obtained his answer. Student 6 first asked a general question (line 1) and, when she did not understand her teammate's first explanation (line 4), she asked a specific question that made clear her confusion (line 5):

1	Student 6	Why [is it] 6.4?
2	Student 7	'Cause I felt like it.
3	Student 6	Come on!
4	Student 7	'Cause you don't put the zeroes. Just put it in. You see how it's right here there's …
5	Student 6	No, why is the decimal point *there*?
6	Student 7	'Cause you have to move it over two [places].

These students' questions seemed to correspond to what Nelson-Le Gall (1985) termed instrumental help seeking (see also adaptive help seeking; Newman, 1991, 1998; Ryan & Pintrich, 1997): help seeking limited to the amount and type of information needed for help seekers to solve the problem themselves.

Why were some students reluctant to seek help or to admit that they needed it whereas other students were willing to seek help and reveal what they did not understand? Several interrelated factors may be students' goal orientations and their self-perceptions of academic and social competence (Ryan, Pintrich, & Midgley, 2001; Ryan & Pintrich, 1997). The students most likely to seek help in the classroom are those with a mastery goal orientation (Ames, 1992a, 1992b), those who have learning goals (Dweck, 1986), or those who have task-focused goals (Nicholls, 1979; Ryan & Pintrich, 1997), and those who believe they are self-efficacious—that they can do well in school and can control their learning through their own efforts (Schunk, 1989). These students tend to focus on learning rather than performance, to show a preference for challenge and an interest in problem solving and learning contexts, to strive toward independent mastery, to attribute failures to insufficient effort instead of ability, and to see errors as a natural and useful source of feedback in the learning process (Nelson-Le Gall, 1992), making it likely that they will ask questions and will persist in seeking help until they understand.

Students with performance-goal or relative-ability-goal orientations, in contrast, focus on looking good compared to others (performance-approach goal) and/or avoiding looking bad or stupid (performance-avoidance goal) and may avoid asking too many questions because it would portray them as incompetent (Middleton & Midgley, 1997; Newman, 1991, 1994; Ryan & Pintrich, 1997). Students with a performance-goal orientation who are also low achievers or who perceive themselves as academically incompetent may be especially likely to avoid seeking help (Butler & Neuman, 1995), and may become so discouraged that they give up trying to understand (Mulryan, 1992). Students may also avoid seeking help in classrooms in which teachers are perceived to value performance more than learning (Midgley & Urdan, 1995; Ryan, Gheen, & Midgley, 1998; Turner et al., 2002; Urdan, Midgley, & Anderman, 1998). Consistent with a performance-oriented approach to classroom instruction (Anderman, Patrick, Hruda, & Linnenbrink, 2002), the teachers in our study stressed grades and test scores, and even made public comparisons among students in terms of performance.

Students may also avoid help seeking for reasons related to social concerns. Students who perceive themselves as socially incompetent may feel threatened by help seeking and thus avoid it (Ryan & Pintrich, 1997). Students whose social-goal orientation focuses on social status (rather than forming relationships with others) may avoid seeking help because it threatens their self-worth (Ryan, Hicks, & Midgley, 1997).

The transcripts of group work in the present study yielded little information about students' goal orientations or their perceptions of their own academic or social competence. A few students made comments indicating that they wanted to learn how to solve the problem ("I want to know how to do it"; "I want to see if I do number 2 right"; "[I'm] trying to do it myself"; "OK, let me do it"; "I'm gonna redo it"), which suggested a learning or mastery orientation. Clues about a possible performance orientation, such as students saying that they wanted to appear more competent, or less incompetent, than other students, occurred even less frequently. A very small number of students described themselves as "smart" but the context suggested that they may have been congratulating themselves on either understanding how to solve the problem or obtaining the correct answer, or both (e.g., "Oh, boy. Now I get it. Smart! Too smart"). Similarly, a very small number of students described themselves as stupid ("Man! Now I was so stupid, I forgot"; "I was doing something stupid"), but it was unclear whether that reflected their self-perception, whether they wanted to avoid looking stupid, or whether that was simply their way of saying they made a mistake. These infrequent student comments did not correspond to students' help-seeking behavior in any systematic way.

More direct and comprehensive information about students' goal orientations could be obtained through surveys or interviews (Midgley et al., 2000), or from stimulated recall, in which students or groups think aloud while viewing or listening to replayed tapes and, in this case, describe the decisions they made about whether to seek, or to persist in seeking, help (Bloom, 1953).

Level of Student Knowledge.   We also examined whether help seeking related to students' actual level of knowledge (as opposed to self-perceptions of their competence). Specifically, we tested the hypothesis that students who asked specific questions had more knowledge about the task than students who asked only general questions. Having some knowledge about how to solve the problem could have enabled students to ask specific questions and could have made it easier to understand and apply any help received.

To compare the knowledge levels of students who asked specific questions and those who asked only general questions, we first compared their pretest scores (recall that students completed a curriculum-specific pretest at the beginning of each phase of the study). In all phases, we found no statistically significant differences in pretest mean scores between students who asked specific questions and students who asked only general questions. Students' mathematical knowledge at the beginning of the curriculum unit, then, did not predict whether students asked specific questions or only general questions on the day we observed group work.

Second, we investigated whether the two subgroups of students had different levels of knowledge about how to solve the problems assigned for group work *on the day we observed them.* As evidence of same-day knowledge about the task, we examined both the accuracy of any work students completed on that day's problems prior to their seeking help and any evidence of at least partial understanding exhibited in the context of their questions.

We distinguished between two categories of students: those who showed some knowledge about how to solve the problem prior to asking questions or in the context of their questions, versus those who showed a total lack of understanding about how to solve the problem.

Students showed that they had some knowledge in two ways. Some students verbalized work that was partially correct prior to seeking help. For example, when calculating the cost of telephone calls, many students recognized that the cost was a function of the number of minutes and the per-minute cost, but did not recognize that they had to treat the first and additional minutes separately due to different per-minute costs; they multiplied the first-minute cost by the number of minutes in the phone call (e.g., "You times 19 times 5"). As another example, when adding fractions with unlike denominators, some students multiplied the denominators to obtain a common denominator ("10 times 5 is 50"), showing that they had some understanding of the concept of a common denominator although not the lowest common denominator. Other students showed some knowledge in the context of their questions. For example, in the question "[It's a] 5-minute call, [so] where'd you get 4?" the help seeker showed that he understood the function of the number of minutes but not the fact that the additional minutes needed to be treated separately.

Students demonstrated a total lack of understanding about how to solve the problem in a variety ways. Some students made errors that showed that they were totally confused or lacked minimal understanding of how to solve the problem, such as adding or multiplying the first-minute and additional-minute costs in the telephone call problems ("You multiply it 38 times 22?"), or adding the numerators and/or denominators of fractions with unlike denominators ("And then you add the two numbers? 3 and 2?"). Other students asked questions that showed a lack of understanding of how to start solving the problem, such as asking what arithmetic operation to use ("Add or subtract?"). Still other students did not perform any independent work on the problems but only copied or echoed other students' answers and/or repeatedly stated that they did not understand ("I don't know how to do this").

Some students provided ambiguous evidence or insufficient evidence about whether they did or did not understand how to solve the problem for us to be able to make a determination about their knowledge level at the time they sought help. For instance, when some students verbalized calculations or answers, we could not determine whether they performed the work themselves or merely repeated work done by others. In other cases, students said nothing at all before asking questions, and their questions gave no insight into their level of understanding. For example, a student who asked "How did you get 29?" in a telephone call problem may understand the basic structure of the problem and be inquiring about the separation of the call into the first and additional minutes, or the student may not understand any part of the problem and be simply asking how her teammates obtained their numbers. Still other students made errors of unknown origin; we could not determine whether they were simply computational errors or errors that reflected a major misunderstanding.

Comparisons of students' knowledge levels showed that (a) students who asked specific questions were more likely than students who asked only general questions to show some knowledge of how to solve the problem (see Fig. 3.6), and (b) students who asked only general questions were more likely than students who asked specific questions to demonstrate a total lack of understanding (see Fig. 3.7). These results show that task-related knowledge on the day of observation significantly distinguished between students who did or did not ask specific questions: Students who asked specific questions had more knowledge than students who asked only general questions.

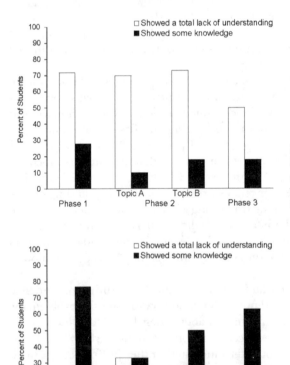

FIG. 3.6. Knowledge levels of students at the time of help seeking: students who asked only general questions.

FIG. 3.7. Knowledge levels of students at the time of help seeking: students who asked specific questions.

Why did knowledge on the day of observation distinguish between students who asked specific questions and students who asked only general questions whereas pretest scores did not? We observed group work at mid-unit, as much as 2 weeks after the pretest was administered. Many students' level of knowledge had changed from the time of the pretest, some more than others. As a consequence, pretest scores were not a good indicator of students' knowledge level prior to their seeking help on the occasions we observed group work. The correlation between pretest scores and same-day knowledge was only moderate in Phase 1 ($r = .49, p = .002$) and was near-zero and nonsignificant in the other phases. These findings show that level of knowledge measured at the beginning of the curriculum unit was not a good gauge of student knowledge midway through the unit, and that current knowledge level, not knowledge at the beginning of the curriculum unit, guided student behavior.

The Role of Groups' Responses to Help Seeking in the Evolution of Help Seekers' Group Work Experiences

Groups' responses to students' help-seeking attempts seemed to play a major role in encouraging or discouraging students' further help-seeking behavior. We examine three kinds of group behavior that may influence students' help-seeking behavior: (a) the level of help received by help seekers, (b) negative socioemotional behavior (of both help seekers and help givers), and (c) directives for the help seeker to copy others' work.

Level of Help Received. As reported earlier in this chapter, students who asked general questions were less likely to receive high-level help than students who asked specific questions. Two findings are noteworthy. The first concerns the nonresponsiveness of groups to general questions compared to specific questions. A large percentage of general questions generated *no* response from the group (ranging from 22% to 32% across the three phases). By comparison, a smaller percentage of specific questions generated no response (ranging from 0% to 25% across the three phases). As a result of the differential responsiveness of the group to general versus specific questions, students who asked general questions were more likely than students who asked specific questions to receive no response to a large number of their help-seeking attempts (59% of students who asked only general questions vs. 30% of students who asked specific questions in Phase 1; 44% vs. 0% in Phase 2 for like denominators; 8% vs. 0% in Phase 2 for unlike denominators; 55% vs. 0% in Phase 3). An extreme example of a group repeatedly ignoring a student appears here. Student 8 sought help eight times: seven times from his group and once from the teacher. The teacher did provide help in response to his request, but the group ignored six of his seven questions.

Student 8   I don't understand. (*no response*)
Student 8   We have to find out if it's add or subtract or times? (*no response*)
Student 8   0.06. Add or subtract? No, (unclear) 19 right? (*no response*)
Student 8   You have to find out if it's add or subtract. (*no response*)
Student 8   I need some help to do number 4. (*no response*)
Student 8   [Teacher's name]! How do you do this page? (*receives response*)
Student 8   I don't understand. (*no response*)
Student 8   I don't understand. (*receives response*)

This student's very last request did generate a response, but instead of helping him, his teammates argued among themselves about the correct number to use, and ignored Student 8, who never said anything further during group work.

The second noteworthy finding is that students who asked general questions were more likely than students who asked specific questions to receive very-low-level help that did not include any calculations or explanation of how to solve the problem (either noncontent responses, Level 1, or answers without any supporting details, Level 2; see Table 3.3). In Phase 1, 35% of students who asked general questions received only very-low-level help compared to 5% of students who asked specific questions. In the other phases, the percentages were 50% versus 33% (Phase 2 for like denominators), 27% versus 25% (Phase 2 for unlike denominators), and 57% versus 33% (Phase 3).

Why did groups respond at such a low level to students who asked only general questions? Groups may have found it too difficult to determine what explanation to give to students who did not make explicit what aspect of the problem they did not understand. Questions and comments such as "I don't get it" and "How do you do it?" provide no clues about which aspects of the problem to explain. In contrast, specific questions such as "Why did you have to subtract 1?" "So you don't add 9 plus 9 [to get the denominator]?" "How did you get 1/6 over here though?" and "Why is the decimal point there?" made it easier for the help giver to formulate a targeted explanation.

Other groups may have been reluctant to provide much help to students who asked general questions because groups perceived the help seekers as unmotivated to learn how to solve the problem, especially when help seekers asked for help before expending any discernable effort. They may have perceived the help seekers as incapable of learning how to solve the problem, viewing the help seekers as having too little understanding to attempt to solve the problem or to formulate a specific question. Or, the groups may have seen in the help-seeker some combination of both of these traits.

We tested still another reason: Students who asked general questions may have had low status in the group (Cohen, 1982, 1994; Cohen, Lotan, & Catanzarite, 1990). We examined several student variables as possible status characteristics: mathematical competence (an indicator of academic status), and gender and ethnic background (diffuse status characteristics; Berger, Rosenholtz, & Zelditch, 1980). None of these student characteristics seemed to operate as status characteristics to explain the low level of help given to students who asked only general questions. As we already stated, students who asked only general questions had similar mean pretest scores to those who asked specific questions. In addition, analyses of students' *relative* mathematics competence in terms of the deviation of their pretest scores from the mean of their group showed that their relative status was not related to whether they asked specific questions or only general questions. Although, as we showed earlier, students who asked general questions exhibited less knowledge than students who asked specific questions on the day we observed group work, this knowledge level likely fluctuated day to day and was not likely to serve as a status characteristic. Finally, the distribution of males and females and the distribution of ethnic backgrounds were very similar among students who asked only general questions and those who asked specific questions. These findings show that the two help-seeker subgroups were equivalent in terms of the status factors we examined.

Regardless of why groups gave low-level help or no help to students who asked only general questions, receiving such responses likely had a detrimental effect on help seekers, possibly discouraging them from seeking further help and changing their help-seeking strategies. Sustaining the repeated unresponsiveness of their groupmates was likely emotionally discouraging for students, and may have served to suppress students' motivation to seek help or even work on the task. Chiu (2000) suggested that ignoring conveys the message that the speaker's proposal (here, the help seeker's question) is unworthy of a response. Even receiving low-level responses may have been discouraging. Chiu (2000, p. 30) suggested that students treat neutral low-level responses such as "Let me think about that for a moment" as criticisms, which can be psychologically threatening to the person receiving them. Receiving low-level help (both non-content responses, Level 1, and answers without any elaboration, Level 2) may also have frustrated help seekers because they could not use the help to learn how to solve the problems or even to gain enough knowledge to phrase specific questions. A number of students who received low-level or no help seemed to give up trying to understand and resorted to copying or asking for answers, or simply stopping work altogether. For example, Student 9 below sought help repeatedly without any response:

Student 9	We need real help. *(no response)*
Student 9	OK, wait up. Let me see, let me see this. I have no idea how you do this. Oh, wait, hold on. Here's your decimal. Multiply this by, oh, here you go, here you go. Erase everything. *(no response)*
Student 9	How do you do this? I don't understand it. *(no response)*
Student 9	I don't know. I just put it that way. *(no response)*

After these help-seeking attempts, she offered an answer that she knew was incorrect ("I got .0136 percent, but I know that's wrong"), but gave up seeking further help.

The Role of Negative Socioemotional Behavior. We found that negative socioemotional behavior functioned in two ways. First, some students who asked general questions—but no students who asked specific questions—received negative socioemotional responses that may have suppressed their further attempts to seek help or actively work on problems. Some groups insulted students when they asked for help. For example, when one student asked for help ("Has anyone done this one yet?"), his teammates responded with a barrage of insults ("We finished that. You're a fool," and "He's stupid"). Another student told his groupmate to "shut up" when he said he needed help. Other help-seeking attempts met with dismissals. For example, when one student said she didn't understand ("I don't get this. I knew how to do it but now I forgot how to do it"), another student retorted with, "You better start learning, huh?" When another student asked, "Hey, how do you do this? Twenty one?" she received the unhelpful, "You do it very carefully." Students who received insults in response to their help seeking tended not to persist, and sometimes reduced their overall participation in group work, which is consistent with previous research finding that rudeness can reduce participation in group discussions (Chiu & Khoo, 2003; Mulryan, 1992; Salomon & Globerson, 1989).

Second, some students who asked general questions—but no students who asked specific questions—initiated negative socioemotional behavior prior to help seeking that seemed to guarantee that groups would not respond when these students sought help. In one example, one student insulted another by suggesting that he was poor ("Are you a poor person?" "I thought so"). Later, when the first student turned to the second student for help ("I don't understand it"), he refused to provide it ("Forget you then. Shit. You don't want to do shit"). In another example, two students insulted a third student by calling her "stupid" and "dumb." Not surprisingly, when one of them asked her for help on a later problem, she refused to provide help ("You got to figure it out on your own"). During group interactions, negative socioemotional behavior clearly impacted the nature of group interactions. It reduced the likelihood both of persistence in asking questions on the part of the help seeker and of receiving a helpful response to questions asked from the help giver.

Directives for the Help Seeker to Copy Others' Work.   Instead of providing help, some groups dictated the work to help-seekers or told them outright to copy other students' work. This often served to suppress further help-seeking attempts, particularly among students who asked only general questions. In the example that follows, instead of explaining to Student 10 how to solve the problem, the group dictated the numbers and arithmetic operations for him to write on his paper (lines 2, 4, 6, 7, 9). He didn't ask any further questions about this problem and copied his teammates' work on the remaining group work problems:

1	Student 10	I don't know how to do this.
2	Student 11	OK. Just copy him, put for the first minute.
3	Student 10	Just copy who?
4	Student 12	First minute. Put the first minute. The first minute is 19 cents. And then the additional minute. Additional minutes, are there is, there is 5 … there's 6 additional minutes.
5	Student 10	How many?
6	Student 12	6 additional minutes, and then 6 times 19. 6 times 19.
7	Student 13	6 times 19.
8	Student 10	Oh, (unclear)? No, 6 times um. 6 times …
9	Student 12	12. Yeah, 12.

In other cases, groups blatantly told students to copy their work without even dictating numbers or calculations. For example, when a student admitted that he "didn't know where the heck we are," one of his teammates told him, "Just copy it. Number 2 and number 4." After receiving instructions to copy, this student verbalized no additional work and said very little during the rest of the group session.

Students who asked specific questions were rarely told to copy others' work. Furthermore, these help seekers did *not* accept others' work without questioning it. In the following example, Student 15 had already asked a specific question about a previous problem ("Where did you get 29 from?") and had received high-level help ("And then each additional minute is 13. So you go … 13 times 29 minutes.… Because it is 30 minutes, and the first minute is 22 cents"). When he expressed confusion about the next problem ("Huh?" in line 2), a teammate told him to copy (line 3) and the group proceeded to dictate the numbers and calculations (line 6) without providing any explanation of how to obtain the numbers.

1	Student 14	That's $1.30, right?
2	Student 15	Huh?
3	Student 16	Just copy it down.
4	Student 14	He knows this.
5	Student 15	I don't know this!
6	Student 17	Put 13 times 10.

Unlike students who only asked general questions, however, Student 15's work and thinking on that problem did not end with the dictated calculations. He later asked the group to return to that problem so that he could understand how to solve it. He asked a question about the component of the problem he did not understand (line 7), and obtained help (lines 8, 10, 12, 14) that he understood (line 15):

7	Student 17	Number 8. I want to know how you got that 10.
8	Student 19	The 10. 'Cause that was, 'cause it was 11 minutes. You got 13 times 10, and add the addition ... the first minute.
9	Student 17	That? Wait a minute. Say that again?
10	Student 19	Ok, the 13 cents you got for the additional minutes.
11	Student 17	Uh-huh [yes].
12	Student 19	Then over here there was 11 minutes.
13	Student 17	Uh-huh. [yes]
14	Student 19	And you don't count it as 11. You count it as 10 minutes. You got 13 times 10. You got that, then you add this many.
15	Student 17	Oh ... ! Now I, now I understand.

Why did groups dictate numbers and calculations or tell students to copy? They may have found it too difficult to figure out what explanations to provide, or they may have believed that help seekers were too incompetent or unmotivated to benefit from high-level help. Or, as in the case of Student 15, they may have believed that the students already understood the problem ("He knows this," line 4) and did not need further explanation. Or groups may have been motivated by the group grade structure; because they did not know which student's paper would be selected for grading, they wanted to ensure that every student's paper gave the correct work.

Other groups, however, gave evidence that they believed that copying was legitimate helping behavior, especially in Phase 1, as exemplified by the following comments: "You can copy my paper when I finish ... It says right there to share answers right, so I'm sharing my answers ... Look at the bottom [of the classroom chart] before 'understanding.' Share ideas, info.

We're sharing" and "Here is my paper if you need help." A number of students considered sharing any kind of work, including answers, to constitute helping behavior.

In summary, receiving no help or low-level help in response to help-seeking attempts, negative socioemotional behavior, and being told to copy others' work (behavior that occurred more frequently among students who asked only general questions than among students who asked specific questions) all seemed to suppress productive help seeking as well as constructive subsequent activity. In addition to reducing help seeking as a result of emotional discouragement, students may have decreased their help seeking to preserve their social status. Students who were concerned about the opinions of their peers (typical of many young adolescents) may have been sensitive to the cues provided by the group about the norms for help seeking and may have adjusted their behavior accordingly. If they interpreted implicit signals (the group responded to their requests with low-level instead of high-level help) or explicit signals (the group refused to help them or directed them to copy) as indicating that the group did not want to help them, then they may have stopped seeking help for fear of antagonizing their groupmates and therefore losing favor.

Help Seekers' Use of Help Received

Students who asked only general questions and those who asked specific questions differed markedly in how they used the help that they received. When they did receive high-level help, students who asked only general questions were likely to use it not to learn how to solve the problem but to make sure that the answers or work on their paper would be correct. Their questions can be seen as executive or dependency-oriented help seeking, in which students request the full solution or the final answer with the intent of having others do the work for them (Nelson-Le Gall, Gumerman, & Scott-Jones, 1983), another manifestation of a performance-goal orientation or the lack of sufficient understanding to use the help received. Students who asked specific questions, in contrast, were likely to use the help to try to learn how to solve the problems. The lower percentage of students who exhibited high-level follow-up behavior (solving problems without assistance from others or providing explanations to others) after receiving high-level help among students who asked only general questions than among students who asked specific questions reflects this contrast, at least in some phases (22% vs. 64% in Phase 1; 56% vs. 83% in Phase 3; in Phase 2, only one student ever carried out high-level follow-up behavior after receiving high-level help, making comparisons impossible). We next give examples of the ways in which help seekers used the high-level help they received.

Some students who asked only general questions and were given high-level help clearly did not understand the help and, consequently, could not use it to learn how to solve the problems. Some of them admitted not understanding. One student, for example, received high-level help ("19 cents, right? That's for the first minute. And then each additional minute is 12 cents. And then you can put for 5 minutes, since the first minute is 19 cents. Then the next 4 will be 12. I just plus that all together") but declared, "I don't [get it]." Another student received high-level help about adding fractions with like denominators ("If this number is the same, then you just put that number here.... And then on top you add those two numbers") but immediately replied "I don't know this. I don't know. I need help." Still another student received high-level help ("See, all you have to do is just move over the two decimal places and you get [the answer]") but repeatedly declared that she didn't understand ("We need help" and "I don't get 21").

Other students did not give any immediate indication of whether they understood the high-level help they received, but they declared their lack of understanding by asking for help on the very next problem ("I don't know how to do [problem] 10"). Still others indicated by the nature of their follow-up questions they had not understood the help they received. For example, a student received high-level help about obtaining the lowest common denominator for fractions with unlike denominators ("You just have to see what the two numbers, like, like, like on the bottom.... You know how, on the bottom, how it goes 8, 4? And then there is a different number on the other bottom there.... You know 4 times 1 equals 4, 4 times 2 equals 8, 4 times 3 equals 12? Then you go 3 times 1 is 3, 2 times 3 is 6, 3 times 3 is 9, like that") but asked "And what if you can't multiply?" which showed her continued confusion about finding common multiples. Additional students did not comment on their understanding but either appeared only to repeat or echo the calculations voiced by others (e.g., "7 plus 11, ah, 18," "That's 6.4. Wait. 6.4%?" "3%? ... We're done.") or asked how to solve subsequent problems without first attempting any work on them (e.g., "How do you do number 10?").

Finally, some students who asked general questions tried to use the high-level help they received, but they could not use it to solve the problem successfully. For example, a student received high-level help about the number of additional minutes ("You have to times it times 29, the leftover minutes. One from 30 is 29") and then tried to apply it himself ("Let me see if I'm doing it right"), but he couldn't obtain the correct answer ("I'm going mixed up around here").

Students who asked specific questions and received high-level help often applied it to the problem at hand by recalculating it from the beginning without assistance from their teammates. Others applied the help received to subsequent problems, again without assistance from others. Some students even showed evidence of their thinking as they used help they received to learn how to solve the problems. In the following example, Student 18 repeatedly indicated that she did not understand why the total number of minutes minus one was used in the calculation of the cost of long-distance telephone calls instead of the total number of minutes:

Student 18	How come, in the first problem, how come you times it times 7?
Student 18	[Student's name]! How come she minus?
Student 18	Why did she minus?
Student 18	You don't times it by 30?
Student 18	No, wait. You times it by 30?
Student 18	Oh, wait. Look, ok, up here, it says you have to minus … OK, the minute call, up here was 4 minutes, but they minused 1.

After one of her teammates explained that the "minus 1" corresponded to the first minute in the telephone call ("Because she had the, the first minute, I think"), she did not merely write down the correct calculations, as many students who asked only general questions had done after receiving help. Instead, she continued thinking about the result ("So it's true, you have to times by 29") and restated the rule in her own words ("[You multiply by 29] 'cause you always minus it. You always minus one minute from [the total number of minutes in] the phone call").

Why were students who asked only general questions less likely to apply the help they received than students who asked specific questions? First, as suggested earlier, students who asked only general questions may not have understood the help they received well enough to apply it. This is not surprising because, consistent with other research (e.g., Ross & Cousins, 1995a, 1995b), students often gave unclear, incomplete, and inadequately labeled explanations (e.g., saying "The next 4 will be 12," instead of "The next 4 *minutes* will be 12 *cents each*"). Furthermore, help seekers may not have had enough knowledge to understand the explanation. Vygotsky (1978, 1987) pointed out the importance of help seekers' knowledge in social interaction, arguing assistance will be most beneficial if it is provided within the learner's "zone of proximal development," the difference between what the learner can achieve independently and what he or she can accomplish with help from someone more competent, an adult or a more capable peer. Vygotsky's concept implies that the help provided must be at a more advanced level than the help seeker's current level of knowledge, but not too advanced or the help seeker won't be able to understand it or use it to solve the problem (Hogan & Tudge, 1999; Tudge, 1992).

In this study, the gap between the knowledge level of students who asked only general questions and the help provided may have been too large. For example, a student who did not know that the cost of a telephone call was a function of the number of minutes in the call and the cost per minute would probably not understand an explanation about obtaining the cost of the "additional" minutes (Phase 1). Similarly, a student who did not understand how to find a common multiple was unlikely to be able to comprehend an explanation about finding equivalent fractions with a common denominator (Phase 2). Students who asked specific questions, on the other hand, showed a higher level of knowledge, which may have made the help they received "proximal" to their knowledge level. For example, a student who already understood the basic structure of the telephone cost problem could benefit from an explanation about the differentiation of the call into separate first-minute and additional-minute entities (Phase 1).

Second, students who asked only general questions may not have tried to apply the help they received because they did not realize the value of testing their understanding or because they lacked the metacognitive skills to actively monitor their comprehension (Garcia & Pintrich, 1994; Weinstein & Mayer, 1986; Zimmerman & Martinez-Pons, 1992). Third, they may have believed that they could not complete the work and were afraid to confirm their own lack of understanding by attempting to solve a problem and failing (Butler & Neuman, 1995; Covington, 1984). Finally, students may not have applied the help they received because they wanted to avoid doing the work (social loafing or the "free rider" effect; Kerr & Bruun, 1983; Salomon & Globerson, 1989). As suggested earlier, students may have become social loafers after trying unsuccessfully to obtain the help that they needed. Importantly, because these students did not apply the help they received, they did not discover what parts of the problem they did or did not understand and therefore could not communicate their difficulties to their teammates (cf. Karabenick & Sharma, 1994; Markman, 1981).

CONCLUSIONS

Throughout this chapter, we show that the nature of students' help seeking had important effects on their experiences during group collaboration and on their learning outcomes. Students who asked specific questions about how to solve the mathematics problems received higher level help, more frequently applied the help received to solve problems without receiving assistance from others, and obtained higher posttest scores than students who only asked general questions or who gave general expressions of confusion.

Both help-seeker characteristics and group work dynamics seemed to influence whether students asked specific questions or only asked general questions. Some utterances made during group work suggested that students who asked only general questions may have done so due to lack of motivation and/or unwillingness to seek help. More strongly related to the type of question asked, however, was level of student knowledge on the days we observed group work, with students asking specific questions exhibiting more task-related knowledge than students asking only general questions. A higher level of knowledge seemed to enable students who asked specific questions to formulate help-seeking requests and to benefit from help received.

Group dynamics also influenced the behavior of help seekers. Receiving low-level help or no help in response to questions, negative socioemotional behavior (especially receiving insults or put-downs in response to questions or indications of confusion), and being directed to copy others' work reinforced students' tendencies to ask general questions. Receiving negative responses from groupmates also served to suppress students' tendencies to seek further help, and caused many students to cease trying to understand how to solve the group work problems. Thus, a downward spiral emerged, with students who asked only general questions failing to receive help they understood or could use to solve problems, being discouraged from further help seeking, and eventually withdrawing from group work and/or resorting to copying other students' answers without ever learning how to solve the problems.

The higher frequency of asking general questions than of asking specific questions and the high frequency of providing low-level help occurred despite instructions given to students to ask clear and precise questions and to be responsive to their teammates' help-seeking attempts, especially by giving explanations rather than answers. To bring about major changes in the interaction among students in cooperative groups may require changing the culture of the classroom to reduce the costs and risks associated with help seeking and help giving. Research by Cobb, Wood, Yackel, and McNeal (1993), for example, showed the importance of creating a classroom culture that focuses on students constructing meaning and understanding of solution methods rather than obtaining correct answers, and that emphasizes the importance of students communicating and explaining their thinking. Encouraging all students, whether help seekers or help givers, to explain their interpretations of problems and their problem-solving strategies and to listen to others' explanations (Cobb, Wood, & Yackel, 1993) may make it easier for help seekers to clarify their own thinking and for help givers to provide targeted explanations. Wood, Cobb, and Yackel (1991) emphasized the importance of teachers refraining from evaluating the accuracy of students' answers, even when incorrect, which communicates the permissibility of making mistakes and likely decreases risks associated with help seeking and with challenging other students' ideas and strategies. Instead, teachers recognize that all students' ideas have merit and deserve to be developed and explored, whether correct or not, and that the process of resolving conflicting answers and approaches provided opportunities for learning (Wood et al., 1991). Another important feature of their approach is the use of flexible scheduling and pacing so that students have time to explain and to question each other's thinking. Other approaches to establishing a classroom culture in which students explain their thinking, connect their ideas to those of other students, and monitor each other's comprehension include Palincsar and Brown's (1989; see also Palinscar, 1986; Palincsar & Brown, 1984) reciprocal teaching method and Hogan and Pressley's (1997) instructional scaffolding approach.

Researchers show that a classroom culture that focuses on learning and mastery instead of performance may increase students' willingness to seek help (Midgley & Urdan, 1995; Ryan et al., 1998; Turner et al., 2002; Urdan et al., 1998). To foster a learning orientation in their classrooms, Ames (1992a, 1992b, 1995) suggested that teachers praise students for effort, accomplishments, and improvement, rather than performance; praise students privately; and avoid making comparisons among students (for additional discussion of reducing normative comparisons in classrooms, see Midgley, 1993; Newman & Schwager, 1992). A classroom focus on learning and mastery may also encourage students to monitor each other's level of comprehension and increase the likelihood that students will try to help each other understand the material, thus relieving some of the help-seeking burden of confused students.

Several factors may prove essential for fostering a classroom culture that emphasizes meaning, learning and mastery, and communication of students' thinking. These include an instructional focus on conceptual understanding, on understanding the underlying concepts or principles and the relationships among them (Hiebert & Lefevre, 1986; Rittle-Johnson & Alibali, 1999; Silver, 1986), and on relational understanding for performing procedures with understanding, which Skemp (1978, p. 9) described as "knowing both what to do and why." A focus on the concepts underlying problems may promote more in-depth student descriptions of their thinking than a focus on procedural knowledge or instrumental understanding (Skemp, 1978). This instrumental understanding (Skemp, 1978) includes knowledge of "the algorithms, or rules, for completing mathematical tasks" (Hiebert & Lefevre, 1986, p. 6), "step-by-step procedures executed in a specific sequence" (Carpenter, 1986, p. 113), and "action sequences for solving problems" (Rittle-Johnson & Alibali, 1999, p. 175). Skemp (1978) called this type of knowledge instrumental understanding.

The foregoing descriptions of classroom culture contrast markedly with the culture of the classrooms in the present study. As described by Webb and Mastergeorge (2003; see also Webb et al., 2004), these teachers did not model classroom discourse and practices that fostered beneficial help seeking and help giving. Instead, the teachers focused solely on procedures for solving problems without addressing underlying concepts. They also assumed the major responsibility for solving problems and placed students in the role of passive responder to teachers' questions. These teachers required students to provide answers to problems but not explanations of their thinking. They focused on the accuracy of answers. They expected students to follow a single prescribed problem-solving method. They publicly praised and compared students and groups. These teachers assigned a large number of problems, creating pressure for groups to cut short help seeking and help giving. And they used normative-based grading practices based almost solely on accuracy of answers to problems. Such a classroom culture weakened the effects of the instructions given to students regarding help seeking and help giving in their cooperative groups.

A classroom culture that values students' communication about their thinking and the sharing of ideas and that stresses learning and mastery and conceptual understanding may increase the effectiveness of specific strategies for encouraging help seeking and help giving in cooperative groups. Specific strategies for increasing students' ability and willingness to ask questions in groups include, for example, (a) assigning students to play the role of listener (also called active listener, learning listener, or listener/facilitator; Hythecker, Dansereau, & Rocklin, 1988; O'Donnell, 1999; Yager, Johnson, & Johnson, 1985), in which the listener is required to ask questions of the student playing the role of summarizer, and (b) requiring students to ask each other specific high-level questions about the material (often called reciprocal questioning; Fantuzzo, Riggio, Connelly, & Dimeff, 1989; King, 1989, 1990, 1992, 1999). Other strategies proposed for reducing the risks of help seeking in whole-class instruction might be adapted for cooperative learning settings, such as students watching videotapes of groups solving problems and discussing places at which students could seek help (Schoenfeld, 1987).

Specific strategies for increasing the elaboration of explanations students provide to each other include, for example, (a) providing instruction in explaining skills (Fuchs, Fuchs, Kazdan, & Allen, 1999; Gillies & Ashman, 1996, 1998; Swing & Peterson, 1982; Webb & Farivar, 1994); (b) providing students with specific prompts to encourage them to give elaborated explanations, to explain material in their own words, and to explain why they believe their answers are correct or incorrect (Coleman, 1998; Palincsar, Anderson, & David, 1993); (c) providing specific instruction in giving conceptual rather than algorithmic explanations (Fuchs et al. 1997); and (d) requiring groups to engage in discussion whenever students exhibit difficulty solving a problem or exhibit discrepancies among answers or solution processes (Mevarech & Kramarski, 1997).

Although cooperative learning settings provide students with opportunities for obtaining beneficial help from their peers, the results we presented here suggest that promoting effective help-seeking and help-giving behavior may require comprehensive attention to the classroom culture as a whole, instead of providing only instructions about communicating within small groups. The challenge for future research and practice is to develop classroom cultures that communicate, encourage and reward effective helping behavior among students. The importance of considering multiple aspects of the classroom context is echoed by other researchers such as Stigler and Hiebert (1997, pp. 19, 20), who cautioned that teaching is "not just a collection of individual features ... [but is a] system rooted in deep-seated beliefs about the nature of the subject, the way students learn, and the role of the teacher" and those who call for an approach to improving teaching that acknowledges teaching's "cultural complexity and embeddedness." Exploring how to develop classroom cultures that value students' communication about their thinking and understanding seems to be a promising direction for making cooperative work effective for all help seekers and help givers.

ACKNOWLEDGMENTS

This work was supported in part by the Spencer Foundation, the Academic Senate on Research, Los Angeles Division, University of California, and by grant 1093264 from WestED to the Center for the Study of Evaluation/CRESST. Funding to WestED was provided by grant ESI-0119790 from the National Science Foundation. However, all opinions in this article are those of the authors.

REFERENCES

Ames, C. (1992a). Achievement goals and the classroom motivational climate. In D. H. Schunk & J. L. Meece (Eds.), *Student perceptions in the classroom* (pp. 327-348). Hillsdale, NJ: Lawrence Erlbaum Associates.

Ames, C. (1992b). Classrooms: Goals, structures, and student motivation. *Journal of Educational Psychology, 84,* 261–271.

Ames, C. (1995). Achievement goals, motivational climate, and motivational processes. In G. C. Roberts (Ed.), *Motivation in sport and exercise* (pp. 161–176). Champaign, IL: Human Kinetics Books.

Anderman, L. H., Patrick, H., Hruda, L. Z., & Linnenbrink, E. A. (2002). Observing classroom goal structures to clarify and expand goal theory. In C. Midgley (Ed.), *Goals, goal structures, and patterns of adaptive learning* (pp. 243–278). Mahwah, NJ: Lawrence Erlbaum Associates.

Bargh, J. A., & Schul, Y. (1980). On the cognitive benefit of teaching. *Journal of Educational Psychology, 72,* 593–604.

Berger, J., Rosenholtz, S. J., & Zelditch, M. (1980). Status organizing processes. *Annual Review of Sociology, 6,* 479–508.

Bloom, B. S. (1953). Thought processes in lectures and discussions. *Journal of General Education, 7,* 160–170.

Bossert, S. T. (1988–1989). Cooperative activities in the classroom. *Review of Research in Education, 15,* 225–252.

Brown, A. L., & Palincsar, A. S. (1989). Guided, cooperative learning, and individual knowledge acquisition. In L. B. Resnick (Ed.), *Knowing, learning, and instruction: Essays in honor of Robert Glaser* (pp. 393–451). Hillsdale, NJ: Lawrence Erlbaum Associates.

Butler, R., & Neuman, O. (1995). Effects of task and ego achievement goals on help-seeking behaviors and attitudes. *Journal of Educational Psychology, 87,* 261–271.

Carpenter, T. P. (1986). Conceptual knowledge as a foundation for procedural knowledge. In J. Hiebert (Ed.), *Conceptual and procedural knowledge: The case of mathematics* (pp. 113–132). Hillsdale, NJ: Lawrence Erlbaum Associates.

Chi, M. T. H. (2000). Self-explaining expository texts: The dual processes of generating inferences and repairing mental models. In R. Glaser (Ed.), *Advances in instructional psychology: Educational design and cognitive science* (pp. 161–238). Hillsdale, NJ: Lawrence Erlbaum Associates.

Chi, M. T. H., & Bassock, M. (1989). Learning from examples via self-explanations. In L. B. Resnick (Ed.), *Knowing, learning, and instruction: Essays in honor of Robert Glaser* (pp. 251–282). Hillsdale, NJ: Lawrence Erlbaum Associates.

Chi, M. T. H., Bassock, M., Lewis, M., Reimann, P., & Glaser, R. (1989). Self-explanations: How students study and use examples in learning to solve problems. *Cognitive Science, 13,* 145–182.

Chiu, M. M. (2000). Group problem-solving processes: Social interactions and individual actions. *Journal for the Theory of Social Behavior, 30,* 27–49.

Chiu, M. M., & Khoo, L. (2003). Rudeness and status effects during group problem solving: Do they bias evaluations and reduce the likelihood of correct solutions? *Journal of Educational Psychology, 95,* 506–523.

Cobb, P., Wood, T., & Yackel, E. (1993). Discourse, mathematical thinking, and classroom practice. In E. A. Forman, N. Minick, & C. A. Stone (Eds.), *Contexts for learning: Sociocultural dynamics in children's development* (pp. 91–119). New York: Oxford University Press.

Cobb, P., Wood, T., Yackel, E., & McNeal, B. (1993). Mathematics as procedural instructions and mathematics as meaningful activity: The reality of teaching for understanding. In R. Davis & C. Maher (Eds.), *Schools, mathematics and the world of reality* (pp. 119–134). Needham Heights, MA: Allyn & Bacon.

Cohen, E. G. (1982). Expectation states and interracial interaction in school settings. *American Review of Sociology, 8,* 209–235.

Cohen, E. G. (1994). Restructuring the classroom: Conditions for productive small groups. *Review of Educational Research, 64,* 1–35.

Cohen, E. G., Lotan, R., & Catanzarite, L. (1990). Treating status problems in the cooperative classroom. In S. Sharan (Ed.), *Cooperative learning: Theory and research* (pp. 203–230). New York: Praeger.

Coleman, E. B. (1998). Using explanatory knowledge during collaborative problem solving in science. *Journal of the Learning Sciences, 7,* 387–427.

Cooper, M. A. (1999). Classroom choices from a cognitive perspective on peer learning. In A. M. O'Donnell & A. King (Eds.) *Cognitive perspectives on peer learning* (pp. 215–234). Hillsdale, NJ: Lawrence Erlbaum Associates.

Covington, M. V. (1984). The self-worth theory of achievement motivation: Findings and implications. *Elementary School Journal, 85,* 5–20.

Dweck, C. S. (1986). Motivational processes affecting learning. *American Psychologist, 41,* 1040–1048.

Eicholz, R. E., O'Daffer, P. G., & Fleenor, C. F. (1989). *Addison-Wesley mathematics* (Grade 7). Menlo Park, CA: Addison-Wesley.

Fantuzzo, J. W., Riggio, R. E., Connelly, S., & Dimeff, L. A. (1989). Effects of reciprocal peer tutoring on academic achievement and psychological adjustment: A component analysis. *Journal of Educational Psychology, 81,* 173–177.

Farivar, S., & Webb, N. M. (1991). *Helping Behavior Activities Handbook.* Los Angeles, CA: Graduate School of Education, University of California. Available from Dr. Noreen Webb, Graduate School of Education & Information Studies, UCLA, Los Angeles, CA 90095.

Farivar, S., & Webb, N. M. (1994). Helping and getting help: Essential skills for effective group problem solving. *Arithmetic Teacher, 41*(9), 522.

Fuchs, L. S., Fuchs, D., Hamlett, C. L., Phillips, N. B., Karns, K., & Dutka, S. (1997). Enhancing students' helping behavior during peer-mediated instruction with conceptual mathematical explanations. *Elementary School Journal, 97,* 223–249.

Fuchs, L. S., Fuchs, D., Kazdan, S., & Allen, S. (1999). Effects of peer-assisted learning strategies in reading with and without training in elaborated help giving. *Elementary School Journal, 99,* 201–219.

Garcia, T. & Pintrich, P. R. (1994). Regulating motivation and cognition in the classroom: The role of self-schemas and self-regulatory strategies. In D. H. Schunk & B. J. Zimmerman (Eds.), *Self-regulation of learning and performance: Issues and educational applications* (pp. 127–153). Hillsdale, NJ: Lawrence Erlbaum Associates.

Gibbs, J. (1987). *Tribes: A process for social development and cooperative learning.* Santa Rosa, CA: Center Source Publications.

Hiebert, J., & Lefevre, P. (1986). Conceptual and procedural knowledge in mathematics: An introductory analysis. In J. Hiebert (Ed.), *Conceptual and procedural knowledge: The case of mathematics* (pp. 1–27). Hillsdale, NJ: Lawrence Erlbaum Associates.

Hogan, D. M., & Tudge, J. R. H. (1999). Implications of Vygotsky's theory for peer learning. In A. M. O'Donnell & A. King (Eds.) *Cognitive perspectives on peer learning* (pp. 39–66). Hillsdale, NJ: Lawrence Erlbaum Associates.

Hogan, K., & Pressley, M. (1997). Scaffolded scientific competencies within classroom communities of inquiry. In K. Hogan & M. Pressley (Eds.), *Scaffolded student learning* (pp. 74–107). New York: University of Albany, State University of New York.

Hooper, S. (1992). Effects of peer interaction during computer-based mathematics instruction. *Journal of Educational Research, 85,* 180–189.

Hythecker, V. I., Dansereau, D. F., & Rocklin, T. R. (1988). An analysis of the processes influencing the structured dyadic learning environment. *Educational Psychologist, 23,* 23–27.

Johnson, D. W., Johnson, R. T., & Holubec, E. J. (1988). *Cooperation in the Classroom, Revised.* Edina, MN: Interaction Book Co.

Karabenick, S. A., & Knapp, J. R. (1991). Relationship of academic help seeking to the use of learning strategies and other achievement behavior in college students. *Journal of Educational Psychology, 85,* 365–376.

Karabenick, S. A., & Sharma, R. (1994). Perceived teacher support of student questioning in the college classroom: Its relation to student characteristic and role in the classroom questioning process. *Journal of Educational Psychology, 86,* 90–103.

Kerr, N. L., & Bruun, S. E. (1983). Dispensability of member effort and group motivation losses: Free-rider effects. *Journal of Personality & Social Psychology, 44,* 78–94.

King, A. (1989). Effects of self-questioning training on college students' comprehension of lectures. *Contemporary Educational Psychology, 14,* 366–381.

King, A. (1990). Enhancing peer interaction and learning in the classroom through reciprocal questioning. *American Educational Research Journal, 27,* 664–687.

King, A. (1992). Facilitating elaborative learning through guided student-generated questioning. *Educational Psychologist, 27,* 111–126.

King, A. (1999). Discourse patterns for mediating peer learning. In A. M. O'Donnell & A. King (Eds.), *Cognitive perspectives on peer learning.* (pp. 87–116). Hillsdale, NJ: Lawrence Erlbaum Associates.

Markman, E. M. (1981). Comprehension monitoring. In W. P. Dickson (Ed.), *Children's oral communication skills* (pp. 61–84). New York: Academic Press.

Mayer, R. E. (1984). Aids to prose comprehension. *Educational Psychologist, 19,* 30–42.

Mevarech, Z. R., & Kramarski, B. (1997). IMPROVE: A multidimensional method for teaching mathematics in heterogeneous classrooms. *American Educational Research Journal, 34,* 365–394.

Middleton, M. J., & Midgley, C. (1997). Avoiding the demonstration of lack of ability: An underexplored aspect of goal theory. *Journal of Educational Psychology, 89,* 710–718.

Midgley, C. (1993). Motivation and middle level schools. *Advances in Motivation and Achievement, 8,* 217–274.

Midgley, C., & Urdan, T. (1995). Predictors of middle school students' use of self-handicapping strategies. *Journal of Early Adolescence, 15,* 389–411.

Midgley, C., Maehr, M. L., Hruda, L. A., Anderman, E., Anderman, L., Freeman, K. E., Gheen, M., et al. (2000). *Manual for the Patterns of Adaptive Learning Scale.* Ann Arbor, MI: University of Michigan.

Mulryan, C. M. (1992). Student passivity during cooperative small groups in mathematics. *Journal of Educational Research, 85,* 261–273.

Nattiv, A. (1994). Helping behaviors and math achievement gain of students using cooperative learning. *Elementary School Journal, 94,* 285–297.

Nelson-Le Gall, S. (1981). Help-seeking: An understudied problem-solving skill in children. *Developmental Review, 1,* 224–246.

Nelson-Le Gall, S. (1985). Help-seeking behavior in learning. In E. V. Gordon (Ed.), *Review of research in education* (Vol. 12, 55–90). Washington, DC: American Educational Research Association.

Nelson-Le Gall, S. (1992). Children's instrumental help-seeking: Its role in the social acquisition and construction of knowledge. In R. Hertz-Lazarowitz & N. Miller (Eds.), *Interaction in cooperative groups: The theoretical anatomy of group learning* (pp. 49–68). New York: Cambridge University Press.

Nelson-Le Gall, S., Gumerman, R. A., & Scott-Jones, D. (1983). Instrumental help-seeking and everyday problem-solving: A developmental perspective. In *New directions in helping* (Vol. 2, pp. 265–283). New York: Academic Press.

Newman, R. S. (1991). Goals and self-regulated learning: What motivates children to seek academic help? In M. L. Maehr & P. R. Pintrich (Eds.), *Advances in motivation and achievement* (pp. 151–183). Greenwich, CT: JAI Press.

Newman, R. S. (1998). Students' help seeking during problem solving: Influences of personal and contextual achievement goals. *Journal of Educational Psychology, 90,* 644–658.

Newman, R. S., & Schwager, M. T. (1992). Student perceptions and academic help-seeking. In D. H. Schunk & J. L. Meece (Eds.), *Student perceptions in the classroom* (pp. 123–146). Hillsdale, NJ: Lawrence Erlbaum Associates.

Nicholls, J. G. (1979). Quality and equality in intellectual development: The role of motivation in education. *American Psychologist, 34,* 1071–1084.

Noddings, N. (1985). Small groups as a setting for research on mathematical problem solving. In E. A. Silver (Ed.), *Teaching and learning mathematical problem solving* (pp. 345–360). Hillsdale, NJ: Lawrence Erlbaum Associates.

O'Donnell, A. M. (1999). Structuring dyadic interaction through scripted cooperation. In A. M. O'Donnell & A. King (Eds.) *Cognitive perspectives on peer learning* (pp. 179–196). Hillsdale, NJ: Lawrence Erlbaum Associates.

Palincsar, A. S. (1986). The role of dialogue in providing scaffolded instruction. *Educational Psychologist, 21,* 73–98.

Palincsar, A. S., Anderson, C., & David, Y. M. (1993). Pursuing scientific literacy in the middle grades through collaborative problem solving. *Elementary School Journal, 93,* 643–658.

Palincsar, A. S., & Brown, A. L. (1984). Reciprocal teaching of comprehension-fostering and comprehension-monitoring activities. *Cognition and Instruction, 1,* 117–175.

Palincsar, A. S., & Brown, A. L. (1989). Classroom dialogues to promote self-regulated comprehension. In J. Brophy (Ed.), *Advances in research on teaching* (pp. 35–72). Greenwich, CT: JAI.

Peterson, P. L., Janicki, T. C., & Swing, S. R. (1981). Ability × treatment interaction effects on children's learning in large-group and small-group approaches. *American Educational Research Journal, 18,* 453–473.

Peterson, P. L., Wilkinson, L. C., Spinelli, F., & Swing, S. R. (1984). Merging the process-product and the sociolinguistic paradigms: Research on small-group process. In P. L. Peterson, L. C. Wilkinson, & M. Hallinan (Eds.), *The social context of instruction* (pp. 126–152). Orlando, FL: Academic Press.

Rittle-Johnson, B., & Alibali, M. W. (1999). Conceptual and procedural knowledge of mathematics: Does one lead to the other? *Journal of Educational Psychology, 91,* 175–189.

Rogoff, B. (1991). Guidance and participation in spatial planning. In L. Resnick, J. Levine, & S. Teasley (Eds.), *Perspectives on socially shared cognition* (pp. 349–383). Washington, DC: American Psychological Association.

Rogoff, N. (1990). *Apprenticeship in thinking: Cognitive development in social context.* Oxford, UK: Oxford University Press.

Ross, J. A., & Cousins, J. B. (1995a). Impact of explanation seeking on student achievement and attitudes. *Journal of Educational Research, 89,* 109–117.

Ross, J. A., & Cousins, J. B. (1995b). Giving and receiving explanations in cooperative learning groups. *Alberta Journal of Educational Research, 41,* 103–121.

Ryan, A. M., Gheen, M. H., & Midgley, C. (1998). Why do some students avoid asking for help? An examination of the interplay among students' academic efficacy, teachers' social-emotional role, and the classroom goal structure. *Journal of Educational Psychology, 90,* 528–535.

Ryan, A. M., Hicks, L., & Midgley, C. (1997). Social goals, academic goals, and avoiding seeking help in the classroom. *Journal of Early Adolescence, 17,* 152–171.

Ryan, A. M., & Pintrich, P. R. (1997). "Should I ask for help?" The role of motivation and attitudes in adolescents' help seeking in math class. *Journal of Educational Psychology, 89,* 329–341.

Ryan, A. M., Pintrich, P. R., & Midgley, C. (2001). Avoiding seeking help in the classroom: Who and why? *Educational Psychology Review, 13,* 93–114.

Salomon, G., & Globerson, T. (1989). When teams do not function the way they ought to. *International Journal of Educational Research, 13,* 89–99.

Saxe, G. B., Gearhart, M., Note, M., & Paduano, P. (1993). Peer interaction and the development of mathematical understanding. In H. Daniels (Ed.), *Charting the agenda: Educational activity after Vygotsky* (pp. 107–144). London: Routledge.

Schoenfeld, A. H. (1987). What's all the fuss about metacognition? In A. H. Schoenfeld (Ed.), *Cognitive science and mathematics education* (pp. 189–215). Hillsdale, NJ: Lawrence Erlbaum Associates.

Schunk, D. H. (1989). Social cognitive theory and self-regulated learning. In B. J. Zimmerman & D. H. Schunk (Eds.), *Self-regulated learning and academic achievement: Theory, research, and practice* (pp. 83–110). New York: Springer-Verlag.

Shavelson, R. J., Webb, N. M., Stasz, C., & McArthur, D. (1988). Teaching mathematical problem solving: Insights from teachers and tutors. In R. Charles & E. Silver (Eds.), *Teaching and assessing mathematical problem-solving: A research agenda* (pp. 203–231). Hillsdale, NJ: Lawrence Erlbaum Associates.

Silver, E. A. (1986). Using conceptual and procedural knowledge: A focus on relationships. In J. Hiebert (Ed.), *Conceptual and procedural knowledge: The case of mathematics* (pp. 181–197). Hillsdale, NJ: Lawrence Erlbaum Associates.

Skemp, R. (1978). Relational and instrumental understanding. *Arithmetic Teacher, 26,* 9–15.

Slavin, R. E. (1987). Developmental and motivational perspectives on cooperative learning: A reconciliation. *Child Development, 58,* 1161–1167.

Slavin, R. E. (1990). *Cooperative learning: Theory, research, and practice.* Englewood Cliffs, NJ: Prentice Hall.

Stigler, J. W., & Hiebert, J. (1997). Understanding and improving classroom mathematics instruction. *Phi Delta Kappan, 79,* 14–21.

Sweller, J. (1989). Cognitive technology: Some procedures for facilitating learning and problem solving in mathematics and science. *Journal of Educational Psychology, 81,* 457–466.

Swing, S. R., & Peterson, P. L. (1982). The relationship of student ability and small-group interaction to student achievement. *American Educational Research Journal, 19,* 259–274.

Tharp, R. G. & Gallimore, R. (1988). *Rousing minds to life: Teaching, learning, and schooling in social context.* Cambridge: Cambridge University Press.

Tudge, J. R. H. (1992). Processes and consequences of peer collaboration: A Vygotskian analysis. *Child Development, 63,* 1364–1379.

Turner, J. C., Midgley, C., Meyer, D. K., Gheen, M., Anderman, E. M., Kang,, Y., & Patrick, H. (2002). The classroom environment and students' reports of avoidance strategies in mathematics: A multimethod study. *Journal of Educational Psychology, 94,* 88–106.

Urdan, T. Midgley, C., & Anderman, E. M. (1998). The role of classroom goal structure in students' use of self-handicapping strategies. *American Educational Research Journal, 35,* 101–122.

Valsiner, J. (1987). *Culture and the development of children's action.* New York: John Wiley.

Vedder, P. (1985). *Cooperative learning. A study on processes and effects of cooperation between primary school children.* Westerhaven Groningen, the Netherlands: Rijkuniversiteit Groningen.

Vygotsky, L. S. (1978). *Mind in society: The development of higher psychological processes.* Cambridge, MA: Harvard University Press.

Vygotsky, L. S. (1981). The genesis of higher mental functioning. In J. V. Wertsch (Ed.), *The concept of activity in Soviet psychology* (pp. 144–188). Armonk, NY: Sharpe.

Webb, N. M. (1989). Peer interaction and learning in small groups. *International Journal of Educational Research, 13,* 21–40.

Webb, N. M. (1991). Task-related verbal interaction and mathematics learning in small groups. *Journal for Research in Mathematics Education, 22,* 366–389.

Webb, N. M., & Farivar, S. (1994). Promoting helping behavior in cooperative small groups in middle school mathematics. *American Educational Research Journal, 31,* 369–395.

Webb, N. M., & Farivar, S. (1999). Developing productive group interaction in middle school mathematics. In A. M. O'Donnell & A. King (Eds.), *Cognitive perspectives on peer learning* (pp. 117–150). Hillsdale, NJ: Lawrence Erlbaum Associates.

Webb, N. M., Nemer, K. M., Kersting, N., & Ing, M. (2004, April). *The effects of teacher discourse on student behavior in peer-directed groups.* Paper presented at the annual meeting of the American Educational Research Association, San Diego.

Webb, N. M. & Mastergeorge, A. M. (2003). The development of students' learning in peer-directed small groups. *Cognition and Instruction, 21,* 361–428.

Webb, N. M., & Palincsar, A. S. (1996). Group processes in the classroom. D. Berliner & R. Calfee (Eds.), *Handbook of educational psychology* (pp. 841–873). New York: Macmillan.

Webb, N. M., Troper, J. D., & Fall, R. (1995). Constructive activity and learning in collaborative small groups. *Journal of Educational Psychology, 87,* 406–423.

Weinstein, C. F., & Mayer, R. F. (1986). The teaching of learning strategies. In M. C. Wittrock (Ed.), *Handbook of research on teaching* (3rd ed., pp. 315–327). New York: Macmillan.

Wilkinson, L. C. (1985). Communication in all-student mathematics groups. *Theory into Practice, 24*(1), 8–13.

Wilkinson, L. C., & Calculator, S. (1982a). Effective speakers: Students' use of language to request and obtain information and action in the classroom. In L. C. Wilkinson (Ed.), *Communicating in the classroom* (pp. 85–99). New York: Academic Press.

Wilkinson, L. C., & Calculator, S. (1982b). Requests and responses in peer-directed reading groups. *American Educational Research Journal, 19,* 107–120.

Wilkinson, L. C., & Spinelli, F. (1983). Using requests effectively in peer-directed instructional groups. *American Educational Research Journal, 20,* 479–502.

Wittrock, M. C. (1990). Generative processes of comprehension. *Educational Psychologist, 24,* 345–376.

Wood, D., Bruner, J. S., & Ross, G. (1976). The role of tutoring in problem solving. *Journal of Child Psychology Psychiatry, 17,* 89–100.

Wood, T., Cobb, P., & Yackel. E. (1991). Change in teaching mathematics: A case study. *American Educational Research Journal, 28,* 587–616.

Yackel, E., Cobb, P., Wood, T., Wheatley, G., & Merkel, G. (1990). The importance of social interaction in children's construction of mathematical knowledge. In T. J. Cooney & C. R. Hirsch (Eds.), *Teaching and learning mathematics in the 1990s* (pp. 12–21). Reston, VA: National Council of Teachers of Mathematics.

Yager, S., Johnson, D. W., & Johnson, R. T. (1985). Oral discussion, group-to-individual transfer, and achievement in cooperative learning groups. *Journal of Educational Psychology, 77,* 60–66.

Zimmerman, B. J., & Martinez-Pons, M. (1992). Perceptions of efficacy and strategy use in the self-regulation of learning. In D. H. Schunk & J. L. Meece (Eds.), *Student perceptions in the classroom* (pp. 185–207). Hillsdale, NJ: Lawrence Erlbaum Associates.

Chapter 4

Helping Behaviors in Collaborative Groups in Math: A Descriptive Analysis

Toni M. Kempler
University of Michigan

Elizabeth A. Linnenbrink
Duke University

Over the last two decades, a number of researchers have explored academic help seeking as an important predictor of student learning (e.g., Karabenick, 1998; Nadler, 1998; Nelson-Le Gall, 1992; Newman, 1990; Ryan, Pintrich, & Midgley, 2001; Webb & Mastergeorge, 2003). Much of this research focused on student help seeking within the context of a traditional classroom, as students seek help from other classmates and the teacher while completing individual assignments. Webb and her colleagues (e.g., Webb, 1982, 1991; Webb & Mastergeorge, 2003; Webb, Troper, & Fall, 1995) extended this work to investigate students' helping behaviors in cooperative group contexts. This research has contributed to our understanding of how different types of help seeking and help giving relate to students' learning when working in small groups.

The current chapter extends the literature on helping behaviors in small groups by exploring how helping behaviors may differ based on the interactions of the group. We take a qualitative approach and pay particular attention to two characteristics of group processes or interactions that may relate to helping behaviors. We first consider the *quality* of the group's socioemotional interactions (positive, negative) in relation to their help-ing behaviors. Second, we consider how the *type* of interaction around the task (cooperation, collaboration) relates to the helping behaviors ob-served in the group. Before turning to this work, we provide a brief theo-retical overview of helping behaviors in academic contexts followed by an overview of the research specifically focused on small group contexts.

HELP SEEKING IN ACADEMIC CONTEXTS

The decision to seek help can be thought of as involving both self-regula-tory and social processes (Nelson-Le Gall, 1985; Ryan & Pintrich, 1998). One must first determine if one needs help by monitoring one's own under-standing. If help is needed, the decision is subsequently made about whether to actually seek help. Both individual and contextual factors are in-volved in influencing whether or not help is sought and the type of help that is sought. Individual characteristics that impact how and why help is sought include perceived social and cognitive competencies and achievement goal orientations (e.g., Butler & Neuman, 1995; Karabenick, 2003; Ryan, Hicks, & Midgley, 1997). Contextual factors include the availability of potential helpers, with regard to their perceived competence and willingness to help (Nelson-Le Gall, 1992; Ryan & Pintrich, 1998), and the norms and rules of the classroom (van der Meij, 1988). Classroom norms are often conceptual-ized in terms of teacher support for help seeking, which has been linked to students' willingness to seek help (e.g., Karabenick & Sharma, 1994; Newman & Schwager, 1993).

In this way, there may be a number of explanations as to why students do not seek help when they need it. For instance, students may not be aware that they need help, they may perceive that seeking help is not supported or that there are no available helpers, or they may decide not to seek help for personal reasons (e.g., fear of appearing incompetent). Once the decision is made to seek help, researchers consider what type of help is sought. Some students seek out help in understanding (autonomous help seeking), whereas others simply seek out the answer as a way to avoid doing the work themselves (dependent help seeking) (Nadler, 1998). These different types of help seeking are thought to vary based on aforementioned individual and contextual factors.

HELPING BEHAVIORS IN GROUP CONTEXTS

One of the touted benefits of small-group learning is that it provides nu-merous opportunities for students to explain and expand on ideas, which is thought to result in deeper understanding and learning (Webb & Palinscar,

1996; Yackel, Cobb, & Wood, 1991). In this literature, helping behaviors are often viewed as an important indicator of the overall quality of the group's social interactions in that groups are believed to be interacting effectively when questions are posed and explanations are provided in response. From a help-seeking perspective, group contexts are viewed as beneficial in that they may afford students additional opportunities to seek help. Some researchers studying small groups have examined how helping behaviors relate to learning in small groups in math (for reviews, see Webb, 1982; Webb & Palinscar, 1996). Webb's research (1991; Webb & Farivar, 1999; Webb, Ing, Kersting, & Nemer, this volume; Webb & Mastergeorge, 2003; Webb et al., 1995) in this area is particularly useful, as she and her colleagues expanded much of the early work on helping behaviors in small groups to focus on the quality of the help received as well as the quality of the help sought.

In investigating the quality of help received, Webb (1991; Webb et al., 1995) differentiated between elaborated and nonelaborated help giving. Elaborated help includes providing higher level responses such as a conceptual explanation or a clear explanation of a procedure. Nonelaborated help includes incomplete types of help giving, such as giving the student the answer, providing a response but not providing enough information to help the receiver make connections, or not responding to the request for help. Receiving nonelaborated help, especially when that nonelaborated help indicates that a student's request for help was ignored, appears to be detrimental for learning. Receiving elaborated explanations is not, however, consistently linked to higher levels of learning in all studies (Webb et al., 1995). Webb and Mastergeorge (2003) recently suggested that these inconsistent findings may result because prior research did not focus on whether students' understanding of the concepts for which they sought help improved. When they examined whether students scored higher on exam questions that were specifically related to the areas in which they had previously sought help, their results suggested that receiving elaborated help *was* associated with higher achievement. Unfortunately, these beneficial elaborated responses are rarely realized because students typically receive low-level, nonelaborated responses (Webb & Mastergeorge, 2003).

Students' follow-up responses to the help they receive is also important, with students who work constructively on problems after receiving help generally scoring higher on posttest measures than students who simply receive the help but do not work to incorporate it in their solving of the current problem or later problems (Webb et al., 1995). Interestingly, students who receive elaborated help are more likely to engage in constructive activity. Thus, it seems important that students both receive elaborated explanations *and* actively use the elaborated explanations to further their understanding.

Recently, the quality of students' requests for help has also been investigated (Webb et al., this volume; Webb & Mastergeorge, 2003). This research suggests that the quality of students' requests for help tends to be low, with students posing primarily general questions or making vague statements of misunderstanding. Specific requests for explanations or requests for specific information about the problem are rare. This pattern of help seeking should be of concern to educators because specific requests for help seem to be beneficial for students' learning, in that higher level responses were given to specific questions more frequently than to general questions. In this way, students seem to benefit from posing specific questions because they receive more complete and elaborated responses to their questions and thus have the opportunity to gain a better understanding of the concept or issue.

Overall, the research on helping behaviors in small groups suggests that students would benefit if they asked more specific questions and received more elaborated responses. However, there is little research on why and when high-quality helping behaviors occur in small-group contexts. One potential avenue for promoting high-quality helping behaviors has been to address the behaviors directly through training. For instance, Swing and Peterson (1982) trained students in general "teaching" behaviors and small-group interaction skills such as monitoring the progress of students in the group, checking other group members' work, and providing explanations to other students when needed. They then asked students to work in four-person groups as part of the individual seatwork portion of direct instruction in math. Students who participated in the training were more likely to provide and receive higher level explanations and to check each other's work than were students in a control condition, suggesting that training can improve the quality and frequency of help giving.

Webb (1991) also suggested that the structure of the group may be important for facilitating adaptive helping behaviors and suggested that fostering interdependence in small groups may encourage group members to provide high levels of help. These interventions tend to emphasize the role of the help giver. It might also be useful to consider how to encourage students to ask specific rather than general questions in group contexts, especially given the potential of specific questions for evoking elaborated responses (Webb & Mastergeorge, 2003). Finally, the quality of the helping behaviors may be based on individual difference factors, such as gender, ability, or personality, or group composition factors, such as the ratio of gender or ability within the group (Webb, 1991).

In the current study, we seek to extend this initial work on promoting high-quality helping behaviors by considering how group processes or group interactions are related to helping behaviors for two groups of sixth-grade students working in small groups in math. We consider two types of group processes: (a) the *quality* of the group's interactions and (b) the *type* of interactions. The *quality* of the group's interactions refers to the group's socioemotional interactions in terms of respect, getting along, and being supportive of one another. We conceptualize the *type* of interaction in terms of collaborative and cooperative interactions. *Collaborative interactions* refer to a particular emphasis on shared cognitions, shared understanding, and opportunities for students to co-construct their understanding of the group task (Yackel et al., 1991). When collaborating, students actively work together to complete the assigned task, while sharing, justifying, and explaining their ideas within the group. In contrast, *cooperative interactions* refer to students dividing the task into smaller components to be completed individually or working on solving the same part of the task and then comparing answers.[1]

The quality of the group's socioemotional interactions may support or undermine high-quality helping behaviors. In particular, negative group interactions such as high levels of disrespect, active discouragement of participation, and low cohesion may undermine helping behaviors. Students may be less likely to seek help as they fear their requests will not be answered, their questions will be criticized, or other group members may use the request as an excuse to take over the task. Indeed, Webb's recent research (this volume) suggests that negative responses (e.g., put-downs) to requests for help may suppress further help seeking. In contrast, groups with a more positive pattern of interaction, where there is a high level of respect and where individuals attend to and respond to other students' comments, may foster adaptive helping behaviors. Students in groups with high-quality social interactions might also feel higher levels of cohesion, which should lead to higher quality responses as students may feel more responsibility to ensure that all group members understand the task.

The type of group interactions also has the potential to impact helping behaviors in small groups. It seems plausible that collaboration among group members may support more adaptive helping behaviors than cooperation. For instance, as all students collaborate on a group task, the group discussions surrounding the task may lessen the need to explicitly seek help, as students have many opportunities to hear and provide explanations and justifications regarding the task without explicitly asking for help (Yackel et al., 1991). This emphasis on explanations and justifications as a means of communication may also enhance the likelihood that when help is sought or given, it will also contain higher quality explanations. In contrast,

---

[1]Within the small-group literature, others use the terms *cooperative* versus *collaborative* to refer to the task structure (Webb & Palincsar, 1996). We do not disagree with these distinctions, but feel that in looking at the relation of students' interactions to helping behaviors, it is more important to focus on the interaction processes in which students engage rather than to focus on the way in which the task was structured.

during cooperation, students have fewer opportunities to participate, observe, and learn from their peers working on and discussing the task. Also, as students work independently, students must explicitly seek help. These explicit questions may make the quality of help received more dependent on the type of question asked and the type of response received. A second distinction is that collaboration may reduce the focus on the self (Ames, 1992), making it less likely that the process of help seeking is short-circuited by concerns about demonstrating one's competence. That is, it seems more likely that students who collaborate on a group task will have higher levels of cohesion and thus will view themselves more as a group and less as individuals, in contrast to students who cooperate.

Accordingly, we examined the potential influence of two group processes on the quality of helping behaviors within the group. First, we considered how the quality of interaction related to help-seeking behaviors, making the distinction between negative group interactions, which included disrespectful behavior, discouraging other group member's engagement, and low cohesion, and positive group interactions, which included active listening, respect, encouragement of group members, and high group cohesion. Second, we examined how the type of interaction, or the process of collaborating or cooperating, supported or hindered helping behaviors.

STUDY DESIGN

Two groups of sixth-grade students ($n = 8$) were videotaped while they worked in their small groups for 1 day of each section of the math unit (for a total of 3 days of videotape lasting 129 minutes for each group). Both groups were heterogeneous with regard to prior math knowledge. Group A consisted of two males (Charles [Caucasian], David [African American]) and two females (Angela [Caucasian], Rochelle [African American]). Group B consisted of two males (Sam and Peter, Caucasian) and two females (Briana [Caucasian], Julie [African American]).[2]

Instruction for the mathematics unit was drawn from the first unit on statistics and graphing from the sixth-grade district-approved mathematics textbook. This mathematics unit focused on teaching students how to read and interpret a variety of types of graphs (e.g., bar graphs, line graphs, stem and leaf plots) and how to calculate basic statistics such as the mean, median, and mode. The unit lasted approximately 5 weeks and was broken into three sections. Each section took about 1½ weeks to complete and followed the same basic sequence: whole class instruction/individual seatwork based on the accompanying teacher's manual (3–4 days), small-group work

---

[2]Please note that all students' names are pseudonyms.

designed to complement and enhance the math curriculum (2–3 days), and a quiz taken from the textbook (1 day). The classroom teachers presented all instructional materials, including the whole class instruction and small-group work. Before students began working on the mathematics unit, they completed a series of activities designed by Cohen (1994) to help students learn how to work together in groups.

The whole class instruction generally involved an introduction to the concepts covered in the unit in the form of an interactive lecture. The small-group instruction, which was the focus of the current study, required that students apply the concepts covered during whole class instruction. For the group tasks, the entire group was given one set of materials that it needed to share in order to solve the group task and members were assigned group roles (facilitator, recorder, materials manager, presenter). Group interdependence was fostered by using the group's score on the group activity, and their individual quiz scores, to award improvement points as feedback. These points were based on Slavin's (1995) Student Teams-Achievement Division and were used so that students had some incentive to ensure that each group member understood the concepts being used to solve the group task.

Each small-group task was designed to be completed during two 50-minute class periods and included both lower order questions (calculate the mean, median, mode) and higher order questions (e.g., after calculating the mean, median, and mode for each graph, students were asked to write a paragraph describing which statistic best represented the data presented in the graph).[3] More specifically, students worked on three different group activities during the mathematics unit. For the first group activity, students were asked to pick three graphs (line graph, bar graph, circle graph) from a packet of graphs taken from newspapers and magazines and then to interpret and describe each graph. They were also instructed that one of the three graphs should be misleading and that they must redraw it so it was no longer misleading. The second group activity required that students make a line plot, bar graph, and stem-and-leaf plot using data provided in a general encyclopedia-type resource book. For each graph, the group was expected to choose the data set and develop a descriptive title and a

---

[3]Following Steiner's (1972) distinction between unitary and divisible tasks, this group task can be best classified as a unitary task. More specifically, Steiner suggests that in contrast to divisible tasks that are designed to be solved by dividing up the task among members of the group, unitary tasks are designed so that they cannot be easily divided into subtasks. There are several types of unitary tasks, and we suggest that ours represents a "discretionary task." Discretionary tasks are those tasks in which the group decides how to go about solving the task. For example, a group can decide to let one group member perform the entire task or the group may opt to give each member equal responsibility on the task by collaborating on the task with equal participation. Our task was not easily divisible but did allow for the possibility that different groups might divide up the task or might work together as a group on the entire task.

paragraph describing why they picked that type of graph to represent the information. The third lesson required students to calculate the mean, median, and mode for each of the graphs from the second assignment. For each of the three graphs, the group was also expected to discuss whether the mean, median, or mode most accurately represented the data. Finally, for the stem-and-leaf plot, the group needed to recalculate the mean, median, and mode without the most extreme value and then discuss whether the extreme value was an outlier and why removing it did or did not change the mode.

In terms of analysis, the videotapes were observed and narratives were prepared in an effort to describe the group's interactions. These narratives were subsequently coded by the coauthors by first differentiating between helping behaviors within the group and those that occurred with others outside of the group, including the classroom teacher. The focus of this chapter is on the help seeking that took place within the group. For this behavior, we focused on the nature of the question, the nature of the response, and unsolicited help giving. Questions were coded as referencing the directions for the task, group roles (e.g., what should I be doing?), surface-level math questions (e.g., a request for a definition or the steps for a procedure), and deeper level math questions (e.g., a request for help in deeper understanding such as understanding how to make sense of the data presented on a graph). Within our work, surface-level questions are similar to Webb's notion of "general questions" in that we classify general and vague questions within this code. However, we also include some specific questions here in that students posed specific question about definitions that would not enhance their conceptual understanding. Deeper level math questions are at a higher level in that these questions demonstrate evidence of more thoughtful questioning of underlying math concepts or an understanding of math processes or concepts. The nature of the response was coded as being nonelaborated (e.g., giving the definition, simply taking over the task, ignoring a question), and elaborated (e.g., providing a thoughtful response and following up the response with additional questions or support to ensure understanding). We also noted the negative or positive response of the recipient to the help provided. Finally, we coded unsolicited help in terms of the type of the help (see preceding description) as well as the response of the recipient to that help.

Narratives were also analyzed for the quality of the group's interactions in terms of positive and negative features of the interactions. Group interactions were characterized as *positive* when there was evidence of active listening (e.g., eye contact, paying attention to other group members), sharing of ideas, respecting group members' efforts and contributions, providing positive feedback, attempting to encourage the persistence or engagement of a team member, and when the group demonstrated evidence of group cohesion (e.g., working together as a team, referring to the group as "we"). In contrast, the group's interactions were coded as *negative* when there were explicit attempts at discouraging an individual's participation on the math task (e.g., criticizing her work on the task, refusing to give him a portion of the task, not responding to questions) or evidence of disrespect (e.g., ignoring a group member, put-downs). In addition, narratives were coded for evidence of low group cohesion, or when the group clearly decided not to work together or did not think of each other as part of a team.

With respect to the type of group interaction, we coded whether the group engaged in cooperative versus collaborative interactions while working on the assigned tasks. Group interactions where students actively interacted and shared ideas when working on solving the math task were coded as collaborative. In contrast, interactions where students made the decision to work independently on different portions of the task were coded as cooperative (e.g., groups divided up the task by drawing separate graphs or by independently calculating the statistics for a specific graph). We also noted group discussions about how to divide the task among some or all of the group members as evidence for cooperative rather than collaborative interactions.

Analysis of the coded narratives indicated that Groups A and B differed in their patterns of helping behaviors and the quality of the groups' interactions. We begin by describing these interactions, focusing on the relation between the quality of the group's interactions and helping behaviors for Groups A and B. We then examine the helping behaviors associated with different types of interactions. Because Groups A and B both engaged in cooperative and collaborative interactions, we draw from the interactions of both Groups A and B in this section.

QUALITY OF GROUP INTERACTION AND HELPING BEHAVIORS

In Group A, negative group interactions were dominant. Students consistently showed little respect for fellow group members and actively worked to discourage the participation of several of the group members. The group also showed low cohesion, rarely referring to their team or group. In contrast, Group B's interactions were distinctly positive. Group B was respectful of their fellow group members, actively encouraged all group members to participate, and seemed to have a high sense of cohesion. Given that Group A had predominantly negative interactions whereas Group B exhibited more positive interactions, we were able to contrast the two groups and compare the helping behaviors based on these differences in the quality of the interactions.

Helping Behaviors During Negative Group Interactions

We began by exploring the relation of Group A's negative interactions to their helping behaviors. We observed four main patterns of helping behaviors. First, the questions that students posed were often surface-level or vague. Second, the quality of help giving was low, as evidenced in the nonelaborated and highly critical responses provided in response to group members' questions. Third, there were more frequent instances of unsolicited help giving; these instances were primarily used to criticize a group member's contributions rather than to encourage understanding. Finally, disrespect and nonelaborated help giving seemed to elicit negative reactions from group members and encourage a cycle of negative interactions within the group.

Help Seeking. The questions posed in Group A were primarily surface-level. Students asked questions that were less specific rather than clearly indicating the aspect of the task that was proving difficult. For example, David asked the group, "This isn't going to work … what am I going to do?" when he confronted the problem of creating a scale for the bar graph where the data to be plotted were in the millions. Vague questions were also frequent when students were unsure what they should be doing on the task or what role they might serve in the group (e.g., "What should I do?"). This use of vague questions was often observed as students attempted to reengage with the task after having been off-task. Similarly, surface-level questions were also dependent, given that these questions merely sought the answer to the question such as the definition of a stem-and-leaf plot or a graph's mean. These questions suggested that students were more interested in simply receiving the answer to a particular question than in becoming involved in solving aspects of the task. These surface-level questions seemed to emerge from both routine and challenging aspects of the group task.

Although deeper questions were rare in Group A, there were a few instances observed as students worked on challenging features of the task. For example, David questioned Charles about the misleading features of a particular graph, asking why the scale of the y axis reached 400 so fast. This question was of higher quality than the aforementioned surface-level examples in that David asked why there was such a large jump in the scale, suggesting a desire to understand *why* the graph was created that way. In a second example, Rochelle asked Angela which statistic best represented a particular graph and *why*. Rochelle's help seeking was also adaptive in that she tried to elicit an elaborated response as she pressed Angela for a justification of her answer. Here, the quality of the questions seemed to be related more closely to the challenging nature of the task rather than to specific negative group interactions. However, as noted previously, not all challenging features prompted deeper questions, as students also asked surface-level questions in response to challenging features.

In addition to the type of question posed, Angela and Rochelle tended to selectively pose questions to each other, thus excluding other group members. This tendency suggested a relation between help seeking and the negative quality of group interaction. Specifically, by not posing questions to the whole group, Angela and Rochelle showed disrespect for Charles and David, suggesting that their potential contributions were not valued. Also, this pattern of help seeking demonstrated evidence for discouraging participation in that Angela made a direct effort to exclude the boys from the math task by not directing any questions to them.

Help Giving.   Group A's help-giving patterns can best be characterized by their nonelaborated responses and highly critical tone. One nonelaborated response seen frequently in Group A was to simply switch tasks in response to a question, without providing any additional follow-up assistance. For example, when students were creating different graphs during the second activity, Angela asked Rochelle about how to place numbers in the hundreds on a stem-and-leaf plot. Rochelle offered to "trade" graphs with her and took over Angela's work on the stem-and-leaf plot while Angela worked on completing the paragraph that Rochelle had been writing. Rochelle never provided an explanation for how to complete the task and Angela did not seek additional help.

Exchanging tasks in response to a question was not always a mutual decision. For instance, David had a question about whether earth had one satellite while plotting earth's data point on the bar graph. Rochelle offered to draw the bar graph and suggested that David could instead finish labeling the names of the planets on the x axis. In this case, David refused to give Rochelle the bar graph. This prompted other group members to suggest that David allow someone else to do the work (e.g., Angela asked David, "David, can't you just let us [work on the bar graph]?" and when he continued to work on the bar graph, Angela added, "David, please"). Angela and Rochelle's actions and pleas communicated their disrespect for David, especially with regard to his capability to equally contribute to the task.

Interestingly, this strategy of switching tasks occurred both when the questions required a simple explanation (e.g., how to label the axis) and when the task was more challenging (e.g., scaling the bar graph or writing a paragraph describing the bar graph). The strategy was effective in resolving the immediate concern by relieving the student of the question. Switching tasks was also more time-efficient in that students continued to make progress on the task without needing to stop to take the extra time to help out their teammate. Unfortunately, the strategy was not useful in alleviating the original question, which undermined the opportunity to learn from one's group members. Also, this strategy often excluded group members from actively participating in the task.

When help was provided in response to a question or misunderstanding, Group A exhibited a highly critical tone. For example as described previously, David had questions when working on drawing the bar graph. After Angela's attempts to take over David's task failed, Angela provided help through the feedback and tips that she provided on his graph. However, Angela's feedback and suggestions were highly critical in their tone.

> Angela: See David. The line in the bar graph is supposed to be up here by the moon. Did you ever guess that? Did you ever figure? (*Sarcastic and elevated tone*).
>
> David: Did you ever figure to shut your mouth?
>
> (Angela rests her head down on her desk and laughs).
>
> David: Stop acting like you got an IQ smaller than a rock.
>
> Angela: I am not the one acting!

In this passage, Angela criticized David's depiction of the data as inaccurate. Her elevated and critical tone suggested that the feedback she provided was harsh. Although Angela's feedback could be useful in terms of advising a better presentation of the data, the critical tone through which the feedback was provided undermined the informational components of the provided help. This example also illustrates how a critical tone used when providing help can spark further negative interactions among group members, in that Angela and David went on to insult one another's ability. It is also probable that these types of negative interactions discouraged David's help-seeking attempts in the future. In this way, there may be a cyclical pattern between negative interactions and helping behaviors.

Unsolicited Help Giving.   In terms of unsolicited help giving there were two noteworthy patterns. First, there was a higher frequency of unsolicited help giving observed in Group A. Second, the unsolicited help was often administered in a threatening manner that did not encourage understanding. Instead of providing task-relevant feedback so that the group member receiving the help (i.e., the recipient) could make adjustments as necessary, the helper often took over the task or grabbed the task from the recipient and then edited their work.

David and Charles were often the recipients of unsolicited help, as Rochelle and Angela frequently attempted to grab the task from them in order to make a change or erase their work without ever voicing specific feedback. This was most likely perceived as threatening to Charles and David, as it discredited the work that they had contributed to the group. For example, Angela offered unsolicited help to David as he worked on the bar graph by telling him that he was not doing the task correctly and then directing him to add little dashes to the axis. However, without awaiting David's own attempt to make this change, Angela leaned over the task and began to make the change for him. Moments later, Rochelle and Angela tried to take the paper from David and began to erase his work.

Angela and Rochelle also made general statements to the group explicitly voicing their intent to "help out" within two of the three taped class sessions. For instance, when David was assigned the role of recorder, Angela immediately let David know that they would clearly need to help him a lot. Similarly, after Charles was allowed to contribute to the writing of the explanation for the bar graph (the teacher's suggestion), Rochelle reassured Angela that she would be sure to check over the work after the paragraph was completed.

These patterns of unsolicited help giving were problematic on two counts. First, this type of help was viewed as unwelcome because the helper simply took the task or began erasing work, which was disrespectful to the recipient. In fact, David's reaction (e.g., "You can show me, but not like I'm an idiot") clearly expressed the threatening nature of this type of unsolicited feedback in terms of implied low math ability and disrespect. Second, the helper typically made the adjustments without explaining or justifying the change, as might be evidenced by a higher quality of unsolicited feedback.

Responses to Helping Behaviors. Students in Group A often ignored the help that was offered even though that meant continuing to struggle with the presented challenge. For example, during the third activity Angela expressed frustration when she had difficulty calculating the mean for the bar graph. It is important to note that this frustration was partially due to her misconception that she needed to add all of the numbers on the scale of the graph when calculating the mean, which ranged from 0 to 420 in intervals of 10. Thus, she attempted to add approximately 42 numbers and made frequent mistakes. However, this frustration might have been averted if she had accepted other group members' attempts to help. For example, in response to Angela's increasing frustration, Charles offered help on seven different occasions. Charles initially tried to offer help by saying that he could work on calculating the mean and tried to show Angela that he could type just as fast as she could on the calculator. After Charles made repeated offers, Rochelle began to suggest to Angela that Charles help her calculate the mean. In later attempts, Charles even asked Angela if she would need the teacher to help out; Angela also refused this intervention. Angela's need for help was not quickly abated; it lasted for over 10 minutes and was characterized by high levels of negative affect, yet Angela continued to ignore the group's offers to help. In this manner, Angela communicated that she was unwilling to accept Charles's help even though that meant continuing to struggle with her presented challenge.

In addition to simply not accepting offers to help, there was also evidence that all of the group members' help was not valued equally. For instance, Angela ignored David's and Charles's offers to help and instead redirected her questions to Rochelle. This was especially noteworthy because Charles often gave accurate, thorough, and high-quality responses to questions. His explanations frequently included examples and justifications for his response. Despite Charles's willingness to provide elaborated help, his group members tended to ignore his recommendations or were rather dismissive of his help. For instance, when Angela had a question about whether to put the stem or leaf first in the stem-and-leaf plot, Rochelle initially gave a nonelaborated response by telling Angela to look it up in the book. Charles, in contrast, overheard Angela's question and offered help, but his help was dismissed:

Charles: I know how to do it, you draw a line, it goes down. You know what I am saying? I could teach you.
Angela: I already know how.
Charles: Remember, here is the stem and here is the leaf (recalling a strategy from class).
(Charles continues a moment later).
Charles: You write the 100s on that side and the one numbers on the other, I think.
Angela: That is what I thought. (and then to Rochelle) Don't you with 3.3 put three on one side and three on the other?

It is interesting that Charles provided Angela with an elaborated response to her question by explaining what the graph would look like and recalling a strategy that would jog her memory. Charles also offered to show her and "teach" her. However, Angela remained dismissive of his attempts to help and continued to persist in asking Rochelle a subsequent question, even though Charles had clearly demonstrated his understanding of the subject matter.

David and Charles reacted to the help they received and the negative exchanges with frustration. David often reacted by vocally expressing his frustration or arguing with a group member. Charles, in contrast, was less vocal about his frustrations around the task. As group members ignored Charles's contributions and offers to help on the task, he reacted by disengaging from the task. These responses were not surprising, given Angela's and Rochelle's negative reactions to Charles's and David's offers to help as well as the highly critical tone and unsolicited help giving employed when answering their questions or providing feedback on their work on the task.

Overall, our analyses suggest that helping behaviors were one mechanism through which negative interactions among group members continued. It seems clear from Angela and Rochelle's initial interactions with Charles and David that they did not have high respect for them. This was seen as Angela and Rochelle disregarded Charles's and David's attempts to participate and ignored their contributions. They also communicated this low respect in their unsolicited help giving and reactions to Charles's and David's attempts to help. As Charles and David reacted to the unsolicited help and refusal to accept their help-giving, they became increasingly disrespectful to Angela and Rochelle. In this way, it seems that there was a reciprocal relation between maladaptive helping behaviors and negative group interactions.

Helping Behaviors During Positive Group Interactions

The helping behaviors observed in Group B stand in stark contrast to those characterized for Group A. Although there were fewer helping behaviors, the positive group interactions exhibited by Group B translated into a more respectful manner of questioning and responsiveness to sought help. First, the questions posed had a tone that communicated a respect for the help giver(s). Second, the help givers demonstrated respect by actively listening and working together to assist the help seeker. In addition, student responses were more elaborated and thorough, suggesting a higher quality of help giving during these positive exchanges. Finally, there was only one instance of unsolicited help giving and few instances of group members negatively reacting to helping behaviors with frustration or disrespect.

Help Seeking. There were far fewer explicit questions posed within Group B. However, the help seeking that was observed was similar to the patterns observed for Group A in that they were primarily surface-level. Students asked for definitions (e.g., "What does statistics mean?") and for the answer to a specific task prompt (e.g., "What is the outlier?"). Sam, in particular, asked especially vague questions by stating, "I don't understand," "I'm confused," and "Explain it to me, tell me what to do." Sam used these questions in an effort to have his three group members help him after he was assigned the role of recorder on the first group task and when trying to reengage himself in the task after a brief absence from the classroom.

Although less prominent than surface-level questions, students in Group B posed some higher level questions. These deeper level questions were posed in response to a challenging feature of the task or as students engaged in more in-depth conversations with the material. For example, Briana asked her group *how* they should go about choosing the best statistic to represent each graph. Also, Peter asked a deeper level question when writing the group's explanation posing, "Why did we choose to use this information (when creating this particular graph)?" Peter's question gets at a deeper level of understanding that specific data may be more appropriate for the type of graph being created. Although this was a feature for both groups, deeper level questioning was a more consistent pattern for Group B in contrast to the isolated examples observed for Group A.

The help seeking observed for Group B was often respectful and inclusive. Questions tended to be addressed to the whole group, rather than to select group members. The manner in which the questions were phrased was also respectful. For example, at the beginning of the third activity Sam asked Peter, "When it is time, can you show me how to do a mean?" and moments later asked a subsequent question, "Peter, if you have time, how do you do mean again?" After Peter responded to the question, Sam again showed respect by thanking Peter for his help. In general, however, the patterns of help seeking for Group B were similar to those observed for Group A. This suggests that the positive quality of group interactions did not have a strong influence on the type and quality of questions posed within the group.

Help Giving.   In response to questions, Group B communicated respect for their fellow group members by actively listening to the questions and responding. There were few questions that were left unanswered or that were ignored. Active listening was seen as group members leaned in to get a better look at the task, made eye contact with the speaker, or as multiple group members worked together to assist the help seeker. The latter behavior also served to communicate respect for the help seeker, as the group gave the question their full attention. For example, Briana asked her group which graph was misleading. In response, Julie, Sam, and Peter all leaned in toward the packet, which had been placed at the center of their desks, as they tried to identify the misleading graph. Each group member then contributed by pointing out a misleading graph and discussing the various suggestions.

In a related pattern, there were also respectful interactions among multiple help givers as they worked together to respond to a specific question. There were a number of occasions in which a group member offered a solution and then the other helper indicated agreement with the solution. For example, as the group worked to identify a misleading graph, Peter responded to Sam's question about why the particular graph they selected was misleading. Here, Briana looked on while Peter explained the misleading features of the graph and then indicated her agreement with Peter's explanation. Briana then added to Peter's explanation by pointing out the next step to the problem, given Peter's response. In another example, the whole group began to puzzle over whether they had created the stem-and-leaf plot correctly, with each group member contributing an idea and/or asking an additional question to help clarify and solve the problem. As part of this conversation, Sam showed respect for Peter saying, "Hold on, I think Peter might be right on this one, because you have to put the small ones on this side and the big ones on this side." In this manner, Group B demonstrated respect by actively listening, recognizing, and subsequently providing positive feedback to a fellow group member's helping behaviors.

The respectful tone among group members also seemed to contribute to the quality of the elaborated help. For instance, when Briana responded to Sam's expressed frustration and question about how to interpret a graph and write the accompanying paragraph, her response coupled elaborated help with respect. Briana provided an elaborated response by talking through an example and showing Sam how she would interpret the graph within the written description. Briana completed her example by adding in the numbers she might pull from the graph to illustrate the decrease in the line graph. During this explanation, Briana communicated respect for Sam by involving him in her explanation. For example, Briana asked Sam a question to help him interpret the line graph, asking, "Do you think this (the line) is going up or down? It's going down, right?" In this way, Briana attended to Sam's frustration by clearly demonstrating how to solve the problem and by engaging in a positive interaction with him around this challenge. It may be that positive interactions coupled with elaborated help exceed the benefits of elaborated help alone. These positive helping exchanges not only further student understanding, but may also promote further help seeking.

There were, however, a few occasions where questions went unanswered or the responses were nonelaborated. Some questions were ignored because of a group member's involvement in solving an earlier question or working on a problem with another group member. For example, one of Sam's questions was ignored because Julie, Briana, and Peter were working on figuring out the task directions. There were also a few examples of nonelaborated help giving. In particular, group members offered nonelaborated responses when Sam asked a number of questions related to his role of the recorder during the first task (e.g., Briana told Sam exactly what to write for one graph description instead of explaining her solution).

Although Group B exhibited primarily positive group interactions, there were also a few examples when the help giving was disrespectful. Julie sometimes hindered her group's attempts to solve a question in an effort to keep the group on-task and to ensure that they were making substantive progress. This was seen during the third activity when Sam asked a question about the graph the group created after having checked over the group's work. When Peter began to offer help in response to Sam's question, Julie rolled her eyes in frustration and stated, "Peter, we don't have time to play, we need to get this done." Julie's frustration may have been effective in pressing her group to make progress, but her comments were disrespectful of her peers in that she did not take Sam's question seriously and she thwarted the help-giving efforts of the other group members. These instances were rare, however, and did not reflect a general pattern for Group B.

Overall, Group B expressed a respectful tone during help-giving episodes. Group members made a joint effort and expressed a willingness to respond to questions. It may be that this positive tone within the group encouraged subsequent help seeking in that the help seekers perceived that questions were welcomed and taken seriously. In addition, help seekers might have felt comfortable posing additional questions because there were a number of group members who were available and willing to help.

Unsolicited Help Giving. In contrast to Group A, there was only one explicit example of unsolicited help giving for Group B. In this example, Sam had been working on editing the paragraph the group had prepared to describe the misleading graph when Briana leaned in and began to erase some of Sam's writing. This unsolicited help giving was disrespectful to Sam and was similar to what was observed when Angela and Rochelle provided unsolicited help to David in Group A. However, the response to this episode of unsolicited help giving differed between Groups A and B. After Sam communicated his frustration by throwing his hands up in the air, Briana was responsive to Sam. She talked with Sam about the changes he had been making to the paragraph. In addition, once Sam recognized his mistake, he began to laugh about it and the group joined in, alleviating a potentially negative situation. This example is a nice contrast to the unsolicited help giving in Group A in that the positive interactions and respect exhibited by Group B eased Sam's initial negative reaction to the unsolicited help.

Overall, positive group interactions, which were characterized by high levels of respect and encouragement of whole-group participation, may have contributed to the lower levels of unsolicited help giving in Group B. In particular, simply taking over the task or reaching in to alter another student's work would not be consistent with the overall emphasis within Group B on respecting one's fellow group members and encouraging their participation.

Responses to Helping Behaviors. In contrast to Group A, Group B's responses to helping behaviors were less negative, taking on a neutral or moderately positive tone in response to the help provided. For instance, students continued in their efforts at solving the problem and working toward a solution instead of reacting negatively to a specific group member. Positive responses were rare; however, there was one example that was noted previously in which Sam responded positively to Peter's help on the task by saying thank you and communicating that he now understood.

There were also a few occasions during the first task when Sam reacted negatively to his group due to his frustration in receiving nonelaborated help. Sam became frustrated when he was ignored, when Briana erased his work, and during a few other nonelaborated help-giving episodes. Sam communicated his frustration by disengaging from the group, putting his head down on the desk, or putting his fingers in his ears to indicate that he was no longer listening to his peers. These instances were rare and only occurred during the first group activity.

Overall, the positive quality of interactions exhibited by Group B seemed to encourage higher quality helping behaviors. In particular, the respectful framing of questions may have encouraged fellow group members to provide elaborated responses and to actively listen to posed questions. These higher quality responses also prompted additional questions and more active involvement. This may be especially useful given the importance of actively applying the help received (Webb et al., 1995). In this way, our analyses suggest that positive group interactions supported and provided the opportunity for adaptive helping behaviors.

In general, our analysis of both Groups A and B suggest that the quality of interaction within the group does in fact influence exhibited helping behaviors. This consideration of the social dynamics of the group helps to extend prior research on helping in small groups, which focused more on the type of request for help, characteristics of individual group members in terms of gender, ability, and personality, and the composition of the group in terms of gender and ability (see Webb, 1991; Webb & Mastergeorge, 2003). In particular, our results suggest that positive interactions facilitate adaptive helping behaviors in that students are more respectful in their requests for help and their responses. This respectful tone seems to facilitate helping behaviors in that group members may be more likely to listen to students' requests for help and students may, in turn, be more likely to seek help based on perceived group norms that help seeking is welcomed.

In contrast, when a group's interaction style is highly negative, there seem to be more frequent occurrences of ignoring requests for help or providing feedback in a way that conveys a negative view of the help seeker. Ultimately, these highly negative responses seem to undermine future help seeking as well as the general interactions within the group. These findings parallel Webb et al. (this volume) research, which suggests that negative socioemotional responses to requests for help suppress further help seeking. It is also possible that the negative responses to help giving limit students' opportunities to apply the help they received, which may ultimately undermine their learning. Given the saliency of negative interactions and their potential relation to future help seeking and engagement in the material, negative interactions may have more influence than positive interactions; positive interactions may support helping behaviors, but may be equally as effective as more neutral interactions. Therefore, it seems that the quality of the group interaction, whether it is primarily positive or negative, relates to patterns of help giving, responses to the help received, and the unsolicited help giving exhibited by the group. In contrast, the quality of help seeking within the group did not appear to be affected by the groups' patterns of interaction.

TYPE OF INTERACTION AND HELPING BEHAVIORS

We also examined how the process of working cooperatively or collaboratively on the group task supported or hindered helping behaviors. In general, Group A was somewhat more likely to cooperate, as they often split up the task to be completed independently by members of the group. In contrast, Group B was more likely to collaborate, as they showed a more consistent pattern for sharing the materials and working together on the task. However, we found it inappropriate to directly compare and contrast Groups A and B, as both groups engaged in cooperative and collaborative interactions across the three tapes. Rather, we focused on examining helping behaviors as they occurred when either group cooperated or collaborated. In the results that follow, we first present the patterns of helping behaviors evident when group members cooperated followed by a description of these behaviors when group members collaborated.

Cooperation

Our analyses suggested that cooperative interactions were related to the quality of helping behaviors. Students who were working cooperatively engaged in more explicit forms of help seeking. When a group member had a question, it was necessary for her to stop her own work on the task and interrupt another group member who was working on a different portion of the task in order to ask for help. When students were cooperating, we also observed that the help seeker typically posed a question to a single group member instead of involving the entire group.

The quality of the helping behaviors during cooperative interactions around the math task seemed to depend both on the type of help seeking and the quality of the group interactions. For instance, when Group B engaged in cooperative interactions on the math task during the second activity, Briana questioned Peter concerning the difficulty she was having with drawing the line plot. Although Briana's request for help was lower level [e.g., "How would you do it (the line graph)? Would you do (draw) it down here?"], it seemed to elicit an elaborated response. In addition, Briana's questions were respectful of Peter in that the question made it clear that she valued his opinion when creating the line graph. In response to her question, Peter turned toward Briana and provided her with the necessary help. In this way, Peter also showed respect for Briana by attending to her question and working to keep her engaged in the task. Thus, both the specificity of Briana's question and the norm of positive group interactions for Group B seemed to contribute to the quality of the helping behaviors.

In contrast, instances of cooperation in Group A were typically disrespectful and discouraged equal participation of all group members. For this group, the negative interactions seemed to undermine any benefit of cooperation for facilitating helping behaviors. In particular, the predominance of disrespect among the members discouraged the posing of subsequent questions as the group cooperated on the math task. For example, Angela's and Rochelle's attempts to dominate the task and tendency to discount the contributions of Charles and David seemed to contribute to the maladaptive pattern of helping behaviors for Group A.

Collaboration

When groups engaged in collaborative interactions, unique patterns of helping behaviors were observed. In describing these helping behaviors, we found it useful to distinguish between explicit and implicit forms of help. Explicit help seeking was used to refer to the voicing of a question to the group, such as that characterized during cooperative interactions. Implicit help seeking or help giving suggested that a question was not posed aloud, but instead questions and helping were integrated within the group's discussion.

Explicit Help Seeking.   Overall, there were fewer explicit questions posed when groups collaborated. This is perhaps because students were collaborating while solving the task and were therefore engaged in sharing their ideas, explaining their thinking, and justifying their opinions. In this way, students did not need to explicitly seek help as frequently when they collaborated. When students did explicitly seek help, we observed two main patterns. First, there were some explicit questions that were posed to seek help for a particular math problem (see Group B's patterns under positive group interaction). In a second pattern of explicit help seeking, questions were used as a way to spark the group's engagement. For example, Briana initiated work on the first task by asking her group, "Which one [graph] do you think is misleading?" In response, the group leaned in together to consider the presented graphs; they recalled the features that indicate that a graph was misleading, and identified a misleading graph. In this example, Briana did not seem to be struggling to figure out this question on her own; rather, she used the question as a form of group self-regulation to attempt to engage her group in the task. This pattern can be contrasted with explicit help seeking during cooperative interactions, where the aim of the question was to receive help on a question that could not be answered without the group's assistance.

Implicit Helping Behaviors. In contrast to cooperative interactions where students needed to explicitly seek help, collaborative interactions appeared to enable questions to emerge as students worked together to solve the task. For example, Group B's collaboration when calculating the mean for the stem-and-leaf plot involved implicit helping behaviors. This collaboration was sparked when Sam and the group noticed that their answer included a repeating decimal. Sam initiated a conversation about the repeating decimal, not with a question, but when he commented, "No, that can't be right." The whole group agreed that the answer could not be accurate, which prompted an exchange lasting over 10 minutes.

This exchange began with Julie's recommendation that she should recalculate the mean, suggesting that perhaps she had made an error when entering the numbers into the calculator. While Briana read the numbers aloud and Julie reentered the numbers, the other group members leaned in to monitor her calculations. However, the group soon realized that the repeated decimal again appeared as their answer. In response, the group decided that there might be a problem with the calculator. The collaboration continued as Briana and Julie calculated the mean again using the calculator while Peter and Sam calculated the mean by hand. Again, the group members monitored one another's calculations.

When their attempts continued to result in a repeating decimal, the group tried to understand the problem by expressing some possible explanations:

Sam:	I think something is wrong with the calculator. Maybe we're not supposed to do it on the calculator …
Briana:	It's right you guys, it's just a little big. (*referring to the answer*)
Sam:	That is what I was thinking. Not really too big, too many 3s.
Peter:	See you got 3 right there, and 9 doesn't go into 3. (showing their long division computations to the whole group)

This collaboration continued as the group decided to move on to another aspect of the task, but returned to the problem of the repeated decimal on two more occasions. During subsequent attempts to explain this problem, the group referred to the fact that other calculations only yielded one decimal point, suggesting that their answer might have been inaccurate.

The exchange just described can be examined with regard to implicit help seeking. In particular, the conversation allowed students to share their ideas and explanations for the repeating decimal throughout their work on the task. During the flow of the conversation, group members voiced agreement, made additional comments, or suggested alternative explanations to the same issue. This allowed the students to hear multiple perspectives on solving the problem. In this way, participation in the group conversation helped students to grapple with their current understanding without posing a direct question or providing explicit help to a struggling group member.

Analyses of similar collaborative interactions suggested three main patterns of implicit helping behaviors. First, challenging features of the task sparked these more subtle forms of helping. For example, problems such as understanding task directions, writing explanations, or selecting the statistic that best represented a graph presented a challenge that encouraged the whole group to join together and help one another. Second, help giving was not elicited by an explicit question, but rather by statements or stated opinions (e.g., Sam prompted the discussion just described when he commented, "No, that can't be right"). Third, monitoring of group work emerged naturally as part of the group conversation making it unnecessary for group members to explicitly check each other's work.

Given these types of collaborative conversations, we suggest that implicit forms of help seeking and help giving encourage a greater frequency and a higher quality of helping behaviors. Specifically, the sharing of ideas and opinions around math problems means that students are more consistently engaging in conversations where they must explain and justify ideas and are confronted with alternative viewpoints, in contrast to students working cooperatively. Because the questions are less explicit, students may feel more comfortable seeking help. That is, the perception that their peers may think they are dumb or might ignore their questions might be partially alleviated in this context. Finally, collaborative interactions may help to reduce unsolicited help giving, as the monitoring of group member's work is implicit in their collaborations.

In general, these results suggest that it is important for help-seeking researchers to study helping behaviors when groups cooperate and collaborate, as the patterns of interactions may vary. We found Webb's (1991) general framework of distinguishing between specific and general questions and elaborated and nonelaborated help to be relevant for both collaborative and cooperative interactions, but suggest that this framework may need to be expanded to include the distinction between explicit and implicit forms of helping behaviors. In particular, our observations suggest that group discussions may provide an opportunity for helping behaviors in a subtle, implicit manner, which is similar to the characterizations of collaborative processes in dyads presented by Yackel et al. (1991). Our results suggest that students who collaborate may not need to be as explicit when seeking or giving help because students hear explanations, alternative points of view, and justifications during collaborative exchanges around challenging problems presented by the task. Future research may want to more carefully explore implicit helping behaviors in group contexts, specifically in terms of how it emerges and to what extent it facilitates learning.

Although our study provides interesting insights into the nature of helping behaviors during small group interaction, we must use caution in drawing strong conclusions from this work. Partly due to our small sample, our analyses have confounded positive group interactions with collaborative interactions. It will be important to expand this work to consider the relation of positive and negative social interactions when groups cooperate and collaborate.

CONCLUSION

Previous research on helping behaviors in group contexts has primarily focused on the types of help seeking and help giving (e.g., Webb, 1982, 1991; Webb & Mastergeorge, 2003; Webb et al., 1995; Yackel et al., 1991). The current study extends this research by exploring the interplay between helping behaviors and group interactions. Our findings suggest that different patterns of helping behaviors are observed when groups collaborate rather than cooperate, with more implicit forms of help seeking becoming more prominent during collaboration. Our analyses also suggest that it is useful to consider both helping behaviors and the quality of the groups' interactions, as higher quality instances of help giving and responses to help giving were observed for groups with positive versus negative interactions.

Suggestions for Practice

It is a common practice among educators to employ small-group work as an instructional practice. Our findings suggest that teachers should encourage students to collaborate and should promote positive interactions within groups, as both have implications for engaging students who avoid seeking help and for encouraging effective group work. For those students who have a tendency to avoid seeking help, negative group interactions may be especially detrimental in that they clearly communicate a more threatening context for posing questions. In contrast, the active listening and respect for fellow group members associated with positive group interactions may create group norms that encourage help seeking. In addition, collaboration is advantageous for avoidant help seekers because help seeking may be less salient and provide a less public way of asking for help. That is, during collaboration, student misunderstandings often surface as the group compares viewpoints and strategies, alleviating the need to explicitly seek help.

Those individuals who avoid seeking help because they are unaware that they need help may also benefit when groups collaborate, in that the group can monitor an individual student's understanding through their whole group discussion. Similarly, students who avoid seeking help because they fear appearing incompetent can participate in the conversation and share their own ideas without needing to be in the threatening position of explicitly asking for help.

We also advocate that teachers encourage collaboration due to the higher quality of discussions and elaborated responses that were evident within these interactions. Using tasks in which materials are shared coupled with expressing expectations for collaboration can encourage higher quality collaboration in small groups. In addition, to encourage higher quality helping behaviors, it is important to provide training and feedback so that students can develop the skills necessary to pose deeper level questions and to provide more elaborated responses. It is important to keep in mind, however, that these suggestions are difficult to implement. In the data used for the current study, the task was designed to encourage collaboration, yet Group A primarily cooperated. Furthermore, both groups received training designed to improve the quality of the interactions within the group. This was clearly more effective for Group B than Group A. It may be that initial training coupled with additional interventions once students begin working in groups may help to encourage collaboration and more positive interactions, which should ultimately enhance the quality of the helping behaviors.

In conclusion, our findings suggest that the quality and type of group interactions are both important in understanding helping behaviors in small groups, with both positive group interactions and collaboration encouraging higher quality helping behaviors. This helps to extend prior research on the nature of helping behaviors in small groups by adding to our understanding of how group processes might contribute to higher quality helping behaviors. We recommend that future research continue to explore the patterns of helping behaviors within this relatively unexplored group context.

REFERENCES

Ames, C. (1992). Achievement goals and the classroom motivational climate. In J. L. Meece (Ed.), *Student perceptions in the classroom* (pp. 327–348). Hillsdale, NJ: Lawrence Erlbaum Associates.

Butler, R., & Neuman, O. (1995). Effects of task and ego achievement goals on help-seeking behaviors and attitudes. *Journal of Educational Psychology, 87*, 261–271.

Cohen, E. G. (1994). *Designing groupwork: Strategies for the heterogeneous classroom* (2nd ed.). New York: Teachers College Press.

Karabenick, S. A. (1998). Help seeking as a strategic resource. In S. A. Karabenick (Ed.), *Strategic help seeking: Implications for learning and teaching* (pp. 1–11). Mahwah, NJ: Lawrence Erlbaum Associates.

Karabenick, S. A. (2003). Seeking help in large college classes: A person-centered approach. *Contemporary Educational Psychology, 28,* 37–58.

Karabenick, S. A., & Sharma, R. (1994). Perceived teacher support of student questioning in the college classroom: Its relation to student characteristics and role in the classroom questioning process. *Journal of Educational Psychology, 86,* 90–103.

Nadler, A. (1998). Relationship, esteem, and achievement perspectives on autonomous and dependent help seeking. In S. A. Karabenick (Ed.), *Strategic help seeking: Implications for learning and teaching* (pp. 61–93). Mahwah, NJ: Lawrence Erlbaum Associates.

Nelson-Le Gall, S. (1985). Help-seeking behavior and learning. In E. Gordon (Ed.), *Review of Research in Education* (Vol. 12, pp. 55–90). Washington, DC: American Educational Research Association.

Nelson-Le Gall, S. (1992). Children's instrumental help-seeking: Its role in the social acquisition and construction of knowledge. In N. Miller (Ed.), *Interaction in cooperative groups: The theoretical anatomy of group learning* (pp. 49–68). New York: Cambridge University Press.

Newman, R. S. (1990). Children's help-seeking in the classroom: The role of motivational factors and attitudes. *Journal of Educational Psychology, 82,* 71–80.

Newman, R. S., & Schwager, M. T. (1993). Students' perceptions of the teacher and classmates in relation to reported help seeking in math class. *Elementary School Journal, 94,* 3–17.

Ryan, A. M., Hicks, L., & Midgley, C. (1997). Social goals, academic goals, and avoiding seeking help in the classroom. *Journal of Early Adolescence, 17,* 152–171.

Ryan, A. M., & Pintrich, P. R. (1998). Achievement and social motivational influences on help seeking in the classroom. In S. A. Karabenick (Ed.), *Strategic help seeking: Implications for learning and teaching* (pp. 117–139). Mahwah, NJ: Lawrence Erlbaum Associates.

Ryan, A. M., Pintrich, P. R., & Midgley, C. (2001). Avoiding seeking help in the classroom: Who and why? *Educational Psychology Review, 13,* 93–114.

Slavin, R. E. (1995). *Cooperative learning: Theory, research, and practice* (2nd ed.). Boston: Allyn & Bacon.

Steiner, I. D. (1972). *Group process and productivity.* New York: Academic Press.

Swing, S. R., & Peterson, P. L. (1982). The relationship of student ability and small-group interaction to student achievement. *American Educational Research Journal, 19,* 259–274.

van der Meij, H. (1988). Constraints on question asking in classrooms. *Journal of Educational Psychology, 80,* 401–405.

Webb, N. M. (1982). Student interaction and learning in small groups. *Review of Educational Research, 52,* 421–445.

Webb, N. M. (1991). Task-related verbal interaction and mathematics learning in small groups. *Journal for Research in Mathematics Education, 22*(5), 366–389.

Webb, N. M., & Farivar, S. (1999). Developing productive group interaction in middle school mathematics. In A. M. O'Donnell & A. King (Eds.), *Cognitive perspectives on peer learning* (pp. 117–149). Mahwah, NJ: Lawrence Erlbaum Associates.

Webb, N. M., & Mastergeorge, A. M. (2003). The development of students' helping behavior and learning in peer-directed small groups. *Cognition & Instruction, 21*(4), 361–428.

Webb, N. M., & Palincsar, A. S. (1996). Group processes in the classroom. In D. Berliner & R. Calfee (Eds.), *Handbook of educational psychology* (pp. 841–873). New York: Macmillan.

Webb, N. M., Troper, J. D., & Fall, R. (1995). Constructive activity and learning in collaborative small groups. *Journal of Educational Psychology, 87*(3), 406–423.
Yackel, E., Cobb, P., & Wood, T. (1991). Small-group interactions as a source of learning opportunities in second-grade mathematics. *Journal for Research in Mathematics Education, 22*(5), 390–408.

Chapter 5

Help Seeking in Cultural Context

Simone Volet
Murdoch University

Stuart A. Karabenick
University of Michigan & Eastern Michigan University

Nelson-Le Gall's (1981, 1985) differentiation between instrumental help seeking (that focuses on understanding) and executive help seeking (designed to avoid work) initiated extensive research on the person and situation determinants of whether, for what reasons, and from whom students seek help when confronted with learning difficulties (e.g., Butler, 1998; Karabenick, 1998; Newman, 2000). There is now substantial evidence that instrumental (also referred to as autonomous) help seeking can be considered an adaptive strategy and an important form of self-regulated learning. Self-regulating students, who employ other learning strategies, are more likely to seek help when necessary (Karabenick, 1998). In an adaptive sequence, students determine they need help, decide to seek it, identify and obtain assistance from knowledgeable sources, and effectively process the assistance they receive (Newman, 1998). Rather than necessarily indicative of dependency, students who seek help in this manner can become less rather than more reliant on others when future difficulties arise.

Research indicates that person and situation factors that influence students' use of other cognitive and metacognitive learning strategies apply to help seeking as well. This includes relations between intentions to seek help and adopted and perceived classroom mastery and performance achievement goals (Karabenick, 2003, 2004; Karabenick & Knapp, 1991; Ryan, Gheen, &

Midgley, 1998; Turner et al., 2002). Despite their similarities, however, because it is inherently social, help seeking is unique among strategies—another agent is necessarily involved at some point in the process, which some have characterized as a form of other regulation (Zimmerman & Martinez-Pons, 1986). Accordingly, sociocultural variables that affect motivation and learning in general (Maehr & Pintrich, 1995; McInerney & Van Etten, 2001; Salili, Chiu, & Hong, 2001; Urdan, 1999; Volet & Järvelä, 2001) have particular relevance for help seeking. This chapter examines how culture-related values influence help seeking. After a review of the literature on person and context approaches to help seeking and on the significance of culture for learning and motivation, in particular social-interactive learning activities, we present the results of a transnational study of help seeking in cultural context.

As we elaborate subsequently, research on help seeking evolved in a Euro-American tradition that places considerable emphasis on independence and individuality (Hofstede, 1980; Triandis, 1994). Students' reluctance to seek help is, accordingly, attributable in part to the threat of deviating from a strong individualistic emphasis that denigrates dependency (Fisher, Nadler, & Whitcher-Alagna, 1982; Nadler, 1998; Nelson-Le Gall, 1981, 1985). Thus, help seeking should be more likely in cultures (or subcultures) with less emphasis on independent achievement and with a higher premium on cooperation. This was confirmed by Nadler (1998), who found stronger help-seeking tendencies among communally reared Israeli kibbutz dwellers than among students socialized in more independent city cultures. Type of task also moderated the difference predictably in that kibbutz dwellers sought more help on group than on individual tasks, whereas city dwellers asked for more help on individual tasks.

Nevertheless, social values, even very pervasive ones, do not necessarily translate directly into rates of help seeking. Shwalb and Sukemune (1998), for example, reported that Japanese students, who are socialized in a culture that emphasizes cooperation, dependency, and empathy, were exceedingly reluctant to seek help by asking questions in college classes (similar to U.S. college students). Instead, they suggest, the absence of classroom help seeking is attributable to Japanese classroom norms that result from rigid socialization into student roles that are consistent with transmission rather than interactive-constructivist modes of instruction: Specifically, teachers talk while students remain passive. Most often, students wanted to ask questions but reported being "too shy or embarrassed," careful to not interrupt the teacher or disturb classroom equanimity. Students were not generally hesitant to seek help, however. They were perfectly willing to approach their peers for assistance in private tutoring sessions. Rather than independence–dependence, social concerns of conformity, impression management, sensitivity to others, and personal relationships are more salient determinants of help seeking in the Japanese context.

Shwalb and Sukemune (1998) highlighted the need to focus on students' school-related socialization and peer relationships, particularly their perception of teachers as supportive (Karabenick & Sharma, 1994) and the relative appropriateness and receptivity of peers' to help requests. Developmental studies in the United States indicate that during early school years students approach teachers they perceive as nice, friendly, and receptive. The importance of benevolence changes, however, as teachers increasingly become viewed with greater ambivalence, especially with the transition to middle school with its increasing press for performance and evaluation (Newman, 1990; Ryan, 1998; Ryan et al., 1998). Seeking help, in other words, becomes more threatening as well as potentially beneficial, and by the seventh grade in the United States at least, negative consequences begin to affect instruction-related help seeking (Newman & Schwager, 1993).

During that same time, students' peers become more capable of providing help (Dorval & Eckerman, 1984) and increasingly more available than are teachers, especially in more impersonal college and university settings (Knapp & Karabenick, 1988). As with teachers, however, seeking help from peers in not without its costs. Although by the seventh grade students who asked for help were viewed by their peers as "smart" rather than "dumb" (Newman & Schwager, 1993), the threat of public embarrassment, especially during whole-class activities, is also salient, as well as perceived needs to reciprocate peer help and other forms of indebtedness (DeCooke, 1992; Fisher et al., 1982; Morris & Rosen, 1973). Help seeking also depends on students' social goals, including whether relationships are based on desires for support and intimacy versus utilitarian social status that involves elements of competition (Ryan & Pintrich, 1997). Increased likelihood of help seeking would also be expected between peers with long-standing communal rather than exchange relationships.

That peers present a more complex picture is suggested by recent research that identified autonomous and avoidant help-seeking patterns of U.S. college students (Karabenick, 2004). An autonomous pattern involved seeking necessary help in the form of explanations from teachers. However, seeking help from peers was not a feature of this autonomous pattern Whether or not to ask peers for help, in other words, was not related to students' autonomy-related help-seeking goals. Similarly, the preference to seek help from peers was unrelated to an avoidance pattern comprised of the following: concern over help seeking as threatening, reluctance to seek help, and a preference for expedient help that consisted of seeking direct assistance in the form of answers rather than explanations (i.e., work avoidance goals). Whether students seek help from peers, in other words, is not predictable from their general approach or avoidant help-seeking tendencies. One reason for the absence of association may be that peers, as a class, are more heterogeneous than are teachers. Asking students to report the likelihood of approaching peers for help, therefore, is to ask for a judgment that is less well specified. Peers differ not only in their characteristics but also in their relationships to students—requiring greater specificity about peer-related variables. As discussed subsequently, in the increasingly multi-cultural instructional settings in many areas of the world, the ethnicity and nationality of students and peers should also be considered. Additional studies are needed, therefore, to examine the role of culture not only with regard to students' generalized intentions to seek help but also, as suggested by help-seeking research in the United States and studies of collaborative research elsewhere, students' intentions or reluctance to seek help as a function peers' (and teachers') culture-related characteristics.

HELP SEEKING FROM A CROSS-CULTURAL PERSPECTIVE

Although few studies have examined help seeking in multicultural instructional contexts, there is considerable research on services for mental health and psychological disorders that is potentially relevant. Asian Americans in the United States have been the main target of such research due to concerns that this group utilizes mental health services at lower rates than all other ethnic groups in the United States, despite their high rate of major mental health problems due to discrimination, oppression, and prejudice (Deng, 2004). Leong, Wagner, and Tata's (1995) review of the literature highlighted differences across ethnic groups in attitudes toward seeking professional help. The importance of cultural barriers was identified, which included cognitive, affective, and value orientation differences between help seekers and help providers (Leong & Lau, 2001). Although cognitive barriers seemed specific to seeking help for mental disorders (e.g., level of psychological distress and stigmas associated with counseling), affective and value orientation barriers could generalize to other forms of help-seeking behavior (e.g., preference for culturally based helpers and perceptions that [mental health] systems do not understand worldviews or cultural differences).

This literature suggests that Asian Americans' reluctance to seek help from professionals in comparison to other groups could be attributed, among other factors, to the importance of not expressing personal difficulties publicly and trying to resolve them within the ingroup (family, close friends). Seeking help beyond the ingroup was found to extend first to professionals from similar backgrounds. A number of studies have found that ethnic and language match between the counselor and their client significantly increased the use of mental health services (e.g., Lin, 1994). Studies involving university students further confirmed that degree of acculturation (Tata & Leong, 1994) and types of problem (Gim, Atkinson, & Whiteley,

1990; Tracey, Leong, & Glidden, 1986) influence the use of counseling services. With regard to types of problems, Gim et al. (1990) and Tracey et al. (1986) found that Asian American university students were most willing to see a counselor for academic concerns but rather reluctant to discuss personal problems. According to the researchers, seeking help regarding academic concerns was perceived as a more acceptable issue to discuss with a counselor than were personal problems. This is consistent with an Australian survey of international students in vocational education, (Volet & Pears, 1994), which revealed that 70% of the students had sought help for academic problems, over 60% of those students had approached friends and/or other students, but only 21% their teachers.

Most of the research on culture-related help seeking for psychological difficulties typically compared the attitudes and practices of different ethnic groups. Only a few studies, however, have assessed dimensions of culture that may explain variations in attitudes and practices in help seeking. For example, research by Gloria, Hird, and Navarro (2001), conducted with university students, measured relations between cultural congruence and perceptions of the institutional climate to help-seeking attitudes by socio-race (majority, minority groups). Their findings are consistent with the research comparing ethnic groups, and they also reported that the cultural context variables accounted for a larger proportion of the variance in the help-seeking attitudes of students from different racial and ethnic backgrounds as compared to the attitudes of white students. The researchers interpreted these findings in terms of perceived "inhospitable climates and cultural contexts of most predominantly White universities" (p. 546).

A major limitation of research on professional help for psychological problems is the almost exclusive focus on the help-seeking practices of ethnic minority groups. Little is known about the attitude of individuals from the ethnic *majority* group (typically Whites, English speakers in the U.S. context) toward helpers from other ethnic backgrounds, even though it would be reasonable to expect that all help seekers prefer helpers with whom they think they have the better chance of being understood. The extent to which this preference extends to seeking help for academic problems, and whether it applies to seeking help from both teachers and peers, is unknown. Clearly, studies are needed that explore these culture-related characteristics.

SIGNIFICANCE OF CULTURE IN RESEARCH ON LEARNING AND MOTIVATION

Whether conceptualized as a form of context (Urdan, 1999) or a social construction (Fiske, Kitayama, Markus, & Nisbett, 1998; Matsumoto, 2001), culture has received increased attention in research on learning and motivation. Different culture-related approaches have been developed, each with unique purposes, possibilities, and limitations. After a brief overview of cross-cultural research on the impact of sociocultural contexts on learning and motivation, we review some recent studies exploring the dynamic aspects of sociocultural contexts in social-interactive learning activities. These studies are relevant to understanding the phenomenon of help seeking in cultural context because they examined how various cultural dimensions relate to students' engagement in another type of social-interactive learning activities, namely, group work.

The cross-cultural perspective has dominated until recently. Its main aim is not to generate new psychological theories but traditionally to refine existing ones (essentially Euro-American) so they can claim universality. The early cross-cultural studies, which simply used countries or ethnic groups as independent variables without seeking an understanding of sociocultural practices, have been widely criticized both conceptually and methodologically (Betancourt & Lopez, 1993; Poortinga, 1996). A major criticism, from both within and outside the field, is that the label of culture is elusive and cannot explain the variations that are found in the dependent variables. Some cross-cultural research has attempted to address the problem by identifying and measuring aspects or dimensions of the target culture assumed to be responsible for variations and then comparing the groups. Some of the most well known explanatory cultural dimensions have tapped into individualist/collectivist values (Hofstede, 1980, 1986; Kagitcibasi, 1994; Triandis, 1994) and independent/interdependent conceptualizations of self-systems (Markus & Kitayama, 1991) in order to explain variations in cognition, motivation, and behaviors related to learning.

Early research (e.g., Volet, Renshaw, & Tietzel, 1994; Volet & Renshaw, 1995) on the impact of students' sociocultural backgrounds on their overall motivation to study revealed differences between groups of international university students from Singapore and Anglo-Australian students studying in Australia. The findings were consistent with specific cultural priorities, sociocultural practices, and values promoted within the respective societies and education systems, as reflected in the Singaporean (e.g., Chew, Leu, & Tan, 1998; Ho, 1989; Kwang, Fernandez, & Tan, 1998) and Australian (e.g., Hill, 1998; Smolicz, 1991, 1999; Willcoxon, 1992) literature, as well as with other cultural and cross-cultural research related to the achievement motivation of students from Chinese-ethnic backgrounds (e.g., Biggs, 1996; Salili, 1995; Salili & Hau, 1999; Yip, 1997). A major limitation of this research is the fact that the cultural elements assumed to contribute to variations in students' motivation were not examined as part of the investigation. Furthermore, because these studies typically relied on snapshot type data (single questionnaire), they may have conveyed an implicit—although not necessarily held—view that individuals' motivational profiles are stable across academic tasks and contexts. Cultural regularities as the product of cultural-historical practices cannot be ignored, and it has been argued that cultural descriptors to refer to research participants are acceptable "provided they are not assumed to imply an essence of the individual or group involved and are not treated as causal entities" (Gutiérrez & Rogoff, 2003, p. 23).

DYNAMIC ASPECTS OF SOCIOCULTURAL CONTEXTS IN SOCIAL-INTERACTIVE LEARNING ACTIVITIES

A major challenge of traditional cross-cultural psychology is to address the issues of the dynamic aspects of culture and variations within cultures. According to Shweder and Sullivan (1990), this problem is critical because variations within cultures are often "much greater than between culture differences." Recent work (Volet, 1999b, 2001c) addressed this issue by investigating the origin and development of variations in phenomena of learning and motivation within their social contexts, over time, and with attention paid to patterns of stability and change within and across contexts. This approach, inspired by cultural and sociocultural perspectives, recognizes that cultural contexts provide "cultural affordances" (Kitayama & Markus, 1999) for the development of attitudes, belief systems, and social practices, but in addition it also assumes that when individuals move across contexts, changes in cognitions and practices can occur due to new configurations of person–context dimensions. The review that follows is relevant to the topic of help seeking in cultural context because it focuses on another social-interactive learning activity, namely, group work, and examined the impact of various sociocultural aspects on engagement in such activities.

One study of the dynamic influences of sociocultural contexts was facilitated by a multilevel perspective of person and context (Volet, 2001c). According to this view, the most macro level consisted of sociocultural societal dimensions, belief systems, and values, assumed to provide relatively consistent and coherent frameworks for the development of overall educational policies and priorities and for the design of curricula and assessment practices. Nested within these frameworks are located the particular sociocultural climates created by various learning environments, discipline approaches, pedagogical emphases, and instructional practices. Finally, at the most micro level is the subculture of the immediate learning activity and local social surroundings that students are currently engaged and participating in. The combination of multilevel layers of contexts produces a multiplicity of sociocultural and educational influences that interact with, and are mediated by, individuals' dispositions, tendencies, and appraisals of the current situation. Although each learning situation is assumed to present a unique configuration of person-in-context dimensions (Volet, 2001c), students are expected to display their habitual behavior until contextual cues become salient or emotionally arousing, signaling that cognitive attention is required (Boekaerts, 2001; Pekrun, 2000). Contextual cues can refer to the nature of the task but also the sociocultural environment in which learning is located. When students are required to engage in group activities, context sensitivity is expected to be under greater alert, because individual habitualized behaviors have to be coordinated with peers' own preferred behaviors. The challenge becomes even greater when group activities involve peers from different cultural-educational backgrounds. In these situations, it is expected that attitudes and practices will reflect the dynamic interactions of students' prior sociocultural and educational experiences, personal preferences and tendencies, and appraisals of contextual cues in the particular situation.

Based on the work on collectivism and individualism of Hofstede (1980, 1986) and other cross-cultural researchers (Triandis, 1995), it was expected that students from Chinese-ethnic backgrounds brought up in an East Asian country would display a greater preference for collaborative modes of working and learning, in comparison to students brought up in an Australia context. The presence at the same university (same program, same classes) of some students from a country classified (on Hofstede's cultural map) as high on collectivism (Singapore), some students from a country classified low on collectivism (Australia), and some students from Singapore living in Australia was viewed as ideal for this investigation on the ground that it would be possible to examine the factors associated with positive and negative appraisals of group work without the confounding effect of individual characteristics and contextual variables found in most cross-cultural studies. Rather than assuming high and low levels of collectivism within groups, students' personal dispositions for interdependence (the aspect of collectivism related to social relationships with people other than family members, in the Triandis [1995] instrument for individual measurement) were assessed. The subgroup of international students from Singapore was expected to rate highest on that measure, on the assumption that they would have had more limited exposure to the individualist values assumed to dominate within Australian society (Smolicz, 1999). It was also predicted that the different subgroups would provide an opportunity to expand the variation in levels of interdependence, and in turn attitudes toward group work, that could be found in a single country study.

These expectations were only partially confirmed. Interdependence differentiated between the three groups in the expected directions, although the two subgroups of Singaporean students (international and local) did not differ. At the individual level, only low to moderate positive correlations were found between interdependence and appraisals of group assignments, suggesting that although interdependence accounted for some variance in students' appraisals, it was not sufficient on its own to explain large variations. The data revealed significant differences in overall appraisals of group assignments, with the subgroup of Australian students from Singaporean backgrounds displaying the most positive attitudes toward group assignments, followed by the subgroup of international students newly arrived from Singapore, and last the subgroup of Anglo-Australians. These findings appeared consistent with other studies exploring students' motivation to participate in culturally mixed group activities (Volet, 2001b; Volet & Ang, 1998; Volet & Mansfield, in press). The issue of willingness to participate in culturally mixed groups is critical in countries with culturally diverse student populations, such as Australia and the United States.

In sum, research using surveys, focus-group interviews, and teachers' records highlighted the significance of personal cross-cultural experience in students' willingness to engage in intercultural encounters. As for group work in general, data from matched subgroups revealed how a presumed substantial amount of personal experience of crossing cross-cultural borders, combined with a high level of interdependence (e.g., Australians from Singaporean backgrounds), produced the most positive appraisals of engaging in group assignments with peers from diverse cultural-educational background, and, reciprocally, how presumed minimal cross-cultural experience, combined with a monolingual background and low level of interdependence (e.g., Anglo-Australians), elicited the least positive appraisals. Furthermore, and consistent with the explanation based on combined cultural dimensions, appraisals of the subgroup of international students from Singapore and Australian students from European backgrounds fell somewhere in between.

Independent evidence that substantial bi-multicultural experience may be associated with positive attitudes toward mixing across cultures was found in teachers' records of the membership of self-selected small groups (Volet, 1999c). In a large class of business students, two-thirds of the Australian students who were members of spontaneously formed culturally mixed groups had a bicultural background, whereas the percentage was only 8% in the Australian-only groups. Interview data (Volet & Ang, 1998) documented the nature of the social barriers perceived by local and international students as inhibiting their interactions. These findings converge with repeated evidence in the Australian literature that local and international students (predominantly from East Asian and Chinese-ethnic backgrounds) tend to study in parallel (Mullins, Quintrell, & Hancock, 1995; Nesdale & Todd, 1993; Smart, Volet, & Ang, 2000), are inhibited in their mutual interactions (Wright & Lander, 2003), and generally prefer the company of peers from similar backgrounds (Kudo & Simkin, 2003; Smart et al., 2000). The view that similarity leads to attraction (Byrne, 1971) is well known in social psychology. Triandis (2001) argued that when there is perceived similarity and interaction takes place, the interaction tends to be rewarding. In contrast, when people see others as dissimilar, they feel anxious, try to avoid interaction, feel they have no control over social encounters, and tend to become more ethnocentric through overemphasizing the virtues of their own cultural practices. Some interventions aimed at promoting productive learning in ethnically diverse groups have been successful but have required extensive support over an extended period of time (Watson, Johnson, Kumar, & Critelli, 1998).

Overall, there is converging evidence in the literature that culture, conceptualized in various ways, contributes to explaining variations in students' engagement in social-interactive learning activities. As a socially mediated strategy, help seeking and help giving during academic study are expected to be similarly influenced by students' sociocultural backgrounds and prior educational practices, degree of personal cross-cultural experience, and perceived affordances in the social environment toward achieving a positive outcome of the help seeking/help giving process. To date, little is known about the relationship between the help-seeking patterns and general social predispositions of subgroups of students from different cultural-educational/linguistic backgrounds or between students' perceived culture-related contextual dimensions and their help-seeking practices, taking into account their personal dispositions. To our knowledge, there have been no systematic studies on how culture affects the ways that students seek and, more importantly, avoid seeking help from peers from different cultural-educational backgrounds. In the context of increasingly multicultural student populations, it is imperative to better understand these social phenomena. Whether students are more likely to seek academic help from peers that they perceive as close or similar to them—even when they know that other students could equally provide the help that they need—and whether the type of help that is sought makes a difference have received little attention in the literature on help seeking. Social psychology research on the contact hypothesis (Allport, 1954; Hewstone & Brown, 1986) and on ingroup/outgroup distinctions (Brewer, 1999; Kashima, 2001; Triandis, McCusker, & Hui, 1990; Wills & DePaulo, 1990) provides useful concepts to address this question.

THE INTERCULTURAL CONTACT HYPOTHESIS AND INGROUP/OUTGROUP DISTINCTIONS

In its earliest and basic form, the contact hypothesis posited that association with persons from a disliked group, or from a culturally different group, leads to the growth of liking and respect for that outgroup (Cook, 1978; Hewstone & Brown, 1986; Williams, 1947). Over the years, an impressive amount of research has been generated to assess that hypothesis but the results have been inconsistent. According to Hewstone and Brown (1986), this is due to major conceptual limitations of that research, in particular the lack of distinction between two forms of contact, interpersonal and intergroup. Although it is widely recognized that intergroup contact can play a role in improving intergroup relations, the contact hypothesis in its simplest form is generally considered too narrow and limited. Research on the experience of international students in their host country has tested (implicitly or explicitly) the contact hypothesis as an intercultural contact hypothesis issue.

The early and more recent extensive literature on the social experience of international students in England (e.g., McKinlay, Pattison, & Gross, 1996; Tajfel & Dawson, 1965), the United States (e.g., Liberman, 1994; Pedersen, 1991), and Australia (e.g., Burke, 1986; Mullins et al., 1995; Smart et al., 2000; Todd & Nesdale, 1997) has provided limited support for the view that by simply having students from different cultural backgrounds studying alongside each other, they will spontaneously interact and learn *about, with,* and *from* each other. This research has revealed how subgroups of students from different cultural-educational backgrounds tend to study in parallel, with the subgroups of international students creating subcultures of conationals who provide a major source of support for each other (Nesdale & Todd, 1993; O'Donoghue, 1996; Pedersen, 1991). For international students away from the familiar social support network available back home, conational groups provide safe cultural-emotional support for personal issues, but also an ideal first point of contact for assistance in an unfamiliar learning environment. Overall, there is converging evidence that in Australia (e.g., Barker, Child, Gallois, Jones, & Callan, 1991; Mullins & Hancock, 1991; Mullins et al., 1995; Nesdale & Todd, 1993; Smart et al., 2000; Todd & Nesdale, 1997; Volet & Ang, 1998), the United Kingdom (Bochner, Hutnik, & Furnham, 1985; Furnham, 1997; Furnham & Alibhai, 1985; Furnham & Bochner, 1982; McKinlay et al., 1996), and the United States (Gareis, 2000a, 2000b; Trice & Elliot, 1993), international students from different cultural-educational backgrounds find it difficult to develop relationships with host nationals and tend to stick with conationals or students with a shared linguistic background. Their status as sojourners distinguishes them from other groups of students from different cultural backgrounds who are permanent residents. The clear distinction made by many international students between their interactions with conationals (or students from similar ethnic backgrounds) and other students—and what they believe they can expect from members of each group (including help)—is consistent with concepts found in the ingroup/outgroup literature.

Research on ingroup/outgroup distinctions can be traced back to Allport's (1954) early work on ingroup attachment and loyalty. Allport stressed how the familiar is typically preferred over the less familiar, but he also mentioned that preference for the ingroup does not necessarily mean hostility toward the outgroups. The rationale for ingroup preference is that ingroup treatment is expected to be more predictable and avoids the emotional risks associated with moving out of one's zone of comfort. Like Allport, Brewer (1999) argued that positive discrimination for the ingroup can be independent of attitude toward the outgroup and is not necessarily associated with outgroup antagonism. The ingroup/outgroup distinction and the tendency for "ingroup bias" are widely considered to be universal (Kashima, 2001).

Research on the nature of social interactions between international and host students converges to show that, overwhelmingly, students prefer interacting with their "own people." Studies in an Australian context (Volet & Ang, 1998) revealed that in order of priority, international students preferred completing academic tasks with their co-nationals, followed by other international students from similar backgrounds. Local Australian students were usually their last choice, unless students knew a particular person from that outgroup, or unless some strategic reason justified a different choice. Students' elicited reasons for their "ingroup bias" were: cultural-emotional connectedness; language (either same language or shared experience of communicating in a second language); prejudice; and some practical considerations. Similarly, the Australian students stated that they preferred interacting with local peers. Their justifications were similar, although, and as could be expected, the issue of cultural-emotional connectedness was stronger among the group of international students.

The explanatory power of the ingroup/outgroup distinction may, however, be reduced for individuals who have extensive experience of crossing cultural borders at the individual level, such as people who are bi-multicultural themselves. Brewer and Miller (1988) argued that it is through repeated contact experiences, where outgroup individuals are responded to in terms of their relationship to the ingroup individual's self, that future interactions with members of that outgroup will be improved. On the basis of their personal cross-cultural experience, bi-multicultural individuals may feel more confident (emotionally, skills-wise) to select interactants on the basis of individual affinity rather than cultural background criteria that ignore the magnitude of intragroup individual differences (Shweder & Sullivan, 1990). Research on university students' attitudes toward mixing across cultures during study supports this view (Volet, 1999a), which found reliable differences between four otherwise comparable groups of students who differed in degree of personal cross-cultural experience. The group of students least confident/willing to mix with students from different cultural-educational backgrounds for group activities was the group with the least amount of intercultural exposure (typically monocultural, monolingual, students born and educated in their country of permanent residence). The students with the most positive attitudes were those with the greatest amount of cross-cultural experience (typically bi-multicultural, bi-multilingual students born and educated in different countries). The group of just arrived international students was located in between, which is consistent with their more marginal cross-cultural experience.

Overall, perceived and experienced diversity in cultural attitudes and practices seems to create social barriers between students. The research already reviewed highlights how students' social interactions are affected by those perceptions. Intra- and intercultural help-seeking practices are assumed to operate on principles similar to those found in relation to social interactions and appraisals of group work. Help seeking is a social-interactive process that requires self-confidence as well as perceived affordances in an intercultural context. The basic assumption is that students most willing to seek help from peers from cultural-educational backgrounds perceived as different from themselves would be those from monocultural, monolingual backgrounds. Reciprocally, students expected to be most willing to seek help from peers from cultural-educational backgrounds perceived as different from them would be those with the greatest amount of personal cross-cultural experience.

In addition, it is expected that students' help-seeking practices are also affected by their perceptions of the affordances of the social learning environment. To date, the issue of affordances of the environment in regard to help-seeking practices has been examined mainly in relation to classroom goal structures. In the context of higher education, where seeking help from peers takes place primarily outside class, the issue of perceived affordances may be critical since the choice of peers is not constrained by classroom activities and instruction. In that perspective, it seems reasonable to assume that students' willingness to seek help outside their ingroup would also be affected by their perceptions of what students from an outgroup may have to offer that peers from the ingroup may not. If both could equally provide assistance, willingness is likely to be affected by more subjective, socioemotional cost-benefit dimensions. For example, the typical outgroup for international students is likely to consist of local students who speak the language of instruction and may have precious local knowledge that the ingroup may not provide. One could assume that the benefits expected from seeking help from that outgroup are sometimes greater than the tendency for ingroup bias. In contrast, the typical outgroup for local students typically consists of international students who do not speak the language of instruction, are less familiar with the learning environment, and therefore are implicitly considered as less likely to be able to provide help until experienced otherwise. Our transnational study of help seeking in cultural context examined these assumptions. More generally, it addressed the empirical gap in understanding help seeking in cultural context.

Intra- and Intercultural Help Seeking: A Transnational Study

Samples and Cultural Subgroups.   The overall aim of this study was to establish how culture, operationalized in various ways, may play a role in help seeking in multicultural university environments. Two research locations (United States and Australia) were expected to provide different configurations of students' subgroups and thus an opportunity to examine patterns of help seeking both within their respective local social learning environments and across social environments with some similar and some different characteristics. Sampling students enrolled in business classes, which have relatively standard curricula (e.g., marketing, finance), increased comparability across countries. Business curricula, as compared to other areas of study, such as the humanities or sciences, also typically enroll relatively large numbers of international students that could be compared with monocultural/monolingual local students. As shown in Table 5.1, the largest subgroup across locations (Monocultural) consisted of students who were monolingual, born and permanent residents of the United States/Australia. The second group consisted of students with mixed culture (Mixed) who were typically permanent residents but born in other countries and speaking another language. The third subgroup (Other) consisted of students from cultures other than that of the host country, typically international students from non-English-speaking countries. As shown in Table 5.1, the percentage of students in the mixed and other subgroups varied by location. Identifying the profile of outgroups for each category of respondents was considered highly relevant to interpret the research findings, because the profiles of students' respective outgroups are expected to provide unique affordances and constraints for students' help seeking, in particular their likelihood of seeking help from peers perceived as similar or dissimilar to themselves.

TABLE 5.1

Frequency (%) of Australian and U.S. Students by Cultural Groups

Location	Local Students		International Students	
	Monocultural[a]	Mixed Culture[b]	Other Culture[c]	Total
Australian	77 (58%)	39 (30%)	16 (12%)	132
U.S.	118 (73%)	12 (7%)	32 (20%)	162
Total	195 (66%)	51 (17%)	48 (17%)	294

[a]Monocultural: local, monolingual (English).
[b]Mixed culture: local, bilingual or multilingual.
[c]Culture other than host country: language other than English.

By classifying students in this manner, the present study differs from other research related to the cultural contact hypothesis and ingroup/outgroup behaviors in that it did not use ethnic labels to identify groups. Our approach is based on the view that cross-cultural research should concentrate on the cultural aspects of groups that are assumed to produce variations in the object of investigation (Betancourt & Lopez, 1993) because intragroup differences are often greater than intergroup differences (Shweder & Sullivan, 1990). This approach is also intended at avoiding stereotyping of particular groups, which has plagued many cross-cultural studies because of the implicit essentialist view of culture underlying that research. Following this line of thought and on the basis of previous research on university students' attitudes and appraisals of working with peers from different cultural-educational backgrounds, degree of personal intercultural experience and potential affordances provided by the ingroup and the outgroup were identified as the most promising candidates influencing intra- and intercultural help-seeking practices in a multicultural, higher education setting.

Characterization of Peer Groups (Help-Seeking Targets). To investigate intra- and intercultural help seeking across cultural contexts, three hypothetical peer groups were characterized in relation to students themselves: a typical *ingroup;* a typical *outgroup;* and an *in-between group* with mixed characteristics. A major advantage of this conceptualization is that the groups are meaningful to all students regardless of their ethnic or cultural background and whether they were local or international students. The three hypothetical peers groups also to some degree mirrored the three subgroups of students (i.e., mono, mixed, and other). They were described to students by means of the following vignettes:

Ingroup (A-type students)

Their first language is the *same* as yours or if different it does not matter since communication is not a problem at all. You *know* these students *very well,* perhaps since your first year at [name] University, perhaps from before. They are likely to have attended primary/secondary schools similar to the ones you attended yourself (either in [United States/Australia] or overseas). You feel that their socio-cultural background and life *experiences are similar* to yours.

In-between group (B-type students)

Their first language is the *same* as yours or if different it does not matter since communication is not a problem at all. You *don't know* these students very well since this may be the first time you are in the same class or you never had the opportunity to interact with them before. They may have attended primary/secondary schools similar to the ones you attended but you are not sure—they may have gone to school elsewhere. Since you don't know them very well, you are *not sure* whether their socio-cultural background and life experiences are similar/different to yours.

Outgroup (C-type students)

Their first language is *not* the same as yours. You *don't know* these students well at all. They are students who lived/went to school in a country other than yours before studying at [name] University (e.g., you lived/went to school in [United States or Australia] before starting your study at [name] University and these students lived/went to school in another country. OR you lived/went to school in another country and these students lived/went to school in [United States or Australia]). You think that their socio-cultural background and life experiences are *different* from yours.

Students were invited to consider the three types of peers in relation to themselves, and were asked first to rate the likelihood that they would approach a student of each type if they had to seek help from another student (i.e., contingent on their need for help): (a) in order to quickly get the answer they needed and they were aware that a student of each type had the answer (expedient type of help), and (b) in order to better understand general ideas or principles or to learn how to solve problems (autonomous type of help). They were then asked to repeat their ratings but this time in relation to help giving in terms of how likely it would be that an A-, B-, or C-Type student would approach someone like himself or herself in order to provide expedient or autonomous help. Ratings were on a scale from 1 = *not at all likely* to 5 = *very likely*. Data for expedient and autonomous help were combined for all subsequent analyses because the ratings were highly correlated and results virtually identical. As a consequence, the results should be interpreted as generalizing across reasons why students seek help.

Help Seeking and Help Giving Across Subgroups and Locations

Seeking Help. Table 5.2 presents the likelihood that students in each of the cultural subgroups would seek help from the three types of peers described in the vignettes (A, B, and C as designated earlier). As expected, and consistent with prior research on social cohesion and group work in culturally mixed groups, when combining samples across locations and subgroups, students were more likely to seek help from peers they knew well and perceived as similar to them in terms of sociocultural background and life experiences (A-*Mean* = 4.4) than those partly (B-*Mean* = 3.7) or very dissimilar from themselves (C-*Mean* = 2.6), $F(2, 294) = 95.0, p < .0001$. A type by subgroup interaction, $F(4, 590)\ 2.99, p < .05$, also indicated that these differences depended on the subgroup. The relevant means associated with the interaction are presented in Fig. 5.1, which shows smaller variation between likelihood ratings as a function of peer type for international than for monocultural students. This is also underscored by examining the differences between the mean likelihood of seeking help from a Type A versus Type C peers (also shown in Table 5.2), where the largest difference (combining Australian and

TABLE 5.2

Mean Likelihood (*SD*) of Australian and US Students Seeking Help from
Peers Differing in Relative Culture-Related Characteristics

Location	Type	Local Students		International Students	Total
		Monocultural	Mixed Culture	Other Culture	
Australia	A	4.3 (1.1)	4.4 (1.1)	3.6 (1.4)	4.2 (1.2)
	B	3.5 (0.9)	3.7 (0.9)	3.2 (0.8)	3.5 (0.9)
	C	2.3 (1.0)	2.7 (1.3)	2.8 (1.1)	2.5 (1.1)
	A – C difference	2.1 (1.4)	1.7 (1.6)	0.8 (2.4)	1.8 (1.6)
U.S.	A	4.6 (0.8)	4.5 (0.8)	4.4 (0.9)	4.6 (0.8)
	B	4.0 (0.8)	3.6 (0.9)	3.7 (0.9)	3.9 (0.9)
	C	2.6 (1.3)	2.8 (1.3)	2.6 (1.1)	2.7 (1.3)
	A – C difference	2.0 (1.4)	1.7 (1.6)	1.7 (1.5)	1.9 (1.4)
All students	A – C difference	2.0 (1.4)	1.7 (1.6)	1.4 (1.8)	1.8 (1.5)

U.S. samples) was evidenced by the dominant monocultural group of students (2.0) and smallest for the international student group (1.4). Although
not statistically significant (i.e., there was to interaction that involved location), the A – C difference as a function of subgroup appears primarily due to
international students in Australia who tended to be simultaneously less
likely to seek help from Type A peers (i.e., other international students) and
more likely to seek help from Type C peers (i.e., dominant subculture students) than were students in the other subgroups.

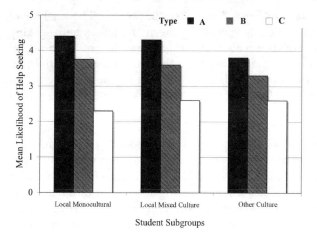

FIG.5.1.
Mean rated likeli-
hood of Australian
and U.S. students
seeking help from
peers as a function
of cultural distance.

One possible explanation for greater differentiation within the sub-group of international students in the U.S. context compared to the Australian context may be that the outgroup for the U.S. international students was dominated by English-speaking, United States-born and educated students (91%) with only a small subgroup of U.S. students from mixed cultures/languages (9%). In contrast, the outgroup for Australian international students was much more diverse, with the English-speaking Australians much less dominant (66%) and included a substantial subgroup of host students from mixed cultural and language backgrounds (34%).

The patterns of responses of international students across locations may therefore be interpreted in terms of affordances that their respective outgroups could offer. Within the Australian context, the perceived outgroup was most likely to include students from mixed backgrounds, who could reasonably be perceived as more approachable given their personal bi/multicultural experience. This mixed outgroup would be hardly noticeable in the U.S. context because of its small size. Therefore, the stronger preference by international students in the United States to seek help from their ingroup could be interpreted in relation to the dichotomous nature of their peer group, combined with the availability of a much larger (in)group of international students—although further subgroupings might be more relevant to the definition of an ingroup. This interpretation assumes, of course, that the effects of sociocultural interactive context transfers to students' interpretations of the vignettes they rated. Students in the United States also rated themselves more likely, overall, to seek help (*Mean* = 3.6) than did students in Australia (*Mean* = 3.4), $F(1,295) = 5.75, p < .02$. The difference across location is consistent with the greater percentage of students from monolingual backgrounds in the United States, that is, the proportion of students with a large pool of peers with similar background to seek help from.

Help-Giving Expectations From Target Peer Groups.   The analysis of help giving, shown in Table 5.3, revealed patterns similar to help seeking overall, although the effects were not as large. Regardless of location and personal cross-cultural experience, students thought that peers with background characteristics similar to their own would be more likely to approach them for help (A-*Mean* = 4.2) than would students from a mixed (B-*Mean* = 3.7) or different cultural-educational background (C-*Mean* = 3.0), $F(2, 294) = 38.1, p < .001$.

Although the order of beliefs regarding being approached are similar to help seeking, the A – C difference scores for the two monocultural groups were much smaller (Australian = 1.4 and U.S. = 1.1) than for help seeking (respectively 2.1 and 2.0). Thus, when reflecting about their own help-seeking practices, students' ingroup–outgroup preferences were more differentiated than when anticipating how others would make decisions about

TABLE 5.3

Mean Rated Likelihood (*SD*) of Australian and US Students Being Approached
for Help by Peers Differing in Relative Culture-Related Characteristics

Location	Type	Local Students		International	Total
		Monocultural	Mixed Culture	Other Culture	
Australia	A	3.9 (1.3)	4.1 (1.1)	3.5 (1.3)	3.9 (1.2)
	B	3.2 (1.0)	3.7 (1.0)	3.2 (0.8)	3.4 (1.1)
	C	2.6 (1.1)	2.8 (1.2)	2.9 (1.2)	2.7 (1.1)
	A – C difference	1.4 (1.6)	1.4 (1.6)	0.6 (2.2)	1.8 (1.6)
U.S.	A	4.4 (1.0)	4.5 (0.7)	4.2 (0.9)	4.3 (1.0)
	B	4.0 (1.0)	3.9 (1.0)	4.0 (0.7)	4.0 (0.9)
	C	3.3 (1.3)	3.4 (1.5)	3.3 (1.1)	3.3 (1.1)
	A – C difference	1.1 (1.5)	1.2 (1.5)	0.9 (1.7)	1.1 (1.6)
All students	A – C difference	1.2 (1.6)	1.4 (1.6)	0.8 (1.8)	1.2 (1.6)

approaching them for help. Interestingly, the patterns of differentiations for
the two subgroups of international students were closer to each other when
help giving (A – C difference scores for Australian students = 0.6, U.S. = 0.9)
than for help seeking (respectively, .0.8 and 1.7). The patterns of differentiation (as well as A and C ratings) by the subgroup of international students in
the Australian context appeared remarkably consistent across help seeking
and help giving (A – C difference score of 0.8 for help seeking and 0.6 for
help giving). This was not the case for the subgroup of international students
in the U.S. context who thought that peers from their outgroup (primarily
U.S. students from monocultural, monolingual backgrounds) would be more
likely to seek help from them than they were themselves prepared to do.
Consistent with the results of help seeking, U.S. (*Mean* = 3.9) more so than
Australian students (*Mean* = 3.3) believed that others were more likely to approach them for help, $F(1,294) = 16.0$, $p < .001$. The lesser exposure to
peers from different and mixed backgrounds in the United States compared
to the Australian context may partly explain this difference, in the sense of increasing the perceived differences with less well-known peers.

To summarize, the results suggest that regardless of their personal
cross-cultural background, individuals located in a learning environment
where the student population tends to be dichotomous (e.g., U.S. sample
with a small in-between, mixed group) tend to differentiate more clearly between help-seeking than help-giving practices and beliefs. In this study, students were more likely to seek help from their ingroup than their outgroup

but the distinction was reduced when students considered how peers would seek help from themselves. In contrast, when the student population was more diverse (e.g., Australian sample with a relatively large in-between, mixed group), help-seeking and help-giving beliefs and practices tended to reflect similar patterns. Overall, the differences in help-seeking and help-giving patterns across locations highlight the significance of individual-context dynamics in responses to social interactive situations. It should also be noted that analyses using language spoken at home (English vs. other languages) and where students attended high school (local vs. elsewhere) instead of cultural subgroups revealed similar patterns of findings for both help seeking and help giving.

Consistency Across Types of Help-Seeking Targets (A vs. C)

A second important issue regarding help seeking in multicultural context is that of consistency across types of targets (A, B, and C); that is, to what degree does the likelihood of seeking help from an A-Type student predict help seeking from a B- or a C-Type student? Greater consistency would indicate general tendencies to seek help independent of target. Alternatively, low or even negative associations would be another way of determining whether help seeking depends on the sociocultural characteristics of sources of assistance. A related question is whether these relationships vary as a function of student subgroups.

As shown in Table 5.4, for the dominant cultural subgroups (i.e., Mono) in both countries, intentions to seek help were moderately consistent between targets that differed either according to degree of personal cultural /language experience (A vs. B, $r = .33/r = .49$) or residence (B vs. C, $r = .42/r = .53$), but far less so when targets differed with respect both to personal cultural/language experience and residence (A vs. C, $r = -.01/r = .14$). This pattern was present, but to a lesser degree, for the mixed-culture students in both countries. A clear difference emerged for international students, however, which evidenced stronger influences of target characteristics. Specifically, although there were moderately consistent tendencies to seek help from their ingroup and those in the host country (A vs. B, $r = .37/r = .40$), there was little consistency when residence and other differences existed (B vs. C, $r = .12/r = -.12$). More evident is the pattern of ingroup preference by international students indicated by the inverse relationship between intentions seek help from A- versus C-Type others ($r = -.34$, $p < .01$ across locations). Although there was a consistent trend among international students in the United States ($r = -.13$), the ingroup bias was clearly present in Australia ($r = -.67$, $p < .01$). Thus, the more international students indicated they would seek help from other international students the less likely they would do so from students in the dominant culture.

TABLE 5.4

Relationship (Correlations) Between Intentions to Seek Help From Target
Peer Groups by Peers Differing in Relative Culture-Related Characteristics

		Local Students		International Students	
Location	Types	Monocultural	Mixed Culture	Other Culture	Total
Australia	A vs. B	.33[b]	.27	.37	.51[c]
	B vs. C	.42[c]	.41[b]	.12	.49[c]
	A vs. C	−.01	.07	−.67	−.06
U.S.	A vs. B	.49[c]	.28	.40[a]	.65[c]
	B vs. C	.53[c]	.24	−.02	.56[c]
	A vs. C	.14	−.07	−.13	.09
All students	A vs. B	.44[c]	.27	.43[b]	.42[c]
	B vs. C	.51[c]	.38[a]	−.01	.41[c]
	A vs. C	.10	−.04	−.34[b]	.02

[a]Significant at $p < .05$.
[b]Significant at $p < .01$.
[c]Significant at $p < .001$.

Relationship of General Help-Seeking Intentions to the Likelihood of Seeking Help From Peers as a Function of Cultural Distance

One of the questions raised earlier concerns the absence in previous studies
of relationships between general help-seeking intentions (both to approach
and to avoid) and seeking assistance from other students (Karabenick,
2004). As noted earlier, one suggestion for the absence of association was
that although teachers are a relatively well-defined group, students are very
heterogeneous, especially in multicultural settings. We could examine this
issue because the present study provided the necessary detail, at least with
regard to the relative sociocultural characteristics of student sources of assistance. The specific questions we asked were: When students indicate they
would seek help when necessary (i.e., general tendency to seek help): (a) Is
that tendency associated with seeking help from students (i.e., informal
sources)? (b) Does the degree of association depend on the socio-cultural
similarity to that of the student? and (c) Is that tendency related to the difference between students' tendency to seek help from similar versus dissimilar peer (i.e., the difference between A and C students)? The relationship
between generalized intentions to seek help when necessary and intentions
to seek help from type A-Type or C-Type students is presented in Table 5.5.

As shown in this table, it appears that for dominant, monocultural
groups in both countries combined, general intentions to seek help when

TABLE 5.5

Relationship Between Generalized Intention to Seek Help When Necessary
and Intentions to Seek Help from Target Peer Groups (A and C)

Location	Type	Local Students Monocultural	Mixed Culture	International Students Other Culture	Total
Australia	A	.26a	.16	.64b	.28[b]
	C	.10	.16	−.29	.09
	A – C	.11	.00	.53[a]	.12
U.S.	A	.29[c]	.03	−.01	.21[b]
	C	.20[a]	.10	−.00	.14
	A – C	−.04	−.11	−.08	.02
All students	A	.28[b]	.13	.25	.26[b]
	C	.17[a]	.13	−.10	.12[a]
	A – C	.04	−.02	.28[a]	.07

[a]Significant at $p < .05$.
[b]Significant at $p < .01$.
[c]Significant at $p < .001$.

necessary are associated the likelihood of obtaining that help from students who are culturally similar to themselves ($r = .28$). The tendency is less evident for seeking help from dissimilar students, again when students in both countries are combined ($r = .17$). It is still statistically significant for the U.S. group ($r = .20$, $p < .05$) but not the Australian group ($r = .10$). For these students, there is no evidence, however, that the tendency to seek help is related to differential help seeking from the two types of students (i.e., the A – C difference score ($r = .11$ and $r = -.04$). The mixed-culture subgroups (Mixed) in both countries showed no indication that tendencies to seek help are associated with either similar or dissimilar others, perhaps because their own group was so heterogeneous. In contrast, the two subgroups of international students displayed different patterns across locations.

No significant relationships were found for the international students in the United States. Most intriguing, however, was the pattern for international students in Australia, for whom general intentions to seek help were directly associated with seeking help from similar peers ($r = .64$, $p < .01$) along with a reduced tendency to seek help from culturally dissimilar others ($r = -.29$). This differential relationship is revealed by the A – C difference score, which was statistically significant ($r = .55$, $p < .05$) despite the relatively small sample size. These findings show evidence that intentions to seek needed help are not necessarily generalizable across culturally disparate sources of assistance, but rather are moderated by students' own cultural background in relation to those sources. One important question is whether some learning environments and teaching practices may influence help seeking patterns with regard to sources of assistance and own background.

Impact of Contextual Dimensions on Help Seeking

Research on the relationship of contextual variables to help-seeking patterns related to academic study is growing. Contextual variables have usually been conceptualized in terms of classroom goal structures. In recent work (Karabenick, 2004), significant relationships between students' help-seeking patterns and perceptions of their classes' achievement goal structures were revealed, even after controlling for students' personal goal orientations. Research on the impact of culture-related context on help seeking is scarce. A recent American study (Gloria et al., 2001), which focused on students' attitudes toward seeking professional for emotional or psychological problems (not academic problems), revealed that cultural context variables accounted for a significant proportion of the variation in students' help-seeking attitudes but more so for racial and ethnic minority (REM) groups than for Whites. A major limitation of that study, however, was the fact that the groups being compared (combining race and socioeconomic background) were located at different universities. Consistent with the focus on intercultural help seeking, an original culture-related measure of the learning environment was conceptualized for the present exploratory study. The 6-item instrument (called perceived press for interaction) measures students' perceptions of the extent to which their learning environment encourages students to mix with peers from different cultural backgrounds. The instrument aimed at examining whether students' likelihood of seeking help from outgroup peers would be related to perceptions that teachers valued, and even initiated, intercultural interactions and activities as an integral part of academic learning. To our knowledge, there has been no systematic study of university students' perceptions of their learning environment in regard to intercultural dimensions and how such views promote or inhibit adaptive interpersonal or intergroup learning processes, such as help seeking. It seemed reasonable to expect that perceived press for cultural interaction would be positively related to intentions to mix with peers from different cultural backgrounds, although natural tendencies for ingroup bias could be expected to moderate this relationship. A measure of perceived class socioemotional support was also included on the grounds that more socially challenging help-seeking behaviors (i.e., intercultural help seeking) may be more likely to take place in learning environments perceived as socially and emotionally supportive, although its effects may be less specifically linked to intercultural interaction but rather increasing the likelihood of help seeking from students in general.

As shown in Table 5.6, there is clear evidence that students in the dominant, monocultural group in Australia ($r = .27$, $p < .05$) and the United States ($r = .23$, $p < .05$), as well as both countries combined ($r = .28$, $p < .001$), who perceived more press for cultural interaction reported being more likely to seek help from students of other cultures. The trend was also present for mixed-cultural students but clearly absent for international students. Perceived press for cultural interaction also reduced the A–C difference score both for monocultural ($r = -.22$, $p < .01$) and mixed culture students ($r = -.34$, $p < .01$) in both locations. Interestingly, although not statistically significant, the association in the mixed cultural group is attributable in part to the lower tendency for those students to seek help from their own group in both locations. Although the extent to which these associations are a function of teacher/class differences (at least in the United States) or variation in perceived press among students within classes is not determinable because of the study design (i.e., single time point). Nevertheless, it seems clear that perceived press does play a role in the help-seeking process by affecting the likelihood of seeking help as a function of helping sources' relative cultural characteristics.

TABLE 5.6

Association Between Perceived Socioemotional Support, Perceived Pressure
for Cultural Interaction, and Intentions to Seek Help
from Type A and Type C Target

		Perceived Pressure for Interaction				Perceived Socioemotional Support			
		Cultural Subgroup				Cultural Subgroup			
Location	Target Type	Mono	Mixed	Other	All	Mono	Mixed	Other	All
Australia	A	.02	−.24	.02	−.04	.04	−.08	.30	.11
	C	.27[a]	.13	−.32	.17[a]	.27[a]	−.11	−.55[a]	.13
	A – C	−.15	.13	.17	−.17[a]	−.16	−.18	.45	−.07
U.S.	A	−.16	−.46	−.13	−.16[a]	.18[a]	−.15	.16	.16[a]
	C	.23[a]	.20	.03	.18[a]	.17	.03	.07	.12
	A – C	−.29[b]	−.39	−.14	−.25[c]	−.05	−.10	.19	.00
Both locations	A	.02	−.25	.11	−.01	.17[a]	−.07	.34[a]	.18[c]
	C	.28[c]	.15	−.11	.20[c]	.24[c]	.09	−.18	.15[b]
	A – C	−.22[b]	−.34[b]	.13	−.17[b]	−.10	−.16	.39[b]	−.02

[a]Significant at $p < .05$.
[b]Significant at $p < .01$.
[c]Significant at $p < .001$.

In contrast to perceived press for cultural interaction, across all students, perceived socioemotional support was related to increased intentions to seek help from similar (A-Type: $r = .18, p < .001$) as well as dissimilar culture peers (C-Type: $r = .15, p < .01$), although the effect was most evenly distributed for U.S. students. The relationships were not uniform across cultural groups, however, with international students in Australia who perceived more support more likely to seek help from other international students but less from outgoups (C-Type: $r = -.55, p < .05$). Combining both locations, international students who perceived more general support were both significantly more likely to seek help from their ingroup ($r = .34, p < .05$), somewhat less likely form their outgroup ($r = -.18$), with the consequence being a greater differential in seeking help as a function of source cultural characteristics (A – C: $r = .39, p < .01$). In summary, it is quite evident that student perceptions of culturally specific and general support are differentially linked to the likelihood of seeking help from sources of assistance that vary in relative cultural characteristics.

DISCUSSION

Results from this transnational study demonstrate the impact of cultural factors on help seeking and provide additional evidence of cultural influences on students' social-interactive learning activities. Furthermore, the pattern of help seeking by diverse student groups in multicultural environments shown here is consistent with generic social processes. In particular, the tendency to prefer culturally similar versus dissimilar helpers reflects the universality of ingroup bias (Kashima, 2001), Byrne's (1971) principle of attraction to similar others, Triandis's (2001) claim that when there is a sense of perceived similarity between people their interactions are perceived as more rewarding and thus get repeated, and that similarity is an important factor in intercultural friendship formation (Kudo & Simkin, 2003).

Thus, it is not unexpected that students would seek help from similar others, given that rewarding interactions are experienced as a function of the substantive amount of shared social knowledge, which increases the ease with which the student interactions occur (Lau, Chiu, & Lee, 2001). It is this shared social knowledge that creates a sense of cultural-emotional connectedness (Volet & Ang, 1998) that individuals understandably want to maintain for their well-being. In transcultural interactions, social challenges emerge because communicators have more limited shared social knowledge and may be anxious about how to establish comfortable levels of intercultural communication. Therefore, unless individuals have strategic reasons to overcome cross-cultural challenges, they will spontaneously choose to interact with people perceived as sharing the same "modes of discourse for negotiating differences in meaning and interpretation" (Bruner, 1990, p. 13). Help-seeking practices appear to operate according to these principles.

The transnational study, however, also revealed that differences in the likelihood of seeking help from familiar versus less familiar students were not the same across specific subgroups. As expected, the strongest ingroup bias was found among monocultural, monolingual students. This is consistent with research on collaborative group interactions on multicultural university campuses (Volet, 1999a, 1999c), which revealed that monocultural, monolingual students were the least prepared to interact and mix with students perceived as different from themselves. Although perceived cultural distance may partially explain students' reluctance to interact with less familiar peers—even if these peers could offer the help that is needed—the contextual affordances provided by less familiar peers may also play a significant role. In this transnational study, the outgroup for local monocultural, monolingual students consisted of international students characterized by a number of disadvantages: (a) The language of instruction was their second language, (b) they were less familiar with local educational practices and they had limited general local knowledge, and (c) they possibly had styles of communication perceived as different from local cultural norms. In combination, these elements apparently converged to create a sense that these students may not be an attractive source of help, regardless of whether they could actually provide the needed help. The fact that the monocultural, monolingual subgroups were dominant in numbers may further explain the patterns of results, because peers from the ingroup were readily available. Furthermore, and although help seeking from peers has been found to be unrelated to avoidance patterns (Karabenick, 2004), one may speculate that there may be a feeling among this group of local students that seeking academic help from peers who are at a disadvantage in regard to academic study would be unreasonable.

The help-seeking patterns of local students from mixed culture backgrounds were not, however, consistent with Volet's (1999a, 1999c) research on students' motivation to mix with peers from different cultural backgrounds for working in groups. In that research, local students from culturally mixed backgrounds, that is, those with presumed extensive experience with crossing cultural borders, displayed significantly more positive attitudes toward culturally mixed groups than toward local students from monocultural, monolingual backgrounds. No such differential preference of cultural subgroups was found with regard to help seeking in the present study. This suggests that the greater perceived affordances provided by international students for group work do not extend to seeking help. Mixing with peers from different cultural-educational backgrounds for group activities should be enjoyable for students who are familiar with crossing cultural borders, potentially creating new opportunities for networking and intercultural learning. As in prior research, this subgroup can be assumed to be least likely to feel anxious about managing uncertainty in intercultural communication (Gudykunst, 1995). Help seeking may be different, however, in the sense that the activity is less conducive to creating opportunities for intercultural learning but rather limited to resolving a problem, which may take minimal interaction. Under such circumstances, it is reasonable to assume that students would use the most cost-efficient strategy and, for reasons similar to their monocultural, monolingual counterparts, approach familiar, predictable peers. In other words, pragmatic concerns of seeking help may outweigh the broader social implications of group work.

The smallest ingroup bias, displayed by international students, can be explained by the interaction of personal and contextual factors. As discussed previously, it is well documented that these students are often in need of assistance with academic matters at the beginning of their study at a foreign university. Because their "outgroup" consists of local students, who have the capacity to provide assistance with language difficulties, local academic knowledge and local social networks are naturally attractive as a source of help for such matters, which would be different if the needed help was of a more personal nature (Bochner, McLeod, & Lin, 1977). It was therefore not surprising to find that international students, in comparison to other subgroups, were found to discriminate less between ingroup and outgroup members as sources of assistance. The fact that the two subgroups of international students consisted of individuals from a diversity of origins limited the possibility of forming genuine ingroups (e.g., conationals). Although international students form a coherent subgroup due to their shared foreignness (Bochner et al., 1977), it is unreasonable to assume that this is sufficient to meet the definition of an ingroup.

The notion of ingroup, as described in the literature, is expected to be limited to people from similar ethnic backgrounds and, in addition, those who share a special bonding. Yet there is converging evidence in the literature on international students that when fellow compatriots are not available to form ingroups, bonding for social support is sought from other foreign students who are perceived as close socioemotionally (Volet & Ang, 1998; Ward, Bochner, & Furnham, 2001). In this transnational study, the profile of the two subgroups of international students did not differ substantially; therefore the differential findings across locations can be attributed to contextual dimensions, such as availability within the Australian context of a more mixed, and thus presumed more approachable, local student population, in comparison to the U.S. context. In sum, although we found evidence of the general inverse relation between cultural similarity and the likelihood of seeking help, this overall effect was moderated by students' own cultural background. Thus, the universality of ingroup bias was supported (Kashima, 2001) but in combination with the influence of differential opportunities for help afforded by peers from diverse backgrounds in relation to the help seeker's own background.

Avoiding ethnic labels to categorize groups, and instead using vignettes to describe hypothetical peer groups as sources of help, was found conceptually and methodologically useful, because these represented the cultural dimensions assumed to produce variations in help-seeking patterns. The impact of unique configurations of person–context dimensions and their dynamic interactions at the experiential interface (Volet, 2001a) were important to understand students' help-seeking and help-giving practices in cultural context. Understanding the role of cultural dimensions in relation to students' intentions or reluctance to seek help as a function of peers' culture-related characteristics is critical for designing learning environments that are more inclusive of all students, and in the context of international education for promoting opportunities for intercultural learning, especially for students from monocultural, monolingual backgrounds.

Evidence that students' perceptions of teachers' encouragement to mix with peers from different cultural backgrounds had some impact on the help-seeking intentions of local students from both monocultural and culturally mixed backgrounds is encouraging. Although the present study could not reasonably independently measure the extent to which this is attributable to differences between teachers/classes (e.g., Karabenick, 2004), the results suggest that teacher-induced intercultural press would pay dividends. If we take as a general principle that one characteristic of powerful learning environments involves ready access to high-quality sources of information, these environments should include providing the least restrictive access to persons who may provide that information. In addition to its other virtues, therefore, minimizing intercultural barriers to adaptive interpersonal contact can be an important asset to effective help seeking, and therefore the chances of academic success. Although cultural barriers to contact may not be problematic when one's own subgroup has sufficient resources for students to draw on, the rapidly changing and increasingly multicultural environments in which learning takes place will make it more difficult to determine whether ingroup resources are sufficient. Therefore, a social self-regulated learning strategy, such as help seeking, will be more successful in the long run when students' can select sources of assistance without regard to cultural strictures. The present study provides evidence that such barriers exist and that efforts toward their mitigation are not only highly desirable but in some cases could be necessary for many students who need help.

REFERENCES

Allport, G. W. (1954). *The nature of prejudice*. Cambridge, MA: Addison-Wesley.
Barker, M., Child, C., Gallois, C., Jones, E., & Callan, V. J. (1991). Difficulties of overseas students in social and academic situations. *Australian Journal of Psychology*, *43*(2), 79–84.

Betancourt, H., & Lopez, S. R. (1993). The study of culture, ethnicity, and race in American psychology. *American Psychologist, 48*(6), 629–637.

Biggs, J. B. (1996). Western misperceptions of the Confucian-heritage learning culture. In D. W. J. Biggs (Ed.), *The Chinese learner: Cultural, psychological and contextual influences* (pp. 45–68). CERC, The University of Hong Kong/ACER.

Bochner, S., Hutnik, N., & Furnham, A. (1985). The friendship patterns of overseas and host students in an Oxford student residence. *Journal of Social Psychology, 125*(6), 689–694.

Bochner, S., McLeod, B. M., & Lin, A. (1977). Friendship patterns of overseas students: A functional model. *International Journal of Psychology, 12*, 277–297.

Boekaerts, M. (2001). Context sensitivity: Activated motivational beliefs, current concerns and emotional arousal. In S. E. Volet & S. Järvelä (Eds.), *Motivation in learning contexts: Theoretical advances and methodological implications* (pp. 17–31). Amsterdam: Elsevier Science.

Brewer, M. B. (1999). The psychology of prejudice: Ingroup love or outgroup hate? *Journal of Social Issues, 55*(3), 429–444.

Brewer, M. B., & Miller, N. (1988). Contact and cooperation: When do they work? In Phyllis A. Katz & Dalmas A. Taylor (Eds.), *Eliminating racism: Profiles in controversy* (pp. 315–326). New York: Plenum Press.

Bruner, J. (1990). *Act of meaning*. Cambridge, MA: Harvard University Press.

Burke, B. D. (1986). Experiences of overseas undergraduate students. *Student Counselling and Research Unit Bulletin 18*, University of New South Wales, Sydney, Australia.

Butler, R. (1998). Determinants of help seeking: Relations between perceived reasons for classroom help-avoidance and help-seeking behaviors in an experimental context. *Journal of Educational Psychology, 90*, 630–643.

Byrne, D. (1971). *The attraction paradigm*. New York: Academic Press.

Chew, S. B., Leu, G. J. M., & Tan, K. H. (1998). *Values and lifestyles of young Singaporeans*. Singapore: Prentice Hall.

Cook, S. W. (1978). Interpersonal and attitudinal outcomes in cooperating interracial groups. *Journal of Research and Development in Education, 12*(1), 97–113.

DeCooke, P. A. (1992). Children's understanding of indebtedness as a feature of reciprocal help exchanges between peers. *Developmental Psychology, 28*(5), 948–954.

Deng, L. Y. R. (2004). *Psychotherapy with Asian-Canadian clients: Cultural barriers and help-seeking*. Retrieved July 1, 2004, from http://www.oise.utoronto.ca/depts/aecdcp/CMPConf/papers/DengPaper.html

Dorval, B., & Eckerman, C. O. (1984). Developmental trends in the quality of conversation achieved by small groups of acquainted peers. *Monographs of the Society for Research in Child Development, 49*(2), 1–72.

Fisher, J. D., Nadler, A., & Whitcher-Alagna, S. (1982). Recipient reactions to aid. *Psychological Bulletin, 91*, 27–54.

Fiske, A., Kitayama, S., Markus, H. R., & Nisbett, R. E. (1998). The cultural matrix of social psychology. In D. Gilbert, S. Fiske & G. Lindzey (Eds.), *The handbook of social psychology* (4th ed., pp. 915–981). San Francisco: McGraw-Hill.

Furnham, A. (1997). The experience of being an overseas student. In D. McNamara & R. Harris (Eds.), *Overseas students in higher education: Issues in teaching and learning* (pp. 13–29). London and New York: Routledge.

Furnham, A., & Alibhai, N. (1985). The friendship networks of foreign students: A replication and extension of the functional model. *International Journal of Psychology, 20*, 709–722.

Furnham, A., & Bochner, S. (1982). Social difficulty in a foreign culture: An empirical analysis of culture shock. In S. Bochner (Ed.), *Cultures in contact: Studies in cross-cultural interaction* (pp. 161–198). Oxford, UK: Pergamon Press.

Gareis, E. (1999). Rhetoric and intercultural friendship formation. *International and Intercultural Communication Annual: Rhetoric in Intercultural Contexts, 22,* 91–117.

Gareis, E. (2000). Intercultural friendship: Five case studies of German students in the USA. *Journal of Intercultural Studies, 21*(1), 67–91.

Gim, R. H., Atkinson, D. R., & Whiteley, S. (1990). Asian-American acculturation, severity of concern, and willingness to see a counsellor. *Journal of Counseling Psychology, 37,* 281–285.

Gloria, A. M., Hird, J. S., & Navarro, R. L. (2001). Relationships of cultural congruity and perceptions of the university environment to help-seeking attitudes by sociorace and gender. *Journal of College Student Development, 42*(6), 545–562.

Gudykunst, W. B. (1995). Anxiety/uncertainty management (AUM) theory. In R. L. Wiseman (Ed.), *Intercultural communication theory* (Vol. 19, pp. 8–58). Thousand Oaks, CA: Sage Publications.

Gutiérrez, K. D., & Rogoff, B. (2003). Cultural ways of learning: Individual traits or repertoires of practice. *Educational Researcher, 32*(5), 19–25.

Hewstone, M., & Brown, R. (1986). Contact is not enough: An intergroup perspective on the "contact hypothesis." In M. Hewstone & R. Brown (Eds.), *Contact and conflict in intergroup encounters* (pp. 1–44). Oxford: Basil Blackwell.

Hill, B. V. (1998). Values education: The Australian experience. *Prospects, XXVII*(2), 1173–1191.

Ho, W. M. (1989). Value premises underlying the transformation of Singapore. In S. K. Singh & P. Wheatley (Eds.), *Management of success: The moulding of modern Singapore* (pp. 671–691). Singapore: Institute of Southeast Asian Studies.

Hofstede, G. (1980). *Culture's consequences: International differences in work-related values.* Beverley Hills, CA: Sage.

Hofstede, G. (1986). Cultural differences in teaching and learning. *International Journal of Intercultural Relations, 10,* 301–320.

Kagitcibasi, C. (1994). Human development and societal development: Linking theory and application. In A. M. Bouvy, F. J. R. van der Vijver, P. Boski & P. Schmitz (Eds.), *Journeys into cross-cultural psychology* (pp. 7–27). Amsterdam: Swets & Zeitlinger.

Karabenick, S. A. (Ed.). (1998). *Strategic help seeking: Implications for learning and teaching.* Mahwah, NJ: Lawrence Erlbaum Associates.

Karabenick, S. A. (2003). Help seeking in large college classes: A person-centered approach. *Contemporary Educational Psychology, 28,* 37–58.

Karabenick, S. A. (2004). Perceived achievement goal structure and college student help seeking. *Journal of Educational Psychology, 96*(3), 569–581.

Karabenick, S. A., & Knapp, J. R. (1991). Relationship of academic help seeking to the use of learning strategies and other instrumental achievement behavior in college students. *Journal of Educational Psychology, 83,* 221–230.

Karabenick, S. A., & Sharma, R. (1994). Perceived teacher support of student questioning in the college classroom: Its relation to student characteristics and role in the classroom questioning process. *Journal of Educational Psychology, 86*(1), 90–103.

Kashima, Y. (2001). Culture and social cognition: Towards a social psychology of cultural dynamics. In D. Matsumoto (Ed.), *The handbook of culture and psychology* (pp. 325–360). New York: Oxford University Press.

Kitayama, S., & Markus, H. R. (1999). Yin and yang of the Japanese self: The cultural psychology of personality coherence. In D. Cervone & Y. Shoda (Eds.), *The coher-*

ence of personality: Social cognitive bases of personality consistency, variability, and organization (pp. 242–302). New York: Guilford.

Knapp, J. R., & Karabenick, S. A. (1988). Incidence of formal and informal help seeking in higher education. *Journal of College Student Development, 29,* 223–227.

Kudo, K., & Simkin, K. A. (2003). Intercultural Friendship Formation: The case of Japanese students at an Australian university. *Journal of Intercultural Studies, 24*(2), 91–114.

Kwang, H. F., Fernandez, W., & Tan, S. (Eds.). (1998). *Lee Kuan Yew: The man and his ideas.* Singapore: Times Editions/Strait Times Press.

Lau, I. Y., Chiu, C.-Y., & Lee, S.-L. (2001). Communication and shared reality: Implications for the psychological foundations of culture. *Social Cognition, 19*(3), 350–371.

Leong, F. T. L., & Lau, A. S. L. (2001). Barriers to providing effective mental health services to Asian Americans. *Mental Health Services Research, 3,* 201–214.

Leong, F. T. L., Wagner, N. S., & Tata, S. P. (1995). Racial and ethnic variation in help-seeking attitudes. In J. G. Ponterotto, J. M. Casas, L. A. Suzuki & C. M. Alexander (Eds.), *Handbook of multicultural counseling* (pp. 415–438). Thousand Oaks, CA: Sage.

Liberman, K. (1994). Asian student perspectives on American university instruction. *International Journal of Intercultural Relations, 18*(2), 173–192.

Lin, J. C. H. (1994). How long do Chinese Americans stay in psychotherapy? *Journal of Counseling Psychology, 41,* 288–291.

Maehr, M. L., & Pintrich, P. R. (Eds.). (1995). *Advances in motivation and achievement: Culture, motivation and achievement* (Vol. 9). Greenwich, CT: JAI Press.

Markus, H. R., & Kitayama, S. (1991). Culture and the self: Implications for cognition, emotion and motivation. *Psychological Review, 98*(2), 224–253.

Matsumoto, D. (Ed.). (2001). *The handbook of culture and psychology.* New York: Oxford University Press.

McInerney, D. M., & Van Etten, S. (Eds.). (2001). *Research on sociocultural influences on motivation and learning* (Vol. 1). Greenwich, CT: IAP.

McKinlay, N. J., Pattison, H. M., & Gross, H. (1996). An exploratory investigation of the effects of a cultural orientation programme on the psychological well-being of international university students. *Higher Education, 31,* 379–395.

Morris, S. C., & Rosen, S. (1973). Effects of felt adequacy and opportunity to reciprocate on help seeking. *Journal of Experimental Social Psychology, 9*(3), 265–276.

Mullins, G., & Hancock, L. (1991). Educating overseas students at the University of Adelaide: how do we rate? *Lumen, 20,* 3–4.

Mullins, G., Quintrell, N., & Hancock, L. (1995). The experiences of international and local students at three Australian universities. *Higher Education Research and Development, 14*(2), 201–231.

Nadler, A. (1998). Relationship, esteem, and achievement perspectives on autonomous and dependent help seeking. In S. A. Karabenick (Ed.), *Strategic help seeking: Implications for learning and teaching* (pp. 61–93). Mahwah, NJ: Lawrence Erlbaum Associates.

Nelson-Le Gall, S. (1981). Help-seeking: An understudied problem-solving skill in children. *Developmental Review, 1,* 224–246.

Nelson-Le Gall, S. (1985). Help-seeking behavior in learning. In E. W. Gordon (Ed.), *Review of research in education* (Vol. 12, pp. 55–90). Washington, DC: American Educational Research Association.

Nesdale, D., & Todd, P. (1993). Internationalising Australian universities: The intercultural contact issue. *Journal of Tertiary Education Administration, 15*(2), 189–202.

Newman, R. S. (1990). Children's help-seeking in the classroom: The role of motivational factors and attitudes. *Journal of Educational Psychology, 82,* 71–80.

Newman, R. S. (1998). Adaptive help seeking: A role of social interaction in self-regulated learning. In S. A. Karabenick (Ed.), *Strategic help seeking: Implications for learning and teaching* (pp. 13–37). Mahwah, NJ: Lawrence Erlbaum Associates.

Newman, R. S. (2000). Social influences on the development of children's adaptive help seeking: The role of parents, teachers, and peers. *Developmental Review, 20,* 350–404.

Newman, R. S., & Schwager, M. T. (1993). Students' perceptions of the teacher and classmates in relation to reported help seeking in math class. *Elementary School Journal, 94,* 3–17.

O'Donoghue, T. (1996). Malaysian Chinese students' perceptions of what is necessary for their academic success in Australia: A case study at one university. *Journal of Further Higher Education, 20*(2), 67–80.

Pedersen, P. B. (1991). Counselling international students. *Counselling Psychologists, 19*(1), 10–58.

Pekrun, R. (2000). A social cognitive, control-value theory of achievement emotions. In J. Heckhausen (Ed.), *Motivational psychology of human development* (pp. 143–163). Oxford, UK: Elsevier Science.

Poortinga, Y. (1996). Indigenous psychology: Scientific ethnocentrism in a new guise? In J. Pandey, D. Sinha & D. P. S. Bhawuk (Eds.), *Asian contributions to cross-cultural psychology* (pp. 59–71). New Delhi/Thousand Oaks/London: Sage.

Ryan, A. M. (1998). *The development of achievements beliefs and behaviors during early adolescence: The role of peer group and classroom contexts.* Unpublished doctoral dissertation, University of Michigan.

Ryan, A. M., Gheen, M., & Midgley, C. (1998). Why do some students avoid asking for help? An examination of the interplay among students' academic efficacy, teachers' social-emotional role and classroom goal structure. *Journal of Educational Psychology, 90,* 528–535.

Ryan, A. M., & Pintrich, P. R. (1997). "Should I ask for help?" The role of motivation and attitudes in adolescents' help seeking in math class. *Journal of Educational Psychology, 89,* 329–341.

Salili, F. (1995). Explaining Chinese students' motivation and achievement: A sociocultural analysis. In M. L. Maehr & P. R. Pintrich (Eds.), *Advances in motivation and achievement: Culture, motivation and achievement* (Vol. 9, pp. 73–118). Greenwich, CT: JAI Press.

Salili, F., Chiu, C. Y., & Hong, Y. Y. (Eds.). (2001). *Student motivation: The culture and context of learning.* New York: Kluwer/Plenum.

Salili, F., & Hau, K. T. (1999). Teachers' evaluative feedback and its relationship with students' perception of ability and effort: An analysis of the effects of culture and context on students' perceptions. *Asia Pacific Journal of Education (Singapore), 19*(2), 60–71.

Shwalb, D. W., & Sukemune, S. (1998). Help seeking in the Japanese college classroom: Cultural, developmental, and social-psychological influences. In S. A. Karabenick (Ed.), *Strategic help seeking: Implications for learning and teaching* (pp. 141–170). Mahwah, NJ: Lawrence Erlbaum Associates.

Shweder, R. A., & Sullivan, M. A. (1990). The semiotic subject of cultural psychology. In L. A. Pervin (Ed.), *Handbook of personality: theory and research* (pp. 399–416). New York: Guilford Press.

Smart, D., Volet, S. E., & Ang, G. (2000). *Fostering social cohesion at university: Bridging the Cultural divide.* Canberra: Australian Education International.

Smolicz, J. J. (1991). Who is an Australian? Identity, core values and the resilience of culture. In M. Secombe & J. Zajda (Eds.), *J.J. Smolicz on education and culture* (pp. 11–49). Canberra, Australia: James Nicholas Publishers.

Smolicz, J. J. (1999). Social systems in plural societies. In M. Secombe & J. Zajda (Eds.), *J.J. Smolicz on education and culture* (pp. 139–157). Canberra, Australia: James Nicholas Publishers.

Tajfel, H., & Dawson, J. (Eds.). (1965). *Disappointed guests: Essays by African, Asian and West Indian students*. London and Oxford: Institute of Race Relations & Oxford University Press.

Tata, S. P., & Leong, F. T. L. (1994). Individualism-collectivism, social-network orientation, and acculturation as predictors of attitudes toward seeking professional psychological help among Chinese Americans. *Journal of Counseling Psychology, 41*, 280–287.

Todd, P., & Nesdale, D. (1997). Promoting intercultural contact between Australian and international university students. *Journal of Higher Education Policy and Management, 19*(1), 61–76.

Tracey, T. J., Leong, F. T. L., & Glidden, C. (1986). Help seeking and problem perception among Asian Americans. *Journal of Counseling Psychology, 33*, 331–336.

Triandis, H. C. (1994). *Culture and social behavior*. New York: McGraw-Hill.

Triandis, H. C. (1995). *Individualism and collectivism*. Boulder, CO: Westview Press.

Triandis, H. C. (2001). Modern education needs cross-cultural psychology. In D. M. McInerney & S. V. Etten (Eds.), *Research on sociocultural influences on motivation and learning* (Vol. 1, pp. 1–13). Greenwich, CT: Information Age.

Triandis, H. C., McCusker, C., & Hui, C. H. (1990). Multimethod probes of individualism and collectivism. *Journal of Personality and Social Psychology, 59*, 1006–1020.

Trice, A., & Elliot, J. (1993). Japanese students in America: II. College friendship patterns. Journal of inter-cultural learning. *Higher Education Research and Development, 17*(1), 5–23.

Turner, J. C., Meyer, D. K., Anderman, E. M., Midgley, C., Gheen, M., & Kang, Y. (2002). The classroom environment and students' reports of avoidance strategies in mathematics: A multimethod study. *Journal of Educational Psychology, 94*, 88–106.

Urdan, T. C. (Ed.). (1999). *Advances in motivation and achievement* (Vol. 11). Stamford, CT: JAI Press.

Volet, S. E. (1999a). Internationalisation of higher education: Opportunities for intercultural development of Chinese and Australian students. In J. Lu (Ed.), *Education of the Chinese: The global prospect of national cultural tradition* (pp. 240–256). Nanjing: Nanjing University Press.

Volet, S. E. (1999b). Learning across cultures: Appropriateness of knowledge transfer. *International Journal of Educational Research, 31*(7), 625–643.

Volet, S. E. (1999c). Motivation within and across cultural-educational contexts: A multi-dimensional perspective. In T. Urdan (Ed.), *Advances in motivation and achievement* (Vol. 11, pp. 185–231). Greenwich, CT: JAI Press.

Volet, S. E. (2001a). Learning and motivation in context: A multi-dimensional and multi-level, cognitive-situative perspective. In S. E. Volet & S. Järvelä (Eds.), *Motivation in learning contexts: Theoretical advances and methodological implications* (pp. 57–82). London: Elsevier.

Volet, S. E. (2001b). Significance of cultural and motivational variables on students' appraisals of group work. In F. Salili, C. Y. Chiu, & Y. Y. Hong (Eds.), *Student motivation: The culture and context of learning* (pp. 309–334). New York: Plenum.

Volet, S. E. (2001c). Understanding learning and motivation in context: A multi-dimensional and multi-level cognitive-situative perspective. In S. E. Volet & S.

Järvelä (Eds.), *Motivation in learning contexts: Theoretical advances and methodological implications* (pp. 58–82). Amsterdam: Elsevier Science.

Volet, S. E., & Ang, G. (1998). Culturally mixed groups on international campuses: An opportunity for intercultural learning. *Higher Education Research & Development, 17*(1), 5–23.

Volet, S. E., & Järvelä, S. (Eds.). (2001). *Motivation in learning contexts: Theoretical advances and methodological implications*. Amsterdam: Elsevier Science.

Volet, S. E., & Mansfield, C. (in press). Motivation and self-regulation in socially challenging learning environments at university: Significance of goals and mental representations. *Higher Education Research & Development*.

Volet, S. E., & Pears, H. (1994). *International students in Technical and Further Education (TAFE) Colleges in Western Australia: Students' reflections on their experience and perceptions of the future of associations between their country and Australia* (Research report). Perth: Murdoch University and TAFE International (WA).

Volet, S. E., Renshaw, P., & Tietzel, K. (1994). A short-term longitudinal investigation of cross-cultural differences in study approaches using Biggs' SPQ. *British Journal of Educational Psychology, 64*, 301–318.

Volet, S. E., & Renshaw, P. D. (1995). Cross-cultural differences in university students' goals and perceptions of study settings for achieving goals. *Higher Education, 30*(4), 407–433.

Ward, C., Bochner, S., & Furnham, A. (2001). *The psychology of culture shock*. East Sussex: Routledge.

Watson, W. E., Johnson, L., Kumar, K., & Critelli, J. (1998). Process gain and process loss: Comparing interpersonal processes and performance of culturally diverse and non-diverse teams across time. *International Journal of Intercultural Relations, 22*(4), 409–430.

Willcoxon, L. (1992). *"Australian values" Asia is your business*. Sydney: Research Institute for Asia and the Pacific, University of Sydney.

Williams, R. M. (1947). *Reduction of intergroup tension*. New York: Social Science Research Council.

Wills, T. A., & DePaulo, B. M. (1990). Interpersonal analysis of the help-seeking process. In C. R. Snyder & D. R. Forsyth (Eds.), *Handbook of social and clinical psychology* (pp. 350–375). Elmsford, NY: Pergamon.

Wright, S., & Lander, D. (2003). Collaborative group interactions of students from two ethnic backgrounds. *Higher Education Research & Development, 22*(3), 237–251.

Yip, K. (1997). *The mediation of Confucian-based ideas on student goal conceptualization in the context of a performance goal orientation*. Singapore: National Institute of Education, Nanyang University.

Zimmerman, B. J., & Martinez-Pons, M. (1986). Development of a structured interview for assessing student use of self-regulated learning strategies. *American Educational Research Journal, 23*, 614–628.

Chapter 6

When Is Seeking Help Appropriate? How Norms Affect Help Seeking in Organizations

Brian A. Sandoval
Fiona Lee
University of Michigan

In 1978, the Perkin-Elmer Corporation won the NASA contract to manufacture the mirror for the Hubble Space Telescope. The success of the Hubble Space Telescope rested on Perkin-Elmer's ability to create a one-of-a-kind mirror with maximum smoothness and precise curvature—it was a technological challenge for the team of engineers entrusted with the Hubble project. To ensure the success of the project, Perkin-Elmer hired renowned technical experts and optical engineers as consultants to assist the Hubble team. However, even though the Hubble team faced many problems during the mirror production process, it resisted seeking help from the experts. For example, when one of the consultants, Roderic Scott, would come by, team members said to each other, "Hey, Rod is out there. Don't let him in. Turn up the radio" (Capers & Lipton, 1993, p. 51). As a result of not seeking help, the engineers failed to resolve serious problems that emerged from the production of the mirror, which in turn led to the installation of a seriously flawed mirror into the telescope.

HELP SEEKING IN EDUCATIONAL
AND ORGANIZATIONAL PSYCHOLOGY

Perkin-Elmer's experience raises an intriguing question—why do individuals resist seeking help even though help is needed and available? This question has been of long-standing interest to educational researchers and practitioners who focus on help seeking in the classroom. Research shows that as children grow older they become more aware of their inadequacies and the need to seek help (Markman, 1977). Yet, like the Hubble engineers, children do not ask their teachers, parents, or peers for help when they have problems (Newman & Goldin, 1990). Furthermore, Karabenick and Knapp (1988) found that help seeking is very low among students who are performing poorly and need it the most. This is alarming because seeking help from others is imperative to learning and problem solving in classrooms (Newman, 1994).

Although much of the research on help seeking focuses on educational contexts, the importance of help seeking for learning, problem solving, and skill acquisition extends far beyond the context of formal education. For instance, when adults encounter mental health problems in their everyday life, their ability to seek help from their friends, family, colleagues, and mental health professionals is critical to their ability to sustain both short-term and long-term psychological well-being (Wills, 1983).

There has also been research showing that individuals rely on help seeking to solve new problems and acquire unique skills in their work. For instance, when people start a new job, they proactively seek help to gather technical information related to their tasks, or normative information about expected behaviors and attitudes (Morrison, 1993). Lee (1997, 1999, 2002) examined help-seeking behaviors in organizations implementing new computer systems. Not surprisingly, in the process of acquiring the necessary skills and behavioral routines to use these new systems effectively, employees frequently encountered problems and questions. Whether and how employees sought help when they encountered problems significantly predicted their satisfaction with the new systems (Lee, Teich, Spurr, & Bates, 1996) and the quality of their performance (Lee, 2002). As the Perkin-Elmer story illustrates, seeking help can be imperative to successful performance in work settings.

Although both educational and organizational psychologists examine the process, antecedents, and outcomes of help seeking, there is little exchange between these literatures. In this chapter we hope to bring the two literatures together to increase the understanding of help seeking in both educational and organizational domains. Specifically, we argue that norms—whether they exist in the classroom, a work team, a business organization, or within a nation—affect whether and how individuals seek help.

We first review the educational psychology literature to demonstrate that norms are critical for eliciting help seeking behaviors in the classroom, even overcoming individual resistances to seeking help. We then provide a brief synopsis of the literature on norms, and in particular individualist and collectivist norms. Next, we argue that individualist norms discourage help seeking because help seeking creates impressions of dependence, incompetence, and inferiority, values inconsistent with individualist norms. Conversely, collectivist norms facilitate help-seeking behaviors because these norms emphasize interdependence, effort, and collaboration. Finally, we discuss how these norms can be managed in organizations such as schools or workplaces to facilitate help seeking.

Norms and Help-Seeking Behavior

There is considerable evidence that norms affect help seeking behaviors in the classroom. In interviews of seventh- and eighth-grade students, Ryan, Pintrich, and Midgley (2001) reported that students referred to rules and norms when asked to describe why they did or did not seek help in the classroom. For example, when students reported norms such as "most of the time at the end of class if you really don't understand something you can go up and ask the teacher," help seeking was facilitated (Ryan, 1996, as cited in Ryan et al., 2001). Similarly, Karabenick and Sharma (1994) found that the proclivity for college students to ask questions was related to the perceived amount of teacher support of questioning not only through explicit rules, but also through implicit norms. For example, students perceived questioning was supported in the classroom if the teacher gave careful and thorough answers, or allocated class time to give students opportunities to ask questions.

There is evidence that there was more help seeking when teachers developed classroom norms that emphasized learning, progress, and improvement, rather than demonstrating relative ability (Ames, 1992). Particularly, students reported feeling more comfortable asking questions in front of their peers when classroom norms supported growth and deemphasized comparison (Ryan, Gheen, & Midgley, 1998). These norms reduced students' focus on their selves and their abilities (Kaplan, Middleton, Urdan, & Midgley, 2002), which in turn reduced their fear that seeking help would highlight their incompetence and inferiority. Newman (1998) similarly found that students sought more help when classroom norms stressed learning and mastery, even if their own personal motivations emphasized the display of high ability.

In addition to norms established by teachers, Kennedy (1997) found that peer academic norms influenced the likelihood of help seeking. Students who reported that their peers had negative reactions to academics were less likely to seek help. Similarly, student concerns about social status with their peers reduced help seeking (Ryan, Hicks, & Midgley, 1997). Ryan and Pintrich (1997) noted that students who were socially unsure had lowered rates of help seeking because they perceived help seeking as jeopardizing their self-worth (Ryan et al., 1997). In short, if peer norms discouraged help seeking, help-seeking behaviors put students at risk of being ostracized.

These studies demonstrate that help-seeking behavior is in large part dependent on the norms established by peers and teachers, and that norms can override individual's proclivity to avoid seeking help. In the next subsections, we discuss how norms have been generally defined and measured in the literature, and then focus on one specific dimension of norms—individualism and collectivism.

Norms

A Definition.   Norms refer to standards of behavior. Every social organization, from a two-person dyad to an entire country, has norms of various kinds that define what is appropriate and inappropriate behavior in that social system. Arriving on time for an appointment or class or waiting in line for a teller at the bank are common norms in America (Lee & Duenas, 1995). These norms, however, are less prevalent in Latin American cultures (Hall, 1966).

Norms are so commonplace we rarely realize we abide by them until they are violated. For instance, in universities there are classroom norms for where students versus professors should sit—everyone expects students to sit in the auditorium and the professor to stand on the stage in the front of the room. It is usually unnecessary to discuss the norm. Indeed, we hardly recognize this norm until it is violated—for example, if the professor should start lecturing while sitting in the middle of the auditorium rather than standing in front of the room.

Indeed, to maintain norms or standards of appropriate behavior, individuals are frequently sanctioned when they violate norms (Festinger, Schachter, & Back, 1950; Hackman, 1992). For example, one might gently remind a late student that he or she is expected to show up to class on time. Or, the individual may be punished by withholding social goods—the professor or other students may begin to frown at the student, or worse, kick the individual out of the class. In all these cases, members of a social group often exert considerable effort to maintain the norms by sanctioning and punishing inappropriate behavior.

According to Jackson (1965), norms can be defined along several dimensions, such as intensity (how strongly members of the social system feels about the norm), range of tolerable behavior (the range of behaviors that the social system deems appropriate and acceptable), and crystallization (the level of agreement about the norm within the social system). For example, norms about violence in the classroom might be high in intensity (members of the class have strong feelings about the appropriateness of violent behaviors), low in tolerable range (any and all violent behaviors would be considered inappropriate), and high in crystallization (everyone in the classroom agrees about the appropriateness of violent behaviors).

Norms at Multiple Levels of Social Organizations. Norms can exist in various kinds of social organizations, from dyads to entire nations. For example, researchers examining marital relationships found that relationship norms such as humor, affection, and validation were positively related to marital satisfaction (Gottman, 1979). Couples with these norms of relating to one another were better able to deescalate the negativity associated with marital conflict (Carstensen, Gottman, & Levenson, 1995).

Norms have also been extensively studied at the level of work groups or work teams. For instance, Edmondson (1999) suggested that teams had different norms of "psychological safety," where members of safer teams were more likely to trust others not to be critical, and less concerned about others judging them negatively for speaking up. As a result, team members were more likely to engage in risky behaviors such as experimenting with new ideas, learning new skills and task, and discussing mistakes and errors. In a study of 51 teams in office furniture manufacturers with approximately 5,000 employees, Edmondson found that teams with norms emphasizing psychological safety had greater instances of team learning behavior and consequently scored better on measures of team performance outcomes.

Organizations as a whole also have norms to guide members' behaviors. Over time an organization learns how to deal with the external environment and internal problems and develops a set of norms, or standards of behavior, that all members of the organization share (O'Reilly & Chatman, 1996; Schein, 1990). For example, individuals learn not to criticize the company or use the competition's products or services. As new members enter the organization they are socialized both formally and informally and learn these norms, as well as how to best maintain them (Morrison, 1993). Over time, norm maintenance occurs through official policies, incentives, penalties, and the example of peers (Schein, 1968, 1996).

Entire nations, countries, and cultures also have norms to guide their members' behaviors. We have norms about appropriate food to eat, clothes to wear, and music to listen to. Norms guide more than our individual behaviors; they also influence how we relate with others. Such relational norms influence what we focus on when we interact with others. The relational norm in East Asian, Latin American, and Middle Eastern cultures is to emphasize interpersonal harmony and be attuned to the socioemotional needs of others (Sanchez-Burks, Nisbett, & Ybarra, 2000). For example, in

Japanese and Indian work settings it is common for managers to attend personal events like funerals, and Latin American workplaces are characterized by a desire to create personable work climates (Sanchez-Burks, 2002). In contrast, the relational norm in Western cultures is to focus on how a relationship can assist an individual's own needs and the task at hand (Sanchez-Burks et al., 2003).

Individualist and Collectivist Norms

Beyond simply delineating the boundaries of appropriate and inappropriate behaviors, norms provide cues about what the social organization values (Feldman, 1984; Orlikowski, 1992; Schein, 1993). This perhaps is most clear in the literature on individualist and collectivist norms. Individualism/collectivism is one of the most extensively researched and theorized dimensions for describing norms. Many large social systems, from large organizations to entire countries, can be differentiated along this dimension (Chatman & Barsade, 1995; Markus & Kitayama, 1991; Triandis, McCusker, & Hui, 1990). In this subsection, we examine how individualist and collectivist norms in social organizations affect help seeking.

Definition and Measurement of Individualism and Collectivism. Individualist norms are characterized by an emphasis on independence. In social systems with individualist norms, individuals are seen as isolated from others, and individual identities are reinforced by differentiating the self from other people (Uleman, Rhee, Bardoliwalla, Semin, & Toyama, 2000). Individuals are motivated to be different from others, to stand out, essentially to "one-up" others. Merit is based on individual effort, individual contribution to an outcome, and how an individual's performance is compared to others (Chatman & Barsade, 1995). In contrast, social systems with collective norms emphasize interdependence between people. Individuals are seen as inextricably tied to one another, and individual identities are defined by one's relationship to others. Individual performance is less important than the performance of a team or group (Singelis, 1994). Individuals are motivated to minimize differences between themselves and others, to maintain equality, and to generally "fit in" (Triandis, 1997).

Individualism and collectivism have been measured in a variety of ways in the psychological literature (Triandis et al., 1990). One method asked individuals to respond to the sentence stem "I am …" Collectivists are more likely to respond with spontaneous self-descriptors that focus on their relationships with others (e.g., "I am a daughter"), whereas individualists are more likely to respond with spontaneous self-descriptors that focus on their autonomous and differentiating traits (e.g., "I am tall") (Rhee, Uleman, & Lee, 1995).

Another way to measure individualism and collectivism is asking individuals to judge the homogeneity of ingroups and outgroups. Because collectivists emphasize interpersonal harmony for the ingroup, they see the ingroup as more homogeneous than outgroups. Individualists, on the other hand, regard the individual as the basic unit of analysis, and hence they see members of the ingroup as heterogeneous because ingroup members are regarded as different and having identities of their own, whereas outgroup members are perceived as all the same (Triandis et al., 1990).

It is important to note that differences in individualism and collectivism also exist at the individual level of analysis. Triandis and Suh (2002) note that all humans have access to both individualist and collectivist cognitive structures, although people in individualist cultures can more readily access individualist cognitive structures, whereas people in collectivist cultures can more readily access to collectivist structures. Chatman and Barsade (1995) found that the collectivist norms of a group affected cooperation behavior, but also found an interaction between collectivist norms and individual collectivism. Clearly, beyond norms, individual tendencies toward individualism or collectivism also affect behaviors.

Individualist/Collectivist Norms and Help Seeking

Evidence suggests that individualist and collectivist norms affect two types of help-seeking behavior: whether people seek help when problems arise, and how they seek help through their verbal and nonverbal behaviors. In this subsection, we review this evidence.

Propensity of Help Seeking. We argue that norms of individualism and collectivism affect the acceptability of help seeking, which in turn affect *whether* individuals engage in help-seeking behaviors. Specifically, seeking help from others when problems arise directly affect one's sense of dependence, incompetence, and inferiority (Lee, 1997). First, by asking another's input into one's problem, the help seeker acknowledges dependence on another person (Druian & DePaulo, 1977). In other words, the help seeker is dependent on the helper to get the task completed successfully. Second, help seeking from others implies that there is a gap in the help seeker's expertise and knowledge, and therefore implicitly acknowledges one's incompetence (Ames & Lau, 1982; Karabenick & Knapp, 1988). Third, by seeking help from another, the help seeker further admits that he or she is inferior to another person. In short, the help seeker acknowledges that the helper is better, more experienced, more skillful, more knowledgeable, and generally more capable in solving the problem at hand.

Appearing dependent, incompetent, and inferior contradicts values prescribed by social organizations with individualist norms. Indeed, individualist norms advocate independence, superiority, and competence, and as such may discourage help-seeking behaviors (Lee, Caza, Edmondson, & Thomke, 2003). In contrast, in organizations with collectivist norms, appearing dependent, incompetent, and inferior is not considered inappropriate. In fact, to the extent that collectivist norms encourage individuals to minimize differences and foster more interdependencies with others, these norms in turn may facilitate help seeking. In sum, help seeking should be more prevalent in organizations with collectivist than individualist norms. Before we review the evidence for this proposition, we first discuss how individualist and collectivist norms can also affect how people seek help.

Help-Seeking Strategies. Besides affecting whether individuals seek help, individualist and collectivist norms may also affect how individuals seek help. Social linguists have shown that requests for help are often couched in various "verbal strategies" to minimize the impositions of the request (Brown & Levinson, 1987; Goffman, 1967; Hallahan, Lee, & Herzog, 1997; Holtgraves & Yang, 1990, 1992). For example, one verbal strategy that help seekers might use is minimizing the request—such as saying "I need a second of your time" rather than "I need your time"—such that the imposition on the helper appears to be smaller. These verbal strategies can affect the probability of getting the help needed. Past research has shown that help seekers who use more strategies tend to appear more polite and considerate, making it more likely that the helper will indeed extend help (Clark & Schunk, 1980). Also, using more verbal strategies can convey information about the specific nature of the request to the helper, also increasing the probability that the helper will extend appropriate help (Lee, 1999).

Norms affect the extent to which verbal strategies are used to couch requests for help (Brown & Levinson, 1987). For example, requesting data and instruments from other researchers might be an established norm and common practice in some academic fields but not in others—thus, the size of the imposition associated with requesting information from a fellow researcher might be different in different fields.

Individualist and collectivist norms, in particular, play an important role in determining the usage of verbal and nonverbal strategies used to request help. Specifically, individuals in collective settings placed more weight on relational factors (such as power) to determine the strategies for seeking help, using more strategies to seek help from a boss than a subordinate. Individuals in individualist settings placed more weight on contextual factors (such as the size of the request) to determine strategy usage, using more strategies to seek help for a large than a small problem. This was true not only for verbal strategies (such as saying "I apologize but ...") but also for nonverbal strategies (such as appearing deferential and circumspect in body language, facial impressions and tone of voice) (Ambady, Koo, Lee & Rosenthal, 1996; Holtgraves & Yang, 1992).

It makes sense that individualist and collective norms have direct bearing on the strategies people use to seek help. Individualist norms are characterized by emphasis on independence, isolation from others, and differentiating the self from other people. Under individualist norms, individuals are less likely to be sensitive to others' face and wants, and less motivated to remedy the imposition on others from requesting help. Thus individuals may seek help more directly without using verbal or nonverbal strategies to couch the request. In contrast, collective norms emphasize interdependence between people, and individual identities are defined by one's relationship to others. In other words, collective norms encourage other-orientedness, consideration of others' face and wants, empathy, and concern for others (Chatman & Barsade, 1995; Markus & Kitayama, 1991; Ting-Toomey, 1988; Triandis, 1989). Because of the increased emphasis on saving others' face within collective norms, it is likely that more verbal and nonverbal strategies will be used to couch the request to seek help. In other words, help seeking occurs more indirectly.

Evidence From Organizational Studies. In a study examining how employees of a large hospital learned to use a new computer system, Lee (1997) found that help-seeking behaviors were higher in medical departments than in surgical departments. Further, content analysis of e-mail messages users sent to system experts revealed that when seeking help, employees in medical departments were more likely to use verbal strategies to couch the request for help: They were more likely to be ingratiating toward the helper, be self-deprecating, and provide more details about the problem they were encountering (Lee, 1999).

Why would help seeking differ between employees in medical and surgical departments, even though the two departments existed within the same hospital, both departments were implementing the same new technology, and employees in both departments had relatively similar tasks? Lee (1997, 1999) argued that these differences emerged because medical and surgical departments had very different organizational norms. Specifically, surgical departments tend to have more individualist norms. In surgical departments, work procedures are more tightly controlled and roles explicitly differentiated such that there is little need for informal interaction among or between the health care providers (Berwick, Godfrey, & Roessner, 1990; Mercadier, 1985). Surgical doctors and nurses tend to work in a more solitary fashion, and spend relatively less time conferring with other nurses or physicians discussing patient care (Lee, 1997).

In contrast, medical departments are characterized by more collectivist norms. Within medical departments, health care providers tend to maintain closer working relations with each other and with other health care givers. For example, physicians and nurses in medicine rely more heavily on constant interactions among themselves to exchange information and obtain advice (Bosk, 1979; Edmondson, 1996; Payer, 1988). In medical departments, doctors and nurses seem to know each other well, and spend more time in informal conference with each other over work-related and non-work-related issues. It is common, for example, for a group of medical physicians and nurses to gather around informally to brainstorm about diagnosis, treatment issues, and other information and advice (Lee, 1997).

These results from the hospital were replicated in laboratory studies where norms were manipulated (Lee, 1997, 1999). In one study, undergraduate participants were asked to work with a partner on a very difficult task. Specifically, participants were asked to perform complex calculations to solve a business problem. Most participants did not have the technical know-how to complete the task, and even those who did would not have adequate time to complete the task. Participants were randomly assigned to individualist or collective norm conditions. In the individualist norm condition, participants were told that the individual with the best performance, regardless of his or her partner's performance, would receive a large monetary reward. Participants were also told that the experimenter could isolate and evaluate each individual's contribution to the task, such that an individual's performance and chance to win the reward were independent of his or her partner's. In contrast, participants in the collective norm condition were told that the team with the best performance would receive a large monetary reward. Participants were told that they would be evaluated as a team, and that each person's work could not be isolated.

Like the studies examining help seeking among medical and surgical employees, the laboratory studies found that participants in the collectivist norm condition were more likely to seek help, and sought help using more verbal strategies to couch the help seeking request (Lee, 1997, 1999). It appears from these studies that organizational norms, specifically norms of individualism and collectivism, affect whether and how individuals seek help.

Norms and Help Seeking Across Cultures and Ethnicity: Theory and Evidence

Individualist and collectivist norms not only operate at the level of a work team (such as dyads in a lab study) or departments (such as medical and surgical departments in a hospital) but also at the level of an entire culture, country, or ethnic group. In a large study, Hofstede (1980) classified 40 countries along the dimension of individualism and collectivism. Collectivist countries were generally in Asia, Latin America, and Africa, whereas individualist countries were generally in the West (e.g., the United States and Western Europe) (see also Markus & Kitayama, 1991).

These cultural differences in individualism and collectivism have implications for help seeking. Individualist norms at the cultural, national, or ethnic level discourage displays of inferiority, incompetence, and dependence. People from individualist cultures are motivated to seek individual achievement (McClelland, 1961), and behaviors that makes one appear or feel inferior, incompetent, and dependent are especially undesirable. As a result, people in these cultures are less likely to seek help when problems arise. In contrast, people from collectivist cultures work to satisfy the expectations of others (Markus & Kitayama, 1991). Collectivist cultures emphasize interdependence and collaboration between people. Individual need for achievement is low, and this motivation is often overshadowed by the motivation to promote the success of the group or team (Earley, 1993; Sagie, Elizur, & Yamauchi, 1996; Singelis, 1994; Triandis, Bontempo, Villareal, & Asai, 1988). Thus, appearing inferior, incompetent, and dependent is of less concerns for individuals in collectivist cultures. As a result, asking for help should be considered more appropriate and acceptable in collectivist cultures (like Japan) than in individualist cultures (like the United States). These relationships, illustrated in Fig. 6.1, are described in more detail next.

Dependence Versus Interdependence. As previously mentioned, when Perkin-Elmer was awarded the contract to build the Hubble Space Telescope, its employees refused to ask for help when problems emerged even though they had access to renowned optical engineers (Capers & Lipton, 1993). Their reluctance to seek help was in part caused by their refusal to appear dependent on outside experts (Lee, 1997). Dependence refers to the need to rely on others' input to accomplish a task that the help seeker cannot accomplish alone. Although Western cultures promote independence, many cultures around the world regard interdependence with others as a positive trait (Markus & Kitayama, 1991).

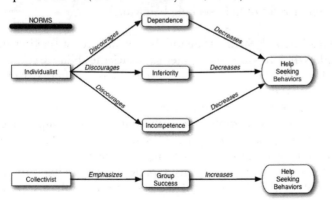

FIG. 6.1. Help seeking, or appearing dependent, incompetent, and inferior, in individualist and collectivist norms.

Asian, Latin American, and African cultures are characterized by an interdependent view of the self and emphasize harmonious interdependence and social harmony (Markus & Kitayama, 1991; Sanchez-Burks et al., 2000). For example, the Japanese recognize concepts like *amae*—a type of dependence—as a cultural ideal (Doi, 1973; Triandis, 1999). In fact, it is appropriate and desirable for Japanese students to depend on their teachers (Azuma, 1986). Shwalb and Sukemune (1998) noted that Japanese students routinely "beg for extra help before examinations" (p. 144). Japanese culture does not construe dependence in a negative light, and in fact encourages dependence in many relationships.

Japanese culture is not alone in its positive evaluation of interdependence. Mexican culture similarly emphasizes reciprocal dependence and a sense of duty among its core traits (Hofstede, 1980; Peck, 1967). In a comparison of family values between Mexican and American students, researchers found that Mexicans placed less emphasis on independence than American participants (Chia et al., 1994). Others suggested that this sense of interdependence emerges from the centrality of interdependent family relationships in Latin American culture (Gabrielidis, Stephan, Ybarra, Dos Santos-Pearson, & Villareal, 1997; Garcia, 1992; Vasquez, 1990).

Differences in the value of independence are apparent even within ethnic groups in the United States. Rotheram and Phinney (1987) suggested that African Americans have a more group-oriented culture that values collective efforts to achieve, and prefer collaboration to competition. Nelson-Le Gall and Resnick (1998) also suggested that African American children are socialized toward interrelatedness with others and collective responsibility. In short, African Americans are more likely to emphasize and encourage individuals to see themselves as dependent and intertwined with others.

Because dependence is not seen as inherently undesirable in collectivist cultures, and in fact these cultures encourage interdependence, seeking help from others should not elicit negative feelings. In fact, help seeking behaviors should be encouraged. Thus, we expect that collectivist cultures should have higher rates of help seeking behavior.

Incompetence Versus Effort. Individuals may also resist seeking help because it implies that they are incompetent and lack the ability to complete the task. The Hubble team at Perkin-Elmer refused to seek help because it would demonstrate their inability to solve problems on their own and display their skill gap. Yet cross-cultural research suggests that cultures with collectivist norms place less emphasis on inherent levels of competence or ability and more emphasis on effort. This may in turn decrease the negativity associated with appearances of incompetence.

For example, compared to Americans, Japanese are more likely to think that effort, not ability, is the source of success, and deemphasize performance evaluation (Holloway, 1988). In interviews of Chinese, Japanese, and American mothers, Stevenson et al. (1990) found that Chinese and Japanese mothers stressed the importance of hard work more than American mothers, whereas American mothers emphasized innate ability more than their East Asian counterparts. Chen and Stevenson (1995) found that Chinese and Japanese high school students were more likely than American students to believe that "studying hard" led to greater performance in mathematics than "having a good teacher." Within the American sample, Asian American students were more likely to endorse "studying hard" as the key to performance than Caucasian American students. Tobin, Wu, and Davidson (1989) found that 20% and 16% of Chinese and Japanese participants, respectively, believed children should learn perseverance at school, but only 5% of American participants thought so.

Similar trends were found in Latin American cultures. Compared to Americans, Mexican American adolescents were more likely to define sport success in terms of effort expended rather than ability (Duda, 1985). Yet as Mexican Americans acculturate to American culture, they are more likely to focus on performance ability and deemphasize effort (Ryska, 2001). In short, as the dominant cultural norm becomes more American and individualist, people value competence more heavily.

Heine et al. (2001) suggest that although individualist norms value self-enhancement, collectivist norms emphasize self-improvement. They found that in individualist cultures motivation increased after success, but motivation in collectivist cultures increased following failure. Individualists tend to see the self as largely stable and immutable (Heine et al., 2001; Dweck, Hong, & Chiu, 1993). This stable view of the self drives individuals to showcase their competence and leads individuals away from self-improvement because it would demonstrate areas of incompetence. Thus, people in cultures with individualist norms are more likely to avoid asking for help, for fear that they will be seen as incompetent.

In contrast, individuals in cultures with collectivist norms view the self as malleable. Failure to successfully accomplish a task, in this context, does not represent a threat to the self since with greater effort success may be possible (Heine et al., 2001). Individuals are therefore motivated to self-improve. This self-improvement motivation suggests that when an individual in collectivist culture encounters a problem, he or she is motivated to seek assistance to accomplish the task. Because individuals from collectivist cultures focus less on a person's innate ability, and consider effort and perseverance to be highly valued traits, those who ask for help in an attempt to solve a problem are seen as hard workers because they are expending extra effort to get the job done.

Inferiority Versus Collaboration. Help seeking can also make individuals feel inferior. For example, by seeking help from experts, engineers on the Hubble Space Telescope project implicitly acknowledge their inferiority to the experts. By seeking help, people in essence acknowledge the superior knowledge and skills of the help giver (Lee, 2002). However, norms found within collectivist cultures may alleviate the negativity associated with feeling inferior. Individuals in collectivist cultures are marked by their desire to foster strong communal bonds and group achievement rather than personal success (Triandis, 1999). Given the reduced emphasis on individual success and ability in collectivist cultures, feelings of inferiority that arise from help seeking should be less aversive.

In addition, concern for the group's goal of success may override concerns about personal success, prompting individuals to seek help to ensure the group succeeds (Earley, 1993). Seeking help in a collectivist culture might demonstrate to other members of the group that a person is concerned about the group's success and is willing to acknowledge a lack of knowledge and seek help in order to contribute.

Fear of appearing inferior may be further attenuated in cultures with collective norms because cooperation is emphasized over competition. Holloway (1988) found that Japanese families promote interpersonal collaboration and deemphasize competition. Mexican culture similarly places a large emphasis on collective needs and goals (Phinney, 1995), and Mexican American children are socialized to complete tasks using cooperative methods (Kagan, 1977). Furthermore, researchers found that although Anglo American children became more competitive with age, Mexican American children became more prosocial, endorsing the cooperative and equal disbursement of rewards (Garcia, 1992; Knight & Kagan, 1977).

The norms that emphasize collaborations in Asian and Latin cultures find their way into the school system as well. Research finds that African Americans, Latin American, and Asian students prefer collaborative classroom environments over competitive ones (Garcia, 1992; Rotheram & Phinney, 1987; Vasquez, 1990). For example, Losey (1995) reported that Mexican American children excelled in classrooms that emphasized reciprocity and collaboration and deemphasized competition. Specifically, in a comparison of cooperative learning and traditional learning, Lampe, Rooze, and Tallent-Runnels (1996) noted that Hispanic children who worked in groups, discussed the material with their group mates, and then reported to other classmates what they had learned, reported higher levels of achievement than students who had learned the material in the traditional individualist format. This emphasis on collaboration over competition in cultures with collectivist norms reduces the negativity associated with appearing inferior, thus promoting more help seeking.

Also, individuals from collectivist cultures may be more inclined to give help—creating an atmosphere that reduces people's hesitation to seek help.

For example, studies have shown that members of cooperative learning groups are more likely to help weaker group members, because they are working for a common goal (Singh, 1991). From a young age, Japanese children are taught to show empathy and sympathy to others, reinforcing the drive to help others (Lewis, 1995; Shwalb & Sukemune, 1998). Similarly Latin American cultures are characterized by the cultural trait of *simpatía,* which stresses social harmony, attending to the well-being and feelings of others, hospitality, and helping others (Levine, Norenzayan, & Philbrick, 2001; Sanchez-Burks et al., 2000; Triandis, Marin, Lisansky, & Betancourt, 1984).

In summary, cultures with collectivist norms emphasize group goals over personal success and collaborative values that encourage helping others. These actions should help create a climate in which individuals feel less avoidant about appearing inferior to others, and thus more willing to seek help from others. Help seeking can make a person appear inferior, incompetent, and dependent. In cultures with individualist norms, this can be highly undesirable. However, cultures with collectivist norms emphasize the connected nature of the self with others, role obligation, and self-improvement to meet the demands of the group. In this context, appearing inferior, incompetent, and dependent is less costly. In fact, help seeking demonstrates a desire to bring the self to a point that best serves the group in its goals, and may be considered a highly valued behavior.

CREATING COLLECTIVIST NORMS IN ORGANIZATIONAL SETTINGS

In this chapter, we argued that norms—individualist versus collectivist—affect whether and how individuals seek help. This has implications first for research in help seeking. Most studies on help seeking focus on domains with relatively individualist norms such as getting help about medical advice (Wills, 1983), performing experimental tasks in a laboratory setting (DePaulo, 1978), or obtaining technical information from engineers (Tyre & Ellis, 1993). All these domains emphasize individual performance and competence, embodying individualist norms. Given theory and evidence suggesting increased help-seeking frequency and more help-seeking strategies in collectivist norms, it might be the case that past research does not show a representative picture of help seeking.

Second, the research on norms and help seeking suggests that one way to increase help seeking behaviors is to change the norms of the social system. For example, Chatman and Barsade (1995) experimentally manipulated norms in work teams by informing team members that rewards were given to individuals (individualist norms) or to entire teams (collectivist norms). This might translate into practices that track the performance of teams rather than individuals, and reward bonuses and promotions to teams rather than individuals. Such practices are likely to facilitate collectivist norms and increase help seeking.

Teams can also be introduced into classrooms to create cooperative and collaborative learning environments that emphasize collectivist norms. Social interdependence, which exists when individuals share common goals and an individual's outcome is affected by the contribution of others, is the theoretical basis of cooperative learning and shares many similarities to collectivism (Deutsch, 1949). Cooperative learning emphasizes the complimentary nature of team members and foments positive interpersonal relationships (Johnson & Johnson, 1998). In a meta-analysis, Johnson and Johnson (1989) found that individuals in a cooperative learning environment performed better than those in a competitive or individualist setting. This might be due to increased help seeking behavior in a cooperative learning environment.

One particular cooperative classroom technique that increases cooperation and team effort is Elliot Aronson's "jigsaw classroom" (Aronson, 1978; Aronson & Patnoe, 1997). Aronson suggested teachers should arrange students to work in small interdependent groups where each child is given a particular task, a piece of the puzzle, which will reveal a complete picture when everyone has contributed their piece. Aronson and his colleagues demonstrated numerous benefits of the jigsaw classroom, such as increased interethnic liking and empathy, minority student achievement (without hampering majority student outcomes), interdependence among students, ability to see things from other students' perspectives, ability to see other students as resources, and willingness to seek help (Aronson & Bridgeman, 1979; Aronson, Bridgeman, & Geffner, 1978; Aronson & Patnoe, 1997).

The jigsaw classroom is an exemplar of collectivist norms, where students learn to rely on one another to complete projects and understand the material. They are less reluctant to ask questions because their peers are perceived as resources, not as competition. The team will only accomplish its goal if all the members are up to par. Team members complement one another, and students are motivated to seek help in order to learn and overcome challenges.

FUTURE DIRECTIONS: EXCHANGES BETWEEN EDUCATIONAL AND ORGANIZATIONAL PSYCHOLOGY

In this chapter, we integrated literature from the educational and organizational literatures to examine how norms affect help-seeking behaviors. Educational psychologists and organizational psychologists have much in common. Both organizational and educational psychologists are fundamentally interested in ways to increase learning, achievement, and performance within a particular social setting. The education literature primarily covers these processes during K–12 and college education, but there is comparatively little work on learning that continues after formal education has ended. The organizational literature, on the other hand, focuses on learning, achievement, and performance in business organizations and other work-related settings. Yet organizational psychologists often overlook schools, even though nearly all adults spent years in these organizations.

The two disciplines could learn from and contribute much to one another. Research from organizational studies can and should be applied to schools. For example, the organizational literature has examined the role that experimentation can play in creating new knowledge. Thomke (1998) described experimentation as a trial and error process that generates new knowledge and learning at every step. Not every attempt at solving the problem will result in success. These failures, however, are an integral part of reaching the final solution and hence are important for performance (Sitkin, 1992). The research shows that many organizations punish failure, which reduces an employees' desire to try novel tasks in the future (Gittell, 2000). Yet experimentation as a learning strategy has been relatively understudied in the educational literature even though this is a critical problem-solving skill in uncertain and new situations (Lee, Edmondson, Thomke & Worline, 2004).

Similarly, the educational literature has extensively focused on the role of performance and mastery goals on academic performance (Ames, 1992; Ames & Archer; 1988; Dweck & Elliott, 1983; Kaplan et al., 2002). Although performance goals emphasize demonstrating ability, mastery goals emphasize self-improvement. Goal orientation also has implications for organizations and job performance. Yet only recently has the organizational literature begun to look at the connection between goal orientation and job performance and satisfaction (e.g., Janssen & Van Yperen, 2004; Van Yperen & Janssen, 2002).

Overall, the fields of educational and organizational psychology have much to contribute to one another and to the literatures on performance, motivation, and learning. The theory and evidence we presented on help seeking provide one such synthesis, highlighting the important role norms play in shaping help-seeking behaviors in different types of social organizations. Specifically, we argued that individualist and collectivist norms differentially emphasize distinct qualities and traits that either encourage or discourage individuals from seeking help. By changing norms, both educators and business practitioners can develop specific interventions to increase help seeking in their classrooms or organizations.

REFERENCES

Ambady, N., Koo, J., Lee, F., & Rosenthal, R. (1996). More than words: Linguistic and nonlinguistic politeness in two cultures. *Journal of Personality and Social Psychology, 70,* 996–1011.

Ames, C. (1992). Classrooms: Goals, structures, and student motivation. *Journal of Educational Psychology, 84,* 261–271.

Ames, C., & Archer, J. (1988). Achievement goals in the classroom, students' learning strategies, and motivation processes. *Journal of Educational Psychology, 84,* 261–271.

Ames, R., & Lau, S. (1982). An attributional analysis of help-seeking in academic settings. *Journal of Educational Psychology, 74,* 414–423.

Aronson, E. (1978). *The jigsaw classroom.* Oxford, England: Sage.

Aronson, E., & Bridgeman, D. (1979). Jigsaw groups and the desegregated classroom: In pursuit of common goals. *Personality and Social Psychology Bulletin, 5,* 438–446.

Aronson, E., Bridgeman, D., & Geffner, R. (1978). Interdependent interactions and prosocial behavior. *Journal of Research and Development in Education, 12,* 16–27.

Aronson, E., & Patnoe, S. (1997). *The jigsaw classroom: Building cooperation in the classroom* (2nd ed.). New York: Addison, Wesley & Longman.

Azuma, H. (1996). Cross-national research: The Hess/Azuma collaboration. In D. Shwalb & B. Shwalb (Eds.), *Japanese childrearing: Two generations of scholarship* (pp. 220–240). New York: Guilford Press.

Berwick, D., Godfrey, A., & Roessner, J. (1990). *Curing health care: New strategies for quality improvement.* San Francisco: Jossey-Bass.

Bosk, C. (1979). *Forgive and remember: Managing medical failure.* Chicago: University of Chicago Press.

Brown, P., & Levinson, S. (1987). *Politeness: Some universals in language usage.* New York: Cambridge University Press.

Capers, B., & Lipton, C. (1993). Hubble error: Time, money and millionths of an inch. *Academy of Management Executive, 7*(4), 41–57.

Cartensen, L. L., Gottman, J. M., & Levenson, R. W. (1995). Emotional behavior in long-term marriage. *Psychology and Aging, 10,* 140–149.

Chatman, J., & Barsade, S. (1995). Personality, organizational culture, and cooperation. Evidence from a business simulation. *Administrative Science Quarterly, 40,* 423–443.

Chen, C., & Stevenson, H. W. (1995). Motivation and mathematics achievement: A comparative study of Asian-American, Caucasian-American and East Asian high school students. *Child Development, 66,* 1215–1234.

Chia, R. C., Wuensch, K. L., Childers, J., Chuang, C., Cheng, B., Cesar-Romero, J., & Nava, S. (1994). A comparison of family values among Chinese, Mexican, and American college students. *Journal of Social Behavior, 9*(2), 249–248.

Clark, H. H., & Schunk, D. (1980). Polite responses to polite requests. *Cognition, 8,* 111–143.

DePaulo, B. M. (1978). Accepting help from teachers: When teachers are children. *Human Relations, 11,* 41–53.

Deutsch, M. (1949). A theory of cooperation and competition. *Human Relations, 2,* 129–152.

Doi, T. (1973). *The anatomy of dependence.* Tokyo: Kodansha.

Druian, P. R., & DePaulo, B. M. (1977). Asking a child for help. *Social Behavior and Personality, 5,* 33–39.

Duda, J. L. (1985). Goals and achievement orientations of Anglo and Mexican-American adolescents in sport and the classroom. *International Journal of Intercultural Relations, 9,* 131–155.

Dweck, C. S., & Elliott, E. (1983). Achievement motivation. In P. Mussen (Ed.), *Handbook of child psychology, Vol. 4, Socialization, personality and social development* (pp. 643–691). New York: Wiley.

Dweck, C. S., Hong, Y., & Chiu, C. (1993). Implicit theories. Individual differences in the likelihood and meaning of dispositional inference. *Personality and Social Psychology Bulletin, 19,* 644–656.

Earley, P. C. (1993). East meets West meets Mideast: Further explorations of collectivistic and individualistic work groups. *Academy of Management Journal, 36,* 319–348.

Edmondson, A. (1996). Learning from mistakes is easier said than done: Group and organizational influences on the detection and correction of human error. *Journal of Applied Behavioral Science, 32,* 5–28.

Edmondson, A. (1999). Psychological safety and learning behavior in work teams. *Administrative Science Quarterly, 44,* 350–383.

Feldman, D. (1984). The development and enforcement of group norms. *Academy of Management Review, 9,* 47–53.

Festinger, L., Schachter, S., & Back, K. (1950). *Social pressures in informal groups: A study of human factors in housing.* New York: Harper & Brothers.

Gabrielidis, C., Stephan, W. G., Ybarra, O., Dos Santos-Pearson, V. M., & Villarel, L. (1997). Preferred styles of conflict resolution: Mexico and the United States. *Journal of Cross Cultural Psychology, 28,* 661–667.

Garcia, E. E. (1992). "Hispanic" children: Theoretical, empirical and related policy issues. *Educational Psychology Review, 4,* 69–94.

Gittell, J. H. (2000). Organizing work to support relational coordination. *International Journal of Human Resource Management, 11,* 517–539

Goffman, E. (1967). *Interaction ritual: Essays on face to face behavior.* Garden City, NY: Doubleday.

Gottman, J. M. (1979). *Martial interaction: Experimental investigations.* New York: Academic Press.

Hackman, J. R. (1992). Group influences on individuals in organizations. In M. D. Dunnette & L. M. Hough (Eds.), *Handbook of industrial and organizational psychology* (Vol. 3, 2nd ed., pp. 199–267). Palo Alto, CA: Consulting Psychology Press.

Hall, E. T. (1966). *The hidden dimension.* New York: Anchor/Doubleday.

Hallahan, M., Lee, F., & Herzog, T. (1997). It's not just whether you win or lose it is also where you play the game: Cross cultural differences in the positivity bias. *Journal of Cross Cultural Psychology, 28,* 768–778.

Heine, S. J., Kitayama, S., Lehman, D. R., Takata, T., Ide, E., Leung, C., & Matsumoto, H. (2001). Divergent consequences of success and failure in Japan and North America: An investigation of self-improving motivation and malleable selves. *Journal of Personality and Social Psychology, 81,* 599–615.

Hofstede, G. (1980). *Culture's consequences: International differences in work-related values.* Beverly Hills, CA: Sage.

Holloway, S. D. (1988). Concepts of ability and effort in Japan and the United States. *Review of Educational Research, 58,* 327–345.

Holtgraves, T., & Yang, J. (1990). Politeness as universal: Cross cultural perceptions of request strategies and inferences based on their use. *Journal of Personality and Social Psychology, 59,* 719–729.

Holtgraves, T., & Yang, J. (1992). Interpersonal underpinnings of request strategies: General principles and differences due to culture and gender. *Journal of Personality and Social Psychology, 62,* 246–256.

Jackson, J. (1965). Structural characteristics of norms. In I. D. Steiner & M. F. Fishbein (Eds.), *Current studies in social psychology* (pp. 301–309). New York: Holt, Rinehart, & Winston.

Janssen, O., & Van Yperen, N. W. (2004). Employees' goal orientations, the quality of leader-member exchange, and the outcomes of job performance and satisfaction. *Academy of Management Journal, 47,* 368–384.

Johnson, D. W., & Johnson R. T. (1989). *Cooperation and competition: Theory and research.* Edina, MN: Interaction Book Company.

Johnson, D. W., & Johnson, R. T. (1998). Cooperative learning and social interdependence theory. In R. S. Tindale, L. Heath, J. Edwards, E. J. Posavac, F. B. Bryant, Y. Suarez-Balcazar, E. Henderson-King, & J. Myers (Eds.), *Theory and research on small groups* (pp. 9–35). New York: Plenum.

Kagan, S. (1977). Social motives and behaviors of Mexican-American and Anglo-American children. In J. L. Martinez (Ed.), *Chicano psychology* (pp. 45–86). New York: Academic Press.

Kaplan, A., Middleton, M. J., Urdan, T., & Midgley, C. (2002). Achievement goals and goal structures. In C. Midgley (Ed.), *Goals, goal structures and patterns of adaptive learning* (pp. 85–108). Mahwah, NJ: Lawrence Erlbaum Associates.

Karabenick, S. A., & Knapp, J. R. (1988). Help seeking and the need for academic assistance. *Journal of Educational Psychology, 80,* 406–408.

Karabenick, S. A., & Sharma, R. (1994). Perceived teacher support of student questioning in the college classroom: Its relation to student characteristics and role in the classroom questioning process. *Journal of Educational Psychology, 86,* 90–103.

Kennedy, E. (1997). A study of students' fears of seeking academic help from teachers. *Journal of Classroom Interaction, 32,* 11–17.

Knight, G. P., & Kagan, S. (1977). Development of prosocial and competitive behaviors in Anglo-American and Mexican-American children. *Child Development, 48,* 1385–1394.

Lampe, J. R., Rooze, G. E., & Tallent-Runnels, M. (1996). Effects of cooperative learning among Hispanic students in elementary social studies. *Journal of Educational Research, 89,* 187–191.

Lee, F. (1997). When the going gets tough, do the tough ask for help? Help seeking and power motivation in organizations. *Organizational Behavior and Human Decision Processes, 72,* 336–363.

Lee, F. (1999). Verbal strategies for seeking help in organizations. *Journal of Applied Social Psychology, 29,* 1472–1496.

Lee, F. (2002). The social costs of seeking help. *The Journal of Applied Behavioral Science, 38,* 17–35.

Lee, F., Caza, A., Edmondson, A., & Thomke, S. (2003). New knowledge creation in organizations. In K. S. Cameron, J. E. Dutton, & R. E. Quinn (Eds.), *Positive organizational scholarship: Foundations of a new discipline* (pp. 194–206). San Francisco: Barrett-Koehler.

Lee, F., Edmondson, A., Thomke, S., & Worline, M. (2004). The mixed effects of inconsistency on experimentation in organizations. *Organization Science, 15,* 310–326.

Lee, F., Teich, J., Spurr, C., & Bates, D. (1996). Implementation of physician order entry: User satisfaction and usage patterns. *Journal of the American Medical Informatics Association, 3,* 42–55.

Lee, Y., & Duenas, G. (1995). Stereotype accuracy in multicultural business. In Y. Lee, L. J. Jussim, & C. R. McCauley (Eds.), *Stereotype accuracy: Towards appreciating group differences* (pp. 157–186). Washington, DC: American Psychological Association.

Levine, R. V., Norenzayan, A., & Philbrick, K. (2001). Cross-cultural helping of strangers. *Journal of Cross Cultural Psychology, 32,* 543–560

Lewis, C. C. (1995). *Educating hearts and minds: Reflections on Japanese preschool and elementary education.* Cambridge, England: Cambridge University Press.

Losey, K. M. (1995). Mexican American students and classroom interaction: An overview and critique. *Review of Educational Research, 65,* 283–318.

Markman, E. M. (1977). Realizing that you don't understand: A preliminary investigation. *Child Development, 48,* 986–992.

Markus, H., & Kitayama, S. (1991). Culture and the self: Implications for cognition, emotion, and motivation. *Psychological Review, 98,* 224–253.

McClelland, D. C. (1961). *The achieving society.* Princeton, NJ: D. Van Nostrand.

Mercadier, M. (1985). Surgery: an international discipline. *American Journal of Surgery, 150,* 237–238.

Morrison, E. W. (1993). Newcomer information seeking: Exploring types, modes, sources, and outcomes. *Academy of Management Journal, 36,* 557–589.

Nelson-Le Gall, S., & Resnick, L. (1998). Help seeking, achievement motivation, and the social practice of intelligence of school. In S. A. Karabenick (Ed.), *Strategic help seeking: Implications for learning and teaching* (pp. 39–60). Mahwah, NJ: Lawrence Erlbaum Associates.

Newman, R. (1994). Adaptive help seeking: A strategy of self-regulated learning. In D. Schunk & B. Zimmerman (Eds.), *Self-regulation of learning and performance: issues and educational applications* (pp. 283–301). Hillsdale, NJ: Lawrence Erlbaum Associates.

Newman, R. S. (1998). Students' help seeking during problem solving: Influences of personal and contextual achievement goals. *Journal of Educational Psychology, 90,* 644–658.

Newman, R., & Goldin, L. (1990). Children's reluctance to seek help with schoolwork. *Journal of Educational Psychology, 82,* 92–100.

O'Reilly, C., & Chatman, J. (1996). Culture as social control: Corporations, cults, and commitment. *Research in Organizational Behavior, 18,* 157–200.

Orlikowski, W. (1992). Learning from notes: Organizational issues in groupware implementation. *The Information Society, 9,* 237–250.

Payer, L. (1988). *Medicine and culture.* New York: Henry Holt.

Peck, R. (1967). A comparison of the value systems of Mexican and American youth. *Revista Interamericana de Psicología, 1,* 41–50.

Phinney, J. S. (1995). Ethnic identity and self-esteem: A review and integration. In A. M. Padilla (Ed.), *Hispanic psychology: Critical issues in theory and research* (pp. 57–70). Thousand Oaks, CA: Sage.

Rhee, E., Uleman, J., & Lee, H. (1995). Spontaneous self-descriptions and ethnic identities in individualistic and collectivistic cultures. *Journal of Personality and Social Psychology, 69*(1), 142–152.

Rotheram, M. J., & Phinney, J. S. (1987). Ethnic behavior patterns as an aspect of identity. In J. S. Phinney & M. J. Rotheram (Eds.), *Children's ethnic socialization: Pluralism and development* (pp. 180–200). Newbury Park, CA: Sage.

Ryan, A. M., Gheen, M., & Midgley, C. (1998). Why do some students avoid asking for help? An examination of the interplay among students' academic efficacy, teacher's social-emotional role and classroom goal structure. *Journal of Educational Psychology, 90,* 528–535.

Ryan, A. M., & Hicks, L., & Midgley, C. (1997). Social goals, academic goals, and avoiding seeking help in the classroom. *Journal of Early Adolescence, 17,* 152–171.

Ryan, A. M., & Pintrich, P. R. (1997). Should I ask for help?: The role of motivation and attitudes in adolescents' help seeking in math class. *Journal of Educational Psychology, 89,* 329–341.

172   SANDOVAL AND LEE

Ryan, A. M., Pintrich, P. R., & Midgley, C. (2001). Avoiding seeking help in the class-room: Who and why? *Educational Psychology Review, 13*(2), 93–114.
Ryska, T. A. (2001). The impact of acculturation on sport motivation among Mexican-American adolescent athletes. *Psychological Record, 51,* 533–547.
Sagie, A., Elizur, D., & Yamauchi, H. (1996). The structure and strength of achievement motivation. A cross-cultural comparison. *Journal of Organizational Behavior, 17,* 431–444.
Sanchez-Burks, J. (2002). Protestant relational ideology and (in)attention to relational cues in work settings. *Journal of Personality and Social Psychology, 83,* 919–929.
Sanchez-Burks, J., Lee, F., Choi, I., Nisbett, R. E., Zhao, S & Koo, J. (2003). Conversing across cultures: East-West communication styles in work and non-work contexts. *Journal of Personality and Social Psychology, 85*(2), 363–372.
Sanchez-Burks, J., Nisbett, R. E., & Ybarra, O. (2000). Cultural styles, relationship schemas, and prejudice against out-groups. *Journal of Personality and Social Psychology, 79,* 174–189.
Schein, E. H. (1968). Organizational socialization and the profession of management. *Industrial Management Review, 9,* 1–15.
Schein, E. H. (1990). Organizational culture. *American Psychologist, 45,* 109–119.
Schein, E. H. (1993). *Organizational culture and leadership.* New York: Random House.
Schein, E. H. (1996). Culture: The missing concept in organization studies. *Administrative Science Quarterly, 41,* 229–240.
Shwalb, D. W., & Sukemune, S. (1998). Help seeking in the Japanese college classroom: Cultural, developmental, and social-psychological influences. In S. A. Karabenick (Ed.), *Strategic help seeking: Implications for learning and teaching* (pp. 141–170). Mahwah, NJ: Lawrence Erlbaum Associates.
Singelis, T. M. (1994). The measurement of independent and interdependent self-construals. *Personality and Social Psychology Bulletin, 20,* 580–591.
Singh, B. R. (1991). Teaching methods for reducing prejudice and enhancing academic achievement for all children. *Educational Studies, 17,* 157–171.
Sitkin, S. B. (1992). Learning through failure: The strategy of small loses. *Research on Organizational Behavior, 14,* 231–266.
Stevenson, H. W., Lee, S., Chen, C., Stigler, J. W., Hsu, C., Kitamura, S., & Hatano, G. (1990). Contexts of achievement: A study of America, Chinese, and Japanese children. *Monographs of the Society for Research in Child Development, 55,* 1–119.
Thomke, S. (1998). Managing experimentation in the design of new products. *Management Science, 44,* 743–762.
Ting-Toomey, S. (1988). Intercultural conflict styles: A face-negotiation theory. In Y. Y. Kim & W. B. Gudykunst (Eds.), *Theories in intercultural communication* (pp. 213–238). Newbury Park, CA: Sage.
Tobin, J. J., Wu, D. Y. H., & Davidson, D. H. (1989). *Preschool in three cultures: Japan, China and the United States.* New Haven, CT: Yale University Press.
Triandis, H. C. (1989). The self and social behavior in different cultural contexts. *Psychological Review, 96,* 506–520.
Triandis, H. C. (1997, May). *Deception during negotiations in cross-cultural perspective.* Paper presented at the 9th Annual Conference of the American Psychological Society, Washington, DC.
Triandis, H. C. (1999). Cross-cultural psychology. *Asian Journal of Social Psychology, 2,* 127–143.
Triandis, H. C., & Suh, E. M. (2002). Cultural influences on personality. *Annual Review of Psychology, 53,* 133–160.

Triandis, H. C., Bontempo, R., Villareal, M. J., & Asai, M. (1988). Individualism and collectivism: Cross-cultural perspectives on self and group relationships. *Journal of Personality and Social Psychology, 54,* 323–338.

Triandis, H. C., Marin, G., Lisansky, J., & Betancourt, H. (1984). *Simpatía* as a cultural script of Hispanics. *Journal of Personality and Social Psychology, 47,* 1363–1375.

Triandis, H. C., McCusker, C., & Hui, C. H. (1990). Multimethod probes of individualism and collectivism. *Journal of Personality and Social Psychology, 59,* 1006–1020.

Tyre, M., & Ellis, S. (1993, August). *Determinants of helping and help-seeking among developers and users of new technologies.* Paper presented at the 53rd Academy of Management Conference, Atlanta, GA.

Uleman, J. S., Rhee, E., Bardoliwalla, N., Semin, G., & Toyama, M. (2000). The relational self: Closeness to ingroups depends on who they are, culture, and the type of closeness. *Asian Journal of Cultural Psychology, 3,* 1–17.

Van Yperen, N. W., & Janssen, O. (2002). Fatigued and dissatisfied or fatigued and satisfied? Goal orientations and responses to high job demands. *Academy of Management Journal, 45,* 1161–1171.

Vasquez, J. A. (1990). Teaching to the distinctive traits of minority students. *The Clearing House, 63,* 299–304.

Wills, T. A. (1983). Social comparison in coping and help seeking. In B. DePaulo, A. Nadler, & J. Fisher (Eds.), *New directions in helping* (Vol. 2, pp. 109–141). New York: Academic Press.

Help Seeking and the Role of Academic Advising in Higher Education

Louise R. Alexitch
University of Saskatchewan

In a study of senior undergraduate students' experiences, Alexitch (1999) noted that a considerable number of students expressed regret about the choices they had made concerning their academic courses and programs. They felt that if they had been better informed about what to expect in their particular programs of study, their decisions and outcomes would have been different:

> I would have liked to know what was available to me and the [grade point average] needed for graduate school upon my first year so that I had a better understanding of what to expect of the programs and of myself. As you can see, it may be too late for me because my grades are well below what is expected to be accepted into graduate school.

> I went into Engineering at first with some pretty high hopes only to realize that this was not for me.... I found myself very unprepared for the big jump from living at home and going to high school to living on my own and trying to keep up with the demands of first-year Engineering. Eventually, I burned out from stress and decided to pursue another field of study that interested me. Because of my time in Engineering, my grades and my self-esteem took a hard blow.

These students (and others like them) indicated that although they were aware of the existence of academic advisors, they had not sought advice on planning their undergraduate education, on developing better academic skills, or on coping with academic demands. It seemed that even after they had begun to experience difficulties, they still had not sought out help from faculty or campus services. As a result, their educational experience and academic performance suffered. The findings of this study raise a number of questions. What factors prevent students from seeking the help that they need? For those students who do seek help, what types of advice do they prefer? Who are the most effective help providers? What can we, as educators and researchers, do to encourage students in higher education to seek guidance when they need it?

Research examining the needs of students in higher education settings (e.g., Alexitch, 1997; Andrews, Andrews, Long, & Henton, 1987; Ender, Winston, & Miller, 1984; Tinsley, de St. Aubin, & Brown, 1982) has revealed that college students seek help on a wide range of issues and topics. They may need advice on identifying their educational aspirations and career goals, on dealing with academic challenges, and on more specific aspects of their academic life such as course selection and meeting institutional requirements (Alexitch, 1994; Holdaway & Kelloway, 1987). Furthermore, this advice may be provided to students in class and out of class by many people (e.g., faculty, peer counselors). In a broad sense, this form of help seeking, which includes some or all of these aspects, is often referred to as *academic advising*.

This chapter focuses on the role of academic advising for students in college and university settings. The chapter is organized into four sections: (a) the nature of academic advising, (b) the characteristics and needs of students who seek academic advising, (c) the providers of academic advising and their effectiveness, and (d) recommendations for improving academic advising in postsecondary institutions.

NATURE OF ACADEMIC ADVISING

Academic advising has been associated with increased student retention (Gallagher & Allen, 2000; McGillin, 2000; Pascarella, 1986), greater satisfaction with college (Frost, 1995; Metzner, 1989), perceiving a college education as important (Metzner, 1989), and better academic performance (Frost, 1995; Kramer, 2000; Metzner, 1989). These findings clearly emphasize the importance of academic advising on students' academic, personal, and career development, making it a crucial form of help provided to postsecondary students. But what is it about academic advising that can have such an effect on students?

What is Academic Advising?

According to Ender et al. (1984), *academic advising* may be defined as *a continuous process, based on repeated contact between a student and advisor, where the student is helped in achieving educational, career, and personal goals.* The relationship with an advisor, ideally, should help a student to acquire the skills and attitudes that will promote intellectual and personal growth. Ender and his colleagues (1984) distinguished academic advising from brief sessions with students that primarily serve an administrative function, which may occur once in a semester (or less often). Indeed, academic advising should not be viewed by the student (or others) as something extra to the process of obtaining an education, but should be considered an integral part of helping a student achieve academic and personal success (Ender et al., 1984).

Similarly, Creamer (2000) considered academic advising to be a form of teaching where the focus is on student academic and personal development, involving the active participation of both the student and advisor. The student should be motivated to make choices based on some self-understanding, and to make use of the opportunities and resources available. This characterization of a student as an active agent in his or her education is closely related to what many researchers (e.g., Karabenick, 2003; Newman, 2000; Zimmerman & Martinez-Pons, 1988) would refer to as a self-regulated learner. The advisor helps students in reaching decisions by integrating information about the institution's programs and resources, and by being sensitive to a student's needs and maturation level.

The academic advising described by Ender et al. (1984) and Creamer (2000) is consistent with the developmental–prescriptive continuum model of academic advising proposed by Crookston (1972). At the *developmental* end of the continuum, the student–advisor relationship is a collaborative relationship, in which the advisor encourages the development of decision-making skills and independence in the student. The advisor's goal is to help the student integrate different aspects of the college experience without focusing solely on academic requirements. Frost (1995) noted that students who had received developmental academic advising were more motivated to succeed, showed greater academic achievement, and took a more active role in planning their academic and career futures. In contrast, a *prescriptive* student–advisor relationship is more directive and unidirectional. Information flows from the advisor to the student, the advice given is more concrete and short-term oriented, and there is an emphasis on outcome (usually academic performance or meeting institutional requirements) rather than on the process of learning.

Developmental and prescriptive academic advising may be considered analogous to adaptive and nonadaptive forms of help seeking observed in classrooms. As with developmental academic advising, in *adaptive help seek-*

ing, the student takes an active role in his or her learning and academic outcomes (Arbreton; 1998; Newman, 1998). For example, the student may ask a course instructor, peer, or other individual for the principles needed to solve a problem, giving him or her the opportunity to develop and practice skills that may be useful for similar problems in the future. In *nonadaptive help seeking,* however, as in prescriptive academic advising, the student is a passive agent, where he or she may ask others to simply provide a solution to a problem. Thus, there is little chance for the student to develop complex strategies for learning and independent mastery, and he or she becomes increasingly dependent on others when problems arise (Karabenick & Knapp, 1991; Newman, 1998).

Is Developmental Academic Advising for Everyone?

Based on the outcome of students who receive developmental versus prescriptive advising, there is general agreement among educators and researchers that developmental advising is preferable to prescriptive advising (Creeden, 1990; Crookston, 1972; Frost, 1991a). In fact, as Table 7.1 shows, the goals of academic advising that are used by National Academic Advising Association (1994) reflect the central features of developmental advising (Habley, 2000).

There is some evidence, however, to indicate that developmental advising may not be suitable to, or even desired by, all students (Alexitch, 1997; Andrews et al., 1987; Fielstein, Scoles, & Webb, 1992). For example, Fielstein et al. (1992) found that students rated the importance of prescriptive advice (e.g., information about course selection, help with enrollment) higher than that of developmental advice (e.g., receiving encouragement, help with developing academic skills). Overall, students' preferences for advising have been found to differ on the basis of gender, age, personality, and previous experience with advising (Alexitch, 1997; Andrews et al., 1987).

The results of studies concerning students' views about particular types of advising led some to question how academic advising is conceptualized, and what developmental academic advising actually entails. Some researchers (e.g., Andrews et al., 1987; Fielstein, et al., 1992; McGillin, 2000) proposed that academic advising may not be unidimensional, but may occur along two independent dimensions: one reflecting person-centered activities such as helping students define their interests and goals, and the second reflecting information-centered activities such as managing and monitoring paperwork related to students' academic progress. Alexitch (1997) found that some students were more concerned with *how* their advisor counseled them (developmental vs. prescriptive), whereas other students were more concerned with *what* was discussed during advising sessions. Again, there seems to be more than one dimension in the con-

TABLE 7.1

Goals of Academic Advisors

Help students to value the learning process and to take full advantage of the knowledge offered by faculty and their academic program, and help students understand the process of applying what they learn to everyday situations.

Review and integrate available information about students' academic needs, performance, aspirations, and difficulties so that students can develop an educational plan that is suited to their abilities, needs, and goals.

Encourage self-reliance in students by helping them to make informed and responsible decisions, to set realistic goals, and to be honest with themselves, concerning their education, career, and lives.

Reinforce students' self-direction by helping students to accomplish the goals and objectives that they have set for themselves, and to identify barriers that may hinder students' progress toward achieving their goals.

Make students aware of, and refer students to, others who can assist students in diverse areas such as admissions, financial aid, housing, health services, special educational needs, course selection, and satisfaction of academic requirements.

Note. Adapted from Habley (2000) and NACADA (1994).

struction of academic advising: one pertaining to mode of delivery or advising style, and the second pertaining to the content or information provided by advising.

Recently, other issues have also surfaced concerning academic advising: how it can be assessed for effectiveness, to what extent advisors should provide information about careers or help with personal problems in addition to providing support for academic development, and who the best individuals are to provide this type of help to students.[1] Despite the debate about the nature of academic advising, the developmental–prescriptive model of advising remains widely accepted. Furthermore, given that the main goals of developmental advising are to help students become self-motivated learners and to achieve their academic potential (Crookston, 1972; Grites & Gordon, 2000), it is still desirable for advisors to try to establish a developmental advising relationship with students. In order to better understand the role of academic advising in higher education, the next section discusses how the students' needs, motivational orientations, and perceptions of help seeking may be related to their general help-seeking tendencies and to their use of academic advising in particular.

---

[1]For a more comprehensive discussion of issues in academic advising, see Gordon, Habley, and Associates (2000).

USERS OF ACADEMIC ADVISING

In the last 30 years, colleges and universities in North America have seen many changes in their student populations (Association of Universities and Colleges of Canada, 1996; Astin, 2000; Upcraft & Stephens, 2000). For example, although the numbers of both men and women enrolled in postsecondary institutions have increased, the rate of increase for women has been more pronounced than that of men. Women now make up the majority of students pursuing undergraduate degrees (Astin, 2000; Statistics Canada, 2003). In addition, there are now more individuals entering college and university later in life (aged 25 years or more) or pursuing degrees on a part-time basis than was typical 20 years ago (Association of Universities and Colleges of Canada, 1996; Upcraft & Stephens, 2000). With respect to ethnic minorities, Upcraft and Stephens (2000) reported that in 1986 ethnic minority students made up 17.9% of the total student enrollment in the United States, but by 1996 the proportion had increased to 25.2%.

With changes in the demographics of the student population have come changes in students' aspirations concerning higher education. For instance, there were more women in the 1990s who expressed an interest in pursuing a graduate level degree than there were in the 1960s; however, the number of men aspiring to higher level degrees was consistent (or had dropped) during the same time period (Astin, 2000). There have also been shifting patterns in the disciplines that students choose to study. Science-based fields such as biology and computer science increased in popularity, whereas there was declining interest in the social sciences, humanities, and teaching (Association of Universities and Colleges of Canada, 1996; Astin, 2000). In addition, students now tend to espouse values that are more materialistic, career-oriented, and utilitarian (Alexitch, 1994; Astin, 2000; Holdaway & Kelloway, 1987). In surveys of incoming students conducted between 1966 and 1996, Astin and his colleagues noted that most students in the 1960s wanted to "develop a meaningful philosophy of life." By the 1990s, however, most students reported that they wanted to be "very well off financially" and that a major benefit of attending college is to "increase one's earning power" (Astin, 2000).

The greater diversity of students and the shifts in their attitudes concerning higher education has important implications for the help that students may need from advisors. For example, a student who is entering a university after being away from school for several years may have clear academic and vocational goals, but may require help with basic academic tasks (e.g., taking notes during lectures, studying for tests). On the other hand, a student who has entered a university directly after high school may need advice on planning his or her educational path and on identifying career interests.

Students' Academic Advising Needs

Several studies (e.g., Sagaria, Higginson, & White, 1980; Weissberg, Berentsen, Coté, Cravey, & Heath, 1982) have found consistently that nonuniversity-related concerns (e.g., social difficulties) are ranked lower in importance by students than are educational or career-related issues. In a needs assessment study conducted with undergraduate students at the University of Georgia, Weissberg et al. (1982) found that students rated the need for career development (e.g., exploring job opportunities, obtaining work experience) more strongly than either academic or personal concerns. The highest ranked academic needs dealt with improving basic academic skills (e.g., study skills, writing), meeting teachers' expectations more effectively, and getting more help from advisors. Similarly, Holdaway and Kelloway (1987) noted that first-year students had difficulty adjusting to the academic workload, the method of instruction, and the expectations of teaching staff, and that many students ended up performing below what they had expected.

The difficulties expressed by the students in these studies are not uncommon and may predict the help students want and expect to receive from academic advisors. The picture, however, becomes more complex when factors such as a student's gender, age, enrollment year, and previous academic experiences are taken into consideration when providing help to a student. For example, in examining the advising needs of undergraduate students, Andrews et al. (1987) found that students who expressed a high need for academic information (e.g., program requirements) from an advisor tended to be younger and more emotionally expressive. In addition, students who were performing poorly expressed a need for personal support (nonacademic help), as well as academic support, from an advisor. In a similar vein, Alexitch (1997) found that students' gender, grades, and satisfaction with previous academic advising were associated with their preferences for advising. Female students preferred a higher level of developmental advising than did male students. Students with lower grades also preferred a more developmental style of advising and wanted more help with basic academic skills (e.g., time management, study skills) than students who had higher grades.

Recent research (e.g., Alexitch, 1999; Kramer, 2000) noted that enrollment year is a crucial factor in determining students' advising needs. That is, students' needs for help in academic, vocational, and personal areas change as they progress through their academic program. This is not surprising, because students are met with different challenges as they move along their educational path, necessitating that they make decisions about the different choices they encounter. As was seen in the Holdaway and Kelloway (1987) study, the issues expressed by the first-year students were concerned with adjusting to, and becoming familiar with, a new academic environment. Alexitch (1999) also noted that incoming students needed help planning their academic program, identifying their interests and goals, and assessing their expectations, whereas senior students indicated that they needed help with making career and postgraduate decisions.

Who Seeks Academic Advising?

Academic advisors can provide undergraduate students with a great deal of guidance and direction in planning their education and their future careers. Unfortunately, although students may acknowledge the importance of receiving advising and meeting with an academic advisor, many do not do so voluntarily—and by their senior year, may even express regrets at not having sought such help (Alexitch, 1999). In a survey of students' use of advising, Creeden (1990) found that 34% of students had not met with an advisor at all, and that even by their senior year, only 19% of students reported having met with an advisor three or more times in their undergraduate career. But why do so few students seek help from academic advisors? What factors determine whether a student seeks academic advising or not?

Students' expectations concerning academic help may be one factor (Alexitch, 2002; Ames & Lau, 1982; Gloria, Hird, & Navarro, 2001; Grayson, Miller, & Clark, 1998; Ryan & Pintrich, 1997). In examining help seeking by college students prior to a major examination, Ames and Lau (1982) found that students were more likely to attend scheduled review sessions if they were given positive information about the review sessions, leading students to expect that the sessions would be useful for their upcoming exam. Of course, expectations about the help available in a given environment may also be shaped by prior experiences with those help providers (Alexitch, 1997; Creeden, 1990). For instance, Alexitch (1997) found that students' prior experience with academic advisors was a significant predictor of their preferences for future academic advising. If those prior experiences with an academic advisor are negative or perceived by students as not useful, it is unlikely they would return for further sessions. At times, dissatisfaction may result from advising sessions not covering the issues (e.g., graduate school, career development) that students' expect to discuss (Creeden, 1990).

These findings, however, do not fully explain why some students who have had little or no experience with seeking help in an academic environment may avoid asking for help even when they are experiencing difficulty. You may recall the experiences of the two students cited at the beginning of the chapter: Even after they encountered significant problems, they did not go to an academic advisor or other campus help provider, but instead tried to manage by changing their goals and lowering their expectations. The result was feelings of regret and a reduction in self-esteem. Beliefs about academic ability, attributions concerning performance, and motivation may affect a student's decision on seeking help. For example, students who believe in their ability to perform better academically, and who feel that their performance can be improved by expending greater effort on an academic task are more likely to seek help when faced with poor performance (Ames & Lau, 1982).

Cultural background, gender, and age also have been identified as playing a significant part in students' attitudes toward seeking help and in their help-seeking behavior. For example, students from minority groups encounter challenges in addition to those faced by the majority of students. They may enter college or university without the requisite academic background, with less support in their home environment, and lacking familiarity with the social and cultural environment of the institution (Frost, 1991a; Nora & Cabrera, 1996). Minority students may end up feeling isolated and out of place, leading them to question their academic abilities and their decision to attend college (Frost, 1991a; Rendon, Jalomo, & Nora, 2000). It is especially problematic for a student if these feelings of academic inferiority are consistent with a stereotype about his or her minority group (Steele, 1997), as in associating African Americans with poor academic ability. Ethnic minority students may avoid seeking help and advice, feeling that this would only emphasize their "different" status, and further confirm their views (and those of others) about their ability to succeed academically (Gloria et al., 2001; Steele, 1997).

Gloria et al. (2001) examined students' gender and culture in relation to attitudes about seeking academic help and psychological counseling in a university environment. The researchers noted that both degree of cultural congruity (i.e., how similar the student's culture was to that espoused by the institution and its staff) and gender were significant contributors to attitudes about help seeking. White students had more positive attitudes about help seeking than did ethnic minority students (i.e., African American, Asian American, Hispanic). The latter students reported more negative perceptions of the university environment, and felt that the help services provided by the university would not reflect or respect their cultural values. In addition, females reported more positive help-seeking attitudes overall than did males, and cultural congruity with a help provider was a more important consideration for females than it was for males. Gloria et al. (2001) suggested that cultural elements may have more influence on the educational, psychological, and social development of female students than of male students.

The Gloria et al. (2001) findings are consistent with those of other studies (e.g., Ames & Lau, 1982; Daubman & Lehman, 1993), in that male students tend to have a more negative view about seeking academic help, and view the consequences of help seeking differently than do female students. Men may view help seeking as a threat to their self-esteem and a confirmation of a lack of ability, whereas women may not see receiving (or even seeking) help from others in such a negative light. As a result, men may be less likely to seek help when they need it than would women (Alexitch, 2002; Ames & Lau, 1982; Daubman & Lehman, 1993; Gloria et al., 2001). In a study of junior undergraduates, Daubman and Lehman (1993) found that men who received help from peers worked less hard, and consequently performed more poorly on a subsequent task, than those who did not receive help. On the other hand, women who received help performed better on a subsequent task than women who did not receive help. Interestingly, all students in this study viewed their help partner favorably, but receiving help clearly had different effects on the task performance and time spent on subsequent tasks of men and women. Thus, the adverse effects on performance may not be due to negative views of the help provider, but rather to the threat to self-esteem that results from having received assistance (Ames & Lau, 1982; Karabenick & Knapp, 1991).

What implications do attitudes and expectations concerning help have for academic advising in higher education? Are men less likely than women to seek out an academic advisor? Does viewing help as a threat to one's self-image also mean that a student will not voluntarily meet with an academic advisor? Alexitch (2002) examined how the threat of seeking help and prior academic performance were related to help-seeking behavioral tendencies and preferences for developmental academic advising. Students who reported poor academic performance or who viewed help seeking as a threat were more likely to endorse nonadaptive strategies for dealing with their academic problems (e.g., dropping courses), were less likely to seek help from others, and preferred less developmental academic advising.

Grayson et al. (1998) conducted a series of qualitative interviews with a small group of university students to obtain students' accounts of seeking advice from academic instructors. In particular, the researchers were interested in students' attitudes about seeking academic help and in determining what students felt prevented them from approaching faculty for help. Students reported that they sometimes avoided seeking help from instructors because they were afraid that others might view them negatively (e.g., impact on their relationships with members of the department) or that they might view themselves negatively. Some students also indicated that they had considered the consequences for the help provider in their decisions to seek advice (e.g., they did not want to waste the time of the instructor). Grayson et al. (1998), however, also found that students' attitudes about seeking advice from faculty depended on the type of problem that the students were experiencing. If students needed help with course work (e.g., clarifying concepts or topics), they were less reluctant to seek help and saw it as less of a threat. If the problem, however, was related to academic motivation (e.g., how to manage one's academic work) or dealt with more serious or broader issues (e.g., progress in one's academic career), then they were more reluctant to seek help.

The results of Grayson et al. (1998) and those of others (e.g., Tinsley, Brown, de St. Aubin, & Lucek, 1984) suggest that students' perceptions of the academic environment, and the roles within it, can affect their help-seeking behaviors. For example, students may feel that getting help for course work from instructors is acceptable and "normal." Instructors communicate that students are expected to seek assistance for course-related matters by setting office hours and inviting students to discuss course content, tests, or assignments. Furthermore, Grayson et al. (1998) speculated that seeking help for general academic problems is more threatening because it may be viewed by the help provider that the student should not be in the university, whereas seeking help for specific issues related to a course does not necessarily reflect a student's overall academic ability. All of this implies that students do not understand the larger role that faculty (and other academic advisors) can play in helping them to address broader academic, career, and personal issues. Unfortunately, it is these very issues that can have a significant impact on students' experiences in college and the likelihood that they will complete their education.

Motivational Orientation in Seeking Academic Advising

Motivational orientation has been related to students' intentions to seek help, the type of help that they seek, and when (or if) students choose to seek help in an academic setting. Simply put, *motivational orientation* may be described as the approach that a student takes to learning, which includes a student's views about the purpose of education and the goals that he or she feels can be accomplished by being academically successful. Students may adopt an intrinsic motivational orientation to learning that is characterized by a desire to be intellectually challenged, an enjoyment of learning for its own sake, and a striving for independent mastery of tasks. In contrast, some students may take an extrinsic motivational orientation to learning that is characterized by a preference for easy academic tasks, viewing education as a means to some other end, a focus on grades (or other indicators of performance), and a desire to please others and gain social approval through schoolwork (e.g., teachers, parents, peers) (Ames & Archer, 1988; Nicholls, 1983; Deci & Ryan, 1985). Ryan and Deci (2000) explained that an intrinsic motivational orientation gives individuals a sense of control and autonomy over tasks ("self-determination"), thereby increasing their sense of satisfaction and interest, whereas an extrinsic motivational orientation can have a number of effects on one's sense of control and well-being. For example, in one type of extrinsic motivation, *introjected regulation,* the individual will perform a behavior not to develop skills or master a task, but to avoid feeling anxious or guilty and to maintain one's sense of self-worth (Deci & Ryan, 1985; Ryan & Deci, 2000).

The two orientations have been referred to by a variety of terms in the literature, such as learning versus grade orientation (Alexitch, 1997, 2002; Eison, Pollio, & Milton, 1986), mastery goal versus performance goal orientation (Ames & Archer, 1988), and task involvement versus ego involvement (Newman, 1998; Nicholls, Cheung, Lauer, & Patashnick, 1989). For the purposes of this chapter, I refer to the two motivational orientations in students as *learning orientation* and *performance orientation,* respectively.

Using elementary school children, Ryan, Hicks, and Midgley (1997) examined the connection between motivational orientation and the perceived threat of help seeking. They found that students who were learning oriented felt less threatened by help seeking than students who were performance oriented. Ryan et al. (1997) explained that because performance-oriented students may be more concerned with how others see them and wanting to appear competent, they see help seeking as a threat to this image and may then avoid seeking help. This does not mean, however, that a performance-oriented student will never seek help. Performance-oriented students do sometimes seek academic help, but the type of help that they seek, and prefer to receive, differs from that sought by learning-oriented students.

A number of studies (e.g., Karabenick, 2003; Karabenick & Knapp, 1991; Newman, 1998, 2000; Ryan & Pintrich, 1997) have uncovered a consistent pattern in the help-seeking behaviors of learning-oriented and performance-oriented students who are faced with challenges or difficulties in an academic setting. Students who strive to master the material presented in school, and who are actively involved in the learning process (i.e., learning-oriented students) will typically engage in adaptive help seeking (Newman, 1998). In contrast, students who are concerned with their performance, and whose goals in school are to outperform their peers and to gain approval from teachers and parents (i.e., performance-oriented students), may engage in nonadaptive help seeking (Karabenick & Knapp, 1991; Newman, 1998). If such a student decides to seek help for a problem, he or she may ask others to simply provide a solution. Nonadaptive help seeking reduces the cost of completing tasks by reducing the risk for failure, but it also increases one's dependency on others because complex strategies for learning are not acquired (Karabenick & Knapp, 1991).

The patterns of help seeking observed in learning- and performance-oriented students can be extended to academic advising. Alexitch (1997) examined how motivational orientation was related to students' experiences with, and preferences for, academic advising from professors.

Students were asked about the style and content of advising that they had previously received from faculty, their satisfaction with the academic advising, and their preferences for receiving academic advising in the future. The findings indicated that motivational orientation played an important role in the academic advising received from professors and, most especially, in students' preferences for academic advising. Students who were highly learning oriented reported meeting with faculty more frequently and for longer sessions, engaged in more academic planning during their advising sessions (e.g., how to prepare for graduate school), and not only had a more developmental advising relationship with their faculty advisors but also expressed a greater preference for a developmental style of academic advising, than students who were less learning oriented. In contrast, students who were highly performance oriented showed a very different pattern of experiences and preferences: Performance orientation did not correlate with level of developmental advising, but was correlated positively with the receiving help with basic academic skills (e.g., study skills, time management). Furthermore, students who were highly performance oriented preferred more discussion on institutional policies, career issues, and basic academic skills.

Therefore, based on the findings of Alexitch (1997) and others (e.g., Eison et al., 1986; Karabenick & Knapp, 1991), learning-oriented students' preferences for developmental academic advising may be viewed as a type of adaptive help seeking in which the goal is to develop broad-based learning skills and independent thinking. In contrast, performance orientation seems to be more closely associated with the content of academic advising sessions, implying a more concrete and limited type of helping relationship—a more nonadaptive type of help seeking.

Motivational orientation may affect not only the type of help that a student requests, but also whether a student chooses to seek help at all. In general, learning-oriented students are more likely to seek help when they need it than are performance-oriented students (Ames, 1983; Newman, 1998; Nicholls et al., 1989; Ryan & Pintrich, 1997). The explanation for this may be that learning-oriented students see help seeking as a normal part of the learning process, and not an indication of failure or a lack of academic ability in themselves (Karabenick & Knapp, 1991; Newman, 1998). This view, however, is not shared by performance-oriented students. For students who are concerned with how others see them or who may have doubts about their ability to achieve, needing help may be a confirmation of poor ability in their eyes. The consequence is that they may avoid approaching others for help, or they may withdraw from a task, course, or program (Ames, 1983; Karabenick & Knapp, 1991; Newman, 1998). These findings also imply that the likelihood of seeking help is dictated by more than just a student's motivational orientation, but may also be affected by a student's perception of control over his or her academic performance. Perceptions of ability and attributions about performance seem to be a crucial element in help seeking by performance-oriented students, whereas these seem to play less of a role for help seeking by learning-oriented students (Ames, 1983; Newman, 1998; Nicholls et al., 1989).

In a recent study, Alexitch (2002) explored how motivational orientation, academic performance, and perceived help-seeking threat were related to help-seeking tendencies and preferred style of academic advising in over 300 junior undergraduate students. As in a previous study (Alexitch, 1997), she found that learning-oriented students were more likely to seek help from formal sources (e.g., faculty) and preferred a more developmental style of academic advising. Grade-oriented students perceived help seeking as a threat, making them less likely to approach formal sources for help, and more likely to engage in nonadaptive strategies when they experienced difficulties (e.g., lowering aspirations, dropping courses). As a consequence, grade-oriented students reported poorer academic performance when compared to learning-oriented students.

Developmental academic advising, with its emphasis on process, autonomy, and skill development, could be regarded as a form of adaptive help. It is not surprising, then, that learning-oriented students, who are likely to engage in adaptive help-seeking strategies and who view learning as a long-term process, have a preference for developmental academic advising. In contrast, because performance-oriented students are more likely to encounter difficulties due to poorer academic performance, and are more likely to attribute their poor performance to a lack of academic ability, they will be less likely to seek help from others. In addition, because performance-oriented students place an emphasis on grades (and similar outcomes) as indicators of learning, when they do seek help, they are more likely to prefer assistance that is helpful only in a short-term, limited fashion, as in prescriptive advising.

PROVIDERS OF ACADEMIC ADVISING

Individual factors, therefore, are significantly related to help-seeking attitudes and behaviors. But who are postsecondary students most likely to seek help from? Karabenick (2003, 2004) noted that perceived threat of help seeking may predict not only whether students will seek help, but also who they approach for help. Will they turn to *informal sources* such as family members, friends, or fellow students, who are not necessarily trained to be academic help providers but may instead offer emotional and psychological support? When do students use *formal sources* of help such as professors, academic advisors, and other campus services, who are specifically trained to offer more structured help to students? Do the individual student factors (e.g., expectations, motivational orientation) affect students' choices of particular help providers?

Tinsley et al. (1982) compared college students' preferences of help providers for career and academic issues (e.g., choosing an area of study, deciding on a career path) and for personal problems (e.g., difficulties getting along with others, lack of self-confidence). Students were presented with seven choices of help providers (close friend, close relative, professional counselor, paraprofessional counselor, clergy, instructor, and academic advisor) and were asked to rate how likely they would be to consult any of these sources for specific problems. Students indicated that they would turn to an academic advisor or instructor for help in choosing a career path and an area of study, or when they had academic difficulties, but for more general life plans they were more likely to go to a close friend or relative (Tinsley et al., 1982). Additional findings, however, indicated that many students preferred to rely on themselves for solving problems or making decisions, rather than seeking out a professional source of help. Tinsley et al. (1982) argued that students may have low expectations of receiving useful help from particular sources, and that students may regard formal help (e.g., academic advisors, instructors, counselors) as a backup to their own (informal) social support network. In a later study, Tinsley and his colleagues (1984) noted that students seemed to be more comfortable with, and attracted to, help providers that they felt possessed attributes similar to those found in a close friend or peer—trustworthy, accepting, and not overly directive. These attributes, especially the latter, are consistent with the model of developmental academic advising.

Additional analyses conducted with data collected by Alexitch (2002) examined the preferences in academic advising style and content for students who tended to seek help from informal sources (e.g., other students) and formal sources (e.g., faculty). She found that preferences for seeking help from either faculty or peers was correlated with less perceived help-seeking threat and with the greater use of effective help-seeking strategies. As Table 7.2 shows, the tendency to seek help from one's peers correlated significantly with a preference for developmental advising, and with a preference for advice on long-term academic planning (e.g., academic goals, preparation for graduate school), career options and choices, and basic academic skills (e.g., study tips, writing). The tendency to seek help from faculty was correlated with these advising topics as well, but students preferred that faculty also provide them with advice on personal issues (e.g., concerns about health) and institutional policies (e.g., program and degree requirements). These findings suggest that students in need of academic advising may use different sources depending on the type of advice sought, and that students recognize that help providers have expertise and knowledge in particular areas.

TABLE 7.2

Correlations of Academic, Help Seeking, and Advising Variables with
Students' Preferences for Help from Peers and Faculty Advisors

| | *Preferred Help Provider* | |
	Students/Peers	*Faculty Advisors*
Academic Variables		
Academic performance	.05	.18[c]
Learning orientation	.09	.43[c]
Performance orientation	.02	−.16[b]
Help-seeking variables		
Adaptive strategies	.40[c]	.37[c]
Nonadaptive strategies	.07	.08
Perceived help-seeking threat	−.17[c]	−.23[c]
Preferred academic advising		
Developmental advising style	.14[b]	.23[c]
Long-term academic planning	.12[a]	.22[c]
Career options and planning	.14[b]	.17[c]
Personal and social issues	.07	.25[c]
Institutional policies and requirements	.06	.11[a]
Basic academic skills	.16[b]	.19[c]

Note. $N = 361$.
[a]Significant at $p < .05$.
[b]Significant at $p < .01$.
[c]Significant at $p < .001$.

Peer Advisors

Peers are important in helping students adjust to the academic and social
demands of college life (Theophilides, Terenzini, & Lorang, 1984;
Thomas, 2000). A student's peer culture may be a key factor influencing his
or her persistence in college, and the development of social ties with other
students may even have a positive effect on academic performance
(Thomas, 2000). Peer advisors are one way to help new students adjust to
many aspects of college life. They may be undergraduate students themselves, often in the final years of their program of study, or
paraprofessionals (e.g., graduate students, students undertaking academic
advising as part of a practicum) (Reinarz, 2000; Teitelbaum, 2000). Peer
advisors also have an advantage over faculty academic advisors in being
able to share their knowledge of campus life and academic experiences with

their younger counterparts. Thus, the assumption is that students may feel less threatened by a peer advisor, because they see the peer advisor as someone who can identify with their problems and experiences.

But how likely are peer advisors to be approached for help with academic difficulties? Reinarz (2000) pointed out that many peer advisors are often limited to support roles in student orientation and in residence halls. Only some peer advisors provide help related to students' education, and that help is often restricted to discussions about a student's progress through an academic program. Moreover, peer advisors may be construed to be *formal* sources of help, much like other campus help providers, having specifically designated roles and duties. As such, students who are experiencing problems may not perceive them in the same way as they would peers with whom they are sharing classes or programs. Knapp and Karabenick (1988) included student tutors as a formal source of help, along with instructors, career counselors, and other campus services. They found that even when formal sources of help were readily available, students still preferred to seek help from informal sources such as friends and classmates.

Faculty Academic Advisors

It is widely recognized that regular faculty–student contact is critical in the academic, career, and social development of students in higher education (Frost, 1991a, 1991b; Kramer, 2000; Reinarz, 2000; Terenzini & Pascarella, 1980; Theophilides et al., 1984). Professors are often the only university or college personnel that students see on a regular basis, and therefore students frequently turn to them first for formal help and advice. As a result, faculty may develop a relationship with students both inside and outside the classroom, and students may approach them for advice on a variety of academic and non-academic matters (Frost, 1991b; Reinarz, 2000). Indeed, Table 7.2 shows that faculty (at least in the eyes of students) may be asked to advise students on a wide variety of topics beyond academic matters, whether in their capacity as course instructors or as academic advisors.

Regardless of the designated role, students generally respond positively to help received from faculty. In a large-scale, cross-institutional survey of students, Habley (2000) found that faculty advisors were satisfactorily meeting students' needs and that students had favorable impressions of their advisors. Alexitch and Page (1997) compared the types of advice sought and provided, and how students rated the usefulness of help received from nonfaculty and faculty academic advisors in a university setting. They noted that students sought advice from faculty advisors on both academic (e.g., program requirements) and career-related (graduate and professional schools) matters. Nonfaculty academic advisors also provided students with information on academic matters, such as program and degree requirements, and on career options. Students reported, however, that faculty advisors provided them with significantly more emotional support than did nonfaculty advisors. Another difference emerged with the perceived usefulness and impact of the advice given to students: Advice received from faculty had a more positive impact, and was perceived by students as more useful, than advice received from nonfaculty advisors.

Positive faculty–student interactions may also help students to develop long-term goals, a greater interest in learning, a richer understanding of the purpose of a university education, and may help students familiarize themselves with the values and culture of the institution (Reinarz, 2000; Terenzini & Pascarella, 1980; Terenzini, Springer, Pascarella, & Nora, 1995). Faculty advising seems to especially affect the cognitive and academic development of students when the contact involves discussion of intellectual matters (Terenzini et al., 1995; Terenzini & Pascarella, 1980). For example, Frost (1991b) reported that faculty–student contact and developmental advising had a positive effect on the critical thinking skills of female college students. Similarly, Kramer (2000) found that students who reported the greatest cognitive development were more likely to perceive faculty advisors as being concerned with student development and to report a close influential relationship with at least one faculty member.

Moreover, an established, developmental advising relationship with faculty and frequent faculty–student contact has been linked to a reduction in student attrition (Frost, 1991a; Pascarella, 1986). Gallagher and Allen (2000) conducted a longitudinal study exploring the effects of regular contact with faculty advisors on first-year students' academic expectations, satisfaction with advising and the institution, and retention. Advisors met with their assigned students periodically throughout the school year. Students' expectations concerning advising (measured in the fall) were compared to their advising experiences (measured in the spring). Gallagher and Allen found that students' advising experiences fell short of their expectations (especially perceived availability of advisor), and that this was one factor in a student's decision to leave the college. Students who had dropped out judged their advisors to be less knowledgeable and concerned about their academic success than students who remained in college.

There is little doubt, then, that faculty and other academic advisors are critical in helping students to have positive experiences in university or college. Many of the findings just cited, however, are correlational rather than causal—that is, students who are already adaptive help seekers and/or learning oriented may be interested in establishing an advising relationship with faculty, and therefore may be benefiting the most from academic advising. The challenge still remains in reaching students who are at risk for academic difficulties, who do not make the most use of their education, or who drop out without completing a degree before seeking any help. As noted earlier in the chapter, students are likely to turn to informal sources (e.g., fellow students) for help when they first encounter difficulties. Although this may be effective for select problems (e.g., particular course assignments), there are certain issues that only academic advisors may be able to address with students. For example, planning one's program of study to meet educational and career goals, and access to information that might be critical in helping one make informed decisions about the future, are more likely to be achieved by meeting regularly with an academic advisor than with a friend. What can an institution and its staff do to reach these students? The final section of this chapter outlines strategies to increase students' use of academic advising both inside and outside the classroom.

INCREASING STUDENTS' USE OF ACADEMIC ADVISING

When we envision a college classroom, we immediately think about how knowledge is imparted to students and how students might master the course content. In addition to conveying academic topics, however, a classroom setting also may be used to accomplish a variety of goals relevant to student development. For example, faculty (or others) may use the classroom to inform students about campus services, social events, and employment opportunities that are available to them. Students may also become aware of the educational and career possibilities in their area of study through the course instructor. Simply informing students, however, will not necessarily motivate those students who feel isolated, who perceive seeking help as a threat to their self-image, who are falling behind, or who take little interest in their education, to actually take advantage of the services and help presented in the classroom.

Changing the learning atmosphere and help-seeking norms in the classroom has proved effective in increasing students' adaptive help-seeking behavior at the elementary and secondary school level (e.g., Arbreton, 1998; Ryan & Pintrich, 1998). Teachers who create a supportive classroom environment by encouraging positive teacher–student and student–student interactions make students feel more comfortable in asking for help (Ryan & Pintrich, 1998). Students are especially more inclined to ask for help when they believe that their teacher views seeking help as an important, and expected, part of the learning process (Arbreton, 1998). In essence, help seeking becomes the norm. This is especially effective in getting students to take a more active approach to their education, and thus in increasing their learning orientation and adaptive help-seeking behaviors.

But can the same thing work in the college classroom? Braxton, Milem, and Sullivan (2000) argued that college students who experience active learning in their courses as a result of regular faculty–student contact, collaborative learning among students, and receiving prompt constructive feedback on their work perceive themselves as gaining knowledge and understanding. This leads to greater satisfaction with college, an increased willingness to devote time to other aspects of the college environment (e.g., student associations, sports), and a greater likelihood of developing supportive relationships with faculty and other students. Overall, students may become better integrated academically and socially into the college environment, and be more likely to complete their education.

In their findings, Braxton et al. (2000) noted that faculty classroom behaviors played an important role in students' active learning—a significant factor in helping students to become academically integrated and intrinsically motivated to learn. As discussed earlier in the chapter, learning orientation is correlated with a greater use of adaptive help-seeking strategies, and with a preference for developmental academic advising (Alexitch, 1997, 2002; Karabenick, 2003). In addition to creating an active learning environment within the classroom, faculty should also emphasize collaboration and deemphasize competition among students. The latter can often lead students to take a performance-oriented approach to their learning, which in turn can lead to a greater reluctance to seek help. For example, Karabenick (2004) found that students who perceived the classroom environment as performance oriented were more likely to engage in avoidance of help seeking.

For those students who are performing poorly (and who need help the most), Ames and Lau (1982) suggested that instructors lead students to believe that past poor performance is a function of a task-specific ability and skills that can be modified by practice, effort, and acquiring new knowledge and skills. They also recommend encouraging students to attend help sessions or office hours of the faculty member to get individualized help. Overall, these strategies heighten students' sense of control and mastery over their learning and academic performance, thereby increasing their confidence and self-esteem.

The college campus, however, is more than just a collection of classrooms, and help may be needed with general academic and career planning and with adjustment to the demands of the college environment. How can educators and administrators also get students to meet with academic advisors on these more general issues? This question becomes especially crucial for students who are new, who do not share the culture and experiences of the majority of college students, or who are academically at risk. For instance, recall that the retention of ethnic minority students poses a particular challenge for many postsecondary institutions. Gloria et al. (2001) recommended that advising services integrate the cultural context of their students into their programming and interventions, thereby, providing advising that is culture specific. Academic advisors may help these students become familiar with the college culture and with the available support services if they are needed. Ideally, academic advisors who are of the same minority group as the students may accomplish these goals more effectively, because they can operate as role models for the students (Frost, 1991a). As with all developmental advising, the goal is to identify the student's needs, interests, and abilities, and to help the student to make realistic academic and career decisions (Frost, 1991a; Priest & McPhee, 2000).

Clark and Halpern (1993) examined the impact of an intensive learning experience on the retention and success of academically unprepared students (based on admission tests). The researchers felt that ethnic minority students, in particular, were at risk for failing and dropping out of college. The program was comprised of an instructional component (full-year pre-university-level course in English or mathematics), frequent faculty–student interactions, small class sizes, and academic and career advising. Over 400 students participated in the program between 1985 and 1990, and most were from ethnic minority groups (e.g., African American, Hispanic, Asian). The outcome of program participants was compared to (a) at-risk students who had enrolled in the college 1 year prior to the program's implementation (1984), and (b) a cohort group who entered in 1985. Clark and Halpern found that the program produced small but significant gains in the student participants when compared to the other two groups. Although they were still having difficulties when compared to the cohort group, program participants were more likely to stay in school at least a second year, were more likely to graduate, and had higher GPAs when compared to the 1984 at-risk students.

Another strategy has been to familiarize a student with academic advising early in his or her academic career. The assumption is that the student may feel more comfortable seeking help when difficulties arise later on, or may even be able to reduce the potential for encountering academic and other difficulties in college. Schwitzer, Grogan, Kaddoura, and Ochoa (1993) examined the impact of a mandatory academic counseling program on students who were at risk for failure and dropping out of college. Using 131 second-year students who met the criteria of poor grade point average, students underwent two phases of the program: one session for assessing their academic attitudes and behaviors (such as study skills), and the second session with a counselor (e.g., psychologist, clinical social worker) to discuss students' academic expectations and experiences, educational goals, academic motivation, and attitudes about instructors. Schwitzer et al. (1993) wanted to determine if these students would return voluntarily for help and further advising. They found that students who committed themselves to return visits after the mandatory sessions made the greatest use of counseling services over time, made modest gains in academic performance, and persisted longer in college, eventually completing their degrees.

Of course, what is also important is the type of advising relationship that students establish once they do meet with an advisor (Alexitch, 1997; Frost,

1991a; Grites & Gordon, 2000). Grites and Gordon (2000) emphasized that "a central mission of advising is to help students understand and appreciate the value of liberal learning, to acquire the capacity for critical thinking, and to make wise curricular choices based on their goals" (pp. 13–14). This point of view is consistent with the goals of developmental advising. But what does an advisor do with a student who is asking questions that reflect nonadaptive help-seeking strategies, who is performance oriented, or who feels more comfortable with prescriptive advising than with developmental advising? Rather than simply providing the answers to students' questions, Grites and Gordon recommended that advisors ask students open-ended, probing, qualitative questions that direct students to think about their choices, interests, and the way in which they approach their education. For example, students have often approached me with the query: What marks do I need to get into graduate school? I usually counter with a question concerning their specific goals (What are you interested in doing?), or their overall feelings about university and their field of study (What do you want to get out of your current program?). During the session, we may at one point discuss the average entrance requirements for most psychology graduate programs in Canada, but the student is left thinking (hopefully) about more than academic performance. This is not to say that advising should not include prescriptive or concrete forms of advice (e.g., program requirements, institutional policies), but the advising relationship should be *primarily* developmental in nature. Although this kind of interaction can be time-consuming, the student is left with the impression that the advisor considers him or her to be an individual with unique academic and career interests, and that he or she is valued by the institution. This is especially critical for students who are either at risk for or who are already experiencing difficulties (Heisserer & Parette, 2002).

Some researchers and educators (e.g., Earl, 1988; Frost, 1991a; Heisserer & Parette, 2002) have advocated a new approach to academic advising, *intrusive advising*, specifically designed for students who are experiencing academic difficulties. Intrusive advising incorporates some prescriptive elements (e.g., monitoring student progress, course selection) and is designed to increase students' decision-making skills and interest in academic and social activities, thereby increasing their chances of success. The overall goal of intrusive advising is to increase students' motivation to learn and to take responsibility for their education. Intrusive advising has had positive effects on student retention, academic performance, and the development of basic academic skills (e.g., study skills, time management) (Frost, 1991a; Heisserer & Parette, 2002). In this advising model, students are encouraged to seek help even before the institution identifies them as having difficulties (Earl, 1988; Frost, 1991a). Regular meetings are set between the advisor and student, wherein students may discuss their academic progress, be taught skills they are lacking, or be referred to other support services. Students are encouraged to become actively involved in their academic and career planning—identifying their strengths as well as weaknesses—and thus to reduce their feelings of isolation or discomfort with seeking help. In essence, students are being taught to be effective help seekers (Frost, 1991a; Heisserer & Parette, 2002).

CONCLUSION

The chapter began with comments made by two senior students who felt that they should have made better use of advising services after they had experienced academic difficulties. If these students not only had sought academic advising but also had established a developmental academic advising relationship with a faculty member early in their undergraduate careers, they might have been able to look back positively on their time in university. Instead, they were left with regrets, doubts about their chosen educational paths, and feelings of wasted effort.

Why had these students not sought out help when it was obvious that they needed it, and when it was readily available (at least from the institution's perspective)? Motivational factors, perceptions of help seeking, and other characteristics such as ethnicity and gender may have operated as barriers to seeking academic advising. From their comments, it was clear that the students had lapsed into using nonadaptive strategies to address their difficulties.

What could faculty and university staff have done to help these students? Advising relationships should have been established when these students entered university. It is during this time that students need help in adjusting to a postsecondary environment, and this is when they begin to make choices concerning their future. As discussed earlier in the chapter, regular contact with a faculty member, both inside and outside the classroom, would likely have had a positive impact on the students. Their concerns could then have been addressed before they became problems. In addition, as they progressed through their programs of study, more general academic and career issues could also have been discussed—helping the students prepare for the choices, opportunities, and other demands that they would have to face as they approached graduation.

Academic advising, as one form of help, can offer a tremendous benefit to all: educators, researchers, institutions, and especially students. Therefore, given the importance of academic advising in higher education, further research needs to be conducted to address many of the issues raised in this chapter. For example, it seems that tailoring academic advising to students' particular expectations, motivational orientation, and cultural background may be effective, and may be received positively by students. But what happens when an advisor tries to deliver developmental advising to a performance-oriented student, one who prefers to engage in nonadaptive help-seeking strategies? The student will probably walk away feeling negatively about the advisor, and it is likely that he or she will not attend further advising sessions. Is mandatory advising necessarily an effective strategy with such students, or should advisors simply meet students' requests even if the help requested produces only limited development of autonomy and problem-solving skills? Another area to address is the current role that faculty members play in providing academic advising to students, and what students expect from faculty academic advisors. Not only have the needs, expectations, and background experiences of students changed in the last 30 years, but the demands placed on faculty have also changed during this time. Higher enrollments at many institutions, greater administrative and research demands, and an overall heavier workload may be having a profound impact on the very people who are effective in helping students.

Ultimately, we must not forget that the goal is to provide students with, and encourage them to establish, an ongoing academic advising relationship that will result in better academic performance, greater satisfaction with the education received, and an increased likelihood of completing a program of study. Our challenge is to determine how we can best accomplish this goal.

REFERENCES

Alexitch, L. R. (1994). *Undergraduate student expectations and perceptions of a university education in the 1990s.* Unpublished doctoral dissertation, University of Windsor, Windsor, Ontario, Canada.

Alexitch, L. R. (1997). Students' educational orientation and preferences for advising from university professors. *Journal of College Student Development, 38,* 333–343.

Alexitch, L. R. (1999). *Survey of students' experiences and program satisfaction: Report to the Dean's Task Force on Curriculum and Program Review.* Saskatoon: University of Saskatchewan, College of Arts and Science.

Alexitch, L. R. (2002). The role of help-seeking attitudes and tendencies in students' preferences for academic advising. *Journal of College Student Development, 43,* 5–19.

Alexitch, L. R., & Page, S. (1997). Evaluation of academic and career counselling information and its relation to students' educational orientation. *Canadian Journal of Counselling, 31,* 205–220.

Ames, R. (1983). Help seeking and achievement orientation: Perspectives from attribution theory. In B. M. DePaulo, A. Nadler, & J. D. Fisher (Eds.), *New directions in helping, Vol. 2: Help seeking* (pp. 165–186). San Diego, CA: Academic Press.

Ames, R., & Archer, J. (1988). Achievement goals in the classroom: Students' learning strategies and motivation processes. *Journal of Educational Psychology, 80,* 260–267.

Ames, R., & Lau, S. (1982). An attributional analysis of student help seeking in academic settings. *Journal of Educational Psychology, 74,* 414–423.

Andrews, M., Andrews, D., Long, E., & Henton, J. (1987). Student characteristics as predictors of perceived academic advising needs. *Journal of College Student Personnel, 28,* 60–65.

Arbreton, A. (1998). Student goal orientation and help-seeking strategy use. In S. A. Karabenick (Ed.), *Strategic help seeking: Implications for learning and teaching* (pp. 95–116). Mahwah, NJ: Lawrence Erlbaum Associates.

Association of Universities and Colleges of Canada. (1996). *Trends 1996: The Canadian university in profile*. Ottawa, Ontario, Canada: AUCC.

Astin, A. W. (2000). The American college student: Three decades of change. In J. Losco & B. L. Fife (Eds.), *Higher education in transition: The challenges of the new millennium* (pp. 7–27). Westport, CT: Begin & Garvey.

Braxton, J. M., Milem, J. F., & Sullivan, A. S. (2000). The influence of active learning on the college student departure process: Toward a revision of Tinto's theory. *Journal of Higher Education, 71,* 569–590.

Clark, J. M., & Halpern, D. F. (1993). The million dollar question: Can an intensive learning experience help lowest-quartile students succeed in college? *Journal of Instructional Development, 20,* 29–39.

Creamer, D. G. (2000). Use of theory in academic advising. In V. N. Gordon, W. R. Habley, & Associates (Eds.), *Academic Advising: A comprehensive handbook* (pp. 18–34). San Francisco: Jossey-Bass.

Creeden, J. E. (1990). Components of good advising: Differences in faculty and student perceptions. *NACADA Journal, 10,* 30–36.

Crookston, B. B. (1972). A developmental view of academic advising as teaching. *Journal of College Student Personnel, 13,* 12–17.

Daubman, K. A., & Lehman, T. C. (1993). The effects of receiving help: Gender differences in motivation and performance. *Sex Roles, 28,* 693–707.

Deci, E. L., & Ryan, R. M. (1985). *Intrinsic motivation and self-determination in human behavior*. New York: Plenum Press.

Earl, W. R. (1988). Intrusive advising of freshmen in academic difficulty. *NACADA Journal, 8,* 27–33.

Eison, J. A., Pollio, H. R., & Milton, O. (1986). Educational and personal characteristics of four different types of learning- and grade-oriented students. *Contemporary Educational Psychology, 11,* 54–67.

Ender, S. C., Winston, R. B., & Miller, T. K. (1984). Academic advising reconsidered. In R. B. Winston, Jr., T. K. Miller, S. C. Ender, T. J. Grites, & Associates (Eds.), *Developmental academic advising: Addressing students educational, career, and personal needs* (pp. 3–34). San Francisco: Jossey-Bass.

Fielstein, L. L., Scoles, M. T., & Webb, K. J. (1992). Differences in traditional and nontraditional students' preferences for advising services and perceptions of services received. *NACADA Journal, 12,* 5–12.

Frost, S. H. (1991a). *Academic advising for student success: A system of shared responsibility* (ASHE-ERIC Higher Education Report No. 3). Washington, DC: George Washington University, School of Education and Human Development.

Frost, S. H. (1991b). Fostering the critical thinking of college women through academic advising and faculty contact. *Journal of College Student Development, 32,* 359–366.

Frost, S. H. (1995). Designing and implementing a faculty-based advising program. *NACADA Journal, 15,* 27–32.

Gallagher, D. J., & Allen, N. (2000). First-year initiatives and results of a year-long advising pilot study: A proposed advising model. *Journal of the First-Year Experience, 12,* 107–128.

Gloria, A. M., Hird, J. S., & Navarro, R. L. (2001). Relationships of cultural congruity and perceptions of the university environment to help-seeking attitudes by socio race and gender. *Journal of College Student Development, 42,* 545–562.

Gordon, V. N., Habley, W. R., & Associates (Eds.). (2000). *Academic advising: A comprehensive handbook*. San Francisco: Jossey-Bass.

Grayson, A., Miller, H., & Clark, D. D. (1998). Identifying barriers to help seeking: A qualitative analysis of students' preparedness to seek help from tutors. *British Journal of Guidance and Counselling, 26,* 237–253.

Grites, T., & Gordon, V. N. (2000). Developmental academic advising revisited. *NACADA Journal, 20,* 12–15.

Habley, W. R. (2000). Current practices in academic advising. In V. N. Gordon, W. R. Habley, & Associates (Eds.), *Academic advising: A comprehensive handbook* (pp. 35–43). San Francisco: Jossey-Bass.

Heisserer, D. L., & Parette, P. (2002). Advising at-risk students in college and university settings. *College Student Journal, 36,* 69–83.

Holdaway, E. A., & Kelloway, K. R. (1987). First year at university: Perceptions and experiences of students. *Canadian Journal of Higher Education, 17,* 47–63.

Karabenick, S. A. (2003). Seeking help in large college classes: A person-centred approach. *Contemporary Educational Psychology, 28,* 37–58.

Karabenick, S. A. (2004). Perceived achievement goal structure and college student help seeking. *Journal of Educational Psychology, 96,* 569–581.

Karabenick, S. A., & Knapp, J. R. (1991). Relationship of academic help seeking to the use of learning strategies and other instrumental achievement behavior in college students. *Journal of Educational Psychology, 83,* 221–230.

Knapp, J. R., & Karabenick, S. A. (1988). Incidence of formal and informal academic help-seeking in higher education. *Journal of College Student Development, 29,* 223–227.

Kramer, G. L. (2000). Advising students at different educational levels. In V. N. Gordon, W. R. Habley, & Associates (Eds.), *Academic Advising: A comprehensive handbook* (pp. 84–104). San Francisco: Jossey-Bass.

McGillin, V. A. (2000). Current issues in advising research. In V. N. Gordon, W. R. Habley, & Associates (Eds.), *Academic advising: A comprehensive handbook* (pp. 365–380). San Francisco: Jossey-Bass.

Metzner, B. S. (1989). Perceived quality of academic advising: The effect on freshman attrition. *American Educational Research Journal, 26,* 422–442.

National Academic Advising Association. (1994). NACADA Statement of Core Values of Academic Advising. Retrieved January 21, 2004, from NACADA Clearinghouse of Academic Advising Resources Web site: http://www.nacada.ksu.edu/Clearinghouse/Research_Related/corevalues.html

Newman, R. S. (1998). Adaptive help seeking: A role of social interaction in self-regulated learning. In S. A. Karabenick (Ed.), *Strategic help seeking: Implications for learning and teaching* (pp. 13–60). Mahwah, NJ: Lawrence Erlbaum Associates.

Newman, R. S. (2000). Social influences on the development of children's adaptive help seeking: The role of parents, teachers, and peers. *Developmental Review, 20,* 350–404.

Nicholls, J. G. (1983). Conceptions of ability and achievement motivation: A theory and its implications for education. In S. Paris, G. Olson, & H. Stevenson (Eds.), *Learning and motivation in the classroom* (pp. 211–237). Hillsdale, NJ: Lawrence Erlbaum Associates.

Nicholls, J. G., Cheung, P. C., Lauer, J., & Patashnick, M. (1989). Individual differences in academic motivation. *Learning and Individual Differences, 1,* 63–84.

Nora, A., & Cabrera, A. F. (1996). The role of perceptions of prejudice and discrimination on the adjustment of minority students to college. *Journal of Higher Education, 67,* 119–148.

Pascarrella, E. T. (1986). A program for research and policy development on student persistence at the institutional level. *Journal of College Student Personnel, 27,* 100–107.

Priest, R., & McPhee, S. A. (2000). Advising multicultural students: The reality of diversity. In V. N. Gordon, W. R. Habley, & Associates (Eds.), *Academic advising: A comprehensive handbook* (pp. 105–117). San Francisco: Jossey-Bass.

Reinarz, A. G. (2000). Delivering academic advising. In V. N. Gordon, W. R. Habley, & Associates (Eds.), *Academic advising: A comprehensive handbook* (pp. 210–219). San Francisco: Jossey-Bass.

Rendon, L. I., Jalomo, R. E., & Nora, A. (2000). Theoretical considerations in the study of minority student retention in higher education. In J. M. Braxton (Ed.), *Reworking the student departure puzzle* (pp. 127–156). Nashville, TN: Vanderbilt University Press.

Ryan, A. M., Hicks, L., & Midgley, C. (1997). Social goals, academic goals, and avoiding seeking help in the classroom. *Journal of Early Adolescence, 17,* 152–171.

Ryan, A. M., & Pintrich, P. R. (1997). "Should I ask for help?" The role of motivation and attitudes in adolescents' help seeking in math class. *Journal of Educational Psychology, 89,* 329–341.

Ryan, A. M., & Pintrich, P. R. (1998). Achievement and social motivational influences on help seeking in the classroom. In S. A. Karabenick (Ed.), *Strategic help seeking: Implications for learning and teaching* (pp. 117–139). Mahwah, NJ: Lawrence Erlbaum Associates.

Ryan, R. M., & Deci, E. L. (2000). Self-determination theory and the facilitation of intrinsic motivation, social development, and well-being. *American Psychologist, 55,* 68–78.

Sagaria, M. D., Higginson, L. C., & White, E. R. (1980). Perceived needs of entering freshmen: The primacy of academic issues. *Journal of College Student Personnel, 21,* 243–247.

Schwitzer, A. M., Grogan, K., Kaddoura, K., & Ochoa, L. (1993). Effects of brief mandatory counseling on help seeking and academic success among at-risk college students. *Journal of College Student Development, 34,* 401–405.

Statistics Canada. (2003). *Report of the Pan-Canadian education indicators program.* Ottawa, Ontario: Author.

Steele, C. M. (1997). A threat in the air: How stereotypes shape intellectual identity and performance. *American Psychologist, 52,* 613–629.

Teitelbaum, H. (2000). Anticipating, implementing, and adapting to changes in academic advising. In V. N. Gordon, W. R. Habley, & Associates (Eds.), *Academic advising: A comprehensive handbook* (pp. 393–408). San Francisco: Jossey-Bass

Terenzini, P. T., & Pascarella, E. T. (1980). Student/faculty relationships and freshman year educational outcomes: A further investigation. *Journal of College Student Personnel, 21,* 521–528.

Terenzini, P. T., Springer, L., Pascarella, E. T., & Nora, A. (1995). Academic and out-of-class influences on students' intellectual orientations. *Review of Higher Education, 19,* 23–44.

Theophilides, C., Terenzini, P. T., & Lorang, W. (1984). Relation between freshman-year experience and perceived importance of four major educational goals. *Research in Higher Education, 20,* 235–252.

Thomas, S. L. (2000). Ties that bind: A social network approach to understanding student integration and persistence. *Journal of Higher Education, 71,* 591–615.

Tinsley, H. E. A., Brown, M. T., de St. Aubin, T. M., & Lucek, J. (1984). Relation between expectancies for a helping relationship and tendency to seek help from a campus help provider. *Journal of Counseling Psychology, 31,* 149–160.

Tinsley, H. E. A., de St. Aubin, T. M., & Brown, M. T. (1982). College students' help-seeking preferences. *Journal of Counseling Psychology, 29,* 523–533.

Upcraft, M. L., & Stephens, P. S. (2000). Academic advising and today's changing students. In V. N. Gordon, W. R. Habley, & Associates (Eds.), *Academic advising: A comprehensive handbook* (pp. 73–104). San Francisco: Jossey-Bass.

Weissberg, M., Berentsen, M., Cote, A., Carvey, B., & Heath, K. (1982). An assessment of the personal, career, and academic needs of undergraduate students. *Journal of College Student Personnel, 23,* 115–122.

Zimmerman, B. J., & Martinez-Pons, M. (1988). Construct validation of a strategy model of student self-regulated learning. *Journal of Educational Psychology, 80,* 284–290.

Chapter 8

Help Seeking in Higher Education Academic Support Services

William Collins
Brian C. Sims
University of Michigan

Give a man a fish, and you feed him for a day.

Teach a man to fish, and you feed him for a lifetime. (Chinese proverb)

The existing help-seeking literature has a number of implications for a broad range of academic support services that can serve to inform both assistance providers and students. This chapter examines that literature with the objective of identifying strategies and research-based insights that can serve to increase the likelihood that college students will take advantage of the institutional sources increasingly available to them. An essential step toward that objective is for educators to understand factors that influence the likelihood and type of student help seeking, as well as how those factors can be used to design effective support programs that minimize the person and situation obstacles that may exist. To provide a broader perspective, we begin with a brief overview of academic support programs in the United States, discussing commonalities and shared goals in relation to student help seeking. The next section offers reasons why college students need help. We then discuss obstacles to students' use of support services, drawing on research from the achievement motivation literature, followed by a list of implications and best practices for support programs. Finally, we offer directions for future research based on an academic support program model at the University of Michigan.

OVERVIEW

Institutionally based academic support for college students in the United States has a long history (Enright & Kerstens, 1980; Maxwell, 1979). In the 1860s, Iowa State College required entering freshmen to be able to read, write, and do arithmetic; students lacking such skills were placed in the college's preparatory department. In 1874, Harvard first offered freshman English due to faculty concern about student preparation in formal writing. In 1915, 350 colleges reported to the U.S. Commissioner of Education that they had college preparatory departments. After World War II, millions of former servicemen attended college on the GI Bill, and government funding allowed the establishment of veterans' guidance centers, reading and study skills programs, and tutoring services to help returning veterans adjust to college demands. These support services eventually were opened to all students.

As college campuses have become more diverse, services that support students academically and that enhance opportunities for improved learning have expanded (Christ, 1971; Noel, 1985; Weinstein & Mayer, 1986). In addition to advising, tutoring, and study skills programs, colleges now routinely offer such services as extended summer orientation programs (Garcia, 1991), learning centers and laboratories (Dempsey & Tomlinson, 1980), collaborative learning programs (Darseneau, 1988; Johnson, Johnson, & Smith, 1991), learning communities (Lenning & Ebbers, 1999; Smith, 1993), supplemental instruction (Martin, Blanc, & De Buhr, 1983), freshman interest groups (Love, 1994; Tinto & Goodsell, 1994), and first-year experience programs (Gardner, 1986). The particular forms of academic support that can be provided vary, but often include some combination of advising, tutoring from faculty or advanced students, study groups, learning communities, collaborative learning groups, supplemental instruction, and freshman interest groups.

Evidence indicates that participation in interventions designed to help students adjust to college results in positive outcomes (Beal, 1980; Wilkie & Kuckuck, 1989), especially for poorly prepared students, significantly improves both grades and college persistence rates, and is strongest during the freshman year of college (Dubois, Kiewra, & Fraley, 1988; Kulik, Kulik & Schwalb, 1983; Walsh, 1985). The Kulik, Kulik, and Schwalb meta-analysis of over 60 published and unpublished studies found a statistically significant effect size for college intervention programs; those participating in college intervention programs had a grade point average that was .27 of a standard deviation higher than for similar students who were not part of the intervention programs.

Common Goals of Support Programs

Despite the wide variety of support offered by institutions, there are three general goals shared by most programs. First, support programs seek to find ways to motivate students to seek help when they need it. Another major goal is to inform students of available resources, or where to go when help is needed. Finally, support programs seek to promote self-regulation and independence on the part of the learner. The particular goals emphasized depend on the type of support program offered. Table 8.1 displays how three general goals of academic support are specific to different types of programs. For example, summer academic programs typically emphasize increasing student awareness about support services, whereas academic counseling services often focus on motivating students to seek help.

Motivating Students to Get Help.   A key challenge borne out of the help-seeking literature is that of motivating students to seek help when they need it (Ryan & Pintrich, 1997; Ryan, Gheen, & Midgley, 1998). An underlying purpose of many support programs is to give students the ability and motivation to ask for help rather than fail in isolation. Educators struggle with the perplexing and complicated question of why some students readily avail themselves of support services, whereas others either resist or delay their participation. An all-too-common observation is that college students wait until they are in trouble before seeking academic help. That is, they have already fallen behind in course assignments, performed poorly on exams, or found course subject matter confusing and difficult to understand before they take steps to get help. On one hand, this can be a commendable trait among students if it reflects their desire to learn on their own and to persist in mastering course content through their independent efforts. On the other hand, it can

TABLE 8.1

Three General Goals of Academic Support and Programs Offered to Meet Them

Goal of Support Program	Types of Programs Offered
Increase awareness of support resources	• Academic advising
	• Academic summer programs
	• First-year experience programs
Motivate students to seek help	• Academic advising
	• Counseling services
Promote self-regulated learning	• Course-specific tutoring
	• Study skills workshops
	• Writing centers

represent unrealistic self-appraisals, exposing them to academic agony that might have been unnecessary had they utilized available assistance earlier. Achievement motivation frameworks provide some important reasons for such delays, which are discussed later in this chapter.

Informing Students of Available Resources.   Recently, there has been growing attention paid to the issues that students face when making the transition to college (Hurtado & Carter, 1997; Tinto, 1993). Researchers have identified a number of factors that affect the college transition process, including a sense of belonging (Bollen & Hoyle, 1990) and perceived social climate (Tinto, 1993). Thus students can fall into the trap of mistakenly assuming that they are "all alone"—that there is no other student with the same set of needs, that there is no one to assist them, or that one form of help is as good as another. In addition, students may not choose the best sources of help.

A major goal of programs designed to support students academically is to inform them about resources where they can find the help they need. First-year experience programs, such as those required of freshman students for credit toward graduation, often focus on making students aware of these resources. Programs typically require students to visit campus assistance centers or assign projects that involve obtaining information about a given center or campus resource, or other ways to acquaint students with what is available to them, which often include services and programs that provide assistance or develop skills and abilities. For example, many universities have comprehensive writing centers with staff and volunteers who help students with their writing by proofreading drafts, conducting workshops, and providing one-on-one tutoring in grammar and editorial services.

The importance of simply informing students about available services is demonstrated by a study of White high school males, in which researchers found that one of the primary deterrents to seeking help was a lack of awareness of services (Timlin-Scalera, Ponterotta, Blumberg, & Jackson, 2003). In addition, students can be quite selective about the sources of help they are inclined to utilize; they may eschew more appropriate sources of help, such as course professors or teaching assistants, and instead turn to less reliable sources such as fellow students, siblings, or even parents, each of which may be better than no help at all, but would rarely be as informed about substantive material as those involved in teaching the course (Knapp & Karabenick, 1988). Students also may be more willing to seek help from sources other than course professors because they are concerned about the risks of self-disclosure to someone involved in the evaluation of their work. One purpose of emphasizing campus resources is to make students aware of appropriate and effective sources of help. From this standpoint, programs that inform students of support options provide a crucial piece of the help-seeking puzzle.

Promoting Self-Regulated Learning.   Another general goal of academic support programs is to promote autonomous learning and the development of skills and abilities needed to succeed in the competitive college environment. Self-regulation includes effective self-monitoring and metacognitive skills that allow students to evaluate their progress and possibly alter their approach to learning. Several researchers have espoused a strategic view of help seeking (Ames & Lau, 1982; Karabenick, 1998; Nelson-Le Gall, 1981), describing it as representing "an adaptive, self-regulating, instrumental response to academic difficulties" (Karabenick & Sharma, 1994).

As Newman (2000) pointed out, starting from infancy, parent–child interactions provide numerous opportunities for children to develop adaptive help seeking and in the process to gain support for building competence and autonomy. That is, interactions with parents allow children to see that difficulty and failure may require assistance to overcome, and that they can count on adults for such assistance. By seeking help in the face of challenging situations, children learn they can maintain task involvement, avert failure, and optimize their chances for mastery and autonomy (Newman, 2000). The same benefits are likely to accrue to college students who take advantage of available help appropriately. Yet many college students were simply good students in unchallenging high schools and as a consequence never really had to develop efficient learning strategies or to seek help strategically. Paradoxically, appropriate help-seeking strategies are important tools used by independent learners (Nelson-Le Gall, 1981), yet students do not always perceive that they need help until too late.

WHY STUDENTS NEED HELP

Effectively accomplishing these goals requires an understanding of why students need help to the first place. Each student is unique, with different patterns of habits, responsibilities, aptitudes, and motivations, and there are several potential reasons why students may need help at any given point in time. For example, a student may be having trouble getting used to the format of her large lecture classes; or, she may need help understanding difficult college material. Two major reasons why students might be in need of academic assistance during college are adjustment and underpreparation.

Adjustment

The traditional college student has recently graduated from high school or secondary school and is embarking on a new journey into adulthood. College life represents increased autonomy and responsibility on the part of the student. However, along with increased autonomy may come potential academic pitfalls. For example, in college there is often less feedback from instructors and greater emphasis on self-regulation. Today's college student must progress through increasingly challenging courses, especially at selective institutions. Their college classmates are often the highest achieving and most motivated students from their respective high schools. Students inevitably find the standards of excellence raised, as a greater proportion of students are highly motivated to achieve academically. What was once done easily now requires a great deal of focus and effort. Indeed, college students—especially those admitted to selective colleges and universities—generally present more impressive academic credentials and have been groomed for college by parents and teachers. As a result, students may overestimate their abilities relative to other students and underestimate the level of performance that is expected by their course professors. Critical thinking and deep processing of information are more likely to be required for success, as well as the ability to apply and interpret course material. The differences between high school and college, in other words, often may require that students change their approaches to learning.

Independent High Achievers

Interestingly, the adjustment difficulties of some high-achieving high school students come from their over-dependence on independence. Their stellar academic performance in high school is a result of setting themselves apart from their peers and demonstrating independence of thought and action. For such students it may seem perfectly natural that in college they would continue to rely on the pattern that has worked well for them in the past, and that is often interpreted to mean working alone and not seeking help from others. Thus many students who were high achievers in high school may not be accustomed to seeking or receiving help, even when circumstances warrant it, resulting in suboptimal academic performance.

Underpreparation

Widespread disparity in the quality of secondary schooling has had an impact on colleges as the American egalitarian tradition has been combined with the necessity of a college degree for an increasing number of careers. Many more good students who attended poor schools now seek the benefits of a post-secondary education. As a consequence, each year, thousands of bright students lacking adequate reading, writing, and critical thinking skills graduate from high schools. Substantial numbers of students from a variety of different socioeconomic backgrounds enter college underprepared for the academic challenges they will face. But students from disadvantaged backgrounds are not the only ones to be challenged by the rigor of college academics.

The National Center for Educational Statistics (2000) reported that 76% of Title IV degree-granting institutions offered at least one remedial course in reading, writing or math, whereas the ACT testing program reported that about half of entering college students must take at least one remedial course in college (ACT, 2003). A subsequent report from ACT concluded that too few students were prepared to enter postsecondary education without remediation when they graduate from high school (ACT, 2004). The report noted that only 26% of ACT-tested students demonstrated readiness for college biology, only 40% were ready for college algebra, and only 68% were ready for English composition. Often, students from urban or rural communities who are highly motivated and industrious bring to college campuses unique perspectives that are valued in the classroom. However, they may also bring with them socioeconomic legacies that represent disadvantaged backgrounds and less preparation for the academic demands of rigorous college education (Brubacher & Rudy, 1997). Thus, the need for academic assistance among students is substantial, and colleges have a concomitant interest in anticipating students' needs for the kinds of help that promote adjustment, achievement, and graduation.

OBSTACLES TO STUDENT USE OF SUPPORT SERVICES

Colleges and universities routinely promote academic excellence and retention by encouraging the development and improvement of study strategies and habits by: (a) promoting self-regulation; (b) providing a support network of resourceful faculty, staff, and students; (c) creating opportunities for cooperative learning; and (d) reducing anxiety. Given the wide range of help resources offered in colleges today, and increasing issues of adjustment and underpreparation, why do many students avoid academic help that is, at least from the institutional perspective, readily available to them? To understand this, we examine the motivational factors, awareness of appropriate sources of help, and identifying when help is needed. Ironically, as we show, the major goals of support programs may engender major obstacles to their possible beneficiaries.

Role of Motivation in Student Use of Support Services

Understanding the role of motivation in help seeking may enhance insight regarding obstacles that prevent students from seeking help. Indeed, help avoidance has been deemed a form of motivated behavior that arises when the benefits to be derived from seeking help are outweighed by the cost of requesting help (Butler, 1998; Nadler, 1997). Major models of achievement motivation are useful for understanding help seeking and help avoidance in the context of academic support services. In particular, achievement goal theory and attribution theory describe how motivational factors may relate to help seeking behavior.

Achievement Goal Theory. Achievement goal theory (see Urdan, 1997, for a review) is concerned with the reasons that students engage in achievement related behavior, as well as the criteria that students use to evaluate progress towards reaching their goals. Researchers have studied goal orientations using somewhat different constructs (e.g., Ames, 1992; Dweck & Leggett, 1988; Maehr & Midgley, 1991; Nicholls, 1984), but the majority of models primarily focus on a common dichotomy. A mastery goal orientation is characterized by a student's focus on learning and understanding, and mastery-oriented individuals use their own progress and improvement as criteria for evaluating success. A performance goal orientation is characterized by students' concern with their ability or performance with social comparison as a criterion for evaluating success. Goal theory predicts that students who operate under a mastery goal orientation tend to focus on learning and task mastery and therefore are more likely to value academic tasks and engage in behaviors that are conducive to learning. In contrast, performance goals are often negatively related to student motivation and self-regulated learning (Dweck & Leggett, 1988; Pintrich & Schunk, 2002).

A considerable amount of research has linked students' mastery and performance goal orientations to various academic help-seeking behaviors in classrooms (e.g., Arbreton, 1998, Karabenick, 2004; Karabenick & Knapp, 1991; Midgley, 2002) and is not reviewed here. Generally speaking, studies indicate the goals that students have in achievement settings are related to help seeking in similar ways as with other learning strategies. That is, highly motivated students are likely to seek help when they need it, just as they are more likely to use elaboration or metacognitive strategies (Karabenick & Knapp, 1991). Thus, *why* students make decisions with respect to the kinds of efforts they make and their decisions about seeking help are very important.

The mastery/performance goal orientation dichotomy parallels work conducted by Nelson-Le Gall (1981), who found that seeking assistance from others was a valuable self-regulating, proactive learning strategy, which led to autonomous achievement. That is, help seeking is an important developmental skill, and focus should be on the motives for seeking help rather than the act itself. As discussed elsewhere in this volume, Nelson-Le Gall (1981) identified two distinct motives for help-seeking behavior. *Executive help seeking* employs others to reduce the cost of achievement by getting others to provide answers, but may actually increase dependency in the long run, as when faced with a similar problem. In contrast, *instrumental help seeking* is designed to increase mastery and competence by procuring only the assistance necessary to accomplish tasks independently.

Those engaged in the providing of academic assistance typically view their effort as being instrumental, whereas students, particularly those needing help "right now," frequently seek executive assistance. That is, *instrumental help seeking* approaches emphasize helping students to master material, show personal improvements, and maintain their interest in and persistence on tasks, whereas *executive help seeking* approaches focus on finding solutions to problems, making comparisons with the progress of others, and may end up causing students to depend more of assistance providers rather than less so. Thus, staff working in academic assistance programs need to be aware of the distinction and also should be prepared to explain to students the goals that will guide their interactions. Students seeking exclusively executive assistance may need to be educated about its true value relative to that of instrumental assistance.

Attribution Theory.   Educational psychologists use attribution theory as a motivational framework to explain how different causal attributions relate to cognitive and behavioral outcomes. Attribution theory (Weiner, 1985, 1986) represents a way to describe how students' explanations of past failure or success outcomes can indirectly affect future achievement through affective reactions, expectancies for success, choice of task, and persistence. Several key studies during the late 1980s and early 1990s provided evidence to support the importance of attributions for self-regulation and achievement behavior, particularly for college students. The attribution process is relevant to college settings in which academic failure may threaten students with loss of control (Perry & Magnusson, 1989). According to Weiner's (1986) achievement motivation theory, causal attributions can mediate a range of responses following failure. For example, a student who attributes failure to a stable, personal cause such as lack of ability would experience more shame, less motivation, and lower control than if he or she had attributed the failure to a changeable, personal cause such as lack of effort.

In a study examining relations between causal attributions for failure and instructional quality, for example, Perry and Magnusson (1989) found that not only are certain attributions more adaptive for dealing with failure, their usefulness may also depend on the quality of instruction in the college classroom. And, in a recent study, Perry, Hladkyj, Pekrun, and Pelletier (2001) investigated relations between students' perceived academic control and their academic achievement and found that high-academic-control students exerted more effort, reported less boredom and anxiety, were more motivated, used self-monitoring strategies more often, and received higher grades than did low-academic-control students. Another potential obstacle arises when students attach negative connotations to help, known as effort–ability covariation (Ames, 1992; Pintrich & Zusho, 2001)—that is, the more students need help to succeed, the lower is their ability. Academic support programs can benefit students by helping them make adaptive attributions for their successes and failures, attributions that lead to positive affective reactions, high expectancy for success, and increased effort and persistence (Weiner, 1985).

Help Avoidance.   Other motivational constructs may represent obstacles to using support resources as well. Students might decide not to seek help as a result of effort abandonment (Feather, 1961, 1963), overconfidence (Yates & Collins, 1979), or stereotype threat (Steele & Aronson, 1995). Yates and Collins (1979) suggested that overconfidence may be a factor, as some students overestimate their true abilities relative to other good students enrolled at the same college. Steele and Aronson (1995) proposed the concept of stereotype threat as one that can have an adverse impact on self-identity and on intellectual performance. Stereotype threat represents being at risk of confirming, as self-characteristic, a negative stereotype about one's group (Steele & Aronson, 1995), and exists when a negative stereotype about a group to which one belongs becomes self-relevant (Steele, 1997). Examples offered to illustrate stereotype threat include women in male-dominated fields such as engineering or African American students in academic settings. Steele and Aronson suggest that stereotype threat functions to downgrade one's personal assessments, identification, and even performance in relevant domains. Stereotype threat is self-evaluative in nature, and among its numerous impacts can be disidentification with otherwise important domains, such as schooling, when the context happens to be academic performance. Thus, even though many students in a given college course might need extra help with subject matter, for particular students, such as women in engineering courses, to seek help could serve to confirm a stereotype in their eyes. Because stereotype threat is self-evaluative in nature, there can exist a self-imposed pressure to withdraw from the domain as personally important or to disprove the stereotype. In either case, such a student might not take advantage of available help to the same degree as others who do not experience threat. Thus, the threat of being perceived as less capable than others could cause some students to disengage from the very resources that should be helpful to them.

Butler (1998) in a summary of help-seeking literature identified two main reasons for avoiding help: (a) help seeking perceived as dependent behavior that conflicts with needs for autonomy (Deci & Ryan, 1985), and (b) help seeking seen as evidence of incompetence and a threat to ability perceptions. Consequently, students may seek help covertly from their peers in order to mask their incompetence rather than to seek help formally from instructors or assistance program staff. Butler also emphasized that students who strive for independence may be more willing to seek help if working alone proved unsuccessful and if help seeking were shown to enhance understanding and support their autonomy in the long run. Thus, there exist qualitatively different reasons for avoiding help.

Karabenick and Knapp (1988, 1991) showed that those who need help the most are often those least likely to seek it and that students with lower self-esteem are more likely to consider help seeking as threatening. These researchers also found that students who perceive themselves as less threatened by help are more likely to seek help, whereas students who are more threatened by the idea of help seeking are not only more likely to avoid doing so, but also more likely to have executive rather than instrumental help-seeking goals (see Karabenick, 2004). Vogel and Wester (2003) examined self-disclosure as it related to help-seeking behavior in clinical settings and found that avoidance factors predicted both attitudes toward help seeking and intentions to seek help. That is, clients who were less likely to seek help found self-disclosure of their present circumstance itself to be distressing, were not confident of the outcomes to be derived from seeking help, or were more concerned with concealing issues of concern. Although these findings relate to counseling situations, it is not unreasonable that they would apply to academic settings as well. If students who need help allow any of these motivations to influence their willingness to seek help, they may find themselves at a distinct disadvantage in terms of academic success relative to students who both recognize their need for help and utilize available help. Based on these motivational obstacles to help seeking, the following section outlines implications for the design and implementation of academic support programs.

IMPLICATIONS FOR SUPPORT PROGRAMS

Implications From Achievement Goal Theory

Because goal theory links students' reasons for wanting to do well with their help-seeking behavior, it may be important for support personnel to identify and understand students' goals on a case-by-case basis. In order to be effective, support programs must provide *realistic* help to students. That is, a student who arrives at a writing center with a rough draft of his mid-term English essay and wants to make sure he gets an "A" probably has a very different goal orientation from that of the student who enjoys regularly attending creative expression workshops at the writing center. It would be unrealistic to try to guarantee the performance outcome of the student with the essay, but improving that student's editing skills might be quite reasonable. Similarly, the student interested in creative expression is likely to be more interested in ongoing feedback and development than in a closed-ended assessment of a particular assignment. The design and implementation of support programs hinge on the understanding of such goals and reasons for seeking help in the first place.

Academic support programs often strive to develop self-regulated learning strategies in students, but students may have something different in mind, particularly if they are struggling. That is, students who find themselves in dire need of help in order to survive academically often want a "quick fix" to their troubles. A challenge for academic support staff is to identify and recognize differences in motivation that can affect the kinds of assistance that students want as well as their willingness to use the help that is available.

Consider the hypothetical (although realistic) cases of Tyshaun and Glyn. Early in the semester, Tyshaun seeks help from her academic advisor to plan her course selection sequences as they relate to fulfilling requirements for her intended academic major. She works with her advisor to identify her academic strengths and weaknesses, and gathers from her advisor information about campus resources that she can use to help address her concerns. For example, she has a long-standing concern about her problem-solving abilities in quantitatively oriented courses and her advisor makes her aware of tutoring help available from graduate student volunteers in the campus engineering lab. Tyshaun also is open to the advisor's suggestions about how to monitor her progress and about diligently following a study schedule.

In contrast, Glyn anxiously meets with his advisor 2 days before the mid-term examination in his economics course. Glyn explains that he hopes to major in business administration and absolutely must do well in this course, but has gotten behind due to other commitments. He feels that by working with a tutor within the next 24 hours he will acquire the information he needs to perform well on the mid-term examination. Glyn is both evasive and impatient as the advisor tries to assess his situation. He feels that the advisor's questions about his study habits in economics amount to wasting time that he could more profitably use with a tutor, if he could find one. After all, he's always had a "good memory" anyway, and if only he had a tutor who could tell him what he needed to study in the time that is left, then he would be able to do well on the examination. He is even willing to study all night if that is what it takes because he believes he must do well on this test to get into the business administration program.

These are but two examples of the wide variety of situations that academic support staff members confront. Tyshaun can be a pleasure to work with in part because she starts early and anticipates her needs. She also demonstrates the kind of motivational orientation we might call instrumental. That is, she seems genuinely to want to do well and to develop her abilities in such a way as to allow her to master not only current assignments, but also future related academic challenges she may face. Glyn, on the other hand, seeks executive help. That is, he wants the kind of help that he can quickly use to address his immediate challenges. He is less concerned with truly developing his abilities and mastering subject matter; rather, he simply wants the information he needs to address the problem currently at hand. Unfortunately, Glyn may also be unrealistic and overextended and does not seem open to understanding that the solution to his problem is not a quick fix; rather, it is one of sustained effort involving self-regulation and effective learning strategies.

Implications From Attribution Theory

As we have seen, whether students attribute their academic successes and failures to ability or effort can be extremely important. One important function that support personnel serve is that of attribution training. Attribution training aimed at getting students to make effort, rather than ability attributions, can go a long way toward motivating students to seek help (Zusho & Pintrich, 2002). Support programs can also work to convince students that seeking help is in fact strategic behavior that leads to success, and not reflective of stupidity or lack of competence.

Moreover, college faculty and academic assistance staff can use knowledge that certain students are less likely to seek help to tailor intervention efforts for such students. Students who shun assistance due to a misplaced sense of independence, for example, may require a different intervention than those who do not seek help because they have simply stopped trying. Karabenick and Knapp (1988) in a study of the relation between help seeking behavior and need for academic assistance found a curvilinear relationship, with those with either high or low need for help less likely to seek help than those with a moderate need for help. They observed that attribution theory (Weiner, 1986) provided a plausible explanation for why the rate of help seeking was low among those with high need. That is, lack of success is likely to result in attributions of low ability, engendering an expectation of future failure and leading to negative emotions such as hopelessness or resignation, as well as low task persistence and even withdrawal. Table 8.2 presents some additional implications of help-seeking research for academic support services.

A Model for Student Academic Development: The Bridge Program

The Bridge Program at the University of Michigan represents an effort to address many of the help-seeking issues just discussed. The Bridge Program, which is open to select students admitted for fall-term enrollment at the University of Michigan, offers students an opportunity to strengthen academic skills, develop a peer support network, and gain firsthand knowl-

TABLE 8.2

Implications of Help-Seeking Research for Academic Support Services

1.	Inform students of the positive outcomes associated with seeking help, (e.g., better grades, facilitated adjustment, retention).
2.	View students as active learners who are likely to seek help for different reasons at different times.
3.	Alert students to those circumstances in which help seeking is likely to be most useful as well as factors that might inhibit help seeking.
4.	Promote climates that disinhibit help seeking by encouraging cooperative, student-centered learning.
5.	Focus helping efforts on individual improvement and mastery rather than on comparison-based coursework.
6.	Consider students' need for help (high or low) and adjust outreach effort accordingly. High need may be accompanied by low self-esteem, making it less likely that the student would seek help.
7.	Be aware that self-disclosure of need for help may be threatening for some students.
8.	Strive to encourage instrumental help seeking among students rather than promoting a reliance on executive help seeking.
9.	Use principles of attribution theory to encourage students to make effort rather than ability attributions.
10.	Encourage students to view help seeking as strategic behavior that leads to academic success.

edge about the nature of student life at a large research institution. A major goal of the program is to develop students into self-regulated learners, individuals with the ability to monitor and control their learning to accomplish their academic goals. Participants enroll in credit-bearing courses during the summer, designed to develop analytical thinking and problem-solving skills as well as effective study and communication skills. Each participant also works with an academic advisor and peer advisor to explore academic goals and career objectives. In addition, students participate in a variety of social activities sponsored by the program.

Each year, Bridge Program participants are asked to complete program evaluation questionnaires, including questions concerning to whom they turned for support and why. Table 8.3 shows the percentages of program participants endorsing a particular reason for meeting with their advisor. Their responses offer some insight into the reasons students have for seeking help. For example, when asked about their reasons for meeting with a program advisor, Bridge participants consistently report "academic advice" as the most common reason. However, nearly three-quarters of these students also indicated that they saw their academic advisor for such concerns as assistance with study skills, with managing course workloads, and with meeting faculty expectations. More than half of them indicated that they saw advisors for help with performance issues (e.g., How can I perform better in this course?) or for help in goals clarification (e.g., What do I want to accomplish by taking this course?). Although faculty should be able to assist in these matters as well, it may be that students often are more willing to turn to advisors because they are seen as less judgmental and also because advisors are not involved in evaluating students' course work or assigning grades. More research is needed in order to investigate student perceptions of campus support programs, as well as applied research that links various types of help seeking to support program goals and objectives.

Our efforts at the University of Michigan make us keenly aware of a wide range of help-seeking options and obstacles common to both students and program staff. Our assistance efforts unfold within a comprehensive program that offers academic advising, course instruction, tutoring, study skills workshops, and the summer academic development program. The comprehensive program's focus is on first-year and sophomore students, but more advanced students can avail themselves of the program's services as well. Typically about 450 new first-year students enter the program each year, and about 1,800 students comprise its overall clientele in a given academic year. About 100 students participate in the summer academic program and their attendance is mandatory, whereas participation in all other program services offered during the academic year is voluntary. In a typical academic year, about 1,100 students will elect to enroll in program instructional courses, over 6,000 advising contacts will be held, and about 300 stu-

TABLE 8.3

Incidence of Summer Bridge Program Students Indicating Various Reasons
for Meeting With Their Advisor ($N = 109$)

Reason for Meeting With Advisor	Percent Indicating Reason
Reason 1: Academic advice (developing an academic plan, course selection)	98%
Reason 2: Academic adjustment issues (study skills development; workload management; understanding faculty expectations and standards)	71%
Reason 3: Performance issues (course difficulty/understanding; performance on tests or assignments)	57%
Reason 4: Self-understanding (abilities; strengths or weaknesses; goals clarification)	51%
Reason 5: Personal adjustment issues (interpersonal relations; emotion or social adjustment)	37%

dents will be provided with academic tutorial assistance upon request. In addition, about 200 students will participate in student development programs such as first-year interest groups for business administration, pre-law, or pre-medical studies.

Among students, it is not unusual for us to see many who fit the profiles described by Karabenick (2003), Butler (1998), or Deci and Ryan (1985). That is, we will see and provide assistance to students who prefer to work alone (i.e., are autonomous), those whose interest is expedient and who therefore seek executive help now, those who are ability focused and seek help through covert means, and those who avoid help because of a presumptive threat to self-esteem. Among staff members who provide assistance to students, we will see some who are so committed to student successful performance that they effectively are providing students with executive assistance rather than the kind of ability development that is deemed to offer better prospects for long-term academic achievement. It can sometimes require substantial involvement to refocus their efforts toward the employment of strategies that promote long-term independence through effective short-term assistance.

Effective resources for such staff may include other staff members with an orientation that employs more instrumental forms of assistance or in-service training that explains the differences between executive and instrumental assistance. For example, in a mathematics course, rather than working out a problem on the blackboard when students have questions, the instructor or tutor can have the students go to the blackboard and work as much of the problem as can be done. Strategic probing of student efforts with questions having to do with problem identification, with the problem-solving goal, or with problem-solving procedures often can prove more beneficial to students than the most thorough and painstaking of illustrations done by the assistance provider about how to solve the problem. However, such procedural knowledge about how to provide assistance needs to be coupled with insight about the variety of motivations students can bring to the help-seeking encounter. That is, assistance providers should be made aware of such research as that indicating that students who are more threatened by the act of seeking help are precisely those more likely to seek executive rather than instrumental assistance (Karabenick, 2003). Such knowledge can serve to help staff members to align their strategies and information with the attitudes and motivations students bring with them.

Successful adjustment and academic achievement in college depends on a variety of student-centered efforts, including task management, performance on tests and assignments, and the development of effective learning strategies and support networks. Research in our program indicates that there is some evidence that students who are more open to receiving help also tend to be more successful academically. The wide variety of assistance programs offered in colleges today means that students have a number of avenues available to them that can help with adjustment to the academic demands to be faced in challenging college environments. Staff working in programs that provide academic support to students in higher education may benefit from an understanding of motivation and how it may be applied to challenges presented by the students they serve.

Students bring with them different motivations for doing academic work, and as a consequence, different helping strategies may be needed in order to assist students effectively. Moreover, the goals of the assistance program may differ from the immediate goals held by the student. Academic assistance at the college level is most effective when it is used in a timely fashion, when students evidence appropriate commitment to their goals, and when they can be helped to see the benefits of instrumental, rather than executive, assistance. By taking advantage of available help, students can gain additional useful perspectives, learn what is expected of them, and deal with feelings of inadequacy or confusion about subject matter. As the demographics of higher education in this country continue to change, so too will the challenges faced by academic support programs that strive to help students overcome obstacles to seeking help with their studies.

We have employed the Motivated Strategies for Learning Questionnaire (MSLQ; Pintrich, Smith, Garcia, & McKeachie, 1993) in research to learn more about college students' beliefs and intention to seek help. Of primary importance, analyses indicate that the more positive students' attitudes were about the value of help seeking when needed, the higher their grades were during the fall term. This suggests that one strategy for academic support programs is to work with students to help them develop more positive attitudes toward taking advantage of help. In a sense, doing so may be considered similar to a medical model approach. That is, students may benefit from approaching their academics with an emphasis on self-monitoring in order to detect potential problem areas early, and then to employ an appropriate intervention and subsequent self-regulation for studying and learning that is both effective and successful.

REFERENCES

ACT, Inc. (2003, August). National data release—ACT scores steady despite record number of test-takers. *ACT Newsroom.* Retrieved February 16, 2004, from http://www.act.org/news/releases/2003/8-20-03.html

ACT, Inc. (2004). *Crisis at the core: Preparing all students for college and work.* Iowa City, IA: ACT, Inc.

Ames, C. (1992) Classrooms: Goals, structures, and student motivation. *Journal of Educational Psychology, 84,* 261–271.

Ames, C., & Lau, S. (1982). An attributional analysis of help-seeking in academic settings. *Journal of Educational Psychology, 74,* 3, 414–423.

Arbreton, A. (1998). Student goal orientation and help-seeking strategy use. In S. A. Karabenick (Ed.), *Strategic help-seeking: Implications for learning and teaching* (pp. 95–116). Mahwah, NJ: Lawrence Erlbaum Associates.

Beal, P. E. (1980). Learning centers and retention. In O. T. Lenning & R. N. Lyman (Eds.), *New roles for learning assistance* (pp. 59–74). San Francisco: Jossey-Bass.

Bollen, K. A., & Hoyle, R. H. (1990). Perceived cohesion: A conceptual and empirical examination. *Social Forces, 69,* 479–504.

Brubacher, J. S., & Rudy, W. (1997). *Higher education in transition* (pp. 399–411). New Brunswick, NJ: Transaction.

Butler, R. (1998). Determinants of help seeking: Relations between perceived reasons for classroom help-avoidance and help-seeking behaviors in an experimental context. *Journal of Educational Psychology, 90*(4), 630–643.

Christ, F. L. (1971). Systems for learning assistance: Learners, learning, facilitators, and learning centers. In F. L. Christ (Ed.), *Interdisciplinary aspects of reading instruction* (pp. 32–41). Los Angeles: Proceedings of the 4th Annual Conference of the Western College Reading Association.

Darseneau, D. F. (1988). Cooperative learning strategies. In C. E. Weinstein, E. T. Goetz, & P. A. Alexander (Eds.), *Learning and study strategies: Issues in assessment, instruction and evaluation* (pp. 103–120). New York: Academic Press.

Deci, E. L., & Ryan, R. M. (1985). *Intrinsic motivation and self-determination in human behavior.* New York: Plenum.

Dempsey, J., & Tomlinson, B. (1980). Learning centers and instructional/curricular reform. In O. T. Lenning & R. L. Nayman (Eds.), *New roles for learning assistance* (No. 2, pp. 41–58). San Francisco: Jossey-Bass.

Dubois, N., Kiewra, K., & Fraley, J. (1988, April). *Differential effects of a learning strategy course with a cognitive orientation.* Presented at the meeting of the American Educational Research Association, New Orleans, LA.

Dweck, C. S., & Leggett, E. L. (1988). A social-cognitive approach to motivation and personality. *Psychological Review, 95,* 256–273.

Enright, G., & Kerstens, G. (1980). The learning center: Toward an expanding role. In O. T. Lenning & R. L. Nayman (Eds.), *New roles for learning assistance* (pp. 1–24). San Francisco: Jossey-Bass.

Feather, N. T. (1961). The relationship of persistence at a task to expectations of success and achievement-related motives. *Journal of Abnormal and Social Psychology, 63,* 552–561.

Feather, N. T. (1963). Persistence at a difficult task with an alternative task of intermediate difficulty. *Journal of Abnormal and Social Psychology, 66,* 604–609.

Garcia, P. (1991). Summer Bridge: Improving retention rates for underprepared students. *Journal of the Freshman Year Experience, 3*(2), 91–105.

Gardner, J. N. (1986). The freshman year experience. *College and University, 61,* 261–274.

Hurtado, S., & Carter, D. F. (1997). Effects of college transitions and perceptions of the campus racial climate on Latino college students' sense of belonging. *Sociology of Education, 70,* 324–345.

Johnson, D. W., Johnson, R. T., & Smith, K. A. (1991). *Cooperative learning: Increasing college faculty instructional productivity.* ASHE-ERIC Higher Education Report No. 4. Washington, DC: George Washington University, School of Education and Human Development.

Karabenick, S. A. (1998). *Strategic help-seeking: Implications for learning and teaching.* Mahwah, NJ: Lawrence Erlbaum Associates.

Karabenick, S. A. (2003). Seeking help in large college classes: A person-centered approach. *Contemporary Educational Psychology, 28*(1), 37–58.

Karabenick, S. A. (2004). Perceived achievement goal structure and college student help seeking. *Journal of Educational Psychology, 96*(3), 569–581.

Karabenick, S. A., & Knapp, J. R. (1988). Help seeking and the need for academic assistance. *Journal of Educational Psychology, 80*(3), 406–408.

Karabenick, S. A., & Knapp, J. R. (1991). Relationship of academic help seeking to the use of learning strategies and other instrumental achievement behavior in college students. *Journal of Educational Psychology, 83*(2), 221–230.

Karabenick, S. A., & Sharma, R. (1994). Seeking academic assistance as a strategic learning resource. In P. Pintrich, D. Brown, & C. E. Weinstein (Eds.), *Student motivation, cognition and learning: Essays in honor of Wilbert J. McKeachie* (pp. 189–211). Hillsdale, NJ. Lawrence Erlbaum Associates.

Knapp, J. R., & Karabenick, S. A. (1988). Incidence of formal and informal help-seeking in higher education. *Journal of College Student Development, 29,* 223–227.

Kulik, C., Kulik, J., & Schwalb, B. (1983). College programs for high-risk and disadvantaged students: A meta-analysis of findings. *Review of Educational Research, 53,* 397–414.

Lenning, O. T., & Ebbers, L. H. (1999). *The Powerful Potential of Learning Communities: Improving Education for the Future.* ASHE-ERIC Higher Education Report Volume 26, No. 6. Washington, DC: George Washington University, Graduate School of Education and Human Development.

Love, A. G. (1994). *Learning Communities fall 1993 evaluation report.* Unpublished report, Temple University, Philadelphia, PA.

Maehr, M. L., & Midgley, C. (1991). Enhancing student motivation: A schoolwide approach. *Educational Psychologist, 26,* 399–427.

Martin, D., Blanc, R., & DeBuhr, L. (1983). *Supplemental instruction: A model for student academic support.* Kansas City: University of Missouri.

Maxwell, M. (1979). *Improving student learning skills.* San Francisco: Jossey-Bass.

Midgley, C. (2002). *Goals, goal structures, and patterns of adaptive learning.* Mahwah, NJ: Lawrence Erlbaum Associates.

Nadler, A. (1997). Personality and help seeking: Autonomous versus dependent seeking of help. In G. R. Pierece, B. Lackey, I. Sarason, & B. R. Sarason (Eds.), *Sourcebook of social support and personality* (pp. 379–407). New York: Plenum Press.

National Center for Education Statistics. (2004). *Remedial education at degree granting postsecondary institutions in fall 2000.* Washington, DC: U.S. Department of Education, Postsecondary Education Quick Information System.

Nelson-Le Gall, S. (1981). Help-seeking: An understudied problem-solving skill in children. *Developmental Review, 1,* 224–246.

Newman, R. S. (2000). Social influences on the development of children's adaptive help seeking: The role of parents, teachers, and peers. *Developmental Review, 20,* 350–404.

Nicholls, J. G. (1984). Conceptions of ability and achievement motivation. In R. Ames & C. Ames (Eds.), *Research on motivation in education* (Vol. 1, pp. 39–73). New York: Academic Press.

Noel, L. (1985). Increasing student retention: New challenges and potential. In L. Noel, R. Levits, & D. Saluri (Eds.), *Increasing student retention: Effective programs and practices* (pp. 000–000). San Francisco: Jossey-Bass.

Perry, R. P., & Magnusson, J. (1989). Causal attribution and perceived performance: Consequences for college students' achievement and perceived control in different instructional conditions. *Journal of Educational Psychology, 81,* 164–172.

Perry, R. P., Hladkyj, S., Pekrun, R. H., & Pelletier, S. T. (2001). Academic control and action control in the achievement of college students: A longitudinal field study. *Journal of Educational Psychology, 93,* 776–789.

Pintrich, P. R., Smith, D. A., Garcia, T., & McKeachie, W. J. (1993). Reliability of the motivated strategies for learning questionnaire (MSLQ). *Educational and Psychological Measurement, 53,* 801–813.

Pintrich, P. R., & Schunk, D. H. (2002). *Motivation in education: Theory, research and application* (2nd ed.). Upper Saddle River, NJ: Merrill Prentice Hall.

Pintrich, P. R., & Zusho, A. (2001). The development of academic self-regulation: The role of cognitive and motivation factors. In A. Wigfield & J. Eccles (Eds.), *The development of achievement motivation* (pp. 250–285). San Diego: Academic Press.

Ryan, A. M., & Pintrich, P. R. (1997). Should I ask for help? *Journal of Educational Psychology, 89*(2), 329–341.

Ryan, A. M.., Gheen, M., & Midgley, C. (1998). Why do some students avoid asking for help? An examination of the interplay among students' academic efficacy, teachers' social-emotional role and classroom goal structure. *Journal of Educational Psychology, 90,* 528–535.

Smith, B. L. (1993, fall). Creating learning communities, *Liberal Education,* pp. 32–39.

Steele, C. M. (1997). A threat in the air: How stereotypes shape intellectual identity and performance. *American Psychologist, 52,* 613–629.

Steele, C. M., & Aronson, J. (1995). Stereotype threat and intellectual test performance of African Americans. *Journal of Personality and Social Psychology, 69,* 797–811.

Timlin-Scalera, R. M., Pinterotto, J. G., Blumberg, F. C., & Jackson, M. A. (2003). A grounded theory of help-seeking behavior among white high school students. *Journal of Counseling Psychology, 50*(3), 339–350.

Tinto, V. (1993). *Leaving college: Rethinking the causes and cures of student attrition.* Chicago: University of Chicago Press.

Tinto, V., & Goodsell, A. (1994). Freshmen interest groups and the first year experience: Constructing student communities in a large university. *Journal of the Freshman Year Experience, 6,* 7–28.

Urdan, T. C. (1997). Achievement goal theory: Past results, future directions. In M. L. Maehr & P. R. Pintrich (Eds.), *Advances in motivation and achievement* (Vol. 10, pp. 99–141). Greenwich, CT: JAI Press.

Vogel, D. L., & Wester, S. R. (2003). To seek help or not to seek help: The risks of self-disclosure. *Journal of Counseling Psychology, 50*(3), 351–361.

Walsh, R. (1985). Changes in college freshman after participation in a student development course. *Journal of College Student Personnel, 26,* 310–314.

Weiner, B. (1985). An attributional theory of academic motivation and emotion. *Psychological Review, 92,* 548–573.

Weiner, B. (1986). *An attributional theory of motivation and emotion.* New York: Springer-Verlag.

Weinstein, C. E., & Mayer, R. E. (1986). The teaching of learning strategies. In M. C. Wittrock (Ed.), *Handbook of research on teaching* (3rd ed., pp. 315–327). New York: Macmillan.

Wilkie, C., & Kuckuck, S. (1989). A longitudinal study of the effects of a freshman seminar. *Journal of the Freshman Year Experience, 1,* 7–16.

Yates, J. F., & Collins, W. (1979). Self-confidence and motivation among black and white college freshmen: An exploration. In A.W. Boykin, A. J. Anderson, & J. F. Yates (Eds.), *Research directions of Black psychologists* (pp. 327–339). New York: Russell Sage Foundation.

Zusho, A., & Pintrich, P. R. (2002). The development of academic self-regulation: The role of cognitive and motivational factors. In A. Wigfield & J. S. Eccles (Eds.), *Development of achievement motivation* (pp. 249–284). San Diego, CA: Academic Press.

Chapter 9

Students' Adaptive and Nonadaptive Help Seeking in the Classroom: Implications for the Context of Peer Harassment

Richard S. Newman
University of California, Riverside

The primary function of classroom teachers is to help students learn. An important aspect of the learning process is asking questions about material one does not understand. When students work independently, monitor task performance, and recognize difficulties they cannot overcome on their own, attempting to remedy these difficulties by requesting assistance from a more knowledgeable individual can be an effective strategy. Unfortunately, students often fail to take the initiative to obtain needed help with schoolwork. Students often sit passively, waiting for the teacher to come to them. They may be afraid that if they ask for help, classmates will think they are incompetent. Or, if they do ask for help, students often do so in what might be considered a nonadaptive way. Sometimes they ask for assistance when it is not necessary—for example, when they have not first attempted the work on their own. They may be more interested in just getting the answer than in understanding the assignment. And sometimes students ask questions simply to get attention from either the teacher or classmates.

For classrooms to be conducive to learning, they must be safe, free of stress, and supportive of positive peer interaction. Another function of teachers then is to help students handle interpersonal challenges that interfere with students' emotional well-being and, ultimately, their learning. At elementary and middle school grades, the demands of maintaining friendships and peer group acceptance often cause children emotional stress. Disagreements and arguments with peers sometimes escalate into aggressive behaviors such as taunts, threats, and exclusion from social activities. A particular type of difficulty children often encounter at school—one that is the focus of this chapter—is peer harassment. Because teachers are not always present when incidents of harassment occur, students have to assess the level of danger and, if necessary, take responsibility for getting help. For many children, knowing when it is appropriate to ask a teacher to intervene presents a dilemma. Especially in situations where the norm is for children to resolve conflict on their own, help seeking can carry with it personal and social costs—for example, being perceived as weak. Sometimes help seeking leads to reprisals from the perpetrator. As a result, students who are harassed often are reluctant to go to adults for assistance, even in the face of real danger. Some students overreact in ways that escalate conflict and danger. And, as in the academic domain, students sometimes seek help unnecessarily. Being seen as a "tattletale" can lead to further interpersonal problems with peers. In sum, help seeking can be a very smart, adaptive way of handling adversity, whether academic difficulty or peer harassment. Also, help seeking can be nonadaptive in both contexts.

A good deal of research has examined help seeking in the academic domain (for reviews, see Newman, 1998a, 2000, 2002). The focus of most of this research, whether stated explicitly or not, has been *adaptive help seeking*. However, defining and operationalizing *adaptiveness* has been problematic. The major purpose of the present chapter is to address issues regarding the construct validity of adaptive help seeking. To this end, it will be important to differentiate adaptive help seeking and several types of *nonadaptive actions* in which children often engage when they encounter academic difficulties. The secondary purpose of the chapter is to focus on peer harassment. In contrast to the literature on academic help seeking, very little research has examined help seeking in the context of harassment. In two recent studies (Newman & Murray, 2005; Newman, Murray, & Lussier, 2001), my colleagues and I have begun to investigate this topic (also see Newman, 2003). In the chapter, I discuss findings from these two studies and explore whether what we know about *adaptive help seeking* and *nonadaptive actions* in the academic domain is useful in understanding how children cope with harassment.

ADAPTIVE HELP SEEKING IN THE ACADEMIC DOMAIN

Theoretical Background Regarding Adaptive Help Seeking

Traditionally, individuals who seek help from others have been characterized as immature and needy, whereas those who can work on their own without requiring help have been characterized as mature and autonomous. Perhaps especially in Western societies, which tend to emphasize self-reliance and individual competitiveness, help seeking among school-aged children has been perceived as an activity to be avoided because of its negative connotation of incompetence, immaturity, and overdependence on others. However, dependence is not the same as overdependence.

In two groundbreaking papers on how students respond to academic difficulties, Nelson-Le Gall (1981, 1985) pointed out that help seeking can be useful, efficacious, and instrumental under certain conditions (see also Ames, 1983). The key is the qualifier "under certain conditions." Nelson-Le Gall described *instrumental help seeking* according to a sequence of six conditions or actions: (a) being aware that one does not know something; (b) deciding to seek help rather than taking an alternative action (e.g., persevering, trying a new strategy, waiting for help, giving up); (c) formulating an appropriate question (i.e., so the request provides the information that is needed but, importantly, no more than what is needed); (d) choosing an appropriate target to whom the question is addressed; (e) successfully carrying out the request for help; and (f) successfully processing the help that is received.

In several papers (Newman, 1991, 1994), I used the term *adaptive help seeking* to refer to the same sequence as described by Nelson-Le Gall (1981, 1985). However, to simplify operationalization of the construct, I emphasized three critical decisions on which adaptive help seeking is contingent: (a) *necessity* of the request (i.e., is it necessary that I ask another person for help?); (b) *content* of the request (i.e., what should I ask?); and (c) *target* of the request (i.e., whom should I ask?). Adaptive help seeking involves the child matching, to the best of his or her ability, the content and target of a request to the specific needs at hand. The most basic element in this definition is *necessity*. The child must realize it is necessary to get help. He or she then formulates a "good" question (i.e., one that will elicit exactly what is needed) that is addressed to a "good" target (i.e., an individual who has the knowledge and motivation to provide exactly what is needed). Adaptive help seeking is a strategy of self-regulated learning (Boekaerts, Pintrich, & Zeidner, 2000; Karabenick, 1998; Newman, 1994; Schunk & Zimmerman, 1998; Zimmerman & Schunk, 1989). More generally, it can be considered an aspect of mature coping, whereby an individual faced with adversity matches a particular action or strategy to a specific stressor (see Brenner & Salovey, 1997; Cohen & Wills, 1985; Fields & Prinz, 1997; Skinner, Edge, Altman, & Sherwood, 2003).

In a further attempt to define the construct, I focused on component skills and resources that adaptive help seeking would seem to require (Newman, 1998a, 2002). Adaptive help seeking is a *strategy*, and as such, can be defined as an integration, or fusing, of "skill" and "will" (Paris, 1988). Accordingly, one can specify certain skills (i.e., cognitive and social competencies) and affective-motivational resources that presumably are required for adaptive help seeking. These include:

1. *Cognitive competencies.* Students can accurately monitor task performance; their confidence in how they perform tasks is well calibrated to external evaluation of their performance (i.e., they know when assistance is necessary); and they are linguistically skillful at formulating requests or questions that will yield precisely the action or information that is needed.
2. *Social competencies.* Students know that others can help; they know who is the best person to approach for help (e.g., a teacher, a peer); and they know how to carry out a request in a socially appropriate way (e.g., they know how to approach, interrupt, engage, and thank the helper).
3. *Affective-motivational resources.* Students' self-perceptions of competence, self-efficacy, personal goals, values, expectations for success, and patterns of causal attribution are associated with a desire for challenge and tolerance for task difficulty; they enjoy working independently, but at the same time, these resources allow them to admit their limitations and attempt to overcome limitations by seeking assistance from those who can help (i.e., they enjoy working collaboratively).

Operationalizing Adaptive Help Seeking

It has been useful, on a theoretical level, to conceptualize adaptive help seeking in terms of component cognitive and social competencies and affective-motivational resources. On an empirical level, researchers have tended to discuss adaptiveness in terms of Nelson-Le Gall's (1981, 1985) six actions and/or Newman's (1991, 1994) three decisions. However, only a few studies have explicitly operationalized adaptive help seeking. In this subsection I review these studies, focusing on the three criteria: necessity, content, and target. First, I discuss research findings that have involved only *necessity* (i.e., independent of content or target of the request). Second, I discuss findings that have involved requests of a particular *content* matched to *necessity* (i.e., independent of target). Little research on help seeking has examined choice of *target*, and no research to my knowledge has examined choice of target *in conjunction with* content and/or necessity. Indeed, most research on academic help seeking has focused on students seeking help from their teacher or an adult experimenter (although see work on peers as helpers: DeCooke & Nelson-Le Gall, 1989; chapters in the present volume by Kempler & Linnenbrink, and by Webb, Ing, Nemer, & Kersting; for work at the college level, see Karabenick, 2004). Hence, I only briefly address this third criterion. Note that although a number of studies have demonstrated relations between individual differences in help seeking and various motivational constructs (e.g., achievement and social goals, perceived competence, self-efficacy), I have limited the present discussion to findings involving achievement goals. Where appropriate, I discuss developmental findings (i.e., adaptive help seeking in relation to age, grade level, or knowledge). At this point in the chapter, I do not differentiate adaptive help seeking from other similar constructs (including instrumental help seeking). In a subsequent section, I do provide a more fine-grained differentiation of constructs.

Necessity. According to this criterion, help seeking is restricted to occasions when assistance is "truly" needed. When their knowledge is lacking or comprehension is incomplete and when there is some ambiguity or confusion inherent in the task at hand, older (and more knowledgeable) students are more aware of difficulties and better at monitoring task performance than younger (and less knowledgeable) students (e.g., Markman, 1981; Pressley, Levin, Ghatala, & Ahmad, 1987).

How has *necessity* been incorporated into research on help seeking? Researchers have used experimental procedures that have simulated one-to-one tutoring (e.g., giving the child a difficult task and an opportunity to request help from an adult experimenter). Several studies have considered initial failure as an objective measure of need. Help seeking following initial failure can be interpreted as appropriate or necessary, whereas help seeking following an initial solution that is correct is inappropriate or unnecessary. Nelson-Le Gall (1987) asked third and fifth graders to define vocabulary words with the option of requesting help. Children gave a tentative, initial answer, were given the option of requesting help, and then were asked for a final answer. Third graders tended to make more unnecessary requests for help than did fifth graders. Using a similar procedure with fifth graders, van der Meij (1990) found that children with relatively poor vocabularies asked significantly more unnecessary questions and tended to ask fewer necessary questions than did children with good vocabularies.

Children increasingly (i.e., with age and knowledge) are able to calibrate subjective judgments of confidence to actual task performance (Newman & Wick, 1987). Lower confidence can be considered an indicator of stronger perceived need for help. Utilizing this approach to examine third and fifth graders' help seeking, Nelson-Le Gall, Kratzer, Jones, and DeCooke (1990) followed the same experimental procedure used by Nelson-Le Gall (1987), although children additionally were asked to judge how confident they were that their tentative, initial answers were correct. Children's subjective judgments of need for help (i.e., confidence ratings) can be compared with objective standards of need (i.e., actual correctness of initial answers). Subjective judgments of need matched objective standards more often among fifth graders (and those with good verbal skills) than among third graders (and those with poor skills). Fifth graders (and those with good skills) sought help more often when they perceived an initial solution to be incorrect than when correct; third graders (and those with poor skills), on the other hand, were just as likely to seek help when they perceived a solution to be incorrect as when they perceived it to be correct.

The majority of help-seeking research has not been experimental and has not taken into account objective or subjective need on specific tasks. These studies have involved self-report data. Typically, students are asked to rate the likelihood of their seeking help, for example, in math class. Wording of items in a conditional sense takes into account students' perceived need for help. So, for example, Ryan and colleagues (Ryan, Gheen, & Midgley, 1998; Ryan, Hicks, & Midgley, 1997; Ryan & Pintrich, 1997; see also Karabenick, 2004; Karabenick & Knapp, 1991) have asked students to rate items such as "If I get stuck on a math problem, I ask someone for help so I can keep working on it" or "I don't ask for help in math even if the work is too hard to solve on my own" (with rating reversed). Similarly, Newman and colleagues (Newman, 1990; Newman & Goldin, 1990) had students rate items such as "When there is something I don't understand and I cannot figure it out myself, I ask the teacher for help." Although experimental studies allow more precise assessment of whether help is necessary for task completion, self-report studies have allowed assessment of students' perceived need for help in the "real world" of classroom learning. In addition to asking students about their help seeking, Ryan, Patrick, and Shim (2005) asked teachers to report how likely it is that the students ask for help in class when it is needed. Students' own reports were largely confirmed by reports of teachers, thus lending an important sense of validity to self-reports.

Content of Request Matched to Necessity.   Not all requests for help, even though they are in response to legitimate need, are adaptive. Given a particular task situation, certain types of requests may be more appropriate (i.e., adaptive) than others. Good, Slavings, Harel, and Emerson (1987) differentiated among four types of informational questions that students ask in the classroom: requests for an explanation, factual information, clarification of information, and confirmation of an answer. Although one cannot infer that requests for explanations are necessarily adaptive without considering the specific needs of the situation, evidence does generally support the value of explanations in classroom discourse (see Webb & Palincsar, 1996). Kearsley (1976) differentiated two types, or forms, of informational requests: open and closed. Open questions (e.g., "What arithmetic operation do I use?" or "How do I do this problem?") are nonspecific, whereas closed questions (e.g., "Does this problem require addition or subtraction?" or "Am I supposed to subtract?" or "This problem requires subtraction, doesn't it?") presuppose some specific knowledge on the part of the questioner. According to van Hekken and Roelofsen (1982), among elementary school-aged children during play, younger children tend to ask open questions, whereas older children tend to ask closed questions. Importance of knowledge on questioning is supported by Smith, Tykodi, and Mynatt (1988). When adults are learning computer skills from a manual, less knowledgeable subjects tend to ask open questions, whereas more knowledgeable subjects ask closed questions.

How has *content* been incorporated, along with *necessity*, into research on help seeking? The experimental procedure of Nelson-Le Gall (1987) and Nelson-Le Gall et al. (1990) was used to examine the effects of grade level and verbal skill on different types of requests for help. Recall that, following an initial answer, children were given the option of requesting help and then were asked for a final answer. Children could request one of two types of help: (a) hint (i.e., indirect help in the form of the target word used in a sentence) or (b) direct answer (i.e., the correct answer supposedly "left behind by another child who had done well on the task"). According to Nelson-Le Gall (1981, 1985), asking for a hint is indicative of "instrumental" help seeking (i.e., it indicates a desire to clarify or refine current knowledge and to learn), whereas asking for a direct answer is indicative of "executive" help seeking (i.e., it indicates either a lack of knowledge or desire for expedient task completion). Perhaps requesting a hint can be likened to a closed question, whereas requesting a direct answer can be likened to an open question. Fifth graders (and children with good skills) asked the experimenter for more hints than direct answers, whereas third graders (and those with poor skills) showed no preference (for similar results, see Nelson-Le Gall & Jones, 1990). Importantly, when fifth graders (and children with good skills) did ask for direct answers, these requests were on trials for which the children felt especially unsure of themselves (i.e., their confidence was low), whereas third graders (and those with poor skills) did not show this relationship between type of request and confidence. In other words, among only the more experienced learners was there evidence of adaptiveness as operationalized in this relatively stringent way (i.e., matching specific type of request to perceived need).

In an experimental study, Newman and Schwager (1995) gave students the option of requesting six types of help: (a) explanations, (b) big hints, (c) little hints, (d) confirmation of an answer, (e) the correct answer, and (f) other. Third and sixth graders were asked to solve a series of mathematical inductive reasoning problems designed to be beyond the students' current level of proficiency. The label for each type of help was printed on a written menu. We included two levels of hints (according to how much mathematical information, relevant to each specific problem, was provided) to explore the precision by which students matched content to perceived difficulty. Again, similar to Nelson-Le Gall's research, big and little hints were somewhat comparable to open and closed questions, respectively. "Other" referred to any question the student wanted to ask. Sessions were individualized, simulating a one-to-one tutorial. For each problem, students could ask an experimenter as many questions as they wanted. All questions were completely answered. Coding of spontaneously generated "other" questions revealed (a) requests for process-related information aimed at understanding how to do the problem and (b) nonspecific, vague statements and questions indicating a lack of understanding (e.g., "My head is hollow!" or "30!?"). Adaptive patterns of help seeking were coded when an independent attempt to solve a problem was followed by an incorrect answer, which in turn was followed by a request for an explanation or hint. These were exhibited infrequently. Sixth graders were more likely than third graders to ask for hints (of both types) and less likely simply to ask for the answer or vaguely express a lack of understanding. We also coded maladaptive patterns of help seeking (e.g., an incorrect answer followed by no additional work or an immediate request for an answer with no independent work). In keeping with predictions from goal theory (see later discussion), maladaptive patterns were exhibited more frequently by students in a performance-goal condition than those in a learning-goal condition.

In a follow-up study with a similar procedure, Newman (1998b) examined help seeking among fourth and fifth graders. Both adaptive and maladaptive patterns were infrequent. Because of the tutorial nature of the procedure, it was fairly common for students to ask for more than one hint per problem; hence, we were able to examine sequences of hints. Interestingly, although there were 33 occurrences of a little hint followed by a big hint (distributed over a good number of students), there was only one occurrence of a big hint followed by a little one. Newman and Schwager (1995) observed the same disproportionality (i.e., 55 occurrences vs. 2). The sequence of little hint followed by big hint suggests students' desire to try to work things out on their own.

In Butler and Neuman (1995), second and sixth graders were asked to solve a series of puzzles; they were given the opportunity to ask an experimenter for either hints or complete solutions. Rather than utilizing an independent measure of students' confidence in prior performance or obtaining a measure of prior failure (cf. Nelson-Le Gall, 1987; Nelson-Le Gall et al., 1990), Butler and Neuman's measure of help seeking was computed as a proportion in such a way that it arguably incorporates "necessity" (i.e., by dividing the number of puzzles for which the child requested help by the number of puzzles that the child did not solve alone). The measure ranges from 0 (i.e., the child never asks for help when he or she does not solve the problem) to 1 (i.e., the child always asks for help when he or she does not solve the problem). They also measured the time elapsed before children who requested help for a puzzle made their first request. Neither the total number of requests for hints, the total number of requests for solutions, nor a proportional measure of necessary help seeking (including hints plus solutions) showed an effect of grade level. However, latency did show a grade effect. Older children took more time before requesting help than did younger children, suggesting more perseverance in the face of difficulty. Using a similar procedure, Butler (1998) had fifth and sixth graders work on difficult math problems for which they could ask for either hints or answers. In this study, a proportional measure of necessary requests for hints, a proportional measure of necessary requests for answers, and a proportional measure of necessary help seeking (including hints plus answers) were computed; again, latency was measured. In an intriguing twist to the procedure, children had the opportunity to "cheat" by copying the answer from an answer sheet. Results involving the three proportional scores, latency, and frequency of cheating are discussed in a later section of the chapter focusing on relations between help seeking and goals.

Choice of Target Matched to Content of Request and/or Necessity. A third criterion for adaptiveness of help seeking involves the suitability of the child's choice of help giver. The adaptive help seeker is able to assess the situation and choose the particular person who is most likely to meet his or her particular needs. So, for example, the "mature help seeker," when stuck on a difficult math problem, knows to go to Mary ("the class math whiz") rather than Mr. Smith ("who may be smart in math but explains things in too complicated a way"). Further, the student is able to ask Mary a question that hones in directly on what he or she does not understand in the problem (cf. Wilkinson & Calculator, 1982). Choice of target obviously is a relevant criterion only in classrooms where students have the option of seeking help from the teacher or peers, where they can choose among teachers and teachers' aides, or where they can choose among different peers. No research to date has operationalized adaptiveness according to matching of both *target* and *content* to *necessity*. There is research, however, suggesting that children are able to differentiate among various characteristics of potential helpers and that this ability increases with age (e.g., see Newman, 2000, 2002).

For example, we know that preschoolers, kindergartners, and first graders believe that individuals are good helpers if they have been helpful in the past (Barnett, Darcie, Holland, & Kobasigawa, 1982). As they come to understand motives, abilities, and behaviors of others, children become aware of different ways that teachers can meet their needs. They show an awareness and appreciation of teachers' kindness and "niceness" (Barnett et al., 1982; Nelson-Le Gall & Gumerman, 1984). By upper elementary grades, children judge teachers as helpful according to their dependability (e.g., willingness to help), interpersonal attunement (e.g., awareness and empathy for others' problems and needs), and dedication (e.g., quality of advice and available time; Furman & Buhrmester, 1985). When Newman and Schwager (1993) asked students if—and why—they go to their teacher for help when they do not understand a math assignment, perceptions of mutual liking and friendship with the teacher emerged as predictors of help seeking across the elementary and middle school grades. In addition to these affect-related factors, teachers' explicit encouragement and support of student questioning predicted help seeking at the upper grades. Presumably, as children become more aware of different ways in which teachers can help them, they become better able to choose between "good" and "poor" helpers.

In spite of generally positive attitudes, children also have negative attitudes regarding adults' helpfulness. As early as Grade 2, children fear negative reactions from teachers if they ask for help (e.g., "I think she might think I'm dumb"; Newman & Goldin, 1990). Perceived costs of going to the teacher are heightened when teachers seem unwilling to help. Comments such as "If you had paid attention, you wouldn't need help" no doubt discourage students from requesting help (van der Meij, 1988). Students come to know which teachers evoke anxiety and fear of "looking dumb" and which teachers are more supportive of questioning. Over the school years, positive and negative attitudes about teachers, and corresponding attitudes about benefits and costs of help seeking, influence in increasingly complex ways children's decisions about what to do when they encounter academic difficulties. In spite of early elementary school aged students being aware of potential costs, their decisions about help seeking seem to depend only on the degree to which they feel they will benefit from the teacher's help and not on perceived costs. For older students, however, perceived costs take on a more prominent role in decision making (Newman, 1990). By middle school, students weigh both benefits and costs, with fear of "looking dumb" in front of teachers and classmates being an especially powerful deterrent to help seeking (Ryan & Pintrich, 1997; Ryan et al., 1998; see also Nadler, 1991, 1998).

In sum, researchers have attempted with only some success to operationalize adaptive help seeking according to necessity and content. Findings suggest that, with age and knowledge, children are increasingly aware of when they need help, and based on this awareness are increasingly likely to request help to deal with the difficulty. Also, with age and knowledge, children seem to be increasingly able to match particular types of requests to particular task demands. The third criterion of adaptive help seeking involves flexibility in the choice of a helper. As children get older, they increasingly are cognizant of characteristics of effective helpers in the classroom and increasingly are influenced by their views regarding costs and benefits of seeking help. However, no research has explicitly taken into account target along with content and/or necessity (although, see Karabenick's [2004] formulation of help-seeking "patterns"). Conceptualizing *adaptive help seeking* according to Newman's (1991, 1994) three criteria has seemed reasonable; however, operationalizing the construct empirically has been problematic.

Elusive Conceptual Issues.   At least five important conceptual questions regarding adaptive help seeking have not been adequately addressed. First, should adaptiveness be defined according to the child's perspective or that of the teacher? The child might make decisions about the necessity, content, or target of a request that are contrary to judgments of an "expert" who may, in fact, be more knowledgeable and/or objective than the child about such decisions. Indeed, how can one know when a child is truly "stumped" (i.e., when he or she has tried his or her best and, having exhausted all strategies and effort, can proceed no further without the teacher's assistance)? Second, should an additional criterion for adaptiveness be that help seeking necessarily leads to success (e.g., the child solving a problem, understanding class material, or completing an assignment)? Again, from whose perspective should success be defined? Third, should a measure of adaptiveness be constrained by classroom factors (e.g., presence of different potential helpers; norms and rules pertaining to whether help seeking is allowed or instead is considered as cheating)? Perhaps the construct is meaningful only if measured in a naturalistic setting (i.e., classroom vs. experiment). Fourth, should adaptiveness take into account the student's academic needs (e.g., task completion and mastery) as well as social needs (e.g., encouragement and enhancement of friendship)? What is adaptive for learning may or may not be adaptive in terms of social relations with peers. For example, the child who wants to learn but feels peer pressure not to look dumb has to reconcile opposing forces. Perhaps even more daunting is what faces the child who wants to learn but whose peer group would ostracize him for pursuing such a goal (cf. Wentzel, 1996). Finally, implicit in the definition of adaptiveness is goal-directedness (i.e., the student enjoys academic challenge, for example, as indicated by preference for hints vs. answers). Should particular goals (e.g., learning goals vs. performance goals; Dweck, 1986; Nicholls, 1979) be explicitly "built into" the definition of adaptive help seeking? Or, should goals be measured independently, with relations between goals and action (i.e., requesting help) tested empirically?

Assuming researchers could agree on answers to these conceptual questions and assuming adaptive help seeking could then be measured in a straightforward way, a major hurdle still remains. "True" adaptive help seeking may be an ideal to which students and teachers strive. However, in the reality of classrooms, adaptive help seeking appears to be rare. Students infrequently ask questions of any type (Dillon, 1988). Most typically, students are reluctant to reveal that they do not understand their work (Newman & Goldin, 1990; Ryan et al., 1997, 1998; Ryan & Pintrich, 1997). Research suggests that reluctance increases over the school years (Good et al., 1987). By high school, students say they put less effort into the goal of getting help with schoolwork than they put into any other classroom goal (Wentzel, 1989). Also, when students do seek help, it may not conform to criteria for adaptiveness. Indeed, adaptiveness can be "compromised" at any or all of the three decision points (i.e., "Is it necessary that I ask another person for help?"; "What should I ask?"; "Whom should I ask?').

The Larger Picture: Nonadaptive Action

In an attempt to facilitate research, it may be useful to take a different approach. *What are the alternatives to adaptive help seeking?* That is, when students encounter difficulties and do *not* seek help adaptively, what *do* they do? Rather than seek help adaptively, students often engage in *nonadaptive help seeking*, or more generally, *nonadaptive action*.

If we consider the first decision on which adaptive help seeking is contingent (i.e., necessity), students can take one of four possible actions:

1. *Adaptive help seeking* (i.e., asking for help when it is necessary).
2. *Nonadaptive help seeking* (i.e., asking for help when it is *not* necessary).
3. *Nonadaptive "other action"* (i.e., *not* asking for help when it is necessary).
4. *Adaptive "other action"* (i.e., *not* asking for help when it is *not* necessary).

Table 9.1 illustrates these four possibilities. Each represents how students calibrate *action* to *need*. Most help-seeking researchers have focused on adaptive and nonadaptive help seeking (i.e., the two left-hand cells). Implicit has been nonadaptive "other action" (i.e., top right cell). Adaptive help seeking (i.e., top left cell) and adaptive "other action" (i.e., bottom right cell) represent actions of academically competent and self-regulated learners (see Boekaerts et al., 2000; Schunk & Zimmerman, 1998; Zimmerman & Schunk, 1989). Several examples of adaptive "other actions" are (a) the student continuing to work independently or (b) the student correctly concluding that the task has been completed and then either moving on to another task or rewarding him-/herself (e.g., by watching TV or going to bed). In the table, I have included terminologies used by four researchers: Ruth Butler, Allison Ryan, Sharon Nelson-Le Gall, and myself. Three of the four actions represented in Table 9.1 map onto different

TABLE 9.1

Calibration of Action to Need (With Different Terminologies)

Is Help Necessary?	Action	
	Seek Help	*Do Not Seek Help*
Yes	*Adaptive help seeking*	*Nonadaptive "other action"*
	Adaptive HS[a]	Passivity
	Autonomous HS[b]	Avoidant-covert action
	Appropriate HS[c]	Avoidance of HS
	Instrumental HS[d]	Passivity
	(Mastery goals)[e]	(Performance-avoidance goals)
No	*Nonadaptive help seeking*	*Adaptive "other action"*
	Nonadaptive HS	ns[f]
	Executive HS	ns
	Dependent HS	ns
	Executive HS	ns
	(Work-avoidance goals)	ns

Note. Terminology according to different researchers (by row in table).
[a]Newman (2002).
[b]Butler (1998).
[c]Ryan et al. (2005).
[d]Nelson-Le Gall (1985).
[e](Probable goal orientation).
[f]ns, Not specified.

achievement goals. In the following subsections, I first discuss achievement goals and then focus on the research of Butler and Ryan.

Achievement Goals Related to Help Seeking.   Achievement goals are highly predictive of students' motivation and behavior in learning situations (see Elliott, 1999; Midgley, 2002; Pintrich, 2000). Students with mastery goals (alternately referred to as learning goals) are motivated to learn; they enjoy developing new skills and prefer challenging work (Dweck, 1986; Nicholls, 1979). Students with performance goals (or ability goals) are interested in maintaining high perceptions of competence; they want to perform better—and certainly not worse—than others (Dweck, 1986; Nicholls, 1979). Recent research in goal theory has differentiated between performance-approach goals (i.e., desire to look competent) and performance-avoidance goals (i.e., desire to not look incompetent; see Midgley, Kaplan, & Middleton, 2001; Pintrich, 2000). Work-avoidance (or expedience) goals have also been related to how students approach academic situations (Meece,

Blumenfeld, & Hoyle, 1988). Individuals with work-avoidance goals try to complete their work quickly, with minimal effort; their priority is to move on to other, preferred activities.

Research on relations between achievement goals and help seeking has focused on the first two of these goals (see Karabenick, 2004; Newman, 1991). Students with mastery goals are relatively likely to engage in adaptive help seeking. That is, they tend to work independently and ask for help when necessary (i.e., following an "honest" effort of their own). When they seek assistance, they request hints and explanations rather than direct answers in order to maintain for themselves the challenge and enjoyment of mastering difficult material. Students with performance (in particular, performance-avoidance) goals often are unwilling to reveal academic difficulties. Because of the salience of social comparison in most classrooms, public disclosure of academic difficulties makes students with performance goals feel vulnerable to negative perceptions by their peers. For these individuals, perceived benefits of help seeking (i.e., learning and academic success) generally are outweighed by perceived costs (i.e., embarrassment about looking incompetent; Nadler, 1991, 1998; see also Karabenick, 1998, 2004).

Research Supporting Differentiation in Table 9.1. Butler's research supports a differentiation among three of the four cells in Table 9.1. Butler (1998) proposed that there are *three* distinct costs associated with help seeking—not just fear of looking incompetent. Further, according to Butler, students' reluctance to seek help can be explained by three qualitatively different, goal-related help-avoidance (HA) orientations: (a) autonomous (or mastery), (b) ability-focused (or performance-avoidance), and (c) expedient (or work-avoidance). Associated with each orientation are particular reasons why students at times do not seek help *as well as* reasons why, at other times, they do seek help. Butler made the following predictions: Students with an autonomous HA orientation refrain from asking for help when help is not necessary because of a desire to learn on their own. At other times, however (e.g., when help is truly necessary), they do seek help in order to overcome obstacles to learning. And, when they seek help, students with this type of orientation will ask for hints rather than direct answers or directions in order to give themselves an opportunity to complete assignments and still feel a sense of accomplishment. Students with an ability-focused HA orientation refrain from asking for help when they sense that classmates are watching because of a desire to mask any academic difficulty they may have. Yet at other times (e.g., when they perceive pressure to get good grades), they are willing to seek assistance. And, when they seek help, these students will employ covert strategies, for example, copying or cheating in order to get the right answer. Students with an expedient HA orientation refrain from seeking help when they think that asking for help will take too long or require too much effort. Yet at other times (e.g., when it enables them to finish quickly without having to put forth much effort), they do seek help. In fact, they may ask directly for the answer to a problem without first trying to figure it out on their own.

To empirically test these predictions, Butler (1998) administered to fifth- and sixth-grade students a questionnaire involving reasons for *avoiding help*. Factor analysis of students' ratings revealed three factors, interpreted as autonomous, ability-focused, and expedient HA orientations. Students were categorized according to whether they exhibited a dominant autonomous, ability-focused, or expedient HA orientation. Based on a second questionnaire (involving reasons for *seeking help*), it was shown that autonomous perceptions for seeking help were highest among students with a dominant autonomous HA orientation; there was a similar correspondence in reasons for *seeking help* and reasons for *avoiding help* for both students with ability-focused and expedient orientations. Butler then had students perform a numerical task (cf. Butler & Neuman, 1995) on which they could obtain different types of help (e.g., hints, answers, or cheating). Requests for hints (i.e., a proportional score that takes into account *necessity*) were most frequent among students with the autonomous orientation; requests for answers (i.e., again, a proportional score) were most frequent and latency was the shortest among students with the expedient orientation; and cheating was most frequent among students (boys only) with the ability-focused orientation.

Research by Ryan supports a differentiation among the same three cells of Table 9.1. Ryan et al. (2005) conducted two studies with students and teachers at Grades 5 and 6. In Study 1, teachers were asked to categorize each of their students into one of three groups according to the following help-seeking tendencies: (a) "generally display appropriate help-seeking skills with their schoolwork (i.e., ask for help when they truly need it but are not overly dependent, do not ask for help the minute they encounter difficulty)"; (b) "ask for too much help with their schoolwork (i.e., need to develop more independence, tend to ask for help the minute they encounter difficulty)"; and (c) "do not ask for help when they need it with their schoolwork (i.e., need to develop help-seeking skills, tend to avoid asking for help altogether even when they need it)." On a questionnaire, students rated how likely they are to not seek help with schoolwork (e.g.,"when I don't understand my schoolwork, I often put down any answer rather than ask for help"). The proportion of students that teachers categorized as "appropriate help seekers," "dependent help seekers," and "avoidant help seekers" was 65%, 13%, and 22%, respectively. Students who were categorized as "avoidant help seekers" had the highest self-ratings of help avoidance.

In Study 2, again, teachers categorized students (i.e., a different group than in Study 1) as one of the three types of help seekers. Students completed several questionnaires: (a) reasons to not seek help (cf. Butler's [1998] autonomous, ability-focused, and expedient reasons), (b) goals (i.e., mastery, performance-approach, performance-avoidance goals), (c) affective experiences in class, (d) social relationship with their teacher, and (e) perceived competence. Students' grades in school and achievement test scores also were collected. The proportion of students who teachers categorized as "appropriate help seekers," "dependent help seekers," and "avoidant help seekers" was 74%, 7%, and 19%, respectively. Thus, consistent across the two studies—and surprisingly—teachers identified most students as appropriate help seekers. This may be attributed to the specific way in which teachers categorized students. Of the two nonadaptive categories, teachers identified more avoidant help seekers than dependent help seekers. In general, avoidant help seekers had the most maladaptive psychological self-profile (i.e., relatively high ability-focused and expedient reasons to not seek help, low mastery goals and high performance-avoidance goals, low perceived competence, relatively little perceived emotional and academic support from their teacher, and relatively little positive affect in class). Students categorized as dependent help seekers comprised the smallest group of students, and on many of the measures did not differ from the appropriate help seekers. However, they were similar to avoidant help seekers in that both groups had relatively low grades and achievement test scores and experienced high amounts of anxiety in class. Ryan et al. (2005) speculated that dependent help seekers may be at-risk, over time, of becoming avoidant help seekers.

In sum, when students encounter academic difficulties, they often respond in ways that are not adaptive for learning. Research on self-regulated learning might benefit from a refocusing on students' help seeking within a context that includes alternative, nonadaptive actions. Table 9.1 is based on the criterion of *necessity* (i.e., students' calibration of *action* to *need*). Differences between the bottom left and top right cells of Table 9.11 are particularly intriguing. Nonadaptive help seeking (i.e., asking for help when it is not necessary) appears to be a qualitatively different sort of action than nonadaptive "other action." The two actions may be representative of two qualitatively different sorts of students, who perhaps are socialized differently and for whom one might expect different academic and social outcomes (for discussion of socialization of help seeking, see Newman, 2000, 2002; Paris & Newman, 1990). Perhaps nonadaptive help seeking is a developmental precursor to nonadaptive "other action." In the following section, I explore whether refocusing our thinking about adaptive help seeking, in particular by differentiating *adaptive help seeking*, *nonadaptive help seeking*, and *nonadaptive "other action,"* can be useful in understanding help seeking in a very different classroom context, namely, peer harassment.

ADAPTIVE HELP SEEKING IN THE CONTEXT OF PEER HARASSMENT

When children are harassed at school, it sometimes is necessary to go to a teacher for assistance. However, at other times it is not necessary. Misreading the situation (i.e., either over- or underestimating danger) and acting "out of sync" can lead to problems. In this section of the chapter, I present a theoretical description of cognitive and social competencies and affective-motivational resources that underlie adaptive help seeking in the context of harassment. The description is necessarily speculative, with only two studies to date having examined help seeking in this domain (Newman et al., 2001; Newman & Murray, 2005). Although neither of the two studies was designed explicitly to examine *adaptive* help seeking, findings can be interpreted according to the framework represented in Table 9.1 (i.e., in a way that differentiates *adaptive help seeking, nonadaptive help seeking,* and *nonadaptive "other action"*).

Theoretical Background Regarding Adaptive Help Seeking

Parallel to the analysis in the academic domain (Newman, 1998a, 2000, 2002), one can specify certain component skills and resources required for adaptive help seeking in the context of harassment. These include:

Cognitive Competencies.   It would seem imperative for students to be able to differentiate among situations that pose different degrees of risk and danger. Children encounter many types of interpersonal conflict, some more normative and acceptable than others. For example, there are struggles for personal control (e.g., children working in a group have opposing views about which problems to do first), conflicts over equal rights (e.g., two children approach the computer at the same time and both want to get on), conflicts involving ambiguous provocation (e.g., a child bumps into a peer and it is not clear whether the bump was accidental or intentional), and rights infractions (e.g., a child takes another's lunch money) (Bernzweig, Eisenberg, & Fabes, 1993; Chung & Asher, 1996; Coie & Dodge, 1998; Erdley, 1996; Graham, Hudley, & Williams, 1992; Hopmeyer & Asher, 1997; Murphy & Eisenberg, 1996). Harassment can involve either relational (i.e., covert) or direct (i.e., overt) aggression (Crick, 1996). Considering just the latter type of incident, it would seem important for students to differentiate different degrees of severity associated with different incidents common to elementary school (e.g., teasing, threats, and actual physical aggression).

Children also must be able to judge different shades of "right" and "wrong" (Astor, 1999). They must have a clear understanding of classroom

factors associated with danger and risk. They must know their school surroundings and be able to recognize danger and risk in different locations
such as the classroom, playground, hallways, and bathrooms (see violence
in "unowned places" on the school campus, Astor, Meyer, & Behre, 1999;
see also Boulton, 1994; Craig & Pepler, 1997; Olweus, 1993a). They must
know whom to "stay away from." Children who are able to accurately monitor and regulate their own safety know their own personal strengths and
limitations; they know what type of conflict they can potentially control
(and what is uncontrollable). They recognize that, when pushed "far
enough," getting help from a teacher may be not only socially acceptable
but necessary.

In general, as children get older, they are better able to cope independently with many interpersonal hassles, without relying on assistance of
adults (see Rubin & Rose-Krasnor, 1992). They increasingly ignore problems or use assertiveness and other prosocial strategies (see Gresham,
Lane, & O'Shaughnessy, 2001; Kochenderfer-Ladd & Skinner, 2002;
Putallaz & Sheppard, 1992; Sullivan, 2000). However, with age, children
are better able to recognize real danger in their surroundings. They become better at distinguishing controllable and uncontrollable stressors and
matching particular coping strategies with particular stressors (Brenner &
Salovey, 1997). At the same time that developing cognitive competencies
help students cope with interpersonal problems with peers, changes in several environmental factors at school (e.g., decrease in teachers' personal involvement with students; increase in class size) may be related to increased
incidence of harassment. Upper elementary and middle school are when
students' concerns about danger and personal safety become increasingly
salient (cf. Eccles & Midgley, 1989; Juvonen, Le, Kaganoff, Augustine, &
Constant, 2004; Pellegrini, 2002).

Social Competencies.   Help seeking is necessarily a social transaction
(Newman, 1998a; see also Jackson, Mackenzie, & Hobfoll, 2000). In addition to cognitive competencies, certain social competencies are also important for adaptive help seeking. Children must believe that teachers can help
them when it is necessary and that teachers can effectively assess and control difficult situations and mete out the "correct" type and amount of
help—whether it is punishment, assistance in conflict resolution, or perhaps encouragement to handle the conflict independently. Ideally, students and teachers have a similar standard of danger and risk. When
teachers expect a student to resolve a conflict on his or her own but the student expects help from the teacher, one can envision difficulties. When
danger is clear-cut (e.g., incidents involving physical aggression), teachers
are expected to be supportive of, and responsive to, a child coming to them
for help. It is likely that students expect this sort of protective response

from their teacher (see Birch & Ladd, 1996; Pianta, 1999). It is likely that both teachers and students believe that incidents on the playground are more serious than ones in the classroom. Their expectation may be that, on the playground, children are on their own whereas the classroom is a place where incidents will be handled by the teacher (Astor et al., 1999).

Social competencies regarding peer relations no doubt are important in adaptive help seeking. In struggles for personal control and conflicts over equal rights, socially competent children are particularly likely to resolve the situation on their own with prosocial strategies (e.g., discussion, sharing, compromise, and assertiveness), whereas children lacking social competence are more likely to depend on help from adults (Eisenberg et al., 1995; see Hartup, 1996; Rubin & Rose-Krasnor, 1992). In more serious situations such as rights infractions, however, socially competent children view help seeking as a reasonable backup strategy (i.e., when prosocial strategies fail to resolve the conflict, Hopmeyer & Asher, 1997). In such situations, if there is more than one adult available to help, students must be able to judge who is the best person to approach. Yet, at times, it may well be preferable for students to rely on friends rather than a teacher (see Espelage & Holt, 2001; Parker & Asher, 1993; Rubin, Bukowski, & Parker, 1998; Ryan, 2001).

Students must know how to carry out a request in a socially appropriate way. How teachers respond to a request for help depends upon their sensitivity to the needs of the child. Students are likely to benefit from communicating to their teacher that they have tried to resolve the incident on their own and have come to realize that they truly need help. One can envision teachers believing that a child is teased because of behaviors under his or her control (e.g., showing off), in which case they may feel unsympathetic and look unfavorably on a request for help. Or, teachers may believe a child is teased due to uncontrollable causes that make it hard for him or her to handle the situation without help (e.g., physical disability). In the latter case, teachers no doubt are more sensitive to the child's plight and more understanding of a request for help (for attributional analysis of victimization, see Graham & Juvonen, 2001; Weiner, 1995).

Affective-Motivational Resources.   Because strong emotions often accompany harassment (e.g., frustration, fear, anger), adaptive help seeking involves mature regulation of emotion (see Brenner & Salovey, 1997; Crick & Dodge, 1996). Students must have the "inner strength" to contain a certain amount of anxiety as they try to accurately determine if perceived hostility in ambiguous situations is due to intentional provocation, or rather, an unintentional accident (see Graham et al., 1992). They must be able to contain anxiety and perhaps fear as they try to resolve conflicts on their own. At times, they must be willing to stand up for themselves with an aggressive response (i.e., reactive aggression, Crick & Dodge, 1996). Yet they must be willing to admit they are incapable of handling certain situations on their own and be able to withstand possibly negative perceptions and feelings from teachers and peers if they do decide to go for help.

Implicit sanctions against help seeking may be especially powerful because of the public nature—and sometimes spectacle—of fights and other overt instances of aggression at school. Bystanders can "egg on" perpetrators and make it particularly difficult for children to seek help (Salmivalli, 2001). These concerns are probably heightened at upper elementary and middle school when the peer group becomes an increasingly important context for socialization (Bukowski & Sippola, 2001; Espelage & Holt, 2001; Ryan, 2001). Harassment is not always overt, however. It can involve relational aggression such as rumors, gossiping, and social ostracism, which can be equally hurtful and dangerous to the psychological well-being of children (Crick, 1996; Underwood, 2002).

Even if they know they need assistance, children require an especially strong sense of self in order to counteract concerns about what others think of them. Indeed, it may be children who are perceived by others—and by themselves—as unpopular or weak who are most likely either to go to the teacher for help prematurely (i.e., when they can in fact handle the situation on their own), persist unsuccessfully at trying to resolve the conflict on their own, or exhibit passivity or submissiveness beyond the point of safety (i.e., when they cannot in fact handle the situation by themselves). Overly dependent help seeking is potentially perceived as "tattling" (see Kochendefer & Ladd, 1997). Although some children may be "too fast" to seek help, other children may be "too slow." Children lacking friends may be especially likely to want to maintain friendship with bullies. When help is truly necessary and they do nothing, unpopular children may become seriously victimized or overreact in aggressive ways that turn into violence (Pellegrini, Bartini, & Brooks, 1999; Perry, Hodges, & Egan, 2001). Children perceived to be popular tend to be seen as socially dominant, aggressive, "tough," and not easy to push around (Rodkin, Farmer, Pearl, & Van Acker, 2000). They may view teasing as relatively minor (and not requiring the teacher's help). Children perceived to be unpopular, on the other hand, may appear to be weak and overly sensitive. Accordingly, they may view teasing as relatively serious (and requiring the teacher's help).

Research on Help Seeking and Harassment

In the following section, I discuss methodology and results from a recent study on harassment and help seeking (Newman & Murray, 2005). Where appropriate, I also refer to our earlier study (Newman et al., 2001). The purpose of this program of research has been to examine whether students' views about help seeking differ according to grade level, perceived popularity, and type of harassment and whether students and teachers view help seeking differently from one another.

Methodology.   In Newman and Murray (2005), participants were students at Grades 4 and 5. We were interested in whether children who are perceived by others as unpopular are more likely than those perceived as popular to go to their teacher for help if they are harassed. Note that *perceived popularity* is a measure of peer reputation (i.e., social visibility; see Cillessen & Mayeux, 2004; Parkhurst & Hopmeyer, 1998); this is a different construct than *sociometric popularity* (i.e., social status; see Coie, Dodge, & Kupersmidt, 1990). According to a peer nomination procedure for perceived popularity, we chose three groups of students who were perceived by their classmates to be "popular," "average in popularity," or "unpopular." The procedure involved students' responses to two questions, "Who has the most friends in your class?" and "Who has the least number of friends in your class?" In addition to students, participants in the study included teachers at Grades 4 and 5.

Materials consisted of a set of vignettes describing three types of overt aggression: (a) *teasing* (e.g., "a boy in your classroom makes fun of your science project and calls you an idiot because you couldn't get it to work"); (b) *threats* (e.g., "a boy who sits next to you threatens to hit you if you take the special chair during silent reading time"); and (c) *physical aggression* (e.g., "as you are going to sharpen your pencil, a boy grabs you and rips a large hole in your new shirt. He then laughs and brags about it"). Half the vignettes in each of the three categories described incidents in the classroom and half on the playground. In individual interviews, participants sorted vignettes (on index cards) into three piles, representing "mild," "moderate," and "severe" incidents. From each pile, the experimenter chose several and asked children, if they were to encounter this situation, (a) whether they would seek help from an adult and (b) why they would, or would not, do so. Children were asked open-ended questions about (a) conditions that would warrant help seeking and (b) conditions that would *not* warrant help seeking. Teachers followed a similar procedure.

Findings.   We found that children generally believe their teacher can help keep them safe if "push comes to shove." Students and teachers alike acknowledged that threats on the playground are more serious than threats in the classroom. The absence of the teacher on the playground contributes to the view that playgrounds can be dangerous. Although there was a general sense of confidence in their teacher as a helper, children admitted they sometimes do not go for help because of mitigating factors, for example, concern that doing so can exacerbate the conflict. It can get them into trouble with their peers and perhaps lead to social exclusion or retribution from the perpetrator. There seemed to be an unspoken fear on the part of students: If they ask for help, will it be forthcoming? Will it be seen as "tattling"? Will it get them into more trouble with the perpetrator? the peer group? or the teacher?

Students' views about harassment and help seeking varied according to perceived popularity. Unpopular students thought teasing was just as serious as threats or actual physical aggression. Students who were popular and average in popularity, on the other hand, thought teasing was less serious than either threats or physical aggression; this view was shared by teachers. Unpopular students thought teasing was more serious than did the other children and teachers, yet they were no different than the other children or teachers in how they perceived threats and physical aggression. When asked if, in fact, they would seek help in the situations portrayed in the vignettes, all three groups of students—*including those who were unpopular*—said they would be just as likely to seek help if they encountered threats or physical aggression and they would be less likely to seek help if teased. When we asked students why they might not seek help in each situation, unpopular children were more likely than their peers to say they would be afraid of retribution from perpetrators.

Discussion of Findings.   Given that unpopular children say they view teasing just as seriously as other types of harassment, their reported reluctance to seek help when teased may mask an underlying sense of danger. They may be well aware, along with the other children, that seeking help is "not a cool thing to do." Unpopular children may be especially fearful that seeking help will backfire, get them in trouble, and make them even less popular. In contrast to unpopular students, average and popular students were less likely to say they would seek help when teased than when threatened or hit; also, they perceive teasing as less serious than the other types of harassment. For average and popular children, who presumably possess a certain amount of toughness and self confidence, it probably is not as necessary to get help if they are teased (see Adler & Adler, 1998; Eder, Evans, & Parker, 1995; LaFontana & Cillessen, 2002; Rodkin et al., 2000).

A number of studies have shown that unpopular children (i.e., individuals not accepted by their peer group; in particular, their social status is either "aggressive-rejected" or "withdrawn-rejected") are at risk of peer victimization (see Rubin et al., 1998). Findings from Newman and Murray (2005) complement these studies. Children who are unpopular, although in a different sense (i.e., they have a reputation of being unpopular or of having little social impact in their peer group), may also be at risk.

How children view the severity of harassment and the need to seek help may contribute to an understanding of the development of victimization.

Although children often find themselves in a dilemma when it comes to weighing costs and benefits of seeking help, the uncertainty may be especially problematic for children who already have a history of social exclusion or rejection. Among children as young as kindergartners and first graders, individuals who are withdrawn and asocial tend to be overly dependent on their teacher (Birch & Ladd, 1998). They use the teacher as a shield to protect themselves from having to deal with normative peer interactions in the classroom, and this has negative ramifications for peer relations. Children perceived by classmates as unpopular may be especially concerned about further social exclusion from their peer group. When they try to handle seemingly minor incidents of harassment on their own, for example, with assertiveness or reactive aggression, but are awkward and unsuccessful, this can reinforce a negative image with peers and lead to further harassment (Boivin, Hymel, & Hodges, 2001; Olweus, 1993b; Schuster, 2001; Smith, Shu, & Madsen, 2001). If they go to their teacher for help, they run the risk of being labeled as a "tattletale" (Kochenderfer & Ladd, 1997). Internalizing taunts and blaming oneself for the cause of harassment can lead to loneliness, low self-esteem, depression, and increased vulnerability (Asher, Parkhurst, Hymel, & Williams, 1990; Ladd & Ladd, 2001). In dangerous situations for which they truly need assistance, some children become submissive (cf. "withdrawn-rejected" children) and perhaps at some point overreact in ways that escalate into violence (cf. "aggressive-rejected" children; Coie & Dodge, 1998; Pellegrini et al., 1999). Both submissiveness and inappropriate aggressiveness are associated with further victimization (Boulton, 1999; Hodges, Malone, & Perry, 1997; Perry et al., 2001; Schwartz, Dodge, Petit, & Bates, 1997).

It is interesting at this point to consider several findings from our earlier study (Newman et al., 2001). In this study, participants were students at Grades 3 and 4. They came from schools in which kindergarten through Grade 3 are lower elementary grades and Grades 4 through 6 upper elementary grades. At lunch time and on the playground, third graders are grouped with younger (and smaller) students, whereas fourth graders are grouped with older (and bigger) ones. (Note: Participants in Newman and Murray [2005] came from schools structured in the same way.) In Newman et al. (2001), in addition to asking students how they would cope with harassment, we questioned them about their self-perceptions (e.g., regarding physical ability; see Marsh, 1992). We were interested in whether children who perceive themselves as lacking physical prowess (and presumably feel ill-equipped to face perpetrators on their own) are relatively likely to seek help. Results showed a significant relation, moderated by grade level, between children's self-perceptions of physical ability and their reports of coping by acquiescing to the perpetrator (and *not* by seeking help from their teacher). At Grade 3, but not Grade 4, children with poor self-perceptions of physical ability were relatively likely to say that, if harassed, they would give in to the perpetrator and do nothing. Lower elementary school aged children may feel especially vulnerable and unsure of what to do if they encounter a situation that might require them to physically stand up for themselves. Those who feel they cannot stand up physically for themselves may acquiesce and hence may be relatively easy targets when confronted by a perpetrator. Upper elementary school aged children who feel this way about themselves do not necessarily give in to bullies. These findings suggest that young children with poor self-perceptions may be especially at risk of developing problems involving psychosocial adjustment associated with harassment (cf. Boulton, 1999; Hodges et al., 1997; Olweus, 1978; Perry et al., 2001).

What is the teacher's role in how students view harassment and help seeking? We know that teachers agree with students that both threats and physical aggression are serious. They disagree with unpopular students regarding the seriousness of teasing. We do not know, however, the impact of teachers' perceptions or behavior on students' help seeking, nor how teachers might influence unpopular students differently than popular students. Teachers may not share students' sensitivities—and indeed sensibilities—regarding fear and danger (see Patrick, Anderman, & Ryan, 2002; Perry & Weinstein, 1998). To the extent that a teacher underestimates potentially adverse effects of harassment, children no doubt are reticent to approach that teacher for assistance. To the extent that teachers have negative perceptions of children who come to them for help, these perceptions potentially are reflected in attitudes and behavior toward individuals who may, in fact, have an especially difficult time dealing with peer harassment at school. For example, if they believe an unpopular child is teased due to something the child has done (e.g., showing off, tattling), teachers may be unsympathetic and perhaps even ignore the child. Unnecessary help seeking may be perceived negatively by teachers as well as peers.

The Larger Picture: Nonadaptive Actions

Peer harassment at elementary school often is accompanied by reports that victims of aggression were reluctant to go to the appropriate authorities (Newman, 2003). Children, in particular, those who are perceived by their peers as unpopular, are sensitive to verbal harassment. How they respond can be critical. It sometimes is appropriate, and perhaps necessary, to go to a teacher for assistance. At other times, it is not necessary. The conceptualization of how students calibrate *action* to *need* in the academic domain (see Table 9.1) may be useful in understanding help-seeking difficulties that certain children encounter in the context of peer harassment.

There would seem to be a stark difference between children who "fit" in the bottom left cell in Table 9.1 (i.e., they tend toward *nonadaptive help seeking*) and children in the top right cell (i.e., they tend toward *nonadaptive "other action"*). One can speculate about general profiles of these two groups of children. Children in the bottom left cell are overly dependent on their teacher. They should handle many peer conflicts on their own but do not. They lack social competence (e.g., assertiveness). They perceive themselves as weak and unable to stand up to bullies. They are perceived as "tattletales." Children in the top right cell are passive and perhaps even submissive. They should rely on their teacher more than they do. They may fear retribution from the perpetrator if they do go to the teacher. They are withdrawn and are seen as an "easy target" for bullies. At some point, however, these children may explode and lash out at those who harass them.

Findings from Newman and Murray (2005) and Newman et al. (2001) suggest a "help-seeking perspective" on development of peer victimization. As in the case of academic difficulty, the two actions (i.e., *nonadaptive help seeking* and *nonadaptive "other action"*) may be representative of two qualitatively different sorts of students, who perhaps are socialized differently and for whom one might expect different outcomes (i.e., in terms of psychological adjustment). Children in our study who were perceived as unpopular should be followed longitudinally. Perhaps these children become, over time, preadolescents and adolescents who fit the dysfunctional profiles characteristic of the bottom left and top right cells. Children who are overly dependent in their help seeking may be at risk of becoming submissive. If so, this developmental progression may parallel what happens in the academic domain, with dependent help seekers becoming, over time, avoidant help seekers (cf. Ryan et al., 2005).

In conclusion, the unfortunate reality of elementary and middle school classrooms is that 40% to 80% of schoolchildren experience peer hostilities such as taunting, threats, social ostracism, and humiliation (Juvonen & Graham, 2001). Confrontations involving verbal and physical aggression and abuse are widely publicized and appear to be on the rise in the United States (APA, 1999). A better understanding of the development of peer victimization can inform programmatic efforts aimed at prevention and intervention. It is important to help children learn to accurately perceive when peer conflict is intentional versus unintentional and to accurately assess the presence of danger. Prosocial problem-solving strategies (e.g., assertiveness, cognitive distancing, or support from friends) can be taught. Training of teachers can stress greater awareness of the "help-seeking dilemma" (i.e., Should I ask for help?) students often encounter at school. Efforts such as these might prevent children from falling into the two nonadaptive cells of Table 9.1. Equally important are interventions for children whose behavior is already characteristic of the bottom left cell and who are at risk, over time, of migrating to the top right cell or "beyond" (i.e., becoming violent).

SUMMARY AND CONCLUSION

Academic difficulty and peer harassment are two very different types of adversity or challenge that students often encounter in the classroom. With schoolwork, students sometimes ask for assistance when it is not necessary; they may be motivated by desire for expedience or may lack confidence needed to work independently. Sometimes students are reluctant to ask for help, afraid that their teacher or classmates will think they are "dumb." As in the academic domain, students who are harassed by peers sometimes seek help unnecessarily; often they are seen as a "tattletale." And sometimes students who are harassed are reluctant to go to adults for assistance, afraid that their teacher will not help them or afraid of retribution by the perpetrator. In both academic and social domains, help seeking under certain conditions can be an adaptive way of handling adversity. Under other conditions, it can be nonadaptive.

The major focus of the chapter was academic help seeking. I discussed research aimed at operationalizing *adaptiveness* and suggested differentiating *adaptive help seeking* from two types of *nonadaptive actions* in which children often engage when they encounter difficulties with schoolwork. The secondary purpose of the chapter was to focus on help seeking in the context of peer harassment. I discussed findings from two recent studies (Newman & Murray, 2005; Newman et al., 2001) and suggested that here too a differentiation between *adaptive help seeking* and *nonadaptive actions* can be useful in understanding how children cope.

The conceptualization represented in Table 9.1 can be applied as a heuristic to two very different types of problems (i.e., academic difficulty and peer harassment) students face in the classroom. However, applying the conceptualization to different domains does not imply that there is an underlying pattern of behavior, or schema, that governs how an individual approaches help-seeking dilemmas in different domains. This is an unanswered—and indeed intriguing—empirical question. That is, to what degree can individuals be characterized according to a traitlike help-seeking disposition? For example, if a child is overly dependent on academic help from his or her teacher (i.e., thus "fitting" into the bottom left cell of Table 9.1), does the same individual tend to "fit" into the same cell as he or she attempts to cope with a bully? Related to domain generality is the issue of stability (i.e., correspondence over time). In particular, to what degree and under what conditions should one expect developmental progression from one cell to another? I have speculated that the child who is overly dependent (i.e., bottom left cell) may tend over time to become avoidant of help seeking (i.e., top right cell). Obviously this also is a question to be addressed empirically.

Several other directions for further research on adaptive and nonadaptive help seeking are noteworthy. First, Table 9.1 represents how students respond to perceived *necessity* of help. The same approach potentially could be expanded to take into account the other two criteria for adaptiveness (i.e., *content* and *target*). Here too, researchers might refocus on nonadaptiveness. For example, which students are likely to have the skills and affective-motivational resources associated with formulating a "bad" question, addressing it to a "poor" target, or not bothering at all to request help? Under what classroom conditions are students likely to be nonadaptive in their choice of content and target? Second, I have alluded to a type of *nonadaptive "other action,"* in the context of peer harassment, that would seem to be different from—and indeed more serious than—avoidant help seeking. In particular, the child who is passive and submissive (i.e., top right cell) may, under certain conditions, overreact aggressively toward perpetrators. Chronic harassment that turns into serious victimization can end in violence (see Perry et al., 2001). Perhaps a parallel problem in the academic domain is pathological cheating (cf. Butler, 1998). Finally, help-seeking research should examine more closely the interaction between student and teacher. The role of the teacher was addressed in academic research by Butler (1998; see also Butler, present volume) and Ryan et al. (2005) and in harassment research by Newman and Murray (2005). To understand children's willingness to seek help in the classroom, it clearly is important to understand teachers' willingness to help. The reciprocal, transactional nature of help seeking, as a "request-and-response unit," should be examined more carefully in future research, in particular, if classrooms are to be made more supportive of children coping with diverse difficulties.

REFERENCES

Adler, P. A., & Adler, P. (1998). *Peer power: Preadolescent culture and identity.* New Brunswick, NJ: Rutgers University Press.

American Psychological Association. (1999). *Warning signs: A youth anti-violence initiative.* Washington, DC: APA.

Ames, R. (1983). Help-seeking and achievement orientation: Perspectives from attribution theory. In B. M. DePaulo, A. Nadler, & J. D. Fisher (Eds.), *New directions in helping: Help seeking,* Vol. 2 (pp. 165–186). New York: Academic Press.

Asher, S. R., Parkhurst, J. T., Hymel, S., & Williams, G. A. (1990). Peer rejection and loneliness in childhood. In S. R. Asher & J. D. Coie (Eds.), *Peer rejection in childhood* (pp. 253–273). Cambridge, England: Cambridge University Press.

Astor, R. A. (1999). Moral reasoning about school violence: Informational assumptions about harm within school subcontexts. *Educational Psychologist, 33,* 207–221.

Astor, R. A., Meyer, H. A., & Behre, W. J. (1999). Unowned places and times: Maps and interviews about violence in high schools. *American Educational Research Journal, 36,* 3–42.

Barnett, K., Darcie, G., Holland, C. J., & Kobasigawa, A. (1982). Children's cognitions about effective helping. *Developmental Psychology, 18,* 267–277.

Bernzweig, J., Eisenberg, N., & Fabes, R. A. (1993). Children's coping in self- and other-relevant contexts. *Journal of Experimental Child Psychology, 55,* 208–226.

Birch, S. H., & Ladd, G. W. (1996). Interpersonal relationships in the school environment and children's early school adjustment: The role of teachers and peers. In J. Juvonen & K. R. Wentzel (Eds.), *Social motivation: Understanding children's school adjustment* (pp. 199–225). Cambridge: Cambridge University Press.

Birch, S. H., & Ladd, G. W. (1998). Children's interpersonal behaviors and the teacher–child relationship. *Child Development, 34*, 934–946.

Boekaerts, M., Pintrich, P. R., & Zeidner, M. (Eds.). (2000). *Handbook of self-regulation.* San Diego, CA: Academic Press.

Boivin, M., Hymel, S., & Hodges, E. V. E. (2001). Toward a process view of peer rejection and harassment. In J. Juvonen & S. Graham (Eds.) *Peer harassment in school: The plight of the vulnerable and victimized* (pp. 265–289). New York: Guilford Press.

Boulton, M. J. (1994). Understanding and preventing bullying in the junior school playground. In P. K. Smith & S. Sharp (Eds.), *School bullying* (pp. 132–159). London: Routledge.

Boulton, M. J. (1999). Concurrent and longitudinal relations between children's playground behavior and social preference, victimization, and bullying. *Child Development, 70*, 944–954.

Brenner, E. M., & Salovey, P. (1997). Emotion regulation during childhood: Developmental, interpersonal, and individual considerations. In P. Salovey & D. J. Sluyter (Eds.). *Emotional development and emotional intelligence: Educational implications* (pp. 168–195). New York: Basic Books.

Bukowski, W. M., & Sippola, L. K. (2001). Groups, individuals, and victimization: A view of the peer system. In J. Juvonen & S. Graham (Eds.) *Peer harassment in school: The plight of the vulnerable and victimized* (pp. 355–377). New York: Guilford Press.

Butler, R. (1998). Determinants of help seeking: Relations between perceived reasons for classroom help-avoidance and help-seeking behaviors in an experimental context. *Journal of Educational Psychology, 90*, 630–643.

Butler, R., & Neuman, O. (1995). Effects of task and ego achievement goals on help-seeking behaviors and attitudes. *Journal of Educational Psychology, 87*, 261–271.

Chung, T., & Asher, S. R. (1996). Children's goals and strategies in peer conflict situations. *Merrill-Palmer Quarterly, 42*, 125–147.

Cillessen, A. H. N., & Mayeux, L. (2004). From censure to reinforcement: Developmental changes in the association between aggression and social status. *Child Development, 75*, 147–163.

Cohen, S., & Wills, T. A. (1985). Stress, social support, and the buffering hypothesis. *Psychological Bulletin, 98*, 310–357.

Coie, J. D., & Dodge, K. A. (1998). Aggression and antisocial behavior. In W. Damon (Series Ed.) & N. Eisenberg (Vol. Ed.), *Handbook of child psychology: Vol. 3. Social, emotional, and personality development* (5th ed., pp. 779–862). New York: Wiley.

Coie, W. M., Dodge, K. A., & Kupersmidt, J. (1990). Peer group behavior and social status. In S. Asher & J. Coie (Eds.), *Peer rejection in childhood* (pp. 17–59). Cambridge, UK: Cambridge University Press.

Craig, W. M., & Pepler, D. J. (1997). Observations of bullying and victimization in the schoolyard. *Canadian Journal of School Psychology, 13*, 41–59.

Crick, N. R. (1996). The role of relational aggression, overt aggression, and prosocial behavior in the prediction of children's future social adjustment. *Child Development, 67*, 2317–2327.

Crick, N. R., & Dodge, K. A. (1996). Social-information processing mechanisms in reactive and proactive aggression. *Child Development, 67*, 993–1002.

DeCooke, P. A., & Nelson-Le Gall, S. (1989). The effects of familiarity on the success of children's help-seeking. *Journal of Applied Developmental Psychology, 10,* 195–208.

Dillon, J. T. (1988). The remedial status of student questioning. *Journal of Curriculum Studies, 20,* 197–210.

Dweck, C. (1986). Motivational processes affecting learning. *American Psychologist, 41,* 1040–1048.

Eccles, J. S., & Midgley, C. (1989). Stage/environment fit: Developmentally appropriate classrooms for early adolescents. In R. Ames & C. Ames (Eds.), *Research on motivation in education* (Vol. 3, pp. 139–181). New York: Academic.

Eder, D., Evans, C. C., & Parker, S. (1995). *School talk: Gender and adolescent culture.* New Brunswick, NJ: Rutgers University Press.

Eisenberg, N., Fabes, R. A., Murphy, B., Maszk, P., Smith, M., & Karbon, M. (1995). The role of emotionality and regulation in children's social functioning: A longitudinal study. *Child Development, 66,* 1360–1384.

Elliott, A. J. (1999). Approach and avoidance motivation and achievement goals. *Educational Psychologist, 34,* 169–189.

Erdley, C. A. (1996). Motivational approaches to aggression within the context of peer relationships. In J. Juvonen & K. R. Wentzel (Eds.), *Social motivation: Understanding children's school adjustment* (pp. 98–125). Cambridge: Cambridge University Press.

Espelage, D. L., & Holt, M. K. (2001). Bullying and victimization during early adolescence: Peer influences and psychosocial correlates. *Journal of Emotional Abuse, 2,* 123–142.

Fields, L., & Prinz, R. J. (1997). Coping and adjustment during childhood and adolescence. *Clinical Psychology Review, 17,* 937–976.

Furman, W., & Buhrmester, D. (1985). Children's perceptions of the personal relationships in their social networks. *Developmental Psychology, 21,* 1016–1024.

Good, T., Slavings, R., Harel, K., & Emerson, H. (1987). Student passivity: A study of question asking in K–12 classrooms. *Sociology of Education, 60,* 181–199.

Graham, S., Hudley, C., & Williams, E. (1992). Attributional and emotional determinants of aggression among African-American and Latino young adolescents. *Developmental Psychology, 28,* 731–740.

Graham, S., & Juvonen, J. (2001). An attributional approach to peer victimization. In J. Juvonen & S. Graham (Eds.) *Peer harassment in school: The plight of the vulnerable and victimized* (pp. 49–72). New York: Guilford Press.

Gresham, F. M., Lane, K. L., & O'Shaughnessy, T. E. (2001). *Interventions for children with or at-risk for emotional and behavioral disorders.* New York: Allyn & Bacon.

Hartup, W. W. (1996). Cooperation, close relationships, and cognitive development. In W. M. Bukowski, A. F. Newcomb, & W. W. Hartup (Eds.), *The company they keep: Friendships in childhood and adolescence* (pp. 213–237). Cambridge, England: Cambridge University Press.

Hodges, E. V. E., Malone, M. J., & Perry, D. G. (1997). Individual risk and social risk as interacting determinants of victimization in the peer group. *Developmental Psychology, 33,* 1032–1039.

Hopmeyer, A., & Asher, S. R. (1997). Children's responses to peer conflicts involving a rights infraction. *Merrill-Palmer Quarterly, 43,* 235–254.

Jackson, T., Mackenzie, J., & Hobfoll, S. E. (2000). Communal aspects of self-regulation. In M. Boekaerts, P. Pintrich, & M. Zeidner (Eds.), *Handbook of self-regulation* (pp. 275–302). San Diego, CA: Academic Press.

Juvonen, J., & Graham, S. (2001).(Eds.) *Peer harassment in school: The plight of the vulnerable and victimized.* New York: Guilford Press.

Juvonen, J., Le, V., Kaganoff, T., Augustine, C., & Constant, L. (2004). *Focus on the wonder years: Challenges facing the American middle school*. Santa Monica, CA: Rand.

Karabenick, S. A. (Ed.).(1998). *Strategic help seeking: Implications for learning and teaching*. Hillsdale, NJ: Lawrence Erlbaum Associates.

Karabenick, S. A. (2004). Perceived achievement goal structure and college student help seeking, *Journal of Educational Psychology, 96,* 569–581.

Karabenick, S. A., & Knapp, J. R. (1991). Relationship of academic help seeking to the use of learning strategies and other instrumental achievement in college students. *Journal of Educational Psychology, 83,* 221–230.

Kearsley, G. P. (1976). Questions and question asking in verbal discourse: A cross-disciplinary review. *Journal of Psycholinguistic Research, 5,* 355–375.

Kochenderfer, B. J., & Ladd, G. W. (1997). Victimized children's responses to peers' aggression: Behaviors associated with reduced versus continued victimization. *Development and Psychopathology, 9,* 59–73.

Kochenderfer-Ladd, B., & Skinner, K. (2002). Children's coping strategies: Moderators of the effects of peer victimization? *Developmental Psychology, 38,* 267–278.

Ladd, B. K., & Ladd, G. W. (2001). Variations in peer victimization: Relations to children's maladjustment. In J. Juvonen & S. Graham (Eds.), *Peer harassment in school: The plight of the vulnerable and victimized* (pp. 25– 48). New York: Guilford Press.

LaFontana, K. M., & Cillessen, A. H. N. (2002). Children's perceptions of popular and unpopular peers: A multimethod assessment. *Developmental Psychology, 38,* 635–647.

Markman, E. M. (1981). Comprehension monitoring. In W. P. Dickson (Ed.), *Children's oral communication skills* (pp. 61–84). New York: Academic Press.

Marsh, H. W. (1992). *Self Description Questionnaire (SDQ) I: A theoretical and empirical basis for the measurement of multiple dimensions of pre-adolescent self-concept. A test manual and research monograph*. Macarthur, New South Wales, Australia: University of Western Sydney, Faculty of Education.

Meece, J. L., Blumenfeld, P. C., & Hoyle, R. H. (1988). Students' goal orientations and cognitive engagement in classroom activities. *Journal of Educational Psychology, 80,* 514–523.

Midgley, C. (Ed.). (2002). *Goals, goal structures, and patterns of adaptive learning*. Mahwah, NJ: Lawrence Erlbaum Associates.

Midgley, C., Kaplan, A., & Middleton, M. (2001). Performance-approach goals: Good for what, for whom, under what circumstances, and at what cost? *Journal of Educational Psychology, 93,* 77–86.

Murphy, B. C., & Eisenberg, N. (1996). Provoked by a peer: Children's anger-related responses and their relations to social functioning. *Merrill-Palmer Quarterly, 42,* 103–124.

Nadler, A. (1991). Help-seeking behavior: Psychological costs and instrumental benefits. In M. S. Clark (Ed.), *Review of personality and social psychology* (Vol. 12, pp. 290–312). New York: Sage.

Nadler, A. (1998). Relationship, esteem, and achievement perspectives on autonomous and dependent help seeking. In S. A. Karabenick (Ed.), *Strategic help seeking: Implications for learning and teaching*. (pp. 61–93). Hillsdale, NJ: Lawrence Erlbaum Associates.

Nelson-Le Gall, S. (1981). Help-seeking: An understudied problem-solving skill in children. *Developmental Review, 1,* 224–246.

Nelson-Le Gall, S. (1985). Help-seeking behavior in learning. In W. Gordon (Ed.), *Review of research in education* (Vol. 12, pp. 55–90). Washington, DC: American Educational Research Association.

Nelson-Le Gall, S. (1987). Necessary and unnecessary help-seeking in children. *Journal of Genetic Psychology, 148*, 53–62.

Nelson-Le Gall, S., & Gumerman, R. (1984). Children's perceptions of helpers and helper motivation. *Journal of Applied Developmental Psychology, 5*, 1–12.

Nelson-Le Gall, S., & Jones, E. (1990). Cognitive-motivational influences on the task-related help-seeking behavior of Black children. *Child Development, 61*, 581–589.

Nelson-Le Gall, S., Kratzer, L., Jones, E., & DeCooke, P. (1990). Children's self-assessment of performance and task-related help seeking. *Journal of Experimental Child Psychology, 49*, 245–263.

Newman, R. S. (1990). Children's help-seeking in the classroom: The role of motivational factors and attitudes. *Journal of Educational Psychology, 82*, 71–80.

Newman, R. S. (1991). Goals and self-regulated learning: What motivates children to seek academic help? In M. L. Maehr & P. R. Pintrich (Eds.), *Advances in motivation and achievement: Goals and self-regulatory processes* (pp. 151–183). Greenwich, CT: JAI Press.

Newman, R. S. (1994). Adaptive help seeking: A strategy of self-regulated learning. In D. H. Schunk & B. J. Zimmerman (Eds.), *Self-regulation of learning and performance: Issues and educational applications* (pp. 283–301). Hillsdale, NJ: Lawrence Erlbaum Associates.

Newman, R. S. (1998a). Adaptive help seeking: A role of social interaction in self-regulated learning. In S. A. Karabenick (Ed.), *Strategic help seeking: Implications for learning and teaching*. (pp. 13–37). Hillsdale, NJ: Lawrence Erlbaum Associates.

Newman, R. S. (1998b). Students' help seeking during problem solving: Influences of personal and contextual achievement goals. *Journal of Educational Psychology, 90*, 644–658.

Newman, R. S. (2000). Social influences on the development of children's adaptive help seeking: The role of parents, teachers, and peers. *Developmental Review, 20*, 350–404.

Newman, R. S. (2002). What do I need to do to succeed … when I don't understand what I'm doing!?: Developmental influences on students' adaptive help seeking. In A. Wigfield & J. Eccles (Eds.), *Development of achievement motivation* (pp. 285–306). San Diego, CA: Academic Press.

Newman, R. S. (2003). When elementary school students are harassed by peers: A self-regulative perspective on help seeking. *Elementary School Journal, 103*, 339–355.

Newman, R. S., & Goldin, L. (1990). Children's reluctance to seek help with schoolwork. *Journal of Educational Psychology, 82*, 92–100.

Newman, R. S., & Murray, B. (2005). How students and teachers view the seriousness of peer harassment: When is it appropriate to seek help? *Journal of Educational Psychology, 97*, 347–365.

Newman, R. S., Murray, B., & Lussier, C. (2001). Confrontation with aggressive peers at school: Students' reluctance to seek help from the teacher. *Journal of Educational Psychology, 93*, 398–410.

Newman, R. S., & Schwager, M. T. (1993). Student perceptions of the teacher and classmates in relation to reported help seeking in math class. *Elementary School Journal, 94*, 3–17.

Newman, R. S., & Schwager, M. T. (1995). Students' help seeking during problem solving: Effects of grade, goal, and prior achievement. *American Educational Research Journal, 32*, 352–376.

Newman, R. S., & Wick, P. L. (1987). Effect of age, skill, and performance feedback on children's judgments of confidence. *Journal of Educational Psychology, 79,* 115–119.

Nicholls, J. G. (1979). Quality and equality in intellectual development: The role of motivation in education. *American Psychologist, 34,* 1071–1084.

Olweus, D. (1978). *Aggression in the schools: Bullies and whipping boys.* Washington, DC: Hemisphere.

Olweus, D. (1993a). Bullies on the playground. In C. Hart (Ed.), *Children on playgrounds* (pp. 85–128). Albany: State University of New York Press.

Olweus, D. (1993b). *Bullying at school: What we know and what we can do.* Cambridge, MA: Blackwell.

Patrick, H., Anderman, L. H., & Ryan, A. M. (2002). Social motivation and the classroom social environment. In C. Midgley (Ed.), *Goals, goal structures, and patterns of adaptive learning* (pp. 85–108). Mahwah, NJ: Lawrence Erlbaum Associates.

Paris, S. G. (1988, April). *Fusing skill and will in children's learning and schooling.* Paper presented at the American Educational Research Association, New Orleans.

Paris, S. G., & Newman, R. S. (1990). Developmental aspects of self-regulated learning. *Educational Psychologist, 25,* 87–102.

Parker, J. G., & Asher, S. R. (1993). Friendship and friendship quality in middle childhood: Links with peer group acceptance and feelings of loneliness and social dissatisfaction. *Developmental Psychology, 29,* 611–621.

Parkhurst, J. T., & Hopmeyer, A. (1998). Sociometric popularity and peer-perceived popularity. *Journal of Early Adolescence, 18,* 125–144.

Pellegrini, A. D. (2002). Bullying, victimization, and sexual harassment during the transition to middle school. *Educational Psychologist, 37,* 151–163.

Pellegrini, A. D., Bartini, M., & Brooks, F. (1999). School bullies, victims, and aggressive victims: Factors relating to group affiliation and victimization in early adolescence. *Journal of Educational Psychology, 91,* 216–224.

Perry, K. E., & Weinstein, R. S. (1998). The social context of early schooling and children's school adjustment. *Educational Psychologist, 33,* 177–194.

Perry, D. G., Hodges, E. V. E., & Egan, S. K. (2001). Determinants of chronic victimization by peers: A review and a new model of family influence. In J. Juvonen & S. Graham (Eds.), *Peer harassment in school: The plight of the vulnerable and victimized* (pp. 73–104). New York: Guilford Press.

Pianta, R. C. (1999). *Enhancing relationships between children and teachers.* Washington, DC: American Psychological Association.

Pintrich, P. R. (2000). The role of goal orientation in self-regulated learning. In M. Boekaerts, P. Pintrich, & M. Zeidner (Eds.), *Handbook of self-regulation* (pp. 451–502). San Diego, CA: Academic Press.

Pressley, M., Levin, J. R., Ghatala, E. S., & Ahmad, M. (1987). Test monitoring in young grade school children. *Journal of Experimental Child Psychology, 43,* 96–111.

Putallaz, M., & Sheppard, B. H. (1992). Conflict management and social competence. In C. U. Shantz & W. W. Hartup (Eds.), *Conflict in child and adolescent development* (pp. 330–355). Cambridge, England: Cambridge University Press.

Rodkin, P. C., Farmer, T. W., Pearl, R., & Van Acker, R. (2000). Heterogeneity of popular boys: Antisocial and prosocial configurations. *Developmental Psychology, 36,* 14–24.

Rubin, K. H., Bukowski, W. M., & Parker, J. G. (1998). Peer interactions, relationships, and groups. In W. Damon (Series Ed.) & N. Eisenberg (Vol. Ed.), *Handbook of child psychology: Vol. 3. Social, emotional, and personality development* (5th ed., pp. 619–700). New York: Wiley.

Rubin, K. H., & Rose-Krasnor, L. (1992). Interpersonal problem solving. In V. B. Van Hassatt & M. Hersen (Eds.), *Handbook of social development* (pp. 283–323). New York: Plenum Press.

Ryan, A. M. (2001). The peer group as a context for the development of young adolescent motivation and achievement. *Child Development, 72,* 1135–1150.

Ryan, A. M., Gheen, M. H., & Midgley, C. (1998). Why do some students avoid asking for help? An examination of the interplay among students' academic efficacy, teachers' social-emotional role, and the classroom goal structure. *Journal of Educational Psychology, 90,* 528–535.

Ryan, A. M., Hicks, L., & Midgley, C. (1997). Social goals, academic goals, and avoiding seeking help in the classroom. *Journal of Early Adolescence, 17,* 152–171.

Ryan, A. M., Patrick, H., & Shim, S. O. (2005). Differential profiles of students identified by their teacher as having avoidant, appropriate, or dependent help-seeking tendencies in the classroom. *Journal of Educational Psychology, 97,* 275–285.

Ryan, A. M., & Pintrich, P. R. (1997). "Should I ask for help?" The role of motivation and attitudes in adolescents' help seeking in math class. *Journal of Educational Psychology, 89,* 329–341.

Salmivalli, C. (2001). Group view on victimization: Empirical findings and their implications. In J. Juvonen & S. Graham (Eds.), *Peer harassment in school: The plight of the vulnerable and victimized* (pp. 398–419). New York: Guilford Press.

Schunk D. H., & Zimmerman, B. J. (1998). *Self-regulated learning: From teaching to self-reflective practice.* New York: Guilford Press.

Schuster, B. (2001). Rejection and victimization by peers: Social perception and social behavior mechanisms. In J. Juvonen & S. Graham (Eds.), *Peer harassment in school: The plight of the vulnerable and victimized* (pp. 290–309). New York: Guilford Press.

Schwartz, D., Dodge, K. A., Petit, G. S., & Bates, J. E. (1997). The early socialization and adjustment of aggressive victims of bullying. *Child Development, 68,* 665–675.

Skinner, E. A., Edge, K., Altman, J., & Sherwood, H. (2003). Searching for the structure of coping: A review and critique of category systems for classifying ways of coping. *Psychological Bulletin, 129,* 216–269.

Smith, K. H., Tykodi, T. A., & Mynatt, B. T. (1988). Can we predict the form and content of spontaneous questions? *Questioning Exchange, 2,* 53–60.

Smith, P. K., Shu, S., & Madsen, K. (2001). Characteristics of victims of school bullying: Developmental changes in coping strategies and skills. In J. Juvonen & S. Graham (Eds.), *Peer harassment in school: The plight of the vulnerable and victimized* (pp. 332–351). New York: Guilford Press.

Sullivan, K. (2000). *The anti-bullying handbook.* Auckland, New Zealand: Oxford University Press.

Underwood, M. K. (2002). Sticks and stones and social exclusion: Aggression among boys and girls. In P. K. Smith & C. H. Hart (Eds.), *Blackwell handbook of childhood social development* (pp. 533–548). Malden, MA: Blackwell.

van der Meij, H. (1988). Constraints on question asking in classrooms. *Journal of Educational Psychology, 80,* 401–405.

van der Meij, H. (1990). Question asking: To know that you do not know is not enough. *Journal of Educational Psychology, 82,* 505–512.

van Hekken, S. M. J., & Roelofsen, W. (1982). More questions than answers: A study of question–answer sequences in a naturalistic setting. *Journal of Child Language, 9,* 445–460.

Webb, N. M., & Palincsar, A. S. (1996). Group processes in the classroom. In D. C. Berliner & R. C. Calfee (Eds.), *Handbook of educational psychology* (pp. 841–873). New York: Simon & Schuster Macmillan.

Weiner, B. (1995). *Judgments of responsibility: A foundation for a theory of social conduct.* New York: Guilford Press.

Wentzel, K. R. (1989). Adolescent classroom goals, standards for performance, and academic achievement: An interactionist perspective. *Journal of Educational Psychology, 81,* 131–142.

Wentzel, K. R. (1996). Social goals and social relationships as motivators of school adjustment. In J. Juvonen & K. R. Wentzel (Eds.), *Social motivation: Understanding children's school adjustment* (pp. 226–247). Cambridge: Cambridge University Press.

Wilkinson, L., & Calculator, S. (1982). Effective speakers: Students' use of language to request and obtain information and action in the classroom. In L. Wilkinson (Ed.), *Communicating in the classroom* (pp. 85–99). New York: Academic Press.

Zimmerman, B. J., & Schunk, D. H. (1989). *Self-regulated learning and academic achievement: Theory, research, and practice.* New York: Springer-Verlag.

Chapter 10

Toward Computer-Based Tutoring of Help-Seeking Skills

Vincent Aleven
Bruce M. McLaren
Kenneth R. Koedinger
Carnegie Mellon University

In today's economic and technological environment, individuals continually face the challenge of acquiring new knowledge and skills. To be successful, people must be "intelligent novices" (Mathan & Koedinger, 2003), able to get up to speed quickly in a new domain. Metacognitive skills are often regarded as key to being a good learner (Bransford, Brown, & Cocking, 2000; Palincsar & Brown, 1984; White & Frederiksen, 1998). Although these skills are crucial in today's society, they are addressed insufficiently in the current educational system.

One such metacognitive skill is help seeking. The ability to seek help at appropriate times from appropriate sources and to learn from the received help is important simply because it is not possible for the school system to prepare students for all future skill needs. Also, it is often very difficult to learn a new set of skills by oneself, without any help—for example, by reading a textbook and doing the exercises, or by searching the Internet and integrating information found in diverse sources. Typically, it is more effective and efficient to selectively enlist the help of a more experienced individual or to post a query to a specialized forum or mailing list on the Internet (Keefer & Karabenick, 1998). Developmental psychologists view help seeking as a key strategy for developing independent ability and skills (Nelson-Le Gall, 1981).

However, there is considerable evidence that many individuals do not seek help effectively (Nelson-Le Gall, 1987) or avoid seeking help altogether (Ryan, Gheen, & Midgley, 1998; Ryan, Pintrich, & Midgley, 2001). A number of studies have shown that students with greater prior knowledge of a given domain exhibit more effective help-seeking behavior (e.g., Miyake & Norman, 1979; Nelson-Le Gall, 1987; Nelson-Le Gall, Kratzer, Jones, & DeCooke, 1990; Puustinen, 1998). The troubling consequence of this finding is that those students who are most in need of help are the least likely to get it at appropriate times (see also Karabenick & Knapp, 1988a). There are social barriers to seeking help, such as fear of being seen as incompetent or not getting full credit for task completion (Nelson-Le Gall, 1981) and the expectation that one should solve problems independently (van der Meij, 1988). Other barriers include inaccurate self-assessment, difficulty in judging when it might pay off to persist in trying to solve a task by oneself rather than seek help, and an inability to formulate good questions. Some forms of help require that one reads and understands technical text and evaluates how to apply the general knowledge found in textual sources to the problem at hand, which can be challenging. Finally, many students tend to be performance oriented (i.e., focused on demonstrating their ability, for example by quickly finishing assigned problems) rather than learning oriented (i.e., focused on developing their ability), thus leading to less effective help seeking (Arbreton, 1998; Karabenick, 2003; Ryan & Pintrich, 1997) and learning (Dweck, 1989).

Although help seeking has been studied extensively in social contexts, it has been studied only to a very limited degree in the context of computer-based interactive learning environments (ILEs), even though such systems are becoming increasingly commonplace at many levels of education (Aleven, Stahl, Schworm, Fischer, & Wallace, 2003; Karabenick & Knapp, 1988b). By ILEs we mean a broad range of instructional software, including, for example, computer-assisted instruction (CAI; see Eberts, 1997; Gibbons & Fairweather, 1998; Larkin & Chabay, 1992), intelligent tutoring systems, (Corbett, Koedinger, & Anderson, 1997), authentic problem-solving environments (CTGV, 1997; Slotta & Linn, 2000), systems geared toward the adaptive presentation of instructional multimedia materials (Brusilovsky, 2001; Dillon & Gabbard, 1998), and systems focused on guided discovery learning (de Jong & van Joolingen, 1998). The current chapter focuses on help seeking within one particular type of ILE, namely, Cognitive Tutors (Anderson, Corbett, Koedinger, & Pelletier, 1995). These types of systems are designed to support guided learning by doing. They offer a rich problem-solving environment, monitor students as they work through problems in this environment, and provide various forms of guidance including hints and feedback. Cognitive Tutors have been proven to be effective in raising students' test scores in actual classrooms. As of the spring of 2004 they were in use in approximately 1,700 schools nationwide. Thus they are a prime example of a successful technological educational innovation.

Although different ILEs are based on very different pedagogical approaches, a feature common to many systems is on-demand help. For example, the Geometry Cognitive Tutor (Aleven & Koedinger, 2002; Koedinger, Corbett, Ritter, & Shapiro, 2000), shown in Figure 10.1, offers two types of on-demand help, in addition to other forms of tutorial guidance such as feedback on students' stepwise problem solutions. We call these two types of help *context-sensitive* and *decontextual* help, reflecting whether or not the help content is tailored, by the system, to the specific learning context. First, at the student's request, the tutor provides context-sensitive hints with information tailored toward the student's specific goal within the problem at hand (see the small window entitled "Hint" in the middle of Fig. 10.1). Typically, multiple levels of hints are available for any given problem-solving step. Second, the tutor offers decontextual help in the form of a glossary window (see the window labeled "Glossary" at the bottom right of Fig. 10.1). The student can use this glossary to browse a set of relevant problem-solving principles and to

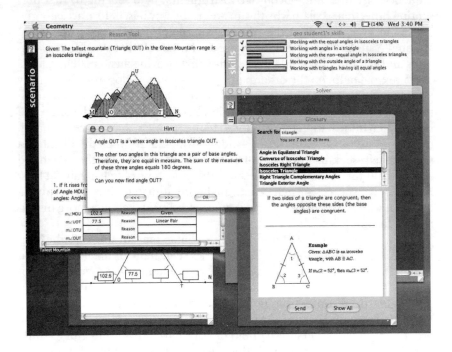

FIG. 10.1.   The Geometry Cognitive Tutor.

selectively display more information about each. Other systems provide similar decontextual help facilities, as well as a variety of others, for example, hyperlinked textbooks, custom-designed hyperlinked background material (Slotta & Linn, 2000), or links to relevant lecture materials (Mandl, Gräsel, & Fischer, 2000). Such decontextual help facilities are much like many sources of help found in the real world. Thus, it is important that students learn to use them appropriately.

The distinction between context-sensitive and decontextual help just given does not align neatly with the difference between executive and instrumental help seeking that has long been made in the literature (see, e.g., Nelson-Le Gall, 1985). Executive help seeking has been defined as focused on supporting performance or completing a task, whereas instrumental help-seeking episodes are concerned with the acquisition of new skills or knowledge. Given that an ILE's goal is to support learning, ideally the help facilities of any given ILE would channel students into instrumental help seeking and would not allow executive help seeking, or perhaps would allow it only as a last resort, to allow students who are really stuck to move on to the next step. The help facilities in the Geometry Cognitive Tutor were designed with these goals in mind. For example, the context-sensitive hints sequences are meant to encourage instrumental help seeking by first presenting hints that explain why the answer is the way it is, before actually giving the answer. However, they do not completely disallow executive help seeking: A student could simply ignore the hint levels that provide explanations and pay attention only to the hints that provide answers. The tutor's decontextual help, on the other hand (i.e., the online glossary of geometry knowledge), never provides answers directly and thus does not seem open to such executive help-seeking strategies. Yet there is a cost to decontextual help: When information is not tailored to the problem-solving step at hand, there is more work to do for the student, which may lower the likelihood that the help-seeking episode will be successful and thereby the likelihood that in the future the student will select the same type of help again (at least if alternative sources of help are available). Ultimately, it is an empirical question which type of help is used more effectively (i.e., in a more instrumental fashion).

Thus, it is important to understand to what extent students use the help facilities of an ILE effectively, that is, to seek help in an instrumental rather than executive manner, and to what extent the proficient use of help facilities helps students learn better. Certainly the literature on help seeking in social contexts, as indicated already, has illustrated the impact of proficient help seeking (or lack thereof) on student learning. On the other hand, researchers in the field of ILEs have only just begun to study help seeking as an important influence on student learning (for a recent overview of the literature, see Aleven et al., 2003). Some studies have provided evidence that the proficient use of the help facilities offered by an ILE can lead to higher learning outcomes (Renkl, 2002; Wood, 2001; Wood & Wood, 1999). For example, Renkl (2002) found that adding on-demand help to a system that presents students examples to study leads to better learning outcomes. Wood and Wood (1999) studied help seeking with a small-scale intelligent tutoring system and found that students with lower prior knowledge tended to have higher learning gains if they used help more frequently.

However, those same studies, as well as others, have presented evidence that students often use the help facilities of ILEs in ways that are not conducive to learning (Mandl et al., 2000). For example, Renkl (2002) identified a group of students with low learning gains who did not use help very frequently. Wood and Wood (1999) found that students with lower prior knowledge were the least likely to use help in an adaptive manner. Unfortunately, such students arguably needed help the most. Aleven and Koedinger (2000), in a classroom study involving the Geometry Cognitive Tutor of Fig. 10.1, found evidence of widespread help abuse (e.g., overuse of help) and to a lesser degree of help avoidance. One goal of this chapter is to present data from this study, documenting students' help use with the Geometry Cognitive Tutor. We believe this evidence to be especially compelling, as it comes from actual classroom use of the tutors.

To interpret these results and adequately address the causes of ineffective help seeking in ILEs, it is important to understand both the system's and the student's contribution to the problem. With respect to the system's contribution, it is important to understand the influence on students' learning of various factors in the design of help systems. Only a small number of studies have been done in this area. These studies found that the effectiveness of on-demand help often depends on the content of the help messages given by the system. For example, in a study in which the subjects tried to learn, by exploration, how to use a simple computer drawing program, Dutke and Reimer (2000) found that explanations of what to do (dubbed "operative help" by Dutke and Reimer) were less effective in supporting learning than explanations of the functioning of the drawing program that the students were trying to master ("function-oriented help"). One could view the central question of that study as: "Which type of help is more instrumental, in the Nelson-Le Gall (1985) sense, operative help or function-oriented help?" Dutke and Reimer's results show that in a context of learning software by task-oriented discovery, function-oriented help is more instrumental or leads to more instrumental help seeking. The distinction between operative help and function-oriented help is orthogonal to that made earlier between context-sensitive and decontextual help. The function-oriented help and operative help used in the Dutke and Reimer study are not context sensitive in the way that the hints of the Geometry Cognitive Tutor are—that is, neither type of help refers to specific information in the given problem or explains how a problem-solving principle applies. It is not clear, however, that greater context sensitivity would be appropriate in a context of discovery learning.

Similarly, studies of the content of feedback messages given by ILEs (i.e., messages that were given at the system's initiative rather than at the student's) have shown an effect of such factors as whether the help message draws attention to the students' goals (McKendree, 1990), the degree of interactivity (i.e., the extent to which students are asked to answer questions when receiving system feedback), and whether the help is couched in abstract or concrete terms (Arroyo, Beck, Beal, Wing, & Woolf, 2001; Arroyo, Beck, Woolf, Beal, & Schultz, 2000).

A second goal of this chapter is to present research aimed at understanding how two additional factors related to the help content may have helped shape students' help-seeking behavior with the Geometry Cognitive Tutor, namely, (a) whether the system's help messages focus solely on domain-specific skills and knowledge or whether they also mix in advice at the metacognitive level, and (b) the number of levels of help given to the students.

In addition to studying how system design may contribute to good or poor help use, it is important to understand the student's contribution. As mentioned, many factors may contribute to poor help-seeking behavior. Our research focuses on the hypothesis that students would learn more effectively, across a range of domains, if they had better help-seeking skills. From this viewpoint, help seeking is a metacognitive skill that must be acquired and that may be open to instruction. (Metacognition is usually regarded as comprising processes of planning, monitoring, and regulating one's own cognition. Help seeking is a learning strategy that is employed when monitoring indicates the need for help and thus is properly regarded as cognition about cognition or as behavioral regulation, that is, as metacognition.) The view that help seeking skills may be open to instruction is consistent with studies that show the success of instructional programs that focus on teaching other types of metacognitive skills, such as self-explanation (Bielaczyc, Pirolli, & Brown, 1995), comprehension monitoring (Palincsar & Brown, 1984), monitoring and heuristically steering problem-solving progress (Schoenfeld, 1987), and self-assessment (White & Frederiksen, 1998). In developing instruction on help-seeking skills, we aim to take advantage of the unique qualities of Cognitive Tutors: Given their proven effectiveness in teaching domain-specific skills and knowledge, it is plausible that they could also help students learn to seek help more effectively. We focus on the hypothesis that such support for help seeking would help students to learn better at the domain level but also would help them to become better help seekers and thus better *future learn-*

ers. The question whether an ILE can be effective in fostering metacognitive skills such as help seeking has not, to our knowledge, been addressed in the literature on ILEs, with the exception of the work of Luckin and Hammerton (2002), who reported preliminary results on "metacognitive scaffolding."

The third goal of this chapter is to present ongoing work aimed at extending the Geometry Cognitive Tutor so that it provides tutoring on students' help-seeking behavior, in addition to assistance with geometry problem solving. The extension to the tutor, called the Help Tutor, will be able to evaluate at any point during a tutoring session whether the student could benefit by asking for help, in light of how difficult the given step is estimated to be at that point in time for that particular student. It will comment when the student makes unnecessary or too-rapid help requests and also when the student refrains from asking for help in situations where it would likely be beneficial. This approach will be implemented within the "model tracing" paradigm that underlies the Cognitive Tutor technology (Anderson et al., 1995). In this paradigm, a tutoring system uses a cognitive model, essentially a simulation model of student thinking that can be executed on the computer, to monitor students' individual approaches to problems and provide guidance as needed. For example, the Geometry Cognitive Tutor employs a cognitive model of problem-solving skill in the domain of geometry to monitor students' solution steps and to provide hints and feedback. Similarly, the planned Help Tutor will use a cognitive model of help seeking to evaluate students' help-seeking behavior. Thus, a key challenge in creating this tutor is the implementation of a detailed model of adaptive help-seeking behavior. We have created an initial model the shares some traits with models of help seeking that have been presented in the literature on help seeking (Nelson-Le Gall, 1981; Newman, 1998) but is considerably more detailed. Further, it is a computational model, meaning that it can be executed on a computer to make predictions about students' help-seeking behavior and to provide tutoring.

In summary, we present data about students' use of the help facilities of the Geometry Cognitive Tutor and document the difficulties that students have in using help effectively. We then present progress made toward addressing those difficulties with respect to both solution approaches outlined, including preliminary data investigating the influence of two factors on students' help use, namely, the mixing of cognitive and metacognitive advice, and the number of hint levels. We also present our initial cognitive model of help seeking that will form the basis for extending the Tutor so that it helps students become better help seekers. Finally, we describe a future experiment to evaluate whether this tutor actually improves students' help-seeking ability and whether they learn better as a result.

THE GEOMETRY COGNITIVE TUTOR

Cognitive Tutors are a form of intelligent instructional software, designed to help students as they learn a complex cognitive skill (Anderson et al., 1995). This type of tutoring software provides support for learning by doing in the form of context-sensitive hints, feedback, and individualized problem selection. Carefully integrated with classroom instruction, Cognitive Tutors for high school algebra and geometry have been shown to be about one standard deviation better than traditional classroom instruction (Koedinger, Anderson, Hadley, & Mark, 1997; Koedinger et al., 2000) and have also been shown to be instrumental in enhancing student motivation (Schofield, 1995). Currently, Cognitive Tutors for Algebra I, Algebra II, and Geometry are disseminated nationwide by a company spun off from our research group (see http://www/carnegielearning.com). As of the 2003–2004 school year, the Algebra I Cognitive Tutor is used in 1,500 schools around the country, and the Geometry Cognitive Tutor in 350 schools.

The Geometry Cognitive Tutor, shown in Fig. 10.1, is an integrated part of a full-year high-school geometry course (Aleven & Koedinger, 2002). Both the tutor and the curriculum were developed by our research group. Following guidelines of the National Council of Teachers of Mathematics (NCTM, 1989), the tutor presents geometry problems with a real-world flavor. In these problems, students are given a description of a problem situation plus a diagram and are asked to calculate unknown quantities such as angle measures, segment measures, the area of two-dimensional shapes, and so on. The tutor offers a rich problem-solving environment in which students can work with both a tabular and a diagrammatic representation of the problem and get assistance from a symbolic equation solver tutor if their solution requires it.

As students enter the values for the unknown quantities into the table (shown on the left in Fig. 10.1), the tutor provides feedback indicating whether the entry is correct or not. In the Angles unit, the unit of the tutor curriculum dealing with the geometric properties of angles (most of the data presented in this chapter pertain to this unit), students are asked also to provide brief explanations for each numeric answer by indicating which geometry theorem or definition justifies it (e.g., "Triangle Sum"). They can either select explanations from the tutor's online glossary, described further in this chapter, or they can type the explanation into the tutor's table. Students are allowed to move on to the next problem only when they provide correct answers and explanations for all steps.

As mentioned, the tutor provides two forms of on-demand help. The tutor's online glossary lists important theorems and definitions of geometry and illustrates each with a simple example diagram (Fig. 10.1, center). This type of help is decontextual: The information that is presented is not tailored to the specific problem that the student is working on. The students can use the glossary freely as they work with the tutor. The glossary also functions as a menu from which students can select the reasons that justify their steps, saving them the effort of typing the name of the theorem. Given that the decontextual help does not directly provide answers, one might regard it as instrumental help as defined by Nelson-Le Gall (1985). Ultimately, though, whether this type of help (or any type of help) is instrumental in helping students learn is an empirical question, the answer to which depends not only on the properties of the help itself but also on whether and how students use it.

Further, the tutor provides context-sensitive hints at the student's request with information on how to complete the next step in the given problem (Fig. 10.1, window in the middle of the figure). For each step, between 5 and 8 levels of hints are available, depending on the specific geometry skill involved. Each hint level provides increasingly more specific advice (see Table 10.1). The hints were designed not just to communicate to the student which problem-solving principle is applicable and how it applies, but also to communicate a strategy for how they might find an applicable principle, if they were not able to recall it from memory. The early hints in each sequence suggest that the student undertake a glossary search using a cue

TABLE 10.1

Example Hint Sequence in the Geometry Cognitive Tutor

	Hint Text	General Hint Plan
1.	As you can see in the diagram, Angles LGH and TGH are adjacent angles. Together they form line HI. How can you use this fact to find the measure of Angle TGH?	Identify key problem feature ("adjacent angles")
2.	Look in the Glossary for reasons dealing with adjacent angles.	Recommend glossary search guided by key feature
3.	Some rules dealing with adjacent angles are highlighted in the Glossary. Which of these reasons is appropriate? You can click on each reason in the Glossary to find out more.	Help reduce glossary search
4.	If two angles form a linear pair the sum of their measures is 180 degrees. Angle TGH and Angle LGH form a linear pair.	Identify relevant problem-solving principle
5.	The measure of Angle TGH plus the measure of Angle LGH is equal to 180 degrees	Discuss how principle can be applied
6.	The measure of Angle TGH is equal to 180 degrees minus the measure of Angle LGH.	
7.	$m\angle TGH = 180° - m\angle LGH$	

identified in the problem (e.g., that the problem involves an isosceles triangle or supplementary angles). An intermediate hint highlights a few potentially relevant geometry rules in the glossary, in case the student was not successful in determining which rule is applicable. The later hints in each sequence discuss how the rule can be applied to find the targeted angle measure. Each hint sequence "bottoms out" by stating a simple algebraic expression that describes how to find the unknown quantity. In other words, the bottom-out hint typically comes very close to giving students the answer for the current step in the problem. Thus, the hint sequences progress from indirect help (hints, really) to direct help. One might say that the earlier help levels provide instrumental help (Nelson-Le Gall, 1985), whereas the last level (the bottom-out hints) provide executive (Nelson-Le Gall, 1985) or expedient (Butler, 1998) help. As before, we caution that judgments as to whether a particular type of help is instrumental or executive are better made after the fact, based on data relating help use and learning outcomes.

Like all Cognitive Tutors (Anderson et al., 1995; Koedinger et al., 1997), behind the scene the Geometry Cognitive Tutor uses a cognitive model to monitor students as they solve problems. The cognitive model represents the skills targeted in the instruction as a set of production rules, following the ACT-R theory of cognition and learning (Anderson & Lebière, 1998). An example of such a skill would be applying the triangle sum theorem to calculate an unknown angle in a triangle, given the measures of the other two angles in the triangle. The cognitive model is an executable simulation of student problem solving. That is, the system can run the model to solve problems step by step in the same manner that students must learn. This executable cognitive model is key to the tutor's ability to monitor and evaluate students' activities, for which it uses an algorithm called "model tracing." When the student attempts to answer a tutor question (e.g., enters a numeric value into the tutor's table), the system runs the model to find out what steps it would take in the same situation and gives feedback to the student by comparing the student's solution step to those generated by the model. Similarly, when the student requests a hint, the system runs the model to generate possible steps, selects the best one, and then produces hint text using templates attached to the production rules in the model that are involved in generating that step.

Cognitive Tutors keep track of the student's knowledge growth over time by means of a Bayesian algorithm called "knowledge tracing" (Corbett & Anderson, 1995). The algorithm is invoked at each problem-solving step to update the tutor's estimates of the probability that the student knows the skills involved in that step. Whether the estimate is incremented or decremented depends on whether the student was able to complete the step without errors and hints. The tutor uses the estimated probability of skill mastery to select problems and make pacing decisions on an individual basis. It displays these estimates in a "skillmeter" window, shown at the top right in Fig. 10.1, to inform the students about their progress. Skills for which the tutor's estimate exceeds a certain threshold (set to .95) are considered to be mastered and are ticked off in the skillmeter window. Once the student has reached mastery for all skills, the tutor advances him or her to the next section of the curriculum. Students tend to be quite aware of this advancement criterion and often keep a close eye on their skillmeter window

STUDENTS' HELP-SEEKING PATTERNS

In this section, we present data about students' help-seeking behavior while using the Geometry Cognitive Tutor. We assess this behavior by comparing it to reasonable predictions about that behavior. We also report how various measures of help use correlate with students' learning outcomes.

Data Collection

The data presented in this section were collected during a classroom study whose goal it was to assess the added value of having students explain their problem-solving steps (Aleven & Koedinger, 2002). The participants were assigned to two conditions, each working with a slightly different version of the tutor. Students in the Explanation condition explained their problem-solving steps (i.e., justified their steps by citing the relevant geometry rule, as already described). Students in the Problem-Solving condition used a tutor version that did not require that they explain their steps (i.e., the table in the tutor interface did not have boxes for entering "Reasons"). In this chapter we are not primarily interested in the effect of having students explain, so we report the results of both conditions together, except where noted.

The study took place in the course of regular instruction with the Geometry Cognitive Tutor in a suburban school in the Pittsburgh area. The study involved the students in two periods of a Geometry Cognitive Tutor course taught by the same teacher and his assistant. The students were mostly 10th graders, that is, 15- and 16-year-olds. In total, 41 students completed the experiment. During the study, about 50% of the time was devoted to classroom and small-group activities. The other 50% of the time the students worked on the tutor's Angles unit, one of the six units that at the time of writing, made up the full-year curriculum of the tutor. The students completed a pretest and posttest before and after their work on the tutor. These tests included questions similar to those encountered on the tutor and included transfer problems as well. The pretest and posttest data indicate that there were significant learning gains, attributable to the combination of work on the tutor and classroom instruction (Aleven & Koedinger, 2002).

As the students worked with the tutor, detailed logs of the student–tutor interactions were collected. The log data were analyzed to explore patterns of students' use of the tutor's help facilities, that is, the tutor's context-sensitive hints and the tutor's (decontextual) online glossary.

Use of Context-Sensitive Help

We looked at a number of variables reflecting the students' use of the tutor's on-demand hints. As mentioned, these hints are context sensitive: They provide information tailored to the particular problem-solving step that the student is working on. We expected that students, to the extent that they were good help seekers, would request help from the tutor when faced with a step that looked unfamiliar or when they had made an error, as indicated by the tutor's feedback, and were not sure how to fix it. We predicted further that good help seekers would use the hints deliberately, that is, read them carefully in order to decide whether they now had enough information to try the step with reasonable confidence or whether they needed to look at a more detailed hint. Finally, we expected that the students, as they became more proficient with a given skill, would request less detailed help from the tutor (i.e., would request to see fewer hint levels).

As it turned out, the students used the tutor's context-sensitive help on 29% of the answer steps and 22% of the explanation steps. By "step" we mean a subgoal in the problem, or equivalently an entry in the tutor's answer sheet. Students requested a hint before their first attempt at answering on 12% of the answer steps and 9% of the explanation steps. We do not have a firm basis for making a numerical prediction as to what the optimal rate of help use *should* be. However, it is clear that help use and errors should to some degree be balanced, that is, should be roughly equal. If students made many errors without asking for help, this would not be good. But neither would it be good if students asked for hints very often while making very few errors. In our data, students made one or more errors on 36% of the numeric answer steps and 37% of the reason steps. Thus, although the frequency of help use was somewhat lower than the error frequency, help use and errors seemed reasonably balanced. After all, it is quite likely that some errors are slips that can be fixed quite easily without requiring assistance from the system. On the other hand, the expectation that students, when faced with an unfamiliar step, would not guess an answer but would request help first was not fully borne out. Regardless of the precise criterion one uses for deeming a step to be "unfamiliar," it seems unlikely that only 1 out of every 10 steps would be unfamiliar when students are working in a novel domain. As further evidence of help avoidance, the students had a tendency to resist asking for a hint, even after making multiple errors on a given step. Details can be found in Aleven and Koedinger (2000).

We also looked for evidence that the tutor's help messages helped to improve students' performance with the tutor, that is, that they made it easier for students to complete tutor problems (see Table 10.2). Overall, students made fewer errors on answer attempts that followed a hint request than on steps where their first action was an answer attempt (82% correct vs. 62% correct). Further, after a student made one or two errors on a step, asking for help as the next action reduced both the number of subsequent errors and the time needed to complete the step (Aleven & Koedinger, 2000). Thus, the help messages aided performance. Similar evidence that the use of context-sensitive help in an intelligent tutoring system aids performance was found in other studies as well (Anderson, Conrad, & Corbett, 1989; McKendree, 1990). It does not necessarily follow, however, that students' help use led to more efficient or effective learning. In order to support that conclusion, one would need to compare learning results obtained with tutor versions with and without hints.

Finally, we looked at a number variables that relate to how deliberately students used the help messages (see Table 10.3). The students spent 1 second or less with as much as 68% of the hints at intermediate levels, meaning that their next action after requesting the hint (often this was the next hint request) occurred in less than 1 second. By "intermediate levels" we mean all levels but the last. Also, students spent an average of 2.3 seconds per intermediate hint, which seems inadequate to read and interpret it and assess whether one knows

TABLE 10.2

Performance on Answer Attempts Immediately Following a Hint

Percent Correct After Intermediate Hint	Percent Correct After Bottom-Out Hint	Percent Correct After Any Hint	Percent Correct When First Action Is Answer Attempt
64%	87%	82%	62%

TABLE 10.3

Deliberateness of Students' Hint Use

Condition	Percent Bottom-Out	Time per Intermediate Hint	Percent Intermediate Hints Used Undeliberately
Explanation	87%	1.9 seconds	69%
Problem-Solving	79%	2.5 seconds	68%
Overall	81%	2.3 seconds	68%

enough to enter the answer. Further, on 81% of the steps on which students requested hints, they asked to see all hint levels including the bottom-out hint. As mentioned, the tutor's bottom-out hints stopped just short of handing students the answer. These data point to frequent use of a strategy in which students click their way through all hint levels as quickly as they can until they reach the bottom-out hint. In other words, the majority of the time, the students choose to use the tutor's context-sensitive hints in (what appears to be) highly executive fashion. This "gaming" behavior has been studied in other work with Cognitive Tutors as well (Baker, Corbett, & Koedinger, 2004).

Summing up the findings with respect to students' use of the tutor's context-sensitive hints, although the students appeared to use the tutor's context-sensitive help with appropriate frequency and although this type of help assisted students in completing the assigned problems, on closer scrutiny, students' help use left much to be desired. In particular, the expectation that the students would use the context-sensitive hints in a deliberate manner was not met. Quite the contrary, the students very frequently used hints to get answers quickly, without careful reflection on the answer. In addition, there was evidence that the students avoided hint use at moments at which it would have been appropriate, namely, when faced with unfamiliar steps or after making multiple errors on a step. The observed preoccupation with bottom-out hints is undesirable. In order to learn from being giving the right answer to a problem (in this case, the bottom-out hint), one needs to construct an explanation of why the right answer is right (Anderson et al., 1989). The finding that students focused on the bottom-out hints was not consistent with our expectation that students would need increasingly less detailed help as they became more proficient. The finding is also inconsistent with results from an earlier study with a Cognitive Tutor for LISP programming, which showed that the average number of hints requested was 1.5 out of 3 hints (Anderson, personal communication).

Use of Decontextual Help

We also looked at the frequency with which the students used the tutor's decontextual help, the online glossary of geometry knowledge. As mentioned, the students could browse this resource freely during their work with the tutor. We expected that for any skill targeted in the instruction, good help seekers would gradually rely less on the tutor's on-demand hints and instead would use the glossary more often. By using the glossary, they would avoid the negative update of the tutor's estimate of their skill mastery that comes with hint use. Thus, glossary use would contribute to their goal of getting their skills "checked off" by the tutor.

As it turned out, however, students used the tutor's online glossary on only 2.7% of the numeric answer steps (see Table 10.4). They used the glos-

TABLE 10.4

Incidence of Decontextual Help: Percentage of Steps on Which the Online Glossary Was Used

	All Use	*Deliberate Use Only*
Numeric answer steps	2.7%	2.0%
Reason steps	43%	15%

Note. Deliberate use was defined as inspecting at least one glossary item for at least 1 second.

sary more frequently when giving reasons for their answers, namely, on 43% of the reason steps. The large discrepancy is likely to be due to the fact that on reason steps, the glossary served as a menu: The students could enter reasons by selecting the name of a geometry rule from the glossary. Much of the glossary use on reason steps, however, appeared to be rapid selection, rather than deliberate reading and interpretation of information about geometry. On only 15% of the reason steps did students spend at least one second with at least one glossary item, a very minimal criterion for deliberate use. It is clearly not possibly for a student in 1 second to learn much from a description of a geometry theorem she or he has not seen before. However, it does seem possible in that amount of time to visually recognize an example diagram.

Clearly, our expectation that the glossary would be a convenient and useful resource was not borne out. The frequency of glossary use on numeric answers steps was very low, even if one considers that glossary use would be appropriate only on steps for which students have some, but incomplete, knowledge.

Correlation Between Help Use and Learning

In order to study the relation between help seeking and learning outcomes, we focused on the measures derived from the student–tutor interactions (which we call *process measures*) listed in Table 10.5. Some means shown in this table are different from those reported earlier because Table 10.5 shows the average of the per-student average whereas the numbers shown earlier are averages over all steps of all students.

It is difficult to predict whether the frequency of help use will correlate positively with learning. On the one hand, one would predict that greater help use would lead to higher learning gains, because students who use help more frequently have more opportunity to benefit from the explanations given in the help messages. On the other hand, frequent help use is likely to be a sign of students' experiencing difficulty during their work on the tutor. It is likely that those who are in trouble more often during training tend to learn less, which would lead to a negative correlation between help seeking

TABLE 10.5

Process Measures Related to Student–Tutor Interactions

Process Measure	Description	Mean ± 1 SD
Success frequency	Percentage of steps that the student got right without making any errors or requesting any hints	55 ± 18
Help frequency	Percentage of steps on which the student asked for help	27 ± 19
Error frequency	Percentage of steps on which the student made one or more errors	36 ± 12
Successful use of help to avoid error	Number of steps where the student used help and did not make an error divided by the number of incorrect steps (i.e., steps where the student used help or made an error)	18 ± 14
Use of help after an error	Percentage of incorrect steps on which the student used help after an error was made (i.e., when students make an error, how often do they ask for help)	40 ± 20

Note.   All measures pertain to numeric answer steps only. Explanation steps are not included.

and learning. We have no good basis for predicting which of these opposing influences will be stronger. We note that Wood and Wood (1999), in a study involving a small-scale intelligent tutoring system for factoring quadratic expressions, found a positive correlation between help use and learning for students with lower prior knowledge.

We considered correlations between process measures and posttest score, with prior geometric knowledge and the pretest scores partialed out (see Table 10.6). Prior geometry knowledge was measured by means of a test administered after the student completed the previous tutor unit, which dealt with the area of various two-dimensional geometric figures. Most of the process measures correlated significantly with the posttest scores. Students who were most successful during training, making fewer errors and completing more steps without errors or hints, tended to do best on the posttest. Students who used help more often tended to do worse, although not if the help was used successfully to solve a step without errors.

Thus, unlike Wood and Wood (1999), we found a negative correlation between help seeking and learning. The negative correlation implies that any learning advantages due to the more frequent use of help messages were not sufficient to enable the more frequent help users, presumably the learners who experienced more difficulties during the learning process, to overcome these difficulties and learn as well as, or better than, students who used help less frequently.

Implications

In short, although there was evidence that students used the tutor's context-sensitive help facility with appropriate frequency and that the help messages helped students in completing problems, there is considerable room for improvement in students' help use. First, there was evidence of widespread "gaming" of the system, with students using the tutor's hints to get to answers as quickly as possible (see also Baker et al., 2004). Second, there was evidence, although not quite as strong, of hint avoidance—that is, of students not requesting a hint when it would likely have been beneficial. Also, the students infrequently used the tutor's online glossary. Under these circumstances, it is hardly surprising that there was a negative correlation between help seeking and learning. Help use aimed at getting answers without reflection on the reasons behind those answers has little potential to improve learning. Therefore, quite possibly, the negative correlation merely reflects the fact that those who are in trouble more often during a learning process tend to have lower learning outcomes.

It is an interesting question why the results reported here differ from those found by Wood and Wood (1999), who as mentioned found a positive correlation between help seeking and learning and did not report the kind of hint abuse that was rampant in our study. There are considerable differences in scale between the studies. While QUADRATIC, the system used by Wood and Wood, comprises about 1 to 1.5 hours of instruction, the Geometry Cognitive Tutor addresses a full-year high-school geometry course. The data reported here relate to the third of six major units that made up the curriculum at the time of the study, which takes about 8.5 hours of work on the tutor. Prior to the study, the students had already spent at least that amount of time working on the previous two tutor units. It is possible that certain tendencies in students' help-seeking behavior do not develop until students work on the tutor over an extended period of time. It would obviously take some time and use for students to fully ab-

TABLE 10.6

Correlations Between Process Measures and Posttest Performance
Controlling for Prior Domain Knowledge and Pretest Performance

Process Measure	r	p
Success frequency	.70	.0001
Help frequency	−.61	.0001
Error frequency	−.66	.0001
Successful use of help to avoid error	−.26	ns
Use of help after error	−.54	.005

sorb the fact that the bottom-out hint virtually provides the answer to a step. Another significant difference may be the fact that the study described here is a classroom study, whereas the Wood and Wood study took place in a lab. Finally, there were a number of differences between the help systems used in the two studies. For example, Wood and Wood had five levels of hints, whereas the Geometry Cognitive Tutor has between five and eight levels of hints for any given step. Also, in QUADRATIC, the system used in the Wood and Wood study, the initial hint level (i.e., the hint level given when the student first asks for help on a step) is contingent upon the student's previous performance, whereas in the Geometry Cognitive Tutor, help always starts at the first level. So, for instance, the approach in the Geometry Cognitive Tutor might encourage rapid hint selection because hints are not customized to performance; that is, many students might find the early hints to be unhelpful. The current data do not allow us to distinguish between these different explanations.

We see two broad possible explanations for the observed ineffective help-seeking behavior. First, the problem may have been mainly with the system. Perhaps the kinds of hints provided by the tutor were too difficult for the population of students who participated in the study; that is, the hints may have been outside their zone of proximal development (Vygotsky, 1978). For example, the hints and glossary may require greater mathematical reading ability than the given student population has. In addition, it may have been too difficult to find relevant information in the glossary (a search facility was added only later). One must know some terminology in order to search effectively. Students may not always have picked up this terminology during classroom instruction. Further, it may have been difficult to interpret information found in the glossary and judge whether that information is relevant to the problem at hand. Better hints and a glossary that is easier to search might have helped.

A second set of explanations focuses on the students. The observed poor hint use may reflect a conscious minimum-effort strategy on the part of students or it may be the result of students' being performance-oriented as opposed to learning-oriented (see, e.g., Arbreton, 1998; Butler, 1998; Karabenick, 2003; Newman & Karabenick, 2004). Alternatively, the poor help use may be the result of poor metacognitive skill. Possibly, these students did not have the habit of trying to understand their own solutions to problems or to understand the help that was given. Maybe these students were not in the habit of looking up things they do not know. With some practice, these students might have been able to use the Geometry Cognitive Tutor more effectively to learn skills involved in geometry problem solving. In the remainder of the chapter, we describe ongoing research aimed at better understanding and addressing these potential causes.

INVESTIGATION OF TWO FACTORS POTENTIALLY INFLUENCING HELP USE

In the current section, we consider two factors related to the content of the tutor's help messages that may have contributed to students' poor help use, namely, (a) the mixing of advice at the cognitive and metacognitive level and (b) the length of the hint sequences. The nature of this work is exploratory; we use data that were not collected specifically to isolate the influence of these two factors. The comparisons therefore are not entirely free of confounds, as we note later. Nonetheless, the comparisons are very useful, because they help zero in on hypotheses that are worthwhile to test in a more carefully controlled study. Without such exploratory work, one is faced with a very wide set of potential hypotheses related to the system design without much guidance as to which ones are most worthy of further study (as argued further in Aleven et al., 2003).

Effect of Mixing Cognitive and Metacognitive Advice

The hint sequences of the Geometry Cognitive Tutor, as illustrated in Table 10.1, mix advice at the cognitive and metacognitive levels. The hints not only explain how to apply a problem-solving principle to a given problem-solving step, but they also advise students on how to find an applicable problem-solving principle, by searching the glossary. There was a good reason for advising students to consult the glossary, namely, that the students learn to use a resource that is like many reference resources found in the real world. In retrospect, however, the resulting hint sequences may have become too involved and may have imposed too much cognitive load, perhaps contributing to the observed poor hint use.

We explore this hypothesis by comparing the hint data between the two conditions in our experiment, the Problem-Solving condition and the Explanation condition. The hints in the Problem-Solving condition mixed advice at the cognitive level with advice at the metacognitive level to a far lesser extent than the hints in the Explanation condition. Consider the hint sequence shown in Table 10.1, which was given only to students in the Explanation condition. The instructions for using the glossary, given at the second and third hint level, constitute advice at the metacognitive level. They explain how the student should go about seeking help, rather than helping directly with the problem-solving step at hand. In the corresponding hint sequence given to the students in the Problem-Solving condition, these two hint levels were omitted. Instead, the following text was added to the first hint of the sequence: "You can look it up in the Glossary." Thus, the comparison is less than ideal: Although the hint sequences in the Problem-Solving condition provide considerably less metacognitive advice than those in the Explanation condition, they do provide some. Further, the hint sequences for the Problem-Solving condition are shorter than those in the Explanation condition, confounding the comparison. Nonetheless, the comparison is useful for exploratory purposes, as argued earlier.

Comparing the hint data between the two conditions (see Table 10.3), we see that the students in the Problem-Solving condition used bottom-out hints less frequently than students in the Explanation condition (79% of steps with hints vs. 87% of steps with hints). The difference is not statistically significant. Further, the students in the Problem-Solving condition spent somewhat more time with the intermediate hints than the students in the Explanation condition (2.5 vs. 1.9 seconds) and had a higher rate of correct answers on their attempts that immediately followed an intermediate hint (69% v. 49%). On the other hand, the rate of deliberate use of intermediate hints (as before, defined as the percentage of hint messages that the student examined for more than 1 second) was the same in each condition (68% in the Problem-Solving condition, 69% in the Explanation condition).

Thus, these data provide some support for the notion that the mixing of advice at the cognitive and metacognitive level may have led to less deliberate help use. But this mixing was not the only cause, as the "nonmixed" hint sequences were not used in a very deliberate manner, either.

Impact of Shorter Hint Sequences With Less Specific Bottom-Out Hints

Another factor that may have invited poor help use is the length of the hint sequences. As mentioned, the hints sequences in the Geometry Cognitive Tutor contained five to eight hint levels. Possibly, the students may have felt that the tutor should get to the point more quickly, which may have contributed significantly to their tendency to skip all hint levels but the last. To test this hypothesis, we have begun to look at data about the student–tutor interactions of different tutor units. For example, we looked at data about student–tutor interactions for the Area unit of the Geometry Cognitive Tutor, which deals with the area of two-dimensional geometric figures. This data set was collected in a different school in a different year, compared to the data from the Angles unit presented earlier.

The hint sequences in the Area unit, illustrated in Table 10.7, have a different underlying hint plan compared to those in the Angles unit. First, the hint sequences in the Area unit do not include any metacognitive advice. That is, there is no advice on how a student should go about finding relevant knowledge when faced with an area problem. Further, the hint sequences in the Area unit are much shorter than those in the Angles unit: Most sequences have three levels. The first level provides the problem-solving principle (often, a formula for finding the area of a particular geometric fig-

TABLE 10.7

Example Hint Sequence in the Area Unit of the Geometry Cognitive Tutor

Hint Text	General Hint Plan
1. The area (A) of a trapezoid can be found using the formula: $A = 1/2 * h * (b + s)$, where h is the height, b is the longer base and s is the shorter base. Which segment in the diagram is the height? Which is the longer base? Which is the shorter base?	Provide problem-solving principle, prompt for mapping of principle to current problem
2. The trapezoid area formula is: $A = 1/2 * h * (b + s)$, where h is the height, b is the longer base and s is the shorter base. In this particular diagram, the height (h) is segment NE, the longer base (b) is segment EV, and the shorter base (s) is segment NA.	Provide problem-solving principle, map to geometric elements of current problem
3. Plug the given values for the height (NE = 304), the longer base (EV = 500), and the shorter base (NA = 207) into the trapezoid area formula: $A = 1/2 * h * (b + s)$	Provide problem-solving principle and show values to be substituted

ure), the second level explains how to map the principle to the step at hand, and the third provides the relevant values to substitute into the formula.

The data indicate that the students working on the Area unit used the hints in a much more deliberate manner than the students working on the Angles unit. Students working on the Area unit:

- Requested to see bottom-out hints on 53% of the steps with hints (Angles: bottom-out hints on 81% of answer steps with hints).
- Spent an average of 26 seconds per intermediate hint and 22 seconds per bottom-out hint (Angles: 2.3 and 6.2 seconds).
- Used only 2.5% of intermediate hints and 10% of bottom-out hints undeliberately, meaning that they looked at them for less than 1 second (Angles: 68% and 54%).

The data show also that in the Area unit, the percentage correct on answer attempts following a hint is lower than the overall percent correct (59% vs. 64%). In other words, there is not the same direct evidence as there was in the Angles unit that the hints help performance. Thus, the data overwhelmingly show that the students in the Area unit used the hints in a far more deliberate manner than the students in the Angles unit. There is no evidence of widespread gaming of the system in the Area unit, as opposed to the Angles unit. There is considerably less evidence that the hints helped performance.

Implications

Although neither comparison presented in this section was entirely free of confounds (the second comparison involved a different group of students in a different school), taken together the two comparisons strongly suggest that it is worthwhile to investigate whether more effective help-seeking behavior would result in the Angles unit if the hint sequences were shortened and did not mix cognitive and metacognitive advice. We plan to test this hypothesis in a controlled experiment with two versions of the Angles unit, the current version and a version with shortened hint sequences (typically three levels per skill) that provide only cognitive advice (i.e., no advice on how to search the glossary).

A MODEL OF GOOD HELP-SEEKING BEHAVIOR

The data about student–tutor interactions with the Geometry Cognitive Tutor indicate that there is considerable room for improvement in students' help-seeking strategies. In a second line of research, we plan to extend the geometry tutor with a Help Tutor aimed at improving students' help use and help-seeking skills, like the proposed (but not implemented) strategy tutor agent described in Ritter (1997). The Help Tutor will give feedback to students on the way they use the tutor's help facilities, so as to get them to use hints and glossary in a deliberate and appropriate manner (Aleven, McLaren, Roll, & Koedinger, 2004).

In order to implement the Help Tutor, we are developing a (prescriptive) model of help seeking with the tutor. This is no easy matter. The relation between help seeking and learning is not fully understood. Wood and Wood (1999) reported examples of individual students whose learning results (working with a computer tutor) seem to be at odds with their help-seeking behavior. For example, they described a student who seemed initially to be overusing the help facilities, yet ultimately had positive learning outcomes.

As a framework for our inquiry, and as a basis for building a computational model, we have developed a conceptual model of help seeking with a computer tutor, shown in Fig. 10.2. The model is based on our experience and intuition with intelligent tutors—in particular, the Geometry Cognitive Tutor—and is informed by models such as those of Nelson-Le Gall and Newman (Nelson-Le Gall, 1981; Newman, 1994); see also Gross and McMullen (1983) for a more detailed model. Such a model needs to be con-

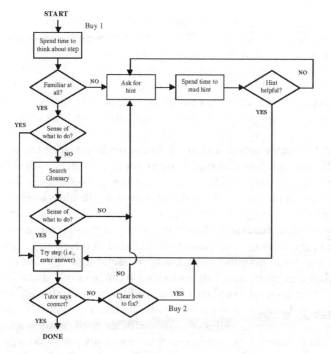

FIG.10.2.
A model of desired help-seeking behavior for a student using an intelligent tutor. The "Bug 1" and "Bug 2" labels mark examples of places where violations of the model can occur, as discussed later in the chapter.

firmed empirically—we are engaged in doing this, as explained later in the chapter.

According to the conceptual model, the ideal student behaves as follows: faced with a step in a tutor problem, the student has three choices: Try the step, go the glossary, or request a hint. If, after spending time considering a problem-solving step, the step looks familiar to the student (i.e., "Familiar at all?" in the flowchart) and she has a good idea of how to solve the step ("Sense of what to do?"), she should proceed with an attempt to solve ("Try step"). If on the other hand, the step looks familiar but the student does not have a clear sense of what to do, she should use the glossary to explore definitions and formulas that may be helpful ("Search Glossary"). After use of the glossary, the student should again reflect on whether she has a good sense of how to tackle the step (the second "Sense of what to do?" from the top of the flowchart). If so, the student should attempt a solution ("Try step"); if not, the student should ask for help ("Ask for hint"). If from the start the step is not recognizable (i.e., "Familiar at all?" in the flowchart), the student should request help ("Ask for hint"). After reading the hint carefully and deliberately ("Spend time to read hint"), the student should then decide whether the hint provides enough information to attempt the step ("Hint helpful?") or whether another hint is needed at this point (the loop back to "Ask for hint" in the flowchart).

After the student tries a step, the tutor will provide feedback to indicate whether the attempt was correct or not. If the tutor feedback indicates the step is correct, the student is done with this cycle of help seeking ("DONE"). On the other hand, if the tutor indicates that the step is incorrect, the student should ponder whether it is clear what to do next ("Clear how to fix?"). At this stage the student is expected to either ask for help, if she or he is unclear what to do ("Ask for hint"), or attempt to solve the step again (the loop back to "Try step").

Thus, the model recommends that students in the initial phase of the acquisition of a skill use hints, then, as they become more proficient with the skill, switch to using the glossary, and finally try to use the skill without the use of hints or the glossary. It may not be immediately clear why the glossary is included in the ideal help-seeking behavior, because the context-sensitive hints provide more information than can be found in the glossary and require less effort on the part of the student. The glossary is included in this strategy because learning to use a resource like the glossary is useful in its own right. Skills learned with the glossary may transfer to a wide range of readily available sources of help in the real world that students must learn to use effectively, such as a web browser, a bookshelf with textbooks, manuals, an encyclopedia, the online help facilities of many software application packages, and so on. These sources are within reach for many people for a large portion of the time. Sources of context-sensitive help on the other hand, although more directly helpful in supporting performance and (perhaps) learning, tend to be more rare and less readily available—the knowledgeable colleague, the teacher, the local guru one floor up, the help line, and so on. Some of these sources, for example, the knowledgeable colleague, can be tapped only with limited frequency without running the risk of overburdening the source and possibly losing it as a result. Within the tutor, this rationale is reflected by the fact that the students can use the glossary freely, but there is a cost associated with the use of context-sensitive hints, at least when hints are requested before an error has been made: As mentioned, the tutor's knowledge-tracing algorithm increments the estimate of skill mastery only when a step is completed without errors or hints.

USING THE HELP-SEEKING MODEL TO TUTOR STUDENTS

In order to build a computational model of the help-seeking flowchart, we had to refine and make concrete some of the abstract components of the flowchart. For example, in order to model the decision points labeled "Familiar at all?" and "Sense of what to do?," which represent acts of self-assessment by the student, we needed to implement a test that determines how well a particular student knows a particular skill at a particular point in time. Item response theory (Hambleton & Swaminathan, 1985) is not suitable because it does not track the effect of learning over time. Instead, we decided to rely on information provided by the Cognitive Tutor's Bayesian knowledge-tracing algorithm. As mentioned, for each skill targeted in the instruction, this algorithm computes a probability that the student has mastered the skill, based on the student's performance so far on problem steps that involve the skill (Corbett & Anderson, 1995). Here, we use a fine-grained notion of skill. An example of a skill is the application of the triangle sum theorem to find the measure of one of the angles in a triangle. Thus, in our model of help seeking, the decisions "Familiar at all?" and "Sense of what to do?" are implemented by comparing the relevant estimate of skill mastery to predefined skill thresholds. For example, if a student's current estimated level for the skill involved in a particular step exceeds a probability threshold, currently set to 0.4, our model assumes "Familiar at all?" = YES. For "Sense of what to do?," a more advanced knowledge level than "Familiar at all?," the threshold is set to 0.6.

For the "Clear how to fix?" step of the flowchart, which determines the student's course of action after making an error, our detailed implementation prescribes that a student with a higher estimated skill level for the particular step (i.e., a skill level above the "Sense of what to do?" threshold of 0.6) retry a step after missing it once. Mid-or lower-skilled students, on the other hand, defined as students whose skill level is equal to or above and below the "Familiar at all?" threshold of 0.4, respectively should ask for a hint. In the future we plan to elaborate "Clear how to fix?" by using heuristics that capture ways that students respond to particular types of common errors. For example, the model may be able to recognize certain types of errors as slips that are easy to fix.

Our implementation of the "Hint helpful?" step predicts that students with different skill levels for a particular step need different amounts of help. Thus, once a hint is first chosen, a student with high skill for the given step is predicted to need one third of the hints, a mid-skill student two thirds of the hints, and a low-skill student all of the hints. These numbers are, of course, rough initial estimates of the amount of help required by students with varying skills. We will refine them as we empirically evaluate our computational model. Ultimately, this particular element of the flowchart is about reading comprehension: The extent to which a hint is helpful depends a great deal on how well a student understood the language of the hint. Thus, in the future we anticipate using results from the reading comprehension literature and also empirically will evaluate tutor data to estimate the difficulty of understanding the tutor's hints.

The help-seeking flowchart is also imprecise in prescribing what the student should do in highly complex and multistep scenarios. For instance, the model is unclear about what a student who repeatedly misses a step or overuses the glossary should do. We have addressed this by introducing thresholds that check for a maximum number of solution attempts or glossary searches that are expected. Thus, for example, a student who exceeds the maximum number of attempts (currently set to 3), while also having seen all the available hints, is expected to ask the teacher for help. When Cognitive Tutors are used in schools, teachers are available to provide help beyond what the Cognitive Tutors can give (see, e.g., Schofield, 1995). The option to ask the teacher for help is not made explicit in our help-seeking model (i.e., there are no production rules that model this step) because that activity could not be monitored by the Help Tutor. However, the Help Tutor will still advise students to ask their teacher if they have exhausted all sources of help.

The various threshold defaults are intuitively plausible but need to be empirically validated. Also, it is likely we will need more fine-grained thresholds, for instance, different "thinking time" thresholds for high, medium, and low skill students. One of the goals of our empirical study, described later, is to refine and extend the use of thresholds in our model.

The Computational Model of Help Seeking

The model described in the previous section forms the basis for a Help Tutor that will serve as an adjunct to an existing Cognitive Tutor. After each student action with the tutor (e.g., requesting a hint, trying a step, inspecting an item in the glossary), the Help Tutor evaluates the action with respect to its model of help seeking. As long as the student's help-seeking behavior conforms to the model (i.e., follows the prescribed steps of the flowchart), no feedback is provided. Deviations from the flowchart on the other hand lead to feedback from the Help Tutor except when the student solves a problem step correctly.

The current initial version of the model consists of 57 production rules. Four key pieces of information are evaluated each time the help-seeking model is run: (a) whether the student took sufficient time to consider their action; (b) whether the action taken by the student is appropriate given the student's mastery (or lack thereof) of the skill involved in the step—for example, a low-skill student should ask for a hint, a high-skill student should try the step, and so on; (c) what the student has already done with respect to this step (e.g., tried and failed multiple times, viewed all the hints); and (d) if the step was attempted, whether the student got it right. Thirty-two of the rules are "bug rules," which reflect deviations of the ideal help-seeking behavior (or "metacognitive bugs"). When the student's behavior matches one of the bug rules, the Help Tutor provides feedback to the student pointing out the observed help-seeking error.

Example of a Student Who Does Not Need Help

Two examples illustrate how our computational model of help seeking operates. In the first example we show how the model handles a hypothetical situation in which a student appropriately does not seek help from the tutor. Suppose a student is presented with a step in a problem involving a skill that she masters quite well. The student carefully ponders the step and then attempts a solution. The tutor feedback indicates that the student's solution step is correct. The student's action corresponds to the following path through the flow chart of help-seeking behavior shown in Fig. 10.2: (1) "Spend time to think about step" = YES, (2) the YES path from both "Familiar at all?" and "Sense of what to do?," (3) doing a "Try step", and (4) "Tutor Says Correct?" = YES. Thus, the student's help-seeking behavior conforms to the model and the Help Tutor remains silent.

Figure 10.3 shows the tree of rules explored by the model-tracing algorithm (Anderson et al., 1995) as it searched for rules matching the student's behavior in this example case. The nodes of the tree represent individual rules considered by the interpreter as it attempts to match the student's action to the ideal action prescribed by the model. The "CHAIN" nodes mark choice points where multiple rules are considered. The matching rule chain is shown in gray; in this case, the student's behavior correctly followed the model. Rules that were considered but that did not match the observed student action are shown in white boxes.

Thus, the matching rule chain contains four rules: an initial rule that starts the chain ("start-new-metacog-cycle"), a rule that identifies the student as having spent an adequate amount of time ("think-about-step-deliberately"), a rule that indicates that the student tried the step, as anticipated by the student's high mastery of the skill at that point in time ("try-step"), and finally a fourth rule that indicates that the student got the step right ("tutor-says-step-was-correct"). In this instance, the student has acted as expected, as indicated by the fact that there is a matching chain of rules that

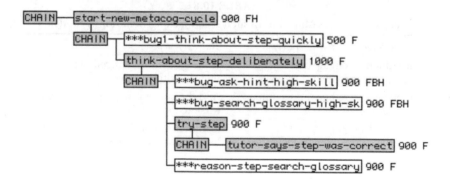

FIG. 10.3.   Production rules that were explored by the Help Tutor as it searched for rules that match a student's example help-seeking behavior. The matching rules (shown in gray) represent desired help-seeking behavior, as captured in the model of Fig. 10.2.

contains only rules that model correct behavior and no "bug rules," that is, rules that model incorrect behavior. (Bug rules have names starting with "bug.") Two of the matching rules are shown in Table 10.8. Given that the student behaved as expected, the Help Seeking Tutor Agent will let her continue without intervening.

Example of a Student Who Abuses Help

Now, consider another hypothetical student, unlike the high-skill student in the previous example, who is faced with an unfamiliar problem-solving step. Suppose further that our student has already tried and missed the step once before. In a second attempt at this step our student, without spending adequate time thinking, ventures an answer and gets it wrong again. In doing so, the student deviates from the help-seeking model in two ways: First, she does not spend enough time thinking about the step (a metacognitive error marked as "Bug 1" in Fig. 10.2). Second, in spite of the fact that it is not clear how to fix the error made on from the previous attempt to solve the step, she does not ask for a hint (marked as "Bug 2"). The bug rules allow the tutor to provide feedback to the student on these metacognitive bugs.

Figure 10.4 shows the tree of rules explored in this metacognitive cycle. Note that, unlike the previous example, an initial rule fires signaling that a solution has already been attempted ("consider-next-action"). This rule indicates that in order to interpret the student action we must not start at the top of the flow chart (indicated by "START" in Fig. 10.2), but rather, we need to start from the decision point immediately after the prior failed solu-

TABLE 10.8

Examples of Rules Matching Desired Help-Seeking Behavior by Students

Rule: think-about-step-deliberately	Rule: try-step
If the student is engaged in a metacognitive problem	If the student is engaged in a metacognitive problem
And the current subgoal is to think about the step	And the current subgoal is to decide what action to take
And the student spent at least min-thinking-time to think about the step	And the students' estimated mastery level for the skill involved in the current step is greater than min-solvable-level
Then—	Then—
Remove the subgoal (next subgoal is to decide what action to take)	Try step
	Set a subgoal to evaluate the result

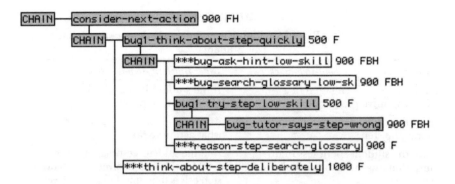

FIG. 10.4.   A chain of rules in the Help-Seeking Tutor Agent's model that represent behavior that deviates from the ideal help-seeking behavior diagrammed in Fig. 10.2.

tion attempt ("Clear how to fix?"). The next rule indicates the student acted too quickly ("bug1-think-about-step-quickly"), another rule indicates that the student was not expected to try the step, given her low mastery of the skill at that point in time ("bug1-try-step-low-skill"), and, finally, a rule fires indicating that the student missed the step ("bug-tutor-says-step-wrong"). The Help Tutor provides the following feedback message, corresponding to the multiple bugs identified in the chain: "Take your time. Think carefully. A hint might help you tackle this difficult step." The bug rules corresponding to the student acting too quickly and trying the step when he or she should not have are shown in Table 10.9.

Note that getting the step wrong in this situation (i.e., the fact that the answer to the geometry problem is incorrect) is not in itself a deviation from the help-seeking model. At a metacognitive level, evaluation of the student's behavior is focused on whether the student conforms to expected (and ideal) metacognitive behavior. A bug at the cognitive level does not necessarily imply a bug at the metacognitive level. However, whether the student gets the step right does matter in the following way: When the student gets a step right, even if there are bugs at the metacognitive level, the Help Tutor will remain silent.

The help-seeking model uses information passed from the cognitive model to perform its reasoning. For instance, the particular skill involved in a step, the estimated mastery level of a particular student for that skill, the number of hints available for that step, and whether or not the student got the step right are passed from the cognitive to the metacognitive model. Metacognitive model tracing takes place after cognitive model tracing. In other words, when a student inputs a value to the tutor, that value is first evaluated at the cognitive level before the student's action is evaluated at the metacognitive level.

TABLE 10.9

Examples of Bug Rules Matching Unproductive Help-Seeking Behavior
by Students

Rule: Bug1-think-about-step-quickly	Rule: Bug1-try-step-low-skill
If the student is engaged in a metacognitive problem	If the student is engaged in a metacognitive problem
And the current subgoal is to think about the step	And the current subgoal is to decide what action to take
And the student spent less than min-thinking-time to think about the step	And the student's estimated mastery level for the skill involved in the current step is less than min-familiarity-level
	And the student has not seen all the hints yet for the current step
Then—	Then—
Remove the subgoal (next subgoal is to decide what action to take)	Try step
	Set a subgoal to evaluate the result
Feedback message: "Take your time. Think carefully."	Feedback message: "A hint might help you tackle this difficult step."

An important consideration in the development of the Help Agent was to make it modular and useable in conjunction with a variety of Cognitive Tutors. The Help Tutor will be a plug-in agent applicable to a wide range of Cognitive Tutors with limited customization. We have attempted to create metacognitive rules that are applicable to *any* Cognitive Tutor, not to a specific tutor. Certainly, there will be some need for customization, as optional supporting tools (of which the glossary is but one example) will be available in some tutors and not others, but many elements of the model will be shared across tutors.

Comparison With Nelson-Le Gall's and Newman's Model of Help Seeking

Our approach to help seeking has some overlap and similarity to earlier research focused on help seeking in social contexts, such as classrooms. In this subsection we compare our model with the general steps in the help-seeking model originally presented by Nelson-Le Gall (1981) and later elaborated by Newman (1994):

1. Become aware of a need for help.
2. Decide to seek help.

3. Identify potential helper(s).
4. Use strategies to elicit help.
5. Evaluate help-seeking episode.

It is informative to consider the similarities and differences between the Nelson-Le Gall model and the help-seeking model presented in this chapter. In the Nelson-Le Gall/Newman model, a learner first must become aware that the task is difficult or that she or he is stuck and in need of help. The ability to assess task difficulty, monitor task progress, and evaluate one's own comprehension and knowledge are important metacognitive functions (Nelson-Le Gall, 1981; Newman, 1998). In the next step of the Nelson-Le Gall/ Newman model, learners must consider all available information and decide whether to seek help. In our help-seeking model, student awareness of the difficulty of the task and need for help is represented by the ideal help-seeking student asking the questions "Familiar at all?" and "Sense of what to do?" In other words, our model, like the Nelson-Le Gall/Newman model, assumes that students with good metacognitive skills will monitor their knowledge and be aware of situations in which help is needed. As described earlier, our model provides a very precise criterion to determine whether to seek help. The Nelson-Le Gall/Newman model encompasses a broad range of factors (besides self-assessment of skill level) that influence the decision to seek help (e.g., fear of embarrassment) but models them in less detail.

In the next step, the learner must find a suitable helper. In most classrooms, the teacher or a fellow student could serve this role. In a social context, selecting the helper may depend on the age of the learner and include the perceived competence and sensitivity of the helper (Knapp & Karabenick, 1988; Nelson-Le Gall, 1981). In our help-seeking model, finding a suitable helper entails the student determining which of the available software help facilities is most appropriate in the current context. In the case of the Geometry Cognitive Tutor, this amounts to a choice between the context-sensitive hints and the glossary. As mentioned, in our model, the choice depends on the student's mastery of the skill involved in the step. A good help seeker will opt for context-sensitive hints early on, when she or he deems mastery of the given skill to be low, and for the glossary when the step is familiar. In the worst case (e.g., repeatedly missing a step, although all hints have been seen), our model assumes the student will seek help from the teacher. This is not depicted explicitly in the model of Fig. 10.2, but it is part of the computational version of the model.

Next in the Nelson-Le Gall/Newman model, the leaner must decide *how* to request help, influenced by the student's knowledge and skills of discourse (Newman, 1998). Essentially, the request must match the task demands. There is no real counterpart to this step in our model of help seeking. Because the student is working with well-defined software functions with specific means to request help, there is no need in our model to consider how to request help.

Finally, in the last step of the Nelson-Le Gall/Newman model, the learner reflects on the help-seeking event to decide if it was helpful and to determine whether further help is required. In our model this behavior is captured by the student asking "Hint helpful?" after receiving a hint and by asking "Sense of what to do?" after using the Glossary.

In summary, there is overlap between the Nelson-Le Gall/Newman model and our model of help seeking. Perhaps the most significant divergence between the models is in the level of specificity. Our model is grounded within an intelligent tutor with specific help functions available to the student. Thus our model is commensurately more detailed but also more bound to a specific tutoring context. The Nelson-Le Gall/New man model does not aspire to the same level of detail or specificity, nor does it aspire to computational rendering. It does however encompass a broader range of factors that may influence students' help-seeking behavior. Ultimately, we intend to empirically test our model with real students in connection with a variety of actual Cognitive Tutors.

Planned Evaluation Studies of the Help-Seeking Tutor Agent

Our goal is to both (a) improve the current model of help seeking and (b) use it for tutoring students to be better help seekers. We plan to do empirical work to achieve both objectives. First, we plan to refine the initial model presented above, as we examine data about student tutor/interactions. For example, various elements of the model may need to be adjusted or refined (e.g., the skill threshold discussed earlier) if it turns out that the model does not distinguish well between productive and unproductive help-seeking behavior or that students deviate so often from the model that it would not be feasible for the Help Tutor to comment on all deviations.

To assist in the evaluation of the frequency with which students deviate from the model, we are developing a *bug taxonomy* that characterizes the range of help-seeking bugs the model can produce. The taxonomy will enable us to aggregate help-seeking problems in broader categories than the fine-grained level of individual bug rules. As an example, the bug category, "Help Abuse" intended to cover general situations in which the student misuses hints provided by the Cognitive Tutor, has a subcategory called "'Clicking Through Hints," which occurs when a student rapidly proceeds from one hint to the next, without sufficient time to read the hints. Another subcategory, "Ask Hint when Skill indicates Trying," characterizes situations in which a student with sufficient skill asks for a hint instead of giving the step a try. Bug instances are categorized in the taxonomy by their specific sequence of rule firings (assuming at least one "bug rule" fires, such as the rule firings illustrated in Fig. 10.4). One useful way we intend to use the taxonomy is to process actual logs of student–tutor interactions (such as those from which the data presented earlier in this chapter were extracted) and determine the percentage of bugs that manifest in each category. This processing can be done automatically, by running the help-seeking model to evaluate the student actions stored in the logs. The resulting data will inform us as to which categories of bugs are most urgently in need of tutoring and which rarely occur. It will also help us to calibrate the various tests and thresholds in the model.

To evaluate whether the model accurately distinguishes between productive and unproductive help-seeking behavior, we will study whether metacognitive behavior that conforms to the model correlates with learning outcomes. We will study also how the various bug categories relate to learning. To a degree, however, the proof of the pudding will be in the eating. That is, we will know that the model is accurate when the Help Tutor actually helps students to learn better. We plan to evaluate whether this is the case in a controlled experiment in which we compare students' learning outcomes obtained with a Cognitive Tutor with the Help Tutor "plugged in" against those obtained with the same Cognitive Tutor running without the Help Tutor.

The planned experiment evaluating the added value of the Help Tutor will indicate whether there is a causal relation between help seeking and learning in an ILE. We know of only one previous study that has addressed the causal relationship, namely, Renkl's (2002) study, in which he compared two versions of a system for example studying, one with and one without on-demand help. This study did find a causal relation. Our study will be different in that it looks at the causal relation within a problem-solving context and will be carried out in an actual classroom. It is different also in that it includes an intervention aimed at improving students' help-seeking behavior. Further, we plan to address a key question, namely, whether students will be better *future* learners as a result of being tutored on help seeking. The Cognitive Tutors provide a convenient platform to investigate such questions because students use them in year-long courses. Thus, we plan to study students' use of help throughout a course to determine if it improves by exposure to the Help Tutor.

CONCLUSION

Many ILEs use on-demand help. As these types of systems are rapidly becoming widespread, it is important to understand the factors influencing the effectiveness of help use and their relation with learning. Examining data from one of the units of the Geometry Cognitive Tutor, we found that widespread gaming of the system (i.e., the use of hints to find answers without taking time to reflect on why the answer is what it is) leads to a negative correlation between help seeking and learning, clearly a sign that the tutor's on-demand hints are not as effective as intended.

To improve the situation, we plan improve the hints themselves, for example, by shortening the hint sequences and not mixing cognitive and metacognitive advice. More importantly, we are developing the Help Tutor, which will provide guidance with respect to students' help-seeking behavior. An initial computational model of help seeking we have developed provides a precise notion of good help-seeking behavior. Using this model to monitor students' help-seeking behavior, the Help Tutor will catch gaming and other unproductive help-seeking behavior. This approach is especially promising in light of the proven effectiveness of Cognitive Tutors in teaching domain-specific skills and knowledge: When used as an adjunct to classroom instruction, the Cognitive Tutors lead to better learning than typical classroom instruction. It is hypothesized that the Cognitive Tutor approach will have similar advantages when used for instruction at the metacognitive level. Our planned evaluation will focus on the hypothesis that exposure to the Help Tutor will help students to learn better at the domain level, even after it has been removed. In other words, we will evaluate whether the Help Tutor prepares students to be better future learners.

ACKNOWLEDGMENTS

The research presented in this chapter is sponsored by the National Science Foundation (NSF) award IIS-0308200. Previously, the research was sponsored by an NSF grant to the Center for Interdisciplinary Research on Constructive Learning (CIRCLE), a research center located at the University of Pittsburgh and Carnegie Mellon University. See http://www.pitt.edu/~circle. Any opinions expressed in this chapter are solely the responsibility of the authors and do not necessarily reflect the official position of the NSF.

REFERENCES

Aleven, V., & Koedinger, K. R. (2000). Limitations of student control: Do students know when they need help? In G. Gauthier, C. Frasson, & K. VanLehn (Eds.), *Proceedings of the 5th International Conference on Intelligent Tutoring Systems, ITS 2000* (pp. 292–303). Berlin: Springer Verlag.

Aleven, V., & Koedinger, K. R. (2002). An effective metacognitive strategy: Learning by doing and explaining with a computer-based cognitive tutor. *Cognitive Science, 26*(2), 147–179.

Aleven, V., McLaren, B., Roll, I., & Koedinger, K. (2004). Toward tutoring help seeking: Applying cognitive modeling to meta-cognitive skills. In J. C. Lester, R. M. Vicario, & F. Paraguaçu (Eds.), *Proceedings of the 7th International Conference on Intelligent Tutoring Systems, ITS 2004* (pp. 227–239). Berlin: Springer Verlag.

Aleven, V., Stahl, E., Schworm, S., Fischer, F., & Wallace, R. M. (2003). Help seeking and help design in interactive learning environments. *Review of Educational Research, 73*(2), 277–320.

Anderson, J. R., Conrad, F. G., & Corbett, A. T. (1989). Skill acquisition and the LISP tutor. *Cognitive Science, 13*, 467–505.

Anderson, J. R., Corbett, A. T., Koedinger, K. R., & Pelletier, R. (1995). Cognitive tutors: Lessons learned. *Journal of the Learning Sciences, 4*, 167–207.

Anderson, J. R., & Lebière, C. (1998). *The atomic components of thought.* Mahwah, NJ: Lawrence Erlbaum Associates.

Arbreton, A. (1998). Student goal orientation and help-seeking strategy use. In S. A. Karabenick (Ed.), *Strategic help seeking: Implications for learning and teaching* (pp. 95–116). Mahwah, NJ: Lawrence Erlbaum Associates.

Arroyo, I., Beck, J. E., Beal, C. R., Wing, R., & Woolf, B. P. (2001). Analyzing students' response to help provision in an elementary mathematics intelligent tutoring system. In R. Luckin (Ed.), *Papers of the AIED-2001 Workshop on Help Provision and Help Seeking in Interactive Learning Environments* (pp. 34–46). Berlin: Springer.

Arroyo, I., Beck, J. E., Woolf, B. P., Beal, C. R., & Schultz, K. (2000). Macro-adapting Animalwatch to gender and cognitive differences with respect to hint interactivity and symbolism. In G. Gauthier, C. Frasson, & K. VanLehn (Ed.), *Proceedings of the 5th International Conference on Intelligent Tutoring Systems, ITS 2000* (pp. 574–583). Berlin: Springer Verlag.

Baker, R. S., Corbett, A. T., & Koedinger, K. R. (2004). Detecting student misuse of intelligent tutoring systems. In J. C. Lester, R. M. Vicario, & F. Paraguaçu (Eds.), *Proceedings of the 7th International Conference on Intelligent Tutoring Systems, ITS 2004* (pp. 531–540). Berlin: Springer Verlag.

Bielaczyc, K., Pirolli, P. L., & Brown, A. L. (1995). Training in self-explanation and self-regulation strategies: Investigating the effects of knowledge acquisition activities on problem solving. *Cognition and Instruction, 13*, 221–252.

Bransford, J. D., Brown, A. L., & Cocking, R. R. (2000). *How people learn: Brain, mind, experience, and school.* Washington, DC: National Academic Press.

Brusilovsky, P. (2001). Adaptive hypermedia. *User Modeling & User-Adapted Interaction, 11*, 87–110.

Butler, R. (1998). Determinants of help seeking: Relations between perceived reasons for classroom help-avoidance and help-seeking behaviors in an experimental context. *Journal of Educational Psychology, 90*, 630–643.

Cognition and Technology Group at Vanderbilt. (1997). *The Jasper Project: Lessons in curriculum, instruction, assessment, and professional development.* Mahwah, NJ: Lawrence Erlbaum Associates.

Corbett, A. T., & Anderson, J. R. (1995). Knowledge tracing: Modeling the acquisition of procedural knowledge. *User Modeling and User-Adapted Interaction, 4*, 253–278.

Corbett, A. T., Koedinger, K. R., & Anderson, J. R. (1997). Intelligent tutoring systems. In M. Helander & T. K. Landauer & P. Prabhu (Eds.), *Handbook of human–computer interaction* (2nd ed., pp. 849–874). New York: Elsevier Science.

de Jong, T., & van Joolingen, W. R. (1998). Scientific discovery learning with computer simulations of conceptual domains. *Review of Educational Research, 68*(2), 179–201.

Dillon, A., & Gabbard, R. (1998). Hypermedia as an educational technology: A review of the quantitative research literature on learner comprehension, control, and style. *Review of Educational Research, 68*, 322–349.

Dutke, S., & Reimer, T. (2000). Evaluation of two types of online help information for application software: Operative and function-oriented help. *Journal of Computer-Assisted Learning, 16*, 307–315.

Dweck, C. S. (1989). Motivation. In: A. Lesgold & R. Glaser (Eds.), *Foundations for a psychology of education* (pp. 87–136). Mahwah, NJ: Lawrence Erlbaum Associates.

Eberts, R. E. (1997). Computer-based instruction. In M. Helander & T. K. Landauer, & P. Prabhu (Eds.), *Handbook of human–computer interaction* (2nd ed., pp. 825–847). New York: Elsevier Science.

Gibbons, A. S., & Fairweather, P. G. (1998). *Computer-based instruction: Design and development.* Englewood Cliffs, NJ: Educational Technology.

Gross, A. E., & McMullen, P. A. (1983). Models of the help-seeking process. In J. D. Fisher, N. Nadler, & B. M. DePaulo (Eds.), *New directions in helping* (Vol. 2, pp. 45–61). New York: Academic Press.

Hambleton, R. K., & Swaminathan, H. (1985). *Item response theory: Principles and applications.* Boston: Kluwer.

Karabenick, S. A. (2003). Seeking help in large college classes: A person centered approach. *Contemporary Educational Psychology, 28,* 37–58.

Karabenick, S. A., & Knapp, J. R. (1988a). Help seeking and the need for academic assistance. *Journal of Educational Psychology, 80,* 406–408.

Karabenick, S. A., & Knapp, J. R. (1988b). Effects of computer privacy on help seeking. *Journal of Applied Social Psychology, 18,* 461–472.

Keefer, J. A., & Karabenick, S. A. (1998). Help seeking in the information age. In S. A. Karabenick (Ed.), *Strategic help seeking: Implications for learning and teaching* (pp. 219–250). Mahwah, NJ: Lawrence Erlbaum Associates.

Knapp, J. R., & Karabenick, S. A. (1988). Incidence of formal and informal academic help seeking in higher education. *Journal of College Student Development, 29,* 223–227.

Koedinger, K. R., Anderson, J. R., Hadley, W. H., & Mark, M. A. (1997). Intelligent tutoring goes to school in the big city. *International Journal of Artificial Intelligence in Education, 8,* 30–43.

Koedinger, K. R., Corbett, A. T., Ritter, S., & Shapiro, L. (2000). *Carnegie learning's Cognitive Tutor™: Summary research results: White paper.* Available from Carnegie Learning, Inc., Pittsburgh, PA. http://www.carnegielearning.com.

Larkin, J. H., & Chabay, R. W. (Eds.). (1992). *Computer-assisted instruction and intelligent tutoring systems: Shared goals and complementary approaches.* Mahwah, NJ: Lawrence Erlbaum Associates.

Luckin, R., & Hammerton, L. (2002). Getting to know me: Helping learners understand their own learning needs through metacognitive scaffolding. In S. A. Cerri, G. Gouardères, & F. Paraguaçu (Eds.), *Proceedings of Sixth International Conference on Intelligent Tutoring Systems, ITS 2002* (pp. 759–771). Berlin: Springer Verlag.

Mandl, H., Gräsel, C., & Fischer, F. (2000). Problem-oriented learning: Facilitating the use of domain-specific and control strategies through modeling by an expert. In W. J. Perrig & A. Grob (Eds.), *Control of human behavior, mental processes and consciousness* (pp. 165–182). Mahwah, NJ: Lawrence Erlbaum Associates.

Mathan, S., & Koedinger, K. R. (2003). Recasting the feedback debate: Benefits of tutoring error detection and correction skills. In U. Hoppe, F. Verdejo, & J. Kay (Eds.), *Proceedings of the 11th International Conference on Artificial Intelligence in Education, AI-ED 2003* (pp. 000–000). Amsterdam: IOS Press.

McKendree, J. (1990). Effective feedback content for tutoring complex skills. *Human Computer Interaction, 5,* 381–413.

Miyake, N., & Norman, D. A. (1979). To ask a question, one must know enough to know what is not known. *Journal of Verbal Learning and Verbal Behavior, 18,* 357–364.

National Council of Teachers of Mathematics. (1989). *Curriculum and evaluation standards for school mathematics.* Reston, VA: Author. http://standards-e.nctm.org/index.htm.

Nelson-Le Gall, S. (1981). Help-seeking: An understudied problem-solving skill in children. *Developmental Review, 1,* 224–246.

Nelson-Le Gall, S. (1985). Help-seeking behavior in learning. *Review of Research in Education, 12,* 55–90.

Nelson-Le Gall, S. (1987). Necessary and unnecessary help seeking in children. *Journal of Genetic Psychology, 148,* 53–62.

Nelson-Le Gall, S., Kratzer, L., Jones, E., & DeCooke, P. (1990). Children's self-assessment of performance and task-related help seeking. *Journal of Experimental Child Psychology, 49,* 245–263.

Newman, R. S. (1994). Adaptive help seeking: A strategy of self-regulated learning. In D. H. Schunk & B. J. Zimmerman (Eds.), *Self-regulation of learning and performance: Issues and educational applications* (pp. 283–301). Mahwah, NJ: Lawrence Erlbaum Associates.

Newman, R. S. (1998). Adaptive help seeking: A role of social interaction in self-regulated learning. In S. A. Karabenick (Ed.), *Strategic help seeking. Implications for learning and teaching* (pp. 13–37). Mahwah, NJ: Lawrence Erlbaum Associates.

Newman, R. S., & Karabenick, S. A. (2004, April). *Achievement goal theory and students' help-seeking orientations: A test of competing models.* Presented at the annual meeting of the American Educational Research Association, San Diego, CA.

Palincsar, A. S., & Brown, A. L. (1984). Reciprocal teaching of comprehension-fostering and comprehension-monitoring activities. *Cognition and Instruction, 1,* 117–175.

Puustinen, M. (1998). Help-seeking behavior in a problem-solving situation: Development of self-regulation. *European Journal of Psychology of Education, 13*(2), 271–282.

Renkl, A. (2002). Learning from worked-out examples: Instructional explanations supplement self-explanations. *Learning & Instruction, 12,* 529–556.

Ritter, S. (1997). Communication, cooperation and competition among multiple tutor agents. In B. du Boulay & R. Mizoguchi (Eds.), *Artificial intelligence in education, Proceedings of AI-ED 97 World Conference* (pp. 31–38). Amsterdam: IOS Press.

Ryan, A. M., Gheen, M. H., & Midgley, C. (1998). Why do some students avoid asking for help? An examination of the interplay among students' academic efficacy, teachers' social-emotional role, and the classroom goal structure. *Journal of Educational Psychology, 90*(3), 528–535.

Ryan, A. M., & Pintrich, P. R. (1997). "Should I ask for help?" The role of motivation and attitudes in adolescents' help seeking in math class. *Journal of Educational Psychology, 89*(2), 329–341.

Ryan, A. M., Pintrich, P. R., & Midgley, C. (2001). Avoiding help in the classroom: Who and why? *Educational Psychology Review, 13*(2), 93–114.

Schoenfeld, A. H. (1987). What's all the fuss about metacognition? In A. H. Schoenfeld (Ed.), *Cognitive science and mathematics education* (pp. 189–215). Hillsdale, NJ: Lawrence Erlbaum Associates.

Schofield, J. W. (1995). *Computers and classroom culture.* Cambridge, England: Cambridge University Press.

Slotta, J. D., & Linn, M. C. (2000). The knowledge integration environment: Helping students use the Internet effectively. In M. J. Jacobson & R. B. Kozma (Eds.), *Innovations in science and mathematics education: Advanced designs for technologies of learning* (pp. 193–226). Mahwah, NJ: Lawrence Erlbaum Associates.

Van der Meij, H. (1988). Constraints on question asking in classrooms. *Journal of Educational Psychology, 80*(3), 401–405.

Vygotsky, L. S. (1978). *Mind in society.* Cambridge, MA: Harvard University Press.

White, B., & Frederiksen, J. (1998). Inquiry, modeling, and metacognition: Making science accessible to all students. *Cognition and Instruction, 16*(1), 3–117.

Wood, D. (2001). Scaffolding, contingent tutoring, and computer-supported learning. *International Journal of Artificial Intelligence in Education, 12,* pp.

Wood, H. A., & Wood, D. J. (1999). Help seeking, learning and contingent tutoring. *Computers and Education, 33,* 153–169.

Implications and Future Research: Where Do We Go From Here?

Richard S. Newman
University of California, Riverside

The chapters in this volume represent diverse topics and raise diverse issues. Contributors have focused on help seeking among elementary and middle school students, high school and college students, and adults working in organizational settings. Most contributors have focused on students seeking academic help (e.g., "How do you do these math problems?") or academic advice or counsel (e.g., "Which courses should I take?"). Others have focused on help with job-related difficulties (e.g., "This doesn't make sense ... let's find out from the expert if we've made this thing correctly") or peer harassment (e.g., "Help! This big kid's been really bugging me"). Help is requested of teachers, peers, advisors, colleagues, and computers. Reported research represents different methodologies, both qualitative and quantitative; some chapters emphasize theory and some are more applied. Our contributors have presented rich accounts of their research and discussed directions in which their work is headed. Rather than summarize each chapter, my aim in this final chapter is to suggest common themes and implications for future research. I have organized the discussion according to (a) achievement goals, (b) construct definition of adaptive help seeking, (c) contextual influences on help seeking, and (d) extensions and application.

ACHIEVEMENT GOALS

The theoretical starting point for most of the research discussed in the chapters is achievement goal theory. Help seeking is a deliberate, goal-directed behavior. Karabenick and Butler provide excellent accounts of how students' goals are related to academic help seeking. Butler and Newman argue that it is time to look beyond the traditional set of mastery and performance goals. Students are motivated also by work-avoidance goals (i.e., desire for expedience). Multiple goal theory has shown that performance-approach goals (i.e., desire to look competent) and performance-avoidance goals (i.e., desire to not look incompetent) need to be differentiated. In addition to achievement-related goals, students' help seeking is related to various social goals. Whether academic or social, goals "reside" in the environmental context (e.g., the classroom, organization) and in the person (e.g., the individual learner, peer group). As illustrated in chapters by Sandoval and Lee and by Volet and Karabenick, "large" contextual entities such as ethnicities and cultures can be characterized according to expectations and goals regarding individuals' achievement. Contextual and personal goals often interact with one another; in fact, it can be argued that they cannot be separated—that is, classrooms, peer groups, organizations, and cultures consist of persons. Still, the distinction can be useful. Contextual goals are established and maintained by teachers and school administrators (e.g., through grading practices and ability grouping) and employers (e.g., through organizational norms and team-related practices); personal goals are socialized at home and in earlier school and work experience (see Newman, 2000). At times, contextual and personal goals conflict, and at other times, they complement one another. Individuals working together—sometimes by choice and sometimes in groupings defined by others—can have conflicting or congruent goals. To understand help seeking, it is necessary to consider these various complexities regarding goals.

Butler reports on a study that relates academic goals to both help seeking and help avoidance. According to Butler (1998), children at Grades 5 and 6 have multiple reasons why, at times, they seek help, and at other times, they do not. Autonomous, performance-related, and expedience-related reasons for *not* seeking help correspond directly to mastery, performance, and work-avoidance goals. Further, these help-avoidance orientations are predictive of (a) reasons why, at other times, students *do* seek help and (b) students' actual behavior. That is, both help seeking and help avoidance can be motivated by a variety of goals. Importantly, Butler's research expands the focus from *help seeking* and *help avoidance* to include *alternative strategies* students often use when faced with academic difficulties (e.g., copying or cheating). My own chapter builds on the same theme.

CONSTRUCT DEFINITION OF ADAPTIVE HELP SEEKING

Because help seeking and help avoidance can take such different forms, it is imperative that researchers carefully operationalize the constructs. I think it is fair to say that all help-seeking researchers as well as educators and organizational leaders interested in facilitating help seeking are interested in *adaptive help seeking,* a construct that can be traced to conceptual papers by Nelson-Le Gall (1981, 1985). In my chapter, I reviewed empirical studies in which adaptiveness has been operationalized according to three criteria (i.e., necessity, content, target). Given the fairly large body of help-seeking research represented in the present volume, in addition to earlier volumes (DePaulo, Nadler, & Fisher, 1983; Karabenick, 1998), it is surprising that so few empirical studies have grappled with the conceptual and methodological issue, "What exactly is adaptive help seeking?" With the aim of advancing help-seeking research, I have categorized students' responses to academic (and social) difficulties as *adaptive help seeking, nonadaptive help seeking,* and *nonadaptive "other actions."*

In the context of computer-based instructional research, Aleven and colleagues are forced to address thorny issues regarding adaptiveness of help seeking. Their research is theory-driven, empirical, and systematic. The interactive learning environment (ILE) described in Aleven's chapter consists of two components: a Cognitive Tutor and a Help-Seeking Tutor Agent. The Cognitive Tutor provides two types of help to high school geometry or algebra students: (a) context-sensitive hints tailored in a sequence from indirect to direct and (b) decontextual "background" help provided in a glossary. Context-sensitive help and decontextual help do not map neatly onto the typology of "executive" or "instrumental" help seeking (see Nelson-Le Gall, 1981, 1985). Both types of help are designed to be instrumental. Help from the glossary is never executive because this type of help never directly provides the final answer; only under certain conditions can context-sensitive help be considered executive (i.e., if the student ignores all hints prior to the last one, which stops just short of providing the final answer). Whether help is executive or instrumental is an empirical question, depending on how the help is used and with what outcome (i.e., learning) the help results.

Aleven's research focuses on (a) whether the Cognitive Tutor can help students learn math and (b) whether the Help-Seeking Tutor Agent can help students learn to adaptively seek help (while they are learning math). The Help-Seeking Tutor Agent is an "adjunct" to (i.e., it is "plugged into") the Cognitive Tutor. The ILE system as a whole distinguishes between students' bugs at the cognitive level (as they solve geometry problems) and metacognitive level (as they seek or avoid help). Explicitly built into the system is the conceptualization of adaptive help seeking as a *mediator* of learning, or, more precisely, a mediator of relations between student characteristics (e.g., base-level math skill) and student learning. This critical notion of mediation, I believe, is implicit but usually overlooked and untested in most research on help seeking. Thus far, in addition to adaptive (i.e., necessary) help seeking, Aleven's findings reveal three help-seeking bugs: (a) help avoidance, whereby the student fails to seek help when it is necessary (i.e., knowing that he or she has made multiple errors); (b) help abuse, whereby the student "clicks through hints" too rapidly or skims the glossary superficially; and (c) help abuse, whereby the student seeks help without first trying the problem on his or her own. In addition to diagnosing bugs, the Help-Seeking Tutor Agent serves an instructional role. For example, if a student needs help but fails to ask for it, the Agent might provide feedback, for example, "Take your time. Think carefully. A hint might help you tackle this difficult step."

As exciting as this program of research is, it is important to note the context in which the help seeking occurs. The helper is a computer. It would be wonderful if the Help-Seeking Tutor Agent's "words" of encouragement and instruction could somehow be provided by a "real person" (cf. role of social interaction; Vygotsky, 1978). Rather than choosing among teachers or among peers, the student must choose between software facilities (e.g., context-sensitive hints or glossary). Still, the ILE is used in real-world classrooms rather than in a lab setting. Typically students work at the computer 50% of class time; the rest of the time, they work in whole-class or small-group activities. Indeed, Aleven and colleagues acknowledge that sometimes students spontaneously step outside the ILE context and ask for help from the teacher! Perhaps the interface of human and machine could be included explicitly in the design of the Tutor Agent, with feedback such as "You have tried your hardest with hints and help from the glossary, but you still are having difficulty. Asking your teacher for assistance might help you tackle this difficult step."

CONTEXTUAL INFLUENCES ON HELP SEEKING

A key element to this volume, as evidenced in the book's subtitle, is context. Contextual influences on help seeking can be examined on several different levels (cf. nested environments; Bronfenbrenner, 1979). In the following discussion, I focus on contextual influences within the immediate setting (i.e., classrooms or place of work) and at levels within which these settings are situated (i.e., schools, organizations, and cultures).

Teachers

To understand contextual influences on academic help seeking, including contextual goals, it is necessary to consider the helper. According to Butler, whether students are willing to ask for help depends "first and foremost" on how teachers talk and communicate with their students, in particular, how they respond to students' requests for help (see Karabenick & Sharma,

1994). Indeed, help seeking is a social transaction embedded in a social relationship. Teachers maintain classrooms that differ in affordances to students (Turner et al., 2002). Teachers differ from one another in the degree to which they provide encouragement for help seeking. Butler raises the question, "Why do teachers respond as they do to students' requests for help?" Teachers are motivated by various personal and professional goals, which are manifest in how they teach and how they themselves seek help from colleagues and administrators. Teachers' goals reflect a larger system of values (or standards of behavior, expectations, or norms) that characterize educational policy and school culture.

An important question is the degree to which teachers are sensitive to students' requests for help. We know that students at different grade levels have different needs. Throughout the elementary grades, a sense of interpersonal connectedness to the teacher predicts help seeking, whereas at the upper grades, a sense that teachers can provide specific, task-focused help also predicts help seeking (Newman & Schwager, 1993). The ideal teacher is sensitive and responsive to individual needs of students. In my own chapter, I discuss research on the role of teachers as helpers in nonacademic situations of peer conflict that sometimes occur at elementary school, namely, peer harassment. Similar to average and popular students, teachers tend to perceive teasing as not very serious, whereas unpopular students perceive teasing to be just as serious as threats or actual physical aggression. How teachers act toward unpopular students and whether their perceptions and actions contribute to unpopular students' reticence to seek help when teased are not clear. A priority for future research on help seeking, whether the focus is academic or social difficulties, is a better understanding of how teachers impact students' help seeking.

Peers

The chapter by Webb and colleagues represents a sophisticated and programmatic investigation of middle school students working in small groups in math class. Past research has shown that elaborated help (e.g., explanations) benefits the child who receives the help if the help is utilized in certain ways (e.g., leads to further work on problems and, if necessary, leads to further help), whereas nonelaborated help (e.g., simply being given the answer) does not usually provide benefits. The chapter focuses on relations between students' requests for help, the type of help they receive, their activity after receiving help, and learning outcomes—in sum, how group dynamics affect help seeking.

According to Webb's findings, receiving explanations is contingent on help-seeking requests that are explicit, precise, and direct—that hone in on the specific problem at hand. Requests that are general and vague often convey confusion or lack of understanding and make it harder for potential helpers to reply with explanations. Why do students make "good" requests for help? For one thing, there may be motivational explanations (e.g., students' persistence, preference for challenge, self-efficacy, and attributions to effort vs. ability). There may be cognitive explanations as well. Good questions require a certain amount of task-related knowledge that is current and accessible (cf. Miyake & Norman, 1979). Adaptiveness and persistence are manifest in flexible questioning (cf. questions that are sequenced from specific to general; Newman, 1998). Requests that are precise tend to elicit high-level (i.e., elaborated) help, which in turn, can be put to good use by the help seeker. Why do students make "bad" requests for help? General requests may mask a student's unwillingness to seek help or desire to dodge responsibility. They can be attributed to nonresponsiveness of group members as demonstrated in help that is not very helpful and negative socioemotional behaviors including directives to copy. Group members may believe the help seeker is not motivated and thus question whether they want to expend effort on the help seeker. General requests tend to elicit low-level help, which can be perceived as criticism and which can discourage further help seeking. If, on top of this, there is rudeness or insults from group members, help-seeking behavior can be quickly extinguished. Stepping outside the microcosm of the small group, consider developmental implications of this sort of group dynamic. One can easily imagine a downward spiral over time that carries over into the classroom as a whole, with certain students becoming increasingly disengaged academically and socially.

The power of positive and negative aspects of group work is reinforced in the chapter by Kempler and Linnenbrink. This research is on sixth graders working in small groups in math class. Similar to Webb's findings, it appears that deeper level requests for help are associated with more elaborated help, which is given in a context characterized by mutual support and respect. The help seeker tends to feel comfortable asking questions and may even laugh about his or her mistake and thank those who helped. Requests that are general and vague elicit help that is nonelaborated and often given with a harsh and critical tone. It is not uncommon for the helper to simply take over the task, discrediting the work of the help seeker. Not surprisingly, the help seeker often ignores the help and becomes frustrated and disengaged. Kempler and Linnenbrink's chapter contains rich descriptions of interpersonal dynamics that typically are out of the earshot of a teacher. Simply assigning students to collaborative activities and assuming they are working together in harmony can be unwise! Indeed, instruction in how to work effectively in groups (see Cooperative Learning Program, described by Webb and colleagues) may be necessary.

Organizations and Culture

Sandoval and Lee (chap. 6, this volume) emphasize the importance in help seeking of contextual norms (i.e., values, goals, standards of behavior, expectations). Norms exist at different levels of organizations, for example, school classrooms, collaborative teams in industry, medical departments in hospitals, and even nations and ethnicities. One way of characterizing norms is according to individualism versus collectivism. In organizations characterized by individualistic norms, workers in ingroups perceive their group as relatively heterogeneous, whereas they perceive outgroups as relatively homogeneous. In organizations characterized by collectivistic norms, workers in ingroups perceive their group as homogeneous and outgroups as heterogeneous. Importantly, workers in ingroups in an individualistic organization tend to be reluctant to seek help from one another; if they do seek help, requests tend to be direct (in the sense that they are not couched in polite and deferential terms). In contrast, ingroup workers in a collectivistic organization tend to be relatively willing to seek help from one another, and when they do so, their requests tend to be indirect and polite. Sandoval and Lee attribute different patterns of help seeking to differences in how workers in the two types of organizations think about independence (vs. interdependence), competition (vs. collaboration), competence (vs. incompetence), superiority (vs. inferiority), importance of effort (vs. ability), and malleability (vs. stability) of personal qualities. According to the analysis of Sandoval and Lee, nations, ethnicities, and cultures can be characterized in either one way or the other, with corresponding predictions regarding help seeking.

Analysis based on organizational norms and the actual mechanisms by which interpersonal group dynamics influence help seeking may hold the greatest promise for understanding and facilitating help seeking (cf. chapters by Webb and colleagues and Kempler and Linnenbrink). Questions that might be addressed in organizational research are:

1. Under what conditions might fear of letting down the group mitigate any potentially positive effects of strong communal bonds in a group?
2. How might the ethnic mix in a group (let's say, a Mexican American is working in a small-group activity with several European Americans) affect help seeking?
3. How might discrepancy between family norms and organizational norms affect help seeking?
4. How might discrepancy between gender norms and ethnic norms affect help seeking?
5. How might organizational norms that would ordinarily support help seeking in a small-group activity be affected by an individual's refusing to work or rudeness toward other group members? Although focused

on ethnicity and academic achievement, research by Steinberg, Dornbusch, and Brown (1992) may be helpful in addressing questions such as these. Their ecological perspective considers multiple "niches" in which students develop. To understand organizational norms and group dynamics of help seeking, it may be necessary to examine the *interplay* between the major contexts in which students (or doctors or engineers) interact (e.g., the family, peer group, classroom, school, organization), rather than examining any one of these contexts alone.

To understand cultural influences on help seeking, Volet and Karabenick have focused on peer group dynamics. Rather than comparing help seeking across cultures, they stress variation within cultures. Like Sandoval and Lee, this research takes into account ingroup versus outgroup distinctions. One would expect individuals to prefer to seek help from those who are similar to them and who pose little threat (i.e., those in the ingroup). Volet and Karabenick considered the makeup of dyads of students (in particular, congruence between ingroup vs. outgroup status of help seeker and help giver). Congruence was defined on three levels. Three groups of students (monocultural/local students, multicultural/local students, and other-cultural/international students) were asked whether they would seek help from (and give help to) another student (who was described as either a monocultural/local student, a multicultural/local student, or an other-cultural/international student). The intriguing aspect of the study's design was its naturalistic sampling in two countries. In both Australia and the United States, there was a reasonably large sample of college students in each of the three cultural groups. Students were asked about hypothetical situations of seeking and giving academic help. In both countries, help seeking was most frequent when congruence was greatest, whether monocultural/local students were paired together, multicultural/local students were paired together, or other-cultural/international students were paired together. Importantly, the strongest ingroup bias was found among monocultural/local students—those who probably have the least experience interacting with students different from them. The smallest ingroup bias was found among other-cultural/international students—those who probably have the greatest experience interacting with students different from them. Implications from the study, for promoting multiculturalism and cooperation in education and in the workplace, are immense.

EXTENSIONS AND APPLICATION

Following the lead of Nelson-Le Gall (1981, 1985), most help-seeking research has examined students seeking academic assistance from classroom teachers. Extensions of this line of research are represented in several chapters in this volume. For example, Aleven and colleagues focus on help seeking in the context of computer-based instruction. Others (e.g., Webb and colleagues, Kempler and Linnenbrink) examine students seeking academic assistance from peers. Although my own work focuses on schoolchildren, I am interested in nonacademic help seeking, in particular, students' response to peer harassment. Following the lead of Karabenick (e.g., Karabenick & Knapp, 1988), a growing body of research has examined college students seeking academic assistance from instructors. Two of our chapters (by Alexitch and Collins and Sims) have extended and applied this focus on college students to include academic advising in higher education. In this final section, I discuss three "extension" chapters: one on peer harassment and two on academic advising in higher education.

Peer Harassment

Based on what we know about how children respond to academic difficulties, I have attempted to analyze children's response to social difficulties, in particular, peer harassment. Although it is reasonable to use the academic literature for gaining insight into a field (i.e., peer harassment) never before examined from a help-seeking perspective, the degree to which there is a "good fit" of the construct *adaptive help seeking* remains to be empirically tested.

As with academic help seeking, there no doubt are cognitive and social skills and affective-motivational resources that a child needs in order to seek help adaptively when harassed. An "established"—although seldom tested—list of skills and resources in the academic realm can serve as a heuristic in thinking about the social realm. In a similar vein, "established"—and in this case, fairly well tested—categories of variables that are related to academic help seeking have served as a guide for two of my studies. In particular, person-related variables (grade level, perceived popularity) and contextual variables (type of harassment, perceptions of teachers) have been shown to be related to help seeking. Perhaps the most important linkage across the academic and social domains is the conceptualization of *nonadaptive help seeking* and *nonadaptive "other action."* The potential importance lies in both theory building (i.e., understanding how students cope with academic and social adversity) and practice. Unnecessary help seeking and avoidance of help seeking are two nonadaptive ways in which children sometimes approach difficulties, whether math problems they do not know how to do or social conflicts they do not know how to handle. Each of the two nonadaptive types of response has its own costs. Differentiating between the two may lead to different types of intervention.

Academic Advising in Higher Education

The complexity of help-seeking research in higher educational settings reflects the complexity of issues with which college undergraduates often require assistance. Students need academic help or advice regarding course selection and career paths. They may need academic help in the form of tutoring or supplemental instruction in study skills, especially when they are entering freshmen without proper preparation in their high school education. They may also need nonacademic help (e.g., personal or emotional support). Help can be informational or relationship based; it can be "prescriptive" (i.e., directive) or "developmental" (i.e., collaborative). There is complexity as well in the individuals who typically provide help: academic advisors, instructors, counselors, and peers. Partially dependent on who provides it, help can be "formal" or "informal." Finally, help can be initiated by the helper (e.g., mandatory advising from the department chair) or by the student. It is evident in the chapters by Alexitch and Collins and Sims that applied, naturalistic, and intervention-based research in a domain with all this complexity is a daunting task.

Although in many ways help-seeking research involving school-aged students is relevant to higher education, in some ways it is not. Developmental issues are important to take into account in all help-seeking research (see Newman, 2000). Dropping out of school no doubt is a much more relevant outcome variable with college students than with elementary or middle school students. The college campus is a complex context, certainly not simply a collection of classrooms. When explaining why they refrain from seeking help, I imagine college students are more likely than school-aged students to say they do not want to waste the time of the teacher or instructor. However, this reason may well mask an undergraduate's fear of looking incompetent—a concern often expressed by schoolchildren of most ages.

Two suggestions for further research on help seeking in higher education come to mind. First, in understanding relations between college students' goals and help seeking, it may be important to take into account the distinction between performance-approach and performance-avoidance goals. Research by Harackiewicz and colleagues (e.g., Harackiewicz, Barron, & Elliot, 1998) demonstrated that the two goals are related differentially to college students' motivation and performance. Second, given the prevalence of cheating (e.g., plagiarism) at the college level, examining nonadaptive, alternative response to academic difficulties may be important (cf. Butler, 1998). Of course, researchers will have to contend with methodological constraints of self-report data (i.e., students' unwillingness to admit cheating).

FINAL THOUGHTS

In conclusion, I want to highlight the three general issues that were raised in diverse ways throughout this volume. Regardless of whether one's focus is help seeking among schoolchildren, college students, or adult workers and regardless of whether one is interested in peer groups, classrooms, organizations, or nations, a better understanding of help seeking requires consideration of: (a) *achievement goals*, (b) *construct definition of adaptive help seeking*, and (c) *contextual influences on help seeking*.

Each of these issues is illustrated in a student–advisor interaction to which Alexitch and Collins and Sims alluded. They noted that when undergraduates seek advice, their goals (e.g., "I simply want the answer, and ... now!") may or may not mesh with goals of advisors (e.g., "Let me take some time and explain this"). One can imagine well-meaning advisors sometimes wanting to provide a "developmental" response and, in the process, turning off a student and inhibiting further help seeking. On the other hand, wanting to make things as easy and expeditious as possible for students, advisors might provide a direct, "prescriptive" response when, in fact, they are passing up an opportunity to engage the student "collaboratively." Interactions such as these reinforce, first, the complex way in which achievement goals can influence help seeking. Goals can be contextual or personal, academic or social. They can be considered as individual difference variables (i.e., dispositions) or as variables that are specific to situations and interpersonal dynamics. Second, defining and operationalizing *adaptive* help seeking is a complex matter: Adaptive from whose perspective? The student or the advisor? Can one infer adaptiveness without taking into account a request's content? Or necessity? Or target? Third, help seeking is contingent on numerous contextual factors, perhaps most notably, the helper.

There is an important practical implication here for educators. Do teachers (or advisors? or computers?) know better than students themselves what they (i.e., the students) need? A common theme throughout a number of chapters in this volume is that "good teachers" (including peer helpers and computers) listen to students. Indeed, as explicitly pointed out by Butler and Webb and colleagues, an important way of changing a classroom culture that does not support student help seeking is for teachers to be more patient, to listen to students' requests for assistance, to not rush to give an answer, to encourage students to explain their work and hone in on what they need, and to value errors as diagnostic information that can be translated into good instruction. More generally, our claim is that contexts supportive of help seeking are conducive to students' learning and to their intellectual and social growth.

REFERENCES

Bronfenbrenner, U. (1979). *The ecology of human development*. Cambridge, MA: Harvard University Press.

Butler, R. (1998). Determinants of help seeking: Relations between perceived reasons for classroom help-avoidance and help-seeking behaviors in an experimental context. *Journal of Educational Psychology, 90,* 630–643.

DePaulo, B., Nadler, A., & Fisher, J. (Eds.). (1983), *New directions in helping: Vol. 2. Help seeking.* New York: Academic Press.

Harackiewicz, J. M., Barron, K. E., & Elliott, A. J. (1998). Rethinking achievement goals: When are they adaptive for college students and why? *Educational Psychologist, 33,* 1–21.

Karabenick, S. A. (Ed.). (1998). *Strategic help seeking: Implications for learning and teaching.* Hillsdale, NJ: Lawrence Erlbaum Associates.

Karabenick, S. A., & Knapp, J. R. (1988). Help seeking and the need for academic assistance. *Journal of Educational Psychology, 80,* 406–408.

Karabenick, S. A., & Sharma, R. (1994). Perceived teacher support of student questioning in college classrooms: Its relation to student characteristics and role in the classroom questioning process. *Journal of Educational Psychology, 86,* 90–103.

Miyake, N., & Norman, D. A. (1979). To ask a question, one must know enough to know what is not known. *Journal of Verbal Learning and Verbal Behavior, 18,* 357–364.

Nelson-Le Gall, S. (1981). Help-seeking: An understudied problem-solving skill in children. *Developmental Review, 1,* 224–246.

Nelson-Le Gall, S. (1985). Help-seeking behavior in learning. In W. Gordon (Ed.), *Review of research in education* (Vol. 12, pp. 55–90). Washington, DC: American Educational Research Association.

Newman, R. S. (1998). Students' help seeking during problem solving: Influences of personal and contextual achievement goals. *Journal of Educational Psychology, 90,* 644–658.

Newman, R. S. (2000). Social influences on the development of children's adaptive help seeking: The role of parents, teachers, and peers. *Developmental Review, 20,* 350–404.

Newman, R. S., & Schwager, M. T. (1993). Student perceptions of the teacher and classmates in relation to reported help seeking in math class. *Elementary School Journal, 94,* 3–17.

Steinberg, L., Dornbusch, S. M., and Brown, B. B. (1992). Ethnic differences in adolescent achievement. *American Psychologist, 47,* 723–729.

Turner, J. C., Midgley, C., Meyer, D. K., Gheen, M., Anderman, E. M., Kang, Y., & Patrick, H. (2002). The classroom environment and students' reports of avoidance strategies in mathematics: A multimethod study. *Journal of Educational Psychology, 94,* 88–106.

Vygotsky, L. S. (1978). *Mind in society: The development of higher psychological processes* (M. Cole, V. John-Steiner, S. Scribner, & E. Souberman, Eds.). Cambridge, MA: Harvard University Press.

Author Index

Subject Index